METHODS AND APPLICATIONS OF ECONOMIC DYNAMICS

CONTRIBUTIONS TO ECONOMIC ANALYSIS

228

ELSEVIER
Amsterdam – Lausanne – New York – Oxford – Shannon – Tokyo

METHODS AND APPLICATIONS OF ECONOMIC DYNAMICS

Edited by
L. SCHOONBEEK
E. STERKEN
S.K. KUIPERS

Faculty of Economics
University of Groningen
Groningen, The Netherlands

1995

ELSEVIER
Amsterdam – Lausanne – New York – Oxford – Shannon – Tokyo

ELSEVIER SCIENCE B.V.
Sara Burgerhartstraat 25
P.O. Box 211, 1000 AE Amsterdam, The Netherlands

ISBN: 0 444 81465 5

This book is printed on acid-free paper.

PRINTED IN THE NETHERLANDS

INTRODUCTION TO THE SERIES

This series consists of a number of hitherto unpublished studies, which are introduced by the editors in the belief that they represent fresh contributions to economic science.

The term "economic analysis" as used in the title of the series has been adopted because it covers both the activities of the theoretical economist and the research worker.

Although the analytical methods used by the various contributors are not the same, they are nevertheless conditioned by the common origin of their studies, namely theoretical problems encountered in practical research. Since for this reason, business cycle research and national accounting, research work on behalf of economic policy, and problems of planning are the main sources of the subjects dealt with, they necessarily determine the manner of approach adopted by the authors. Their methods tend to be "practical" in the sense of not being too far remote from application to actual economic conditions. In additon they are quantitative.

It is the hope of the editors that the publication of these studies will help to stimulate the exchange of scientific information and to reinforce international cooperation in the field of economics.

The Editors

Preface

This book consists of the invited papers that have been presented at a workshop on Methods and Applications of Economic Dynamics. The workshop, held in December 1993 at the University of Groningen, was organized by the Center for Cyclical and Structural Research, or in Dutch, Centrum voor Conjunctuur- en Structuur Onderzoek (CCSO). The CCSO is a research group of economists and econometricians of the University of Groningen and the University of Twente. The group works on the field of empirical general economics and has developed for the Dutch economy a number of large-scale macroeconometric models.

We would like to take the opportunity here to express our gratitude towards all participants of the workshop for their contribution to the discussions. In particular, we mention the following persons who, as invited discussants, gave a strong stimulus to the discussions during the workshop: Willem Boeschoten, Peter Broer, Nanne Brunia, Henk Don, Johan Graafland, Jan Jacobs, Joan Muysken, Herman Nieuwenhuis, Jarig van Sinderen, and Götz Uebe.

We gratefully acknowledge the financial support of the Nederlandsche Bank NV, the Koninklijke Nederlandse Akademie van Wetenschappen, and the Department of Economics of the University of Groningen. Without this support, the workshop would not have been organized.

The continuous skilful advise and kind help of Erik Frambach while making the book with the TEX-system and making the figures has been indispensable. In addition, Suwarni Bambang Oetomo assisted in an excellent way in typing parts of the manuscript.

Finally, during the workshop, Liers Baars has taken care of a lot of things that, for sure, would have gone wrong without her.

Lambert Schoonbeek
Elmer Sterken
Simon Kuipers

Contributors

Anton P. Barten, Catholic University of Louvain, Belgium

Michiel Boutillier, University of Evry-Val d'Essonne and Banque de France, France

Andries S. Brandsma, European Commission, Belgium

Anthony Garratt, London Business School, United Kingdom

Manfred Gilli, University of Geneva, Switzerland

Stephen G. Hall, London Business School, United Kingdom

Frederik Huizinga, Central Planning Bureau, The Netherlands

Alexander Italianer, European Commission, Belgium

Pascal Jacquinot, Banque de France, France

Peter Kooiman, Central Planning Bureau, The Netherlands

Gerard H. Kuper, University of Groningen, The Netherlands

Rahim Loufir, OFCE, France

Pierre Malgrange, CEPREMAP-CNRS, France

Anton van Schaik, Tilburg University, The Netherlands

Lambert Schoonbeek, University of Groningen, The Netherlands

Peter N. Smith, University of Warwick, United Kingdom

Elmer Sterken, University of Groningen, The Netherlands

Kenneth F. Wallis, University of Warwick, United Kingdom

Clifford R. Wymer, University of Rome, La Sapienza, Italy

Contents

Methods and Applications of Economic Dynamics
L. Schoonbeek, E. Sterken and S.K. Kuipers (editors)

Chapter 1

Introduction and overview

Lambert Schoonbeek and Elmer Sterken

The papers in this volume deal with methods and applications of economic dynamics in empirical macroeconomic models. In particular, they contribute to a number of aspects concerning the modeling, analysis and economic interpretation of (i) the long run, (ii) short- and medium-run adjustment dynamics, and (iii) more specifically, stability of models. In this introductionary chapter we place the papers into the perspective of some developments in empirical macroeconometric model-building and macroeconomic theory.

Nowadays, the use of fully fledged dynamic macroeconometric models is common practice all over the world. The models are used to produce forecasts of key macroeconomic variables, to analyze the impact of economic policy measures, and to investigate the structure of the economy described by the model. Bodkin *et al.* (1991) present a detailed description of the history of macroeconometric model-building, and Uebe *et al.* (1986) give a bibliography of several hundreds of models. Most of the traditional Keynesian macroeconometric models are focused on short- or medium-term forecasting and policy analysis, say for a period of one quarter up to two or three years. The models are estimated and calibrated such that the recent past can be reproduced satisfactorily and the immediate future can be predicted with some level of confidence. In the sixties and seventies not much attention was given to the long-run properties in general. The size and complexity of the models increased rapidly, on the one hand because model users became interested in more detailed and disaggregated information, on the other hand as a result of new insights of macroeconomic theory. The availability of ever larger and more powerful computers facilitated this development greatly. Models with hundreds of equations and variables included were no exception.

During the last decade one can observe in the literature an increasing attention for the medium-run and long-run dynamic properties of macroeconometric models, see e.g. Hargreaves (1992). This is accompanied with a greater attention for the role of economic theory in these models. There are several, interrelated, explanations for this attention. First, in the seventies after the first oil-crisis, it turned out that the existing models with their Keynesian emphasis on the demand side, were unable to produce adequate short-term forecasts. In particular, they could not explain the observed combination of high inflation and high unemployment rates. It was felt that a more careful modeling of the supply side, which has a large impact on the medium- and long-run dynamic properties of a model, was needed. Second, the Lucas critique attacked macroeconomic models with respect to the assumption that the parameters of the model's equations remain constant, even if, for instance, it is announced that the government or central bank will change its policy. Subsequently, a lot of attention has been paid to the incorporation of forward-looking rational, or model-consistent, expectations in macroeconomic and macroeconometric models. Models with forward-looking expectations need sensible long-run terminal conditions, as these conditions form the model's anchor. It is known that the terminal conditions of such a model can have a strong impact on the short- and medium-run dynamics. In one breath we remark here that demand-oriented macroeconomic models are attacked from a theoretical point of view for a lack of sound microeconomic foundations. It is argued that aggregate macroeconomic relations should be based on dynamic rational and/or optimizing economic behavior of the economic agents involved. Third, in the late seventies growth theory revived. Solow's neoclassical growth model is increasingly popular since that date. It seems that many Keynesian and neoclassical theorists accept the neoclassical growth model as long-term anchor of economic activity. However, a lively point of debate is the speed of adjustment towards long-run growth paths. Classical economists assume this speed of adjustment to be large, sometimes enforced by using rational expectations, while (new-)Keynesians adhere to a slow speed of adjustment, market imperfections, etc. Another question is whether technological progress should be considered as being exogenous or endogenous. In Solow's model it is exogenous, "falling like manna from heaven", but in the new endogenous growth theory, which emerged in the late eighties, technological progress itself is explained endogenously within a consistent microeconomic context. Fourth, policy measures of governments are increasingly directed towards medium-term goals – e.g. an improvement of the economic structure, sustainability of the government debt, or a more flexible working of the labor market – rather than towards stabilization of short-term business cycles. This change in economic policy is in line with the idea that general equilibrium modeling is a more suited device for long-term analysis. Fifth, econometric theory has dealt with long-run equilibrium relations and adjustment towards long-run paths since a couple of decades. See Sargan (1964) for a seminal paper. However, since Engle and Granger (1987) have published their main cointegration and error correction results a renewed attention can be observed. One of the very attractive features of this type of models is that from the outset a consistent and clear distinction is made between the long-run equilibrium and short-run adjustment dynamics. The underlying idea is that economic theory is particularly useful in the specification of the long-run equilibrium, whereas the short-run adjustment dynamics are more or less *ad hoc*, i.e. primarily data based. Partial adjustment models have become less popular in favor of error-correction systems and macroeconometric model-builders are forced to specify explicit proper long-run relations, see e.g. the Bank of England model (1993). A practical problem encountered in the application of cointegration models is the fact that the length of available time series of aggregate economic variables is often relatively short. This reduces the power of the statistical tests involved appreciably.

There is the problem on what the real long run and corresponding equilibrium concept should be. Basically, this amounts to the problem which of the variables of a model should be kept fixed and which of them should vary endogenously. In general, the larger the number of endogenous variables of a model is, the more complex the analysis will be. Macroeconomic theory distinguishes some alternative options here, which in part seem to have been introduced in order to make the relevant models analytically tractable, see e.g. Turnovsky (1977). Deleau *et al.* (1990) discuss the following three main options: (i) the *short* long run: prices and the capital stock are fixed. For instance, in the IS/LM model and its open economy version (Mundell-Fleming) this concept is used to describe equilibrium. Most of the time it is assumed that equilibrium on the money market takes place before equilibrium on the goods market. (ii) the *medium* long run: prices are flexible, but the capital stock is still fixed. Examples are Keynesian demand systems extended with a standard Phillips curve. Equilibrium analyses often focus on stationary states. (iii) the *long* long run: prices and the capital stock are flexible. Adjustment processes for all variables are taken into account. For fully fledged macroeconometric models, in which all variables move together, (iii) obviously is the relevant long-run concept. The appropriate related equilibrium concept is the steady-state growth path in which all variables exhibit constant growth (some variables, e.g. interest rates, may have a zero growth rate). If the actual values of the variables of a model coincide with the steady-state values, then there is no endogenous tendency to leave the steady-state path. Steady-state growth paths preserve the invariance of the production structure (balanced growth). Moreover, they keep stock-flow ratio's constant. Existence of a steady-state growth solution requires that certain restrictions, in particular homogeneity conditions, should be met. For analytical purposes, one of the attractive features of such a solution is that it involves the analysis of two separated sets of just *static* functional relations: one set related to growth rates, the other one related to initial levels. The fact that these relations do not involve time lags greatly facilitates the analysis. Other simplifying attractive features are that certain variables might become equal (e.g. supply equals demand) or that certain terms might become zero. For an interesting methodological discussion of equilibrium concepts used in macroeconomics, we refer to Vercelli (1991).

Discussing the long run, one is naturally led to the question of stability of a model. In general, economists will disqualify a model that is highly unstable, in the sense that its variables explode rapidly without limit, as it floats to absurd interpretations. In fact, usually at least some form of stability of a model is wanted. This opinion seems to be supported by empirical evidence that over long periods of time the development of most industrialized economies is relatively stable. See Vercelli (1991) for a critical examination of this opinion, however. In its strict form it is required that the (steady-state) equilibrium of a model is stable. This view rests on the well-known observation of Samuelson (1947, p. 5), that "unstable equilibria, even if they exist, are transient, and non-persistent", and thus not very interesting. In a somewhat less strict form, which applies to non-linear models only, it is not necessary that the (steady-state) equilibrium itself is stable. Rather it is only required that inherent divergent movements of the model variables are turned back, say "stabilized", for instance through the introduction of economically meaningful upper- and lower limits. An example is Hicks' model of cyclical growth, see Gandolfo (1980). Finally, we notice that in models with forward-looking rational expectations (saddlepoint) stability is important as the model needs to converge on the terminal conditions. For a critical account of the stability properties of models with rational expectations, see Vercelli (1991).

Let us consider now how one can analyze the dynamic and long-run properties of a given non-linear macroeconometric model. First, we notice that in general two different types of sources of dynamics prevail simultaneously within a model: (a) lags in budget constraints and (stock-flow) identities, and (b) behavioral lags. Type (a) lags imply dynamics that are intrinsic to any consistent model, cf. Turnovsky (1977). For logical reasons they *must* be included in the model. Type (b) lags are more specific, depending on the particular model or problem under consideration. An example is a Keynesian consumption function in which the consumption expenditures react with some specific (*ad hoc*) distributed lag on disposable income. Another example is a lagged explanatory variable in the short-run dynamic part of an error-correction equation. We also mention here the lag of the error term, i.e the disequilibrium error, which is included in such a type of equation. It is useful to start a dynamic analysis of a model with a careful inspection of its individual equations in order to get an impression of the presence of these two sources of dynamics. Second, due to their size and complexity, it is usually not trivial to get a good insight into the dynamic properties of a complete large-scale model. In fact, some authors conclude that the models behave in practice often as a black-box, see e.g. Kuh and Neese (1982). Helpful tools are still being developed in the literature though. Deleau and Malgrange (1975) classify methods to analyze properties of a given model into two types, i.e. external analysis and internal analysis. Methods are labeled external in case they are concerned with (reduced form) properties of the model as a whole and if no systematic attempt is made to explain these properties in terms of, using again the above terminology, the inner part of the black-box. Methods of internal analysis, on the contrary, precisely try to unravel the inner part of the black-box. The emphasis is on the explanation and economic interpretation of the properties of a model in terms of key variables, (structural form) equations and/or submodels.

An example of external analysis is the calculation of dynamic multipliers. Especially, long-run properties of a model are investigated through inspection of the long-run multipliers. Other closely related examples are deterministic or stochastic simulation experiments. In long-run deterministic simulations, for instance, the model computes endogenous paths given (extended) smoothed numerical values for the exogenous variables. Inspection of these paths provides insight into the stability and oscillatory behavior of the model. Furthermore, it can reveal inconsistencies that are caused by, for instance, the omission of important dynamic feedbacks, like fiscal or financial closure rules, etc. A drawback of this approach is that the results obtained might depend heavily on the chosen numerical values of the exogenous variables. A further example of external analysis consists of the linearization of a model around a reference solution. Next, the eigenvalues of the linearized model are calculated in order to determine whether the model is dynamically stable and/or exhibits cyclical behavior. A clear argument against this approach is that the original model is non-linear, which implies that the results obtained with the linearization only hold locally around the reference solution. However, in practice it turns out that many macroeconometric models do not have severe non-linearities. Under such circumstances, the approach works reasonably well.

An example of internal analysis is the application of graph-theoretical methods with respect to the structural form of a model. Doing so, one can identify in a systematic way the main (dynamic) causal links within a model, and investigate whether the model possibly can be decomposed in a number of more or less separate subsystems. Another example is the so-called structural sensitivity analysis of a model. This means that the model is exposed in a systematic way to deliberately chosen perturbations of its parameters. The goal is to identify those parameters and parts of the model that are mostly responsible for the model's dynamic behavior, the model's eigenvalues, etc. See Kuh *et al.* (1985) for an excellent comprehensive study of internal analysis.

A somewhat different line of research is the explicit analytical study of the long-run properties of macroeconometric models. Interesting questions are for instance: are the individual equations of the model compatible with steady-state properties that can be rationalized by neoclassical theory? What is the impact of technical progress? Does the model as a whole possess a consistent steady-state growth solution? As discussed above, existence of a steady-state growth solution implies that certain homogeneity conditions must hold. Analysis of these restrictions sheds an interesting light on the overall consistency of the model. In case a macroeconometric model indeed possesses a steady-state solution, it is interesting to write down this solution in detail in order to carry out comparative dynamic and static analysis. We observe, however, that in practice the vast majority of econometric models does not possess such a solution, which extremely hampers this approach. In some cases, in particular if only a few of the restrictions are violated, a way out of the problem can be to modify the specification of the model at hand a bit in order to guarantee that all restrictions are satisfied, cf. Wallis and Whitley (1987). In this context we also draw the attention to the class of relatively small continuous time macroeconometric models dating back to the model of the United Kingdom developed by Bergstrom and Wymer (1976). The models of this type are specified in such a way that they possess a steady-state growth solution based on (neoclassical) economic theory. For a more recent model with continuous time, see e.g. Gandolfo and Padoan (1990). Finally, the use of so-called core models or maquettes can be mentioned. These are relatively small transparent models (with discrete time) that capture the most important elements of large-scale macroeconometric models. Usually the core models possess a steady-state growth solution. They are used as a benchmark to explain observed (long-run) dynamic behavior of large-scale models. See e.g. Deleau *et al.* (1984, 1990).

A final recent approach to examine the dynamics of a macroeconometric model consists of a detailed analysis of model anchors, which are parts of the model that drive the long-run solution. Generally speaking the working of the labor and goods market forms the central part of Keynesian models. Recent approaches, founded on the economic theoretical work of Layard and Nickell (1986) focus on the formation of prices and wages in the context of imperfect competition. In particular, the level of wages is assumed to be determined in a process of collective wage bargaining, whereas prices are set using mark-up factors over unit labor costs. From these two elements one is able to determine a long-run equilibrium rate of unemployment, i.e. the Non-Accelerating Inflation Rate of Unemployment (NAIRU). Since the NAIRU is expressed in terms of variables labeled exogenous (like the wedge), one is able to interpret the dynamic development of the NAIRU in a straightforward way. Next, it is interesting to investigate the convergence properties of the actual unemployment implied by the model towards the NAIRU. Studies that follow this route with respect to models of the United Kingdom are e.g. Joyce and Wren-Lewis (1991) and Turner (1991).

After having sketched these developments in the literature, let us now turn to the contributions of this volume. We will briefly summarize the topics addressed in order to give the reader an impression of what follows.

The first two theoretical chapters deal with a number of general aspects concerning the construction and analysis of dynamic macroeconometric models. In Chapter 2, Huizinga and Kooiman systematically analyze the advantages and disadvantages of different specifications of econometric models which incorporate sensible long-run equilibria and short-run adjustment dynamics. In particular, they compare a general autoregressive distributed lag model with a general error-correction model, assuming that both models have the same long-run equilibrium. The correspondence between the models is scrutinized observing that each model can be reparameterized as a special case of the other. Next, the stability properties are examined. Doing so, the focus is on error-correction models, especially on the case where the error terms of these models do not converge to zero as a result of a lack of sufficient feedbacks. Finally, Huizinga and Kooiman argue that an error-correction specification should only be used in case the error term has an unambiguous economic interpretation.

Wymer observes that, although almost all existing macroeconometric models with continuous time are specified as a non-linear model, they are usually estimated by using a linearized form. In addition, their dynamic analysis is mostly done by using "linear" techniques, like eigenvalue (sensitivity) analysis and linear optimal control. Pointing out the weaknesses of this approach, Wymer advocates in Chapter 3, as an alternative, the consistent use of non-linear techniques. He discusses how non-linear estimation methods can be developed that are basically straightforward generalizations of well-established linear methods. With respect to non-linear dynamics, he observes that in some of the existing continuous time models features can be identified which suggest that the models might easily exhibit chaotic behavior. Wymer describes the tools that are needed to investigate this complex type of dynamics, and shows the similarities of these tools with more traditional linear methods (like eigenvalue analysis). The chapter concludes with a brief discussion of non-linear optimal control.

The next two chapters investigate some methodological issues concerning the external and internal analysis of models. In Chapter 4, Barten considers the problem of extracting the eigenvalues of, possibly non-linear, macroeconometric models. As known, the eigenvalues can be determined by calculating the roots of the characteristic equation associated with the (linearized) model. In practice, this can be an enormous task. Barten proposes a simple alternative approach, illustrating it with some small typical examples. First, he simulates the model in order to generate time paths of endogenous variables. Second, an autoregressive form is fitted on these time paths. Then it is shown that the roots associated with the autoregressive form are reasonable approximations of the eigenvalues of the model, in the sense that they provide roughly the same kind of information.

Gilli discusses in Chapter 5 the use of graph-theoretical methods in the analysis of macroeconometric models. To begin with, he reviews causal-ordening tools – like the reduced graph, the minimal graph and the reachability matrix – that can be used to reveal the logical structure of static as well as dynamic models. These tools are particularly useful, as it turns out that macroeconometric models often possess a kind of hierarchical structure. Insight into this structure is interesting, amongst others from an economic point of view. Next, Gilli considers the problem of the determination of the rank of a given matrix. Using nonoriented graphs he derives an upper bound for the rank. It is shown that this problem is closely related to the choice of the normalization of the equations of a model, which in practice is often relevant with respect to the numerical solution of the model.

The subsequent six chapters consider in detail aspects of the dynamic properties of a number of well-documented existing macroeconometric models. The investigations demonstrate the application of a whole range of techniques which can be helpful in order to understand and control better the dynamics of a model. In Chapter 6, Boutillier and Jacquinot analyze the dynamics of MEFISTO, a large-scale macroeconometric model of the French monetary and financial system. The model has error-correction specifications for almost all behavioral equations. This feature enables Boutillier and Jacquinot to investigate, by using graph-theoretical methods, the causality structure within, respectively, a short-run, medium-run, and long-run version of the model. It turns out that from a causality point of view, MEFISTO is a fully hierarchical model in the long run. In the short- and medium run there is a large overall interdependence, although small local blocks still can be identified. Subsequently, the eigenvalues of MEFISTO are computed. Using the causality results, a sensitivity analysis of the eigenvalues is carried out. In this way, a large number of the eigenvalues can be assigned to single equations or small local blocks, which is useful to explain the dynamics of the whole model.

Brandsma and Italianer discuss the problem of the breakdown of large-scale models in (deterministic) simulation experiments. Large systems are not able to support every conceivable set of shocks to the exogenous variables. Traditional methods, like multiplier analysis, do not give an overall answer to this problem. Brandsma and Italianer advocate in Chapter 7 a two step procedure: first construct a maquette and after that apply stochastic simulation as a complement to deterministic analysis. Their example is the Quest model of the European Commission, a model with error-correction mechanisms and model-consistent expectations. The construction of a maquette needs compression of the stochastic information of the original model. Therefore, a method is developed which produces standardized shocks for the error terms of the maquette of Quest. Stochastic simulation with the maquette reveals some insight into the dynamics of Quest. Especially the wage-price block and its interaction with labor demand in the supply block turn out to be essential. Finally, simulations with and without EMU, reveal larger stability in the first case.

Hall and Garratt elaborate some recent developments with respect to expectations formation in large-scale macroeconometric models. They argue in Chapter 8 that rational expectations, although appealing to analyze the long run, are not appropriate to investigate the adjustment dynamics of the short- and medium run. One reason being, for instance, that the expected jumps in the expectations variables are not observed in practice. An alternative approach, recently implemented and tested by the authors, is the inclusion of learning behavior in the models, such that in the short run expectations errors can be made but in the long run there is convergence on a rational expectations equilibrium. Hall and Garratt develop a general framework for this approach which involves the use of Kalman filters. They also discuss applications of it, among others with respect to the London Business School model of the United Kingdom, and in turn examine the impact of the use of different learning rules on the adjustment dynamics.

Smith and Wallis consider the long-run sustainability of fiscal policy in macroeconometric models with forward-looking expectations. They focus in Chapter 9 on the problem of instability, in particular of government debt, in the case of an unanticipated permanent fiscal expansion. A sensible solution for this problem can be the incorporation of a financial closure rule aimed at stabilizing the government debt: for instance, a policy reaction function in which the tax rate changes as a function of the ratio of government debt to national income. Smith and Wallis first review the work that has been carried out following this route with multi-country models. Next, they introduce with success a financial closure rule in the NIESR model and STR model of the United Kingdom. Finally, they investigate the effects of delay in the implementation of a financial closure rule in Murphy's model of Australia.

The long-run steady-state structure of MULTIMOD is analyzed in Chapter 10 by Loufir and Malgrange. MULTIMOD is a 450-equation multi-national macroeconometric model developed at the International Monetary Fund. The behavioral equations of the model are almost systematically described by error-correction specifications. It is known that the model satisfies one exogenously given reference steady-state growth solution by construction, namely through an appropriate choice of residuals. More generally, Loufir and Malgrange discuss that the model satisfies relevant homogeneity conditions, which implies that it is consistent with a general long-run steady-state growth *system*. This system enables them to compute directly (asymptotic) long-run multipliers of (arbitrary) exogenous shocks. The computed results turn out to be plausible. Only in some experiments numerical problems arise, which seems to be related to the fact that the model has two very close steady-state solutions.

Chapter 11, by Schoonbeek and Sterken, considers the dynamics of wage formation in the Netherlands within the context of the macroeconometric model CESAM. It is argued that the long-run properties of this model are largely influenced by the wage-unemployment response. The latter is studied in detail. First, following the recent literature on wage level bargaining and the NAIRU, the wage level approach is investigated. Using cointegration techniques this approach is extensively tested for, but rejected after 1989. This implies that real wages, productivity, unemployment, and the wedge do not form a long-run equilibrium process in levels. Next, a more satisfactory Phillips-type wage growth equation is estimated, which supports the idea of hysteresis in unemployment.

The last two chapters focus on some of the main driving forces of long-run dynamics, i.e. capital accumulation and technical progress. In Chapter 12, Kuper presents a dynamic putty-clay vintage model of investments. The model is firmly based on economic theory. Using a nested production function with three inputs – labor, capital and energy –, and embodied as well as disembodied technical progress, the model equations are derived from an intertemporal optimization problem faced by the firms. Dynamics arise as a result of adjustment costs associated with investments, which depend on the size of the existing capital stock. Kuper examines in detail the long-run equilibrium properties of the model in relation to the type of technical progress, and the dynamic responses to deliberately chosen price shocks. Finally, in order to illustrate the empirical validity, the model is fitted using data of manufacturing industries in the Netherlands.

The final Chapter 13, by Van Schaik, is an empirical study of economic growth. Two issues, analyzed in an earlier study with a dataset of a small number of industrialized countries, are investigated again in detail using another much larger dataset encompassing 107 countries covering the period 1950–1986. The first issue is whether technical progress is endogenous or exogenous. Van Schaik estimates different variants of growth equations and concludes that technical progress is endogenous. This confirms the conclusion obtained before with the other dataset. The second issue concerns the earlier conclusion that the convergence in productivity towards the productivity in the United States has disappeared after 1973. It turns out that this observation must be qualified: there are exceptions among the richest as well as the poorest countries. Finally, given his findings, Van Schaik proposes to incorporate technical progress in macroeconometric models in an endogenous way, rather than exogenously as is common practice in the existing models.

References

Bank of England (1993), "The Bank of England macroeconomic model, spring 1993 version", Technical report, Bank of England, London.

Bergstrom, A.R. and C.R. Wymer (1976), "A model of disequilibrium neoclassical growth and its application to the United Kingdom", in A.R. Bergstrom, editor, *Statistical inference in continuous time economic models*, North-Holland, Amsterdam.

Bodkin, R.G., L.R. Klein, and K. Marwah, editors (1991), *A history of macroeconometric model-building*, Edward Elgar, Aldershot.

Deleau, M., C. Le Van, and P. Malgrange (1990), "The long run of macroeconometric models", in Champsaur, P. *et al.*, editors, *Essays in honor of Edmond Malinvaud, volume II, macroeconomics*, MIT Press, Cambridge.

Deleau, M. and P. Malgrange (1975), "Méthodes d'analyse des modèles empiriques", *Annales de l'INSEE*, **20**, 3–34.

Deleau, M., P. Malgrange, and P-A. Muet (1984), "A study of short-run and long-run properties of macroeconometric models by means of an aggregative core model", in P. Malgrange and P-A. Muet, editors, *Contemporary macroeconomic modelling*, Basil Blackwell, Oxford.

Engle, R.F. and C.W.J. Granger (1987), "Co-integration and error correction: representation, estimation, and testing", *Econometrica*, **55**, 251–276.

Gandolfo, G. (1980), *Economic dynamics: methods and models*, North-Holland, Amsterdam.

Gandolfo, G. and P.C. Padoan (1990), "The Italian continuous time model: theory and empirical results", *Economic Modelling*, **7**, 91–132.

Hargreaves, C.P., editor (1992), *Macroeconomic modelling of the long run*, Edward Elgar, Aldershot.

Joyce, M.A.S. and S. Wren-Lewis (1991), "The role of the real exchange rate and capacity utilisation in convergence to the NAIRU", *The Economic Journal*, **101**, 497–507.

Kuh, E. and J. Neese (1982), "Econometric model diagnostics", in G.C. Chow and P. Corsi, editors, *Evaluating the reliability of macro-economic models*, John Wiley, New York.

Kuh, E., J.W. Neese, and P. Hollinger (1985), *Structural sensitivity in econometric models*, John Wiley and Sons, New York.

Layard, R. and S. Nickell (1986), "Unemployment in Britain", *Economica*, **53**, S121–S169.

Samuelson, P.A. (1947), *Foundations of economic analysis*, Harvard University Press, Cambridge.

Sargan, J.D. (1964), "Wages and prices in the United Kingdom: a study in econometric methodology", in P.E. Hart, G. Mills, and J.K. Whitaker, editors, *Econometric analysis for national economic planning*, Butterworth, London.

Turner, D.S. (1991), "The determinants of the NAIRU response in simulations on the Treasury Model", *Oxford Bulletin of Economics and Statistics*, **53**, 225–242.

Turnovsky, S.J. (1977), *Macroeconomic analysis and stabilization policy*, Cambridge University Press, Cambridge.

Uebe, G., G. Huber, and J. Fischer (1986), *Macro-econometric models – an international bibliography*, Gower Press, Aldershot.

Vercelli, A. (1991), *Methodological foundations of macroeconomics: Keynes & Lucas*, Cambridge University Press, Cambridge.

Wallis, K.F. and J.D. Whitley (1987), "Long-run properties of large-scale macroeconometric models", *Annales d'Economie et de Statistique*, **6/7**, 207–224.

Methods and Applications of Economic Dynamics
L. Schoonbeek, E. Sterken and S.K. Kuipers (editors)

Chapter 2

Integrating dynamics and equilibrium in (large) models[1]

Frederik Huizinga and Peter Kooiman

1 Introduction

One of the main current research projects at the Dutch Central Planning Bureau (CPB) consists of the construction of a model that is suitable for both the short and medium term and the long term. The rationale behind this effort is that many current policies and policy proposals are aimed at improving the structure of the economy. Thus, these policies aim to change the equilibrium of the economy. However, the new equilibrium obviously is not reached overnight, and these policies may in effect have very different short and medium-term effects. In particular, the short/medium and long-term welfare effects of these policies may be of opposite sign, following the saying of "no pain, no gain", and it is this trade-off between "current pain" and "future gain" that often makes it unclear whether a policy should be adopted, or at least makes the proposal controversial.

A proper economic analysis of such a policy, or of a certain exogenous shock of a similar nature, obviously requires a discussion of both the equilibrium or long-run effects and the process of transition towards the new equilibrium. Also, obviously, these two elements of the analysis should be internally consistent. For this reason, it is advisable that both elements be carried out with the same model. Such a model, therefore, must be able to describe the short and medium-term as well as the long-term effects of that policy or exogenous shock.

---

1. The authors thank R. van Stratum and N. Draper for helpful comments.

This overall task has led us to a research project to develop a model that integrates the more empirically oriented traditional macro models with the more theoretically oriented general-equilibrium models. As a start, we want to build a model that integrates the main elements of FKSEC, the Dutch CPB's short and medium-term macro model and MIMIC, the CPB's long-term general-equilibrium model, cf. Central Planning Bureau (1992) and Gelauff (1992).

Before engaging in the actual work of building a new model we decided, as a first step, to develop a general idea about the framework to be chosen as a basic structure for the model and its equations. In this paper we therefore investigate the suitability of alternative modeling frameworks for the integration project. To this end we compare these frameworks with respect to ease of combining equilibrium and dynamics, ease of incorporating the relevant economic theory, and overall transparency of the resulting model structure, both with respect to the long-run equilibrium behavior and the transitional short and medium-term dynamics.

To limit our focus, in this paper we do not deal with issues of estimation or testing, nor do we concern ourselves with explicit or implicit theoretical foundations for either the long or short run. For the moment we simply assume that the available structural models for the short and medium run and for the long run adequately represent our current theoretical and empirical notions about the relevant relationships, and we concentrate on the issue of their integration within a unified modeling framework.

Our knowledge of the properties of such frameworks is still relatively limited. For instance, while some form of error-correction model seems like a logical candidate for an overall framework, and much empirical work on error correction has already been performed, most of the error-correction literature deals with single equations. As far as we know, little has been written on the use of error correction in large-scale models, and even less on the relative advantage of using error correction as a framework for large-scale models compared to possible alternative frameworks.

A natural point to start with is the question what exactly is the relationship between economic theory, equilibrium and dynamics. Granger (1986) asked himself the same question and his answer was:

"At the least sophisticated level of economic theory lies the belief that certain pairs of economic variables should not diverge from each other by too great an extent, at least in the long run. Thus, such variables may drift apart in the short-run or according to seasonal factors, but if they continue to be too far apart in the long-run, then economic forces, such as a market mechanism or government intervention, will begin to bring them together again."

For Granger, this answer naturally led to his research into cointegration.[2] For every model that imposes a deterministic long-run relationship between two macroeconomic variables, but allows deviations from this relationship in the short run, will display cointegration. More generally, any model that imposes a trend-stationary long-run relationship on certain variables imposes that these variables are cointegrated. Thus there appears to be a strong link between economic theory, equilibrium and cointegration. Allowing for the deficiencies of informal, general statements, one can say that the contribution of theory to equilibrium economics lies in providing a reasoned belief that certain cointegrating vectors exist for certain sets of variables.[3]

Moreover, the statement that certain sets of variables are cointegrated not only says something about the long run, but also about the process of adjustment, namely that it can be described by an error-correction model. This property of cointegrated variables is called the Granger Representation Theorem.

The Granger Representation Theorem, of course, does not say that the error-correction model is the only way to describe a dynamic process. Therefore, in this paper, we compare the error-correction model to other representations in a systematic way and discuss their relative advantages and disadvantages.

The remainder of the paper is as follows. In the next section we set up the Autoregressive Distributed Lag Model (ADLM) and the Error-Correction Model (ECM) as two logical candidate frameworks for the integration project. The third and fourth sections discuss stability issues in these models and, in particular, analyze the consequences of some type of instability that is likely to arise from the Dutch CPB's standard operating policy to keep government policy exogenous. The following section discusses some general advantages and disadvantages of the ADLM and ECM systems and also briefly mentions the relationship between these models and first-difference models. The last section summarizes our conclusions.

2 The ADLM and ECM systems

In line with the above Granger quote we shall start with the assumption that the following long-term relationship exists between the joint set of variables $\{y_t, x_t\}$, indexed by time t, that we consider in our (discrete time) short and long-term macroeconomic models[4]

2. In the quote it is not assumed that the original series are integrated, which many authors state as an additional requirement for cointegration. However, Campbell and Perron (1991) in their survey of the cointegration literature do not make this additional requirement and simply require that a (linear) combination of these variables is trend-stationary.

3. To keep the exposition simple and intuitive, we abstract from non-linear relationships. However, the cointegration literature also allows for non-linearities, and we briefly mention them in Section 5.

4. Note that it may not always be optimal for agents to reach equilibrium as indicated by (1), for instance in the case of adjustment costs. It may be a matter of philosophy how to define equilibrium

$$By_t + \Gamma x_t = 0 \tag{1}$$

Here y_t is an $(n \times 1)$ vector of endogenous variables, x_t an $(m \times 1)$ vector of exogenous variables, and B and Γ are $(n \times n)$ and $(n \times m)$ matrices of coefficients. We shall assume throughout the paper that B is nonsingular, and that the structural form (1) is identified. The associated reduced form is $y_t + \Pi x_t = 0$, where $\Pi = B^{-1}\Gamma$. For ease of exposition we assume that the long-term relationships between y_t and x_t are linear, so that they can properly be represented as in (1).

One may wonder under what circumstances a long-run solution to a dynamic model can be represented by a static system, such as (1), in particular when the model contains stock-flow identities. Assume, for example, that the model contains the identity $K_t = (1-\delta)K_{t-1} + I_t$, where K_t and I_t are the capital stock and the flow of (net) investment, and δ is the rate of depreciation. If we consider a polynomial growth rate $\rho(t)$ for I_t we obtain $K_t = (1+\rho(t))/(\delta+\rho(t))I_t$ as the equilibrium relationship for K_t, which only fits into the format of (1) when $\rho(t) = \rho_0$, i.e. under steady growth. We shall return to this issue in Section 4.

In the remainder of this paper we shall assume that (1) is completely known to the modeler. This sets us apart from the mainstream concerns in the literature on cointegration, which largely focuses on the problems involved in the identification and estimation of unknown cointegrating relationships between non-stationary variables. Indeed, as stated in the introduction, our more modest goal is only to investigate the suitability of alternative model frameworks for the integration of given notions about, on the one hand, the short and medium-term relationships, and, on the other hand, the long-run relationships between y_t and x_t. Thus, the known matrices B and Γ represent our prior theoretical and empirical understanding of the long-run equilibrium. For ease of exposition we also leave out the usual random term in all equations and deal with deterministic systems only; however, the analysis for the stochastic case is essentially the same.

To derive a dynamic system consistent with the equilibrium (1) we consider two ways. First, we start with (1) and transform it into a dynamic relationship in such a way that we incorporate our understanding of the short and medium term. This boils down to writing down an Autoregressive Distributed Lag Model (ADLM) consistent with (1). The second way starts with a short-run model that represents our understanding of the short and medium run, and we add the long-run relationship (1) as a target. This boils down to writing down an Error-Correction Model (ECM) consistent with (1). In the remainder of this section we shall derive the ADLM and ECM systems associated with (1), and discuss their formal relationship. In doing so we closely follow the setup in Davidson (1984) and build on his results.

in this case. For the purpose of this paper we say that in such a case agents never reach equilibrium because of adjustments costs, and then possibly analyze the degree of disequilibrium caused by these adjustment costs.

The ADLM system

Transforming equation (1) into a dynamic relationship consists of two steps: replacing matrices B and Γ by matrix polynomials in the lag operator and adding variables that are important for the short run but do not play a role in the long run (assuming such variables exist). The resulting dynamic relation can be written as

$$B(L)y_t + \Gamma(L)x_t + E(L)z_t = 0 \tag{2}$$

in which z_t is a $(q \times 1)$ vector of exogenous variables that are assumed to have only a temporary effect (or, more precisely, that do not enter the equilibrium conditions[5] $By_t + \Gamma x_t = 0$), and

$$B(L) = \sum_{i=0}^{p} B_i L^i,\ \Gamma(L) = \sum_{i=0}^{p} \Gamma_i L^i,\ E(L) = \sum_{i=0}^{p} E_i L^i \tag{3}$$

are matrix polynomials in the lag operator ($Ly_t = y_{t-1}$) of dimension $(n \times n)$, $(n \times m)$ and $(n \times q)$, respectively. The highest non-zero lag occurring in (3) is p. Assuming that all three polynomials are of lag order p is not restrictive; we just fill up the shorter lags with zero matrices to bring them to lag length p.

System (2) is the general equation of an ADLM. For our purposes we like to impose some restrictions on this ADLM. First, in a deterministic steady state without growth, we want to impose that the variables obey (1). Denoting by $X(1)$ the sum of the lag matrices X_i in the general matrix lag polynomial $X(L)$, the deterministic non-growth steady-state version of (2) is $B(1)y_t + \Gamma(1)x_t + E(1)z_t = 0$. Assuming that this equation determines all values of y_t, $B(1)$ is invertible and the solution for y_t can be written as $y_t + B(1)^{-1}\Gamma(1)x_t + B(1)^{-1}E(1)z_t = 0$. The requirement that the non-growth steady-state solution of (2) obeys (1) then amounts to the requirement that $B(1)^{-1}\Gamma(1)x_t + B(1)^{-1}E(1)z_t = \Pi x_t$. Because we want this equation to hold for all steady-state values of x_t and z_t, it implies that $B(1)^{-1}\Gamma(1) = \Pi$ and that $E(1) = 0$. This in turn implies that the ADLM can be written as

$$B(L)y_t + \Gamma(L)x_t + E'(L)\Delta z_t = 0 \tag{4}$$

with $\Delta z_t = z_t - z_{t-1}$, $B(1)^{-1}\Gamma(1) = \Pi$, and $E'(L)$ an unrestricted lag polynomial of order $p-1$.

The requirement that $B(1)^{-1}\Gamma(1) = \Pi$ amounts to the condition that $B(1) = FB$ and $\Gamma(1) = F\Gamma$ for some nonsingular matrix F. One obvious way to achieve

5. The vector z contains variables that do not appear in the equilibrium system at all. We assume there are no endogenous variables for which no equilibrium relation is specified. Hence z contains only exogenous variables. In addition, it may be that, at the level of the individual equation, the ADLM contains endogenous and exogenous variables that are not included in the corresponding equilibrium equation. We will say something about that case in the discussion on ADLM* models below.

this is by setting $F = I$, so that $B(1) = B$ and $\Gamma(1) = \Gamma$. This way, the sums of the coefficients on the current and lagged variables in (4), (and also (2)), equal the corresponding coefficients in (1). We will refer to a model in which this condition is imposed as an ADLM*. So, an ADLM* is a dynamic model in which we simply added lags to the equilibrium conditions we started with.

Second, we generally require of the dynamics of (4) that the system is stable, that is all roots of $|B(\lambda)| = 0$ must lie outside the unit circle, and that the dynamic properties for the short and medium term roughly conform to our current knowledge about them.

The ECM system

The second method we consider to integrate dynamics and equilibrium is adding a restriction on the long term to a dynamic model. The way we do this is through an error-correction model. Following Davidson (1984), this model is written as follows

$$A_1(L)\Delta y_t + A_2(L)\Delta x_t + A_3(L)\Delta z_t + C(L)(B^* y_{t-1} + \Gamma^* x_{t-1}) = 0 \tag{5}$$

where $A_1(L)$, $A_2(L)$, $A_3(L)$ en $C(L)$ are, respectively, $(n \times n)$, $(n \times m)$, $(n \times q)$ and $(n \times n)$ matrix polynomials in the lag operator of order $p - 1$. The first part of the model, involving the Δ terms, we call the first-difference component and the second part the error-correction component. By setting $C(L) = 0$, we get a general first-difference model, which therefore can be considered as a submodel of system (5). $B^* y_t + \Gamma^* x_t = 0$ is the equilibrium relationship between y_t and x_t. We define $e_t = B^* y_t + \Gamma^* x_t$. Therefore, e_{t-1} is the error or the deviation from equilibrium in the previous period. $C(L)$ is the feedback matrix polynomial. It determines how the past deviations from equilibrium exert their influence onto the first-difference component of the model. The coefficients of the A, C and (B^*, Γ^*) matrices are often interpreted as the impact, feedback and equilibrium coefficients of the model. Note that we have, again, divided the vector of exogenous variables (x_t, z_t) into the subvectors x_t and z_t. As in the ADLM, x_t denotes the subvector of exogenous variables that enter the equilibrium conditions, and z_t the subvector of exogenous variables that do not.

Although systems (4) and (5) look somewhat different and are also based on somewhat different approaches, there is no basic difference between them. This is so, because either system can always be reparameterized as a version of the other. To show this, we first replace all Δ's by $(1 - L)$, so that (5) is also written in levels, and combine coefficients. The resulting version of (5) is

$$\begin{aligned}(A_1(L) - (A_1(L) - C(L)B^*)L)y_t \; &+ \; (A_2(L) - (A_2(L) - C(L)\Gamma^*)L)x_t \\ &+ \; A_3(L)(1 - L)z_t = 0 \end{aligned} \tag{6}$$

System (6) is, in fact, an ADLM system, so that it immediately follows that every ECM system can be written as an ADLM system. The two systems are identical if all the (lag) coefficients are the same for all variables. For the coefficients on y_{t-i}, $i = 0, \ldots, p$, this requires that

$$\begin{aligned} B_0 &= A_{1,0} \\ B_i &= A_{1,i} - A_{1,i-1} + C_{i-1}B^* \quad i = 1, \ldots, p-1 \\ B_p &= -A_{1,p-1} + C_{p-1}B^* \end{aligned} \tag{7}$$

and for the coefficients on x_{t-i}, $i = 0, \ldots, p$,

$$\begin{aligned} \Gamma_0 &= A_{2,0} \\ \Gamma_i &= A_{2,i} - A_{2,i-1} + C_{i-1}\Gamma^* \quad i = 1, \ldots, p-1 \\ \Gamma_p &= -A_{2,p-1} + C_{p-1}\Gamma^* \end{aligned} \tag{8}$$

and for the coefficients on Δz_{t-i}, $i = 0, \ldots, p-1$,

$$E_i' = A_{3,i} \quad i = 0, \ldots, p-1 \tag{9}$$

Since we can always find matrices $A_{1,i}$, $A_{2,i}$, $A_{3,i}$, C_i, B^* and Γ^* that satisfy (7), (8) and (9), it must be the case that every ADLM can also be rewritten as an ECM. However, while there is one ADLM reparameterization for every ECM namely (6), the reverse is not true, because the ECM contains many more coefficients than an ADLM. To be precise, an ECM contains n^2p extra coefficients, so that we need n^2p extra restrictions to identify the system. A standard way to obtain restrictions is to include only the error term of the previous period in the equation, i.e. to set $C_i = 0$ for $i = 1, \ldots, p-1$. This gives us $n^2(p-1)$ restrictions. The remaining n^2 extra restrictions can, for instance, come from a set of restrictions on the matrices (B^*, Γ^*) that identify the structural form of the errors e_t.

Despite this multitude of extra coefficients, we can already say something useful about the properties of the ECM even without any restrictions on its coefficients. By summing equations (7) and (8), we get

$$B(1) = C(1)B^* \tag{10}$$

$$\Gamma(1) = C(1)\Gamma^* \tag{11}$$

For an ADLM, the conditions that in a non-growth steady state equation (1) holds are $E(1) = 0$ and $B(1)^{-1}\Gamma(1) = B^{-1}\Gamma$. In an ECM the first condition is automatically fulfilled by including z_t only in the first-difference component. Equations (10) and (11) indicate that in an ECM the second condition becomes $(C(1)B^*)^{-1}(C(1)\Gamma^*) = B^{-1}\Gamma$. This latter condition can be split up into two parts: the matrix $C(1)$ has to be invertible and the matrices B^* and Γ^* have to obey $B^* = GB$ and $\Gamma^* = G\Gamma$ where G is an arbitrary invertible matrix. If we further impose the same set of identification restrictions on $B^*y_t + \Gamma^*x_t = 0$ as on (1), $G = I$ and thus $B^* = B$ and $\Gamma^* = \Gamma$.

So, one very straightforward way to impose the condition that in a non-growth steady state equation (1) holds in an ECM consists of setting $B^* = B$ and $\Gamma^* = \Gamma$, and making sure that $C(1)$ is invertible. In the remainder of the paper we assume that indeed $B^* = B$ and that $\Gamma^* = \Gamma$.[6] The intuition about the condition that $C(1)$ is invertible will be discussed at length in the following section. For now we just say that it means that the system needs to have a full set of feedback mechanisms.

The result that ADLM and ECM systems are observational equivalent implies that the choice between the two types of models does not restrict or augment the types of economic processes we can describe. In this respect, both types of models are perfectly equivalent.[7] The choice must, therefore, be based on the degree to which the model structure helps to impose the theoretical restrictions that do define the model in a straightforward and intuitive way; the way in which it helps the empirical estimation, calibration and validation of the model; the degree of flexibility and user friendliness in practical use, such as prediction and simulation; and the degree to which the model structure helps to understand the results of these exercises.

The ADLM system*

Before we go on, we want to say a bit more about ADLM* systems. As mentioned above, these models basically consist of adding a lag structure to each of the individual equilibrium equations. This is a rather pedestrian way to build dynamic models. However, if we do not know a whole lot more about the model than that eventually a given equilibrium will be reached, and that in the short run there are some lags, it seems like a sensible way to proceed.

To get a better grip on what such a model looks like, first notice that the restrictions $B(1) = B$ and $\Gamma(1) = \Gamma$ imply that all variables in the ADLM* equations that are not included in the corresponding equilibrium equations can always be written purely in first-difference form. This is so, because their coefficients in level form add to zero. Second, if lagged endogenous variables occur in their own equation, the diagonal elements $(B_0)_{ii}$ of B_0 in general are not equal to 1 if the corresponding diagonal elements $(B)_{ii}$ of B are normalized to 1 in equation (1). To obtain the more standard version one could renormalize the ADLM* so that $(B_0)_{ii} = 1$, but for our purposes this is not necessary. Third, if $(B)_{ii} = 0$ for some equation i, then the ADLM* version of that equation is already in error-correction form. A typical example is a price equation, where the price is determined by an equilibrium condition on the quantities. For example, if the equation determining the wage is $ur_t = urn$,

6. Note that this is not restrictive compared to $B^* = GB$ and $\Gamma^* = G\Gamma$, since the matrix G can always be included in $C(L)$. For instance, one interesting decomposition of $C(L)$ is $C(L) = C'(L)B^{-1}$. This leads to an error-correction component of the form $C'(L)(y_t + B^{-1}\Gamma x_t)$, i.e. error correction in terms of reduced-form errors, as opposed to the structural-form errors $By_t + \Gamma x_t$.
7. Other model structures exist that are observationally equivalent as well, such as the Bewley and the Bårdsen representations. See e.g. Banerjee *et al.* (1993).

where ur_t and urn are the actual and the natural rate of unemployment, then the ADLM* equation is $b(L)w_t+$ (first-difference terms) $+c(L)$ $(ur_t - urn) = 0$, where w_t is the wage and $b(L)$ and $c(L)$ are scalar polynomials in the lag operator. Since w_t does not occur in its own equilibrium equation, the restriction $b(1) = 0$ must hold, so that the equation can always be written as: $b'(L)\Delta w_t =$ (first-difference terms) $+c(L)$ $(ur_t - urn)$ for some scalar lag polynomial $b'(L)$, which fits into the ECM format.

Now consider a reparameterization of an ADLM* system in ECM form. Since $B(1) = B$ and $\Gamma(1) = \Gamma$ are imposed in the ADLM*, and $B^* = B$ and $\Gamma^* = \Gamma$ in the ECM, it follows from (10) and (11) that $C(1) = I$.[8] The reverse is also true: from (10) and (11) it follows that the ADLM version of an ECM with $C(1) = I$, $B^* = B$ and $\Gamma^* = \Gamma$ is an ADLM* system. This again indicates that the ADLM* simply is an equation by equation dynamic version of the equilibrium model.

As for the coefficients of the A_1 and A_2 matrices, (7) and (8) give

$$\begin{aligned} A_{1,i} &= \sum_{j=0}^{i} B_j - \sum_{j=0}^{i-1} C_j B \\ A_{2,i} &= \sum_{j=0}^{i} \Gamma_j - \sum_{j=0}^{i-1} C_j \Gamma \end{aligned} \tag{12}$$

These equations indicate that the ADLM* system has a nice ECM reparameterization if $B(L)$ and $\Gamma(L)$ contain at most one lag. Then, by choosing $C_0 = I$ and $C_j = 0$ for $j > 0$, we get $A_{1,0} = B_0$, $A_{2,0} = \Gamma_0$ and $A_{1,j} = A_{2,j} = 0$ for $j > 0$ (since B_i and Γ_i sum to B and Γ). This results in a clear separation in terms of lags between the impact and feedback coefficients. In general, we can maintain such a division as long we let the error-correction terms for each equation start from the longest non-zero lag of the corresponding ADLM* equation.

If, on the other hand, the non-zero elements of $B(L)$ and $\Gamma(L)$ extend beyond those of $C(L)$, (12) indicates that the elements of $A_1(L)$ and $A_2(L)$ may follow a rather erratic pattern. This may include sudden sign reversals for some elements in $A_1(L)$ and $A_2(L)$ compared to those in $B(L)$ and $\Gamma(L)$. For instance, suppose that for some variable in some equation the lag coefficients in ADLM* form are $\frac{1}{4}$, $\frac{1}{4}$, $\frac{1}{4}$ and $\frac{1}{4}$ at lags 0, 1, 2 and 3. Suppose we reparameterize that equation in ECM form with the error-correction term occurring only at lag length 1 with a coefficient of 1. Then (12) indicates that the coefficients for the first difference of that variable are $\frac{1}{4}$, $-\frac{1}{2}$ and $-\frac{1}{4}$ at lag lengths 0, 1 and 2. This makes a straightforward interpretation of the ECM equation difficult, as we discuss further in Section 5.

Finally, if the ADLM* system is considered to be too limited, we can go back to the more general ADLM version (4) with $B(1) = FB$ and $\Gamma(1) = F\Gamma$. The ECM reparameterization then has $C(1) = F$. This is not surprising because, in terms of

8. Note that this unit coefficient in all EC equations results from not having renormalized the ADLM* to have unit coefficients on the diagonal entries of B_0.

levels, the off-diagonal elements of F also pick up the variables of other equilibrium equations. Here the ECM version appears to be at an advantage, as it probably is easier to think about off-diagonal elements in $C(1)$ than in F.

3 Stability

In this section, we look at stability issues in ADLM and ECM systems. In the ADLM system, there is not much to say: the model is stable if all roots of $|B(\lambda)| = 0$ lie outside the unit circle. In the ECM, (6) indicates that stability requires, likewise, that all the roots of

$$|A_1(\lambda)(1-\lambda) + C(\lambda)B\lambda| = 0 \tag{13}$$

lie outside the unit circle.

However, note that stability of y_t stands or falls with the stability of the errors e_t. So, we might as well analyze the stability of e_t directly. Moreover, analyzing stability from the point of view of the errors, while not fundamentally different, may be more convenient. The reason is that if we allow the exogenous variables to grow over time, in most cases y_t also grows with the exogenous variables, while if the model is well behaved, e_t should remain fairly constant. Finally, the direct analysis of the error terms also allows us to say something more about the nature of the disequilibrium if the model is not stable.

As stated above, the disequilibrium error e_t is defined as

$$e_t = By_t + \Gamma x_t \tag{14}$$

It follows that

$$\Delta y_t = B^{-1}\Delta e_t - \Pi \Delta x_t \tag{15}$$

Substituting this into ECM (5) gives

$$A_1(L)B^{-1}\Delta e_t + C(L)e_{t-1} + (A_2(L) - A_1(L)\Pi)\Delta x_t + A_3(L)\Delta z_t = 0 \tag{16}$$

which is a dynamic equation in e_t. Its characteristic equation is

$$|A_1(\lambda)B^{-1}(1-\lambda) + C(\lambda)\lambda| = 0 \tag{17}$$

which, not surprisingly, is just a rewritten version of (13).

In general, there are three possibilities:

(a) All roots lie outside the unit circle. In this case the model is stable, and if we run the model long enough with constant exogenous variables x_t and z_t, e_t will ultimately go to zero.

(b) There is at least one root $\lambda \neq 1$ within or on the unit circle. This implies that the model is unstable in the sense that e_t will either increase without bound or be oscillatory.

(c) All roots either lie outside the unit circle or are equal to 1, with at least one root equal to 1.

The first case is straightforward and requires no further clarification. The second case is problematic, because the model does not have a long-run solution even though the incorporation of such a long-run solution is a central goal of the project. Checking for instability is, however, in principle straightforward: just run the model for a long period and check whether it explodes (or oscillates) or not. If it does, one could analyze which coefficients of the model are the principal causes of the model's instability and adjust them.[9] This procedure, however, is not the focus of this paper, and therefore, we simply assume that this type of instability does not occur.

The third case is, from the point of view of integrating dynamics and equilibrium, the most subtle. The problem is not that the model does not stabilize, but that the level at which it stabilizes may have nothing to do with equilibrium. Moreover, the point at which the model stabilizes depends on the initial conditions and on the shock(s) given to the model.

An ADLM system contains one or more unit roots if and only if the determinant of $B(1)$ is zero, that is if $B(1)$ is singular. Since $B(1) = B$ in ADLM* systems, and B has been assumed to be invertible, we can immediately conclude that such models do not contain any unit roots. From (13) it follows similarly that an ECM system has one or more unit roots if and only if the determinant of $C(1)$ equals zero. Notice that in both cases the condition is one about the sum of the matrix entries of $B(L)$ and $C(L)$. Since both $B(1)$ and $C(1)$ are square, we can also restate the conditions for the presence of unit roots by saying that $B(1)$ or $C(1)$ must have less than full rank.

The intuition for this result for the ADLM case is straightforward: if $B(1)$ is singular, the level of y_t in a stationary steady state is not uniquely determined. For the ECM case, the mathematical intuition is, of course, the same, but we can also provide a more structural intuition within the spirit of the ECM. First, consider the case where $C(L) = C_0$, i.e. $C(L)$ consists of only a single constant matrix. Each column of this matrix C_0 can be thought of as a feedback mechanism from the corresponding element of the disequilibrium vector e_t to the dynamics of the model. More precisely, the ith column of C_0 is the derivative of the change in y_t with respect to the ith entry in the disequilibrium vector e_{t-1}. If C_0 is of full rank, all its columns are linearly independent, so that the model contains n linearly independent feedback

9. For a recent paper that connects stability to individual coefficients, see Schoonbeek (1992). See also Kuh *et al.* (1985).

mechanisms. In other words, the model contains as many feedback mechanisms as variables to be steered back towards equilibrium. This implies that the vector y_t can be brought back fully towards equilibrium.

If $C(L)$ is a lag polynomial of order one or higher, the same intuition applies to $C(1)$. The columns of $C(1)$ are the long-term partial derivatives of the change in y_t with respect to the entries in the disequilibrium vector e_{t-1}. If $C(1)$ is of full rank, the model therefore again contains n linearly independent feedback mechanisms, the effects of which may be spread out over time. It is also interesting that, as to the existence of unit roots, the properties of the lag polynomials $A_1(L)$, $A_2(L)$ and $A_3(L)$ are irrelevant.

If $C(1)$ does not have full rank, we miss at least one feedback mechanism, and the model is no longer able to bring all elements of y_t back to their equilibrium values. More formally, if $C(1)$ is not of full rank, then there exists at least some vector $e_{t-1} \neq 0$ such that $C(1)e_{t-1} = 0$. Moreover, the same holds true for any multiple of that vector. This means that there exist an infinite set of states of disequilibrium that do not send any net (long-run) impulse towards the dynamics of the system. Such states of disequilibrium can, therefore, exist forever, so that the model no longer contains a single long-run solution.

In simulation exercises, this lack of feedback mechanisms implies that the model can stabilize on any of the infinite number of disequilibrium steady states, depending on the nature and size of the shock. In stochastic simulation exercises, it may result in a roaming about of the model, much like a drunk man roams about when he no longer commands all of his feedback mechanisms.

How do we know whether the $C(1)$ matrix has full rank? In general we have to resort to calculating its determinant, but a useful necessary condition is that the matrix should not have any zero rows or columns. This implies that a necessary condition for stability is that every equation of the ECM system should contain at least one error term, and that every error term should be included in at least one equation. We will call this necessary condition the order condition for a full set of feedback mechanisms.

The most straightforward way to assure full rank of $C(1)$ is to restrict it to being a diagonal matrix without any zero entries on its diagonal. While this method may appear rather mechanical, it has two subcases of special interest. First, suppose we take an ADLM* system and reparameterize it as an ECM. We already know that in the resulting ECM, $C(1) = I$. Thus the resulting ECM has a $C(1)$ matrix of full rank. This basically restates the fact that an ADLM* system cannot contain any unit roots.

The fact that the ECM reparameterization of an ADLM* system has $C(1) = I$ yields an important further implication. It implies that the ECM reparameterization of a mixed model with both ADLM* and error-correction equations must have a $C(1)$ matrix in which the rows that correspond to the former ADLM* equations contain a 1 on the diagonal entries and zero's elsewhere. This means that the $C(1)$ matrix automatically has full rank when the submatrix of $C(1)$ obtained by deleting the "ADLM* " rows and columns has full rank. The conclusion is that if we want to build a model in which we choose between an ADLM* or an error-correction specification on an equation by equation basis (as we will suggest later on in the paper), and also want to be sure that the resulting model has no unit roots (has a full set of feedback mechanisms), we only have to check that the submatrix (of the implicit full $C(1)$ matrix) corresponding to the equations that are actually written in error-correction form has full rank.

The second special case concerns identities. Since an identity is a special case of an ADLM* specification, the result in the previous paragraph also holds for identities. So identities can also be ignored when checking for the rank of the $C(1)$ matrix. An identity is obtained within the ECM framework by applying the restrictions $C_0 = I$, $A_{1,0} = B$, $A_{2,0} = \Gamma$, $A_{3,0} = 0$ and furthermore C_i, $A_{1,i}$, $A_{2,i}$ and $A_{3,i}$ equal to zero for $i = 1, \ldots, p-1$ to the proper row of the ECM.

Finally, we note that, even if a model contains equations in ADLM* form (or as a subcase, identities), it may still be convenient to analyze the model in its complete error-correction reparameterization. This is so, because many interesting properties of the ECM are related to the $C(1)$ matrix, and as the above analysis shows, reparameterizing ADLM* equations into error-correction form implies virtually trivial additions to that $C(1)$ matrix. Therefore, we continue our analysis within the framework of the ECM.

Stability of the model does not imply, however, that e_t goes to zero for arbitrary x_t and z_t. For that to be true, (16) has to be homogeneous. For arbitrary x_t and z_t, this implies that $A_1(L)\Pi = A_2(L)$, and $A_3(L) = 0$. That is, $A_{1i}\Pi = A_{2i}$ and $A_{3i} = 0$ for all i. If x_t and z_t are growing linearly, with $\Delta x_t = g_x$ and $\Delta z_t = g_z$, this condition is relaxed to

$$A_1(1)\Pi g_x = A_2(1)g_x + A_3(1)g_z \tag{18}$$

Under this condition, the ECM displays "trend neutrality", i.e. $e_t = 0$ under steady growth.[10] To interpret (18), first suppose that $A_3(1)g_z = 0$. Then (18) implies that the sum of the impact coefficients must, in terms of reduced form (i.e. up to a linear transformation of the whole system), equal the corresponding equilibrium coefficients. This implies that the first-difference component of the ECM equals the first difference of an ADLM* system, again up to a linear transformation. The intuition that $A_3(1)g_z$ does not have to equal zero for trend neutrality is that $A_3(1)g_z$ can make up for divergence between the coefficients in $A_1(1)^{-1}A_2(1)$ and $B^{-1}\Gamma$

10. Note, however, that there are many cases in which this is not to be required. In an intertemporal optimization model with discounting and adjustment costs, for example, it is generally not optimal to fully adjust to a growing target.

(an example is the constant term in a wage change equation if the coefficients for productivity do not add up to 1, but we still want a stable labor-income ratio).

4 Singular $C(1)$ matrices

This section deals with the possibility that the $C(1)$ matrix does not have full rank. This might simply happen by accident in the course of estimation, but also by design. The latter may occur if an agent is modeled as simply not reacting to deviations from his equilibrium relationship. An important example of such an agent in the Dutch CPB models is the government, whose policies are always treated as exogenous. The reason for this is that the CPB wants to analyze the effect of government policies. If the models predict that the effect of the policies is to destabilize the economy, then the government may, of course, change its policy in response to this information (or in response to the actual occurrence of this destabilization), but such an evolution of policy is generally not modeled.

We shall not attempt to derive fully general and rigorous results for the case of a nonsingular feedback matrix. Such results are given in Davidson (1991) for the general stochastic VAR model, and in Davidson and Hall (1991) for the stochastic ECM system of equations. Instead, we shall mainly be concerned with getting an intuitive understanding of the consequences of a nonsingular $C(1)$ matrix for the feedback mechanism operating in the ECM system.

If the $C(1)$ matrix does not have full rank, (16) is an unstable dynamic system because there is at least one unit root. We now want to ask two questions about the nature of this disequilibrium. First, under which conditions is the disequilibrium constrained so that if x_t and z_t are polynomial of degree d, so is y_t? Second, under which conditions is only a subset of variables affected by the disequilibrium situation?

As a partial answer to the first question, we state the following theorem which can be proved along similar lines as in Davidson (1991, Corollary 2.1).

Theorem 1: Let x_t and z_t be polynomials of degree d. Then sufficient conditions for the solution for e_t in (16) to converge to a polynomial of degree at most d are that:
(i) the roots of (17) all lie outside the unit circle or are equal to 1;
(ii) the number of unit roots of (17) equals the nullity of $C(1)$.
Moreover, if these conditions hold, y_t will converge to a polynomial of degree d.

Rather than proving this theorem, we provide some intuition by considering the simple case in which $A_1(L) = A_{10}$ with A_{10} invertible, and $C(L) = C_0$. Then (17) can be rewritten as

$$\left|\frac{1-\lambda}{\lambda}I + BA_{10}^{-1}C_0\right| = 0 \tag{19}$$

which shows that the number of unit roots of (17) in this case equals the number of zero eigenvalues of $BA_{10}^{-1}C_0$. Furthermore, the nullity of C_0 equals the nullity of $BA_{10}^{-1}C_0$. So, the second requirement in the above theorem in this case reduces to the requirement that the number of zero eigenvalues of $BA_{10}^{-1}C_0$ must be equal to its nullity, i.e. this matrix must be non-defective with respect to its zero eigenvalues.

As an illustration, we give a simple example. Suppose that the equilibrium relationships are $y_{i,t} = 0$ for all i and the ECM is

$$\begin{aligned} \Delta y_{1,t} &= 0 \\ \Delta y_{i,t} &= -y_{i-1,t-1} \quad i = 2, \ldots, n \end{aligned} \tag{20}$$

Since (20) is homogeneous, clearly one solution is $y_{i,t} = 0$ for all i. However, depending on the initial conditions, other solutions are possible as well. For instance, $y_{1,t}$ can be a non-zero constant, in which case the solution for $y_{i,t}$ will be a polynomial of degree $i - 1$. The matrix $BA_{10}^{-1}C_0$ for system (20) is (take $B = A_{10} = I$)

$$\begin{pmatrix} 0 & & & & \\ 1 & 0 & & & \\ & 1 & 0 & & \\ & & \cdot & \cdot & \\ & & & 1 & 0 \end{pmatrix} \tag{21}$$

which consists of a single $(n \times n)$ elementary Jordan block with eigenvalue 0. It is exactly the presence of such Jordan blocks that causes the solution of a first-order difference equation to involve higher-order polynomials. The Jordan form of a general matrix involves such elementary Jordan blocks if and only if it is defective with respect to its zero eigenvalues, hence the above condition. That matrix (21) is defective with respect to its zero eigenvalue can also easily be checked since all n eigenvalues are zero, while the nullity is only 1.

Now change the first equation of (20) to $\Delta y_{1,t} = \Delta y_{n,t}$. Matrix $C(1)$ is still singular, but suddenly all errors are driven to zero, except for the last one, which is merely a constant. The matrix $BA_{10}^{-1}C_0$ becomes

$$\begin{pmatrix} 0 & & & 1 & 0 \\ 1 & 0 & & & \cdot \\ & 1 & 0 & & \cdot \\ & & \cdot & \cdot & \cdot \\ & & & 1 & 0 \end{pmatrix} \tag{22}$$

The characteristic polynomial of this matrix is $\lambda^n - \lambda = 0$, which yields a single zero eigenvalue. The nullity of (22) is still 1, so the matrix is no longer defective with respect to its zero eigenvalue.

The crucial difference between these two cases is that in the first case none of the error terms can feed back to their own first differences, while in the latter case, all of them can, except for the last one. In other words, the system changed from being completely recursive to being almost completely simultaneous.

In the remainder of this section we assume that the conditions stated in Theorem 1 hold. Further, we restrict ourselves to x_t and z_t being either constants or growing linearly. Our questions now concern the nature of the individual elements of the error vector e_t in a steady state or steady growth situation.

Steady state

If x_t and z_t are constants, then, by assumption, y_t and e_t also converge to constants. So, in the steady state (16) reduces to

$$C(1)e_0 = 0 \tag{23}$$

When $C(1)$ has full rank, the only solution is obviously $e_0 = 0$, as we found before. However, when $C(1)$ has less than full rank the solution space is a linear subspace of dimension n minus the rank of $C(1)$. The intuition is that each reduction in the rank of $C(1)$ represents a missing feedback mechanism in the system, which adds a degree of freedom to the possible set of steady-state relations between y_t and x_t. It depends on the initial conditions to which steady state e_t converges, i.e. the lagged values of e_t.

In principle, this implies that all values of the vector y_t are indeterminate. Even if $C(1)$ is such that

$$C(1) = \begin{pmatrix} P & 0 \\ Q & R \end{pmatrix} \tag{24}$$

with P a $(p \times p)$ submatrix of full rank, y_t may be completely indeterminate. In this case the first p (structural) error terms are all driven to zero (assuming that the system stabilizes somewhere), but this does not imply that a subset of y_t remains on track as well. Denoting with r_t the reduced-form errors, we have

$$r_t = y_t + \Pi x_t = B^{-1}e_t \tag{25}$$

so that the "loose" errors, in general, enter all elements of y_t. The condition for this not to happen is that B mirrors $C(1)$ in the sense that the zero block in $C(1)$ also occurs in B at the same range. Then $Br_t = e_t$ also implies that the first p reduced-form errors are zero, and thus, that the first p elements of y_t are on target.

This means that the first p equilibrium equations also do not contain any of the remaining $n-p$ "loose" elements of y_t.

Note that if $R = 0$ in (24) then the last $n-p$ error terms do not enter the system at all. In that case we get a nice separation of the error vector into two components: all the included error terms are driven to zero, while all the excluded error terms go to constants that depend on the initial conditions.

Steady growth

Now suppose that $\Delta x = g_x$ and $\Delta z = g_z$. Then $(A_2(1) - A_1(1)\Pi)g_x + A_3(1)g_z$ is a constant vector, and we denote it simply by g. Since, by assumption, e_t is at most linear under steady growth, we can write $e_t = e_0 + g_e t$, with e_0 the vector with values of the errors at time zero and g_e the vector with constant growth rates of e_t. For a general matrix lag polynomial $X(L)$, we define $X^{(r)}$ as

$$X^{(r)} = \sum_{i=0}^{\infty} X_i i^r \tag{26}$$

We can now write

$$\begin{aligned} C(L)e_{t-1} &= \sum_{i=0}^{p-1} C_i e_{t-1-i} \\ &= \sum_{i=0}^{p-1} C_i[e_0 + g_e(t-1) - g_e i] \\ &= C(1)[e_0 + g_e(t-1)] - C^{(1)}g_e \end{aligned} \tag{27}$$

Substituting into (16) gives

$$g + A_1(1)B^{-1}g_e + C(1)e_0 + C(1)g_e(t-1) - C^{(1)}g_e = 0 \tag{28}$$

which has to be satisfied for all t. Equating the coefficients of this polynomial in t to zero gives two sets of n equations

$$\begin{pmatrix} g \\ 0 \end{pmatrix} + \begin{pmatrix} C(1) & A_1(1)B^{-1} - C^{(1)} \\ 0 & C(1) \end{pmatrix} \begin{pmatrix} e_0 \\ g_e \end{pmatrix} = \begin{pmatrix} 0 \\ 0 \end{pmatrix} \tag{29}$$

which, as assumed, has a solution in (e_0, g_e). If $C(1)$ is of full rank, (29) reduces to $g_e = 0$ and $e_0 = -C(1)^{-1}g$. If at the other extreme $C(L) = 0$, e_0 is indeterminate, but g_e is determined if $A_1(1)$ is of full rank.

In general, suppose that $C(1)$ is of rank $n - r$, with $0 < r < n$. Then the second set of equations in (29) implies that $g_e = Nu$, where N is an $(n \times r)$ matrix whose columns span the nullspace of $C(1)$ and u is an arbitrary $(r \times 1)$ vector. Substituting this into the first set of equations leads to

$$g + (C(1)\ :\ (A_1(1)B^{-1} - C^{(1)})N)\begin{pmatrix} e_0 \\ u \end{pmatrix} = 0 \tag{30}$$

which is a system of n equations and $n+r$ unknowns. Since by assumption (30) has a solution (e_0, u) for general g, the inner matrix must be of full rank. Since $C(1)$ has rank $n-r$, it must be the case that the second component of the inner matrix has rank r and that its columns are independent of the columns of $C(1)$. This in turn implies that u is fully determined, and so g_e is fully determined. Moreover, in general, all elements of g_e may be non-zero. So, as soon as $C(1)$ fails to have full rank, for instance, if one agent fails to react to any disequilibrium errors, we may expect the whole system to be affected, in the sense that all disequilibrium errors may grow linearly. As for the vector e_0, all we can say is that it lies in a linear subspace of dimension r. The actual solution for e_0 depends on the initial conditions.

Similarly to the steady-state case, there is, however, an important subcase, in which we can separate e_t into a subvector that remains constant and a subvector that grows linearly. Suppose, again, that there are certain error terms to which nobody reacts, i.e. suppose there are r columns of $C(L)$ that are completely zero. By reordering the equations, we may assume that these zero columns occur at the right-hand side of $C(1)$ so that $C(1)$ may be partitioned as $(C(1)_1\ :\ 0)$, where $C(1)_1$ is $(n\times(n-r))$ and the 0 block is $(n\times r)$. Partition $A_1(1)B^{-1} - C^{(1)}$ accordingly into $((A_1(1)B^{-1})_1 - C(1)_1\ :\ (A_1(1)B^{-1})_2)$, and partition vector e_0 into the subvectors $e_{0,1}$ and $e_{0,2}$ and vector g_e into the subvectors $g_{e,1}$ and $g_{e,2}$ with the first set of components containing the first $n-r$ elements and the second set of components the remaining r. Substituting into (29), we see that the middle square matrix then also contains r zero columns. The vector $e_{0,2}$ is, therefore, completely undetermined. Taking the zero columns out, (29) is reduced to

$$\begin{pmatrix} g \\ 0 \end{pmatrix} + \begin{pmatrix} C(1)_1 & (A_1(1)B^{-1})_1 - C_1^{(1)} & (A_1(1)B^{-1})_2 \\ 0 & C(1)_1 & 0 \end{pmatrix}\begin{pmatrix} e_{0,1} \\ g_{e,1} \\ g_{e,2} \end{pmatrix} = \begin{pmatrix} 0 \\ 0 \end{pmatrix} \tag{31}$$

If $C(1)_1$ has full column rank, the second set of equations implies that $g_{e,1} = 0$. The first set of equations then becomes

$$g + (C(1)_1 : (A_1(1)B^{-1})_2)\begin{pmatrix} e_{0,1} \\ g_{e,2} \end{pmatrix} = 0 \tag{32}$$

The middle matrix is now $(n \times n)$ again. A solution to (32) exists if this matrix is invertible, i.e. if $(C(1)_1 : (A_1(1)B^{-1})_2)$ is of full rank. Then all included error terms are driven to well determined constants, i.e. constants which are independent of the initial conditions (assuming the model is stable). All of the excluded error terms are growing linearly with well determined growth rates but with constants that depend on the initial conditions.

In terms of the reduced-form errors $r_t = B^{-1}e_t$, a similar condition can be found by inserting $I = B\,B^{-1}$ into (29), giving

$$\begin{pmatrix} g \\ 0 \end{pmatrix} + \begin{pmatrix} C(1)B & A_1(1) - C^{(1)}B \\ 0 & C(1)B \end{pmatrix} \begin{pmatrix} r_0 \\ g_r \end{pmatrix} = \begin{pmatrix} 0 \\ 0 \end{pmatrix} \tag{33}$$

where r_0 is the vector with values of the reduced-form errors at time zero and g_r the vector with constant growth rates of r_t. Now suppose that r elements of r_t are not included in any equation – i.e. the levels of the corresponding elements of y_t do not occur in the model –, so that r columns of $C(1)B$ and of $C^{(1)}B$ are zero. By rearranging the order of the equations, we can partition $C(1)B$ into $((C(1)B)_1 : 0)$. Then, by the same argument as before, a solution to (33) can be found if $((C(1)B)_1 : A_1(1)_2)$ is of full rank, where $A_1(1)_2$ is the second set of columns of a similarly partitioned $A_1(1)$. If this can be done, the included elements of y_t are, up to well-determined constants, all driven to their steady states, while the excluded elements of y_t deviate from their steady states by linear terms, the constants of which depend on the initial conditions.

In the introduction to this section it was mentioned that in the Dutch CPB models the government is modeled in such a way that it does not (endogenously) react to any disequilibria. This corresponds to the case where not a column, but a row in $C(L)$ is zero. In this case we have to go back to the general statement that g_e has to lie in the nullspace of $C(1)$. The only elements of g_e that are zero for all g are the elements that correspond to the columns of $C(1)$ that are linearly independent of all other columns of $C(1)$. If there are no zero columns in $C(1)$, i.e. if all error terms are included somewhere, then at least two error terms will grow linearly and possibly more.

Integral control

The above results can easily be generalized to a model with integral control. To illustrate this we generalize the "zero columns" case. The general model with integral control is

$$A_1(L)\Delta y_t + A_2(L)\Delta x_t + A_3(L)\Delta z_t + C(L)e_{t-1} + D(L)e^*_{t-1} = 0 \tag{34}$$

where

$$e^*_t = \sum_{i=0}^{\infty} e_{t-i} \tag{35}$$

If we again allow for e_t to grow at most linearly over time, we can write for e^*_t

$$e_t^* = e_0^* + (e_0 + \frac{1}{2}g_e)t + \frac{1}{2}g_e t^2 \tag{36}$$

Substitution of (15) and (36) into (34) gives, similarly to (29)

$$\begin{pmatrix} g \\ 0 \\ 0 \end{pmatrix} + \begin{pmatrix} D(1) & C(1) - D^{(1)} & A_1B^{-1} - C^{(1)} - \frac{1}{2}D^{(1)} + \frac{1}{2}D^{(2)} \\ 0 & D(1) & C(1) + \frac{1}{2}D(1) - D^{(1)} \\ 0 & 0 & D(1) \end{pmatrix} \begin{pmatrix} e_0^* \\ e_0 \\ g_e \end{pmatrix}$$

$$= \begin{pmatrix} 0 \\ 0 \\ 0 \end{pmatrix} \tag{37}$$

First, notice that if $D(1)$ is of full rank, then both the growth rate and the level of the errors are zero and $e_0^* = -D(1)^{-1}g$. If $D(L) = 0$, we get the previous ECM. If certain cumulated errors are completely omitted from the model, then we can, after rearranging the equations, form a partition of $D(1)$ such that $D(1) = (D(1)_1 : 0)$, and try the matrix $(D(1)_1 : C(1)_2)$, where $C(1)_2$ is the second part of the similarly partitioned matrix $C(1)$. If this matrix is of full rank, the included accumulated errors are constant, while the remaining errors are constant in levels. If $(D(1)_1 : C(1)_2)$ still has certain columns fully zero, we can make a further partitioning and try the matrix $(D(1)_1 : C(1)_{2,1} : (A_1B^{-1})_3)$, where $C(1)_{2,1}$ is the block of the non-zero columns in $C(1)_2$ and $(A_1B^{-1})_3$ is the component of A_1B^{-1} corresponding to the zero columns in $C(1)_2$. If this matrix has full rank, then the included accumulated errors are constant, the remaining errors are constant insofar as they are included, and the then remaining errors are growing as a linear function of t.

5 Advantages and disadvantages of ADLM and ECM systems

As noted in the beginning of the paper, ADLM and ECM systems are basically equivalent, and the choice between them has therefore to be based on the relative advantages they provide in terms of insight, transparency and ease in practical use. In this section we say a bit about this topic. We also include a first-difference model, as that model has been the main type of model used at the Dutch CPB in the past.

ADLM

The main advantage of the ADLM system is, probably, that it is reasonably straightforward: just add lags to the equilibrium equations and, maybe, add some variables that have short-term effects. The intuition in the resulting model is also clear and can even be improved by rewriting $B(L)$ as $B \times B'(L)$, where $B'(L) = B(L)/B(1)$, where the operators $\times$ and $/$ denote multiplication and division at the level of the individual matrix entries. That is, for each variable, the lag polynomial is written as the product of the sum of the lag coefficients (which equals the corresponding coefficient in B in equation (1)) and a lag polynomial of which the sum of the lag coefficients equals 1. In this way, the equilibrium and dynamic aspects of (4) can be separated, at least optically.

The most important disadvantage of the ADLM approach is that, because of multicollinearity problems, system (4) is very difficult to estimate directly. Its first-difference version can be estimated more easily, which has been the practice followed in building the CPB's short and medium-term macro model FKSEC, but then the information about levels is lost, unless we include additional terms representing the proper constants of integration (as discussed below). Either way, the restrictions $B(1) = B$ and $\Gamma(1) = \Gamma$ need to be included in the estimation process. Thus, although the equilibrium and dynamic aspects of (4) can be separated optically, this is not the case during estimation.

ECM

A clear advantage of the ECM system is that, as an overall framework, it is well suited to our central goal, namely the integration of dynamics and equilibrium in the same model. Dynamics, equilibrium and feedback mechanisms are, in fact, the basic building blocks for an ECM. The explicit separation of dynamics and equilibrium relations is not only attractive from the point of view of insight into the structural relationships within the model, but also from the practical point of view of the ease of tinkering with the model after it has been built. Adjustment of the impact coefficients in order to conform to new insight about the short-run dynamics of the model does not alter the equilibrium relationships and generally does not alter the steady state of the model. In the ADLM version of the model, adjustment of one coefficient also leads to adjustment of $B(1)$ and $\Gamma(1)$ and, therefore, to a change in the steady-state properties, unless other coefficients are adjusted as well in a compensating manner.

A second advantage of the ECM is that it is clearly well suited to the analysis of the disequilibrium error e_t. Since equilibrium is part of the focus of the model, the time-path of the deviations from this equilibrium during forecasting and simulation exercises is also of interest and it is handy that they are automatically calculated along the way. From a theoretical point of view, the ECM is also well suited to study the properties of these disequilibrium errors in more general terms, as we have seen in the previous sections.

A third advantage is that it is fairly straightforward to incorporate non-linear equilibrium relationships. We will not analyze this case, but, for instance, the ECM

$$A_1(L)\Delta y_t + A_2(L)\Delta x_t + A_3(L)\Delta z_t + C(L)F(y_{t-1}, x_{t-1}) = 0 \tag{38}$$

is linear in parameters despite being still non-linear in the equilibrium relationships if F is a non-linear function. In ADLM form the equilibrium relationships would also have to be linearized in order to still obtain a model that is linear in parameters.

A fourth advantage of the ECM is that the estimation procedure is fairly straightforward, especially with the justification and aid provided by the new cointegration literature (see e.g. Banerjee *et al.* (1993) and the references therein).

The most important disadvantage of the ECM may actually be the flip side of one of its advantages, namely its flexibility. As demonstrated earlier, the ECM has n^2p extra coefficients. On the one side, this creates flexibility in modeling. But the flip side is that we also have to find n^2p extra restrictions to define the model. These restrictions must be found in the $A(L)$ and the $C(L)$ polynomials. The problem here is, however, that these polynomials are not as different as their names, impact coefficients and feedback coefficients, suggest. For both of them in fact determine the dynamics of the model. But about this dynamics we have rather little insight, and thus also little knowledge to determine which set of coefficients is most reasonable.

In the actual practice of estimation, this problem does not appear to be overwhelming. Error-correction models with sparse sets of coefficients already appear to perform reasonably well. However, this does not mean that the problem has disappeared, for the interpretation issue may very well still exist. That is, as descriptions of data generating processes, error-correction models generally perform well, but as a structural description of economic processes the verdict is less clear.

In fact, the error-correction model may even be rather misleading. For example, suppose that, for some scalar variables y_t, $x_{1,t}$ and $x_{2,t}$, the equilibrium equation is

$$y_t = x_{1,t} + x_{2,t} \tag{39}$$

and that the true dynamics are represented in ADLM* form as

$$y_t = x_{1,t-1} + x_{2,t-2} \tag{40}$$

The conventional ECM is then[11]

$$\Delta y_t = -\Delta x_{2,t-1} - (y_{t-1} - x_{1,t-1} - x_{2,t-1}) \tag{41}$$

Splitting up this equation in the usual impact and error-correction components, this specification seems to suggest a negative relation between y_t and $x_{2,t}$ in the

11. Of course, other ECM specifications are possible as well (see Section 2). This one, however, is the sparsest one and the one most closely related to the error-correction literature in which it is generally assumed that errors enter with lag one.

short run while in fact the $\Delta x_{2,t-1}$ term only serves to cancel the effect of the error-correction term in the first period after a shock in $x_{2,t}$. In this case, the ADLM specification is far more intuitive than the ECM version.

The problem in this case appears to be that the numerical value of the error-correction term is not a "sufficient statistic" for its effect. The degree to which the error term pulls y_t not only depends on its value but also on whether the error was caused by a shock in $x_{1,t}$ or by a shock in $x_{2,t}$. There are, so to speak, two dimensions to the equilibrium error, namely its numerical value and the cause for that error to occur in the first place. The effect of the error depends on both dimensions, but as an explanatory variable in an equation, the error-correction term can only indicate its numerical value. The other dimension, therefore, has to be included in the first-difference component of the model. As a result, the clean interpretation of the error-correction model as consisting of neatly separated impact and error-correction components is lost. Including the long-run equilibrium in a dynamic model through an error-correction mechanism may thus come at a high cost to the interpretability of the short-run dynamics.

The above example may be considered contrived. However, as shown in Section 2, the problem of the "wrong sign" on the first-difference terms may occur whenever the lag length of that first-difference variable exceeds that of the EC component. We also showed that one solution is to make the lag of the EC component at least as long as the lags on the first-difference components. This seems, however, also somewhat contrived: for, why would agents take so long in reacting to the disequilibrium errors?

We believe that at a more abstract level, the problem is that the application of the ECM system in this case is too mechanical. The error term does not have a clear independent economic interpretation as a feedback mechanism. Error-correction terms that do have such an independent economic meaning generally also are considered to be sufficient statistics for the force they represent. Examples are unemployment, utilization rates, inventories stocks and wealth. These variables sum up a state of affairs which, if out of equilibrium for some reason, provokes a reaction that will restore that equilibrium.[12]

Proceeding along this line of thought we consider the ECM to be functional if the error-correction term has a clear economic meaning. (Often, this means that we can

12. Basically, we are complaining about the lack of clear micro-foundations of the general error-correction system. This lack of micro-foundations is also discussed by Nickell (1985) and Alogoskoufis and Smith (1991), although from a somewhat different angle. They conclude that the interpretation of error-correction models is strongly intertwined with the treatment of expectations. While this certainly seems plausible and while their setup does lead to neat error-correction equations in terms of observed variables, the equations they obtain are, in fact, only reduced forms, not structural equations. The separation of impact and error-correction components is purely artificial and based on a decomposition of a single expectations variable into two pieces, one involving first differences and one involving levels.

give it a name.) If we cannot do this, we prefer the ADLM formulation. Whether we are able to find such an economic error term depends, in general, on the equation at hand. This implies that our preference for an ADLM or ECM specification cannot be decided at the level of the overall model, but lies at the level of the individual equations.

First differences

Both the ADLM and the ECM are basically models in levels. Traditional CPB models, however, have mostly been specified in first differences. A natural question to ask is, what is the relationship between first-difference models and ADLM/ECM systems, and can they be made equivalent?

In a deterministic world, taking first difference of a model does not change the model. So, model (4) is equivalent to

$$B(L)\Delta y_t + \Gamma(L)\Delta x_t + E'(L)\Delta^2 z_t = 0 \tag{42}$$

For given series of the exogenous variables x_t and z_t, and given values of y_t for $t = 0$, -1, -2, ..., equations (4) and (42) generate exactly the same values of y_t for $t = 1$, $2, \ldots, T$. This is no longer true when we apply additive shocks ε_t to (4) and (42). Assuming that (4) is stable the effect of the shocks will vanish over time. This is not the case in (42), where the effect of the shocks is permanent. Also, in practical modeling equations such as (4) and (42) will not generally fit the available data exactly, so that a residual has to be added, which, from the formal point of view, can be identified with the shocks ε_t, so that equivalence of (4) and (42) no longer holds.

Clearly, in taking the first difference of (4) augmented with shocks or residuals, we should also take the first difference of those shocks or residuals, and add $\Delta\varepsilon_t$ instead of ε_t to (42) in order to restore full equivalence. Moreover, if we want that in a deterministic steady state without growth the variables obey (1), we have to impose that $B(1)\Pi = \Gamma(1)$ and that $B(1)$ is invertible. This requirement is automatically fulfilled if the first-difference model is the first difference of ADLM (4) (with $B(1)^{-1}\Gamma(1) = \Pi$) or of an ECM with nonsingular $C(1)$ and $B^* = B$ and $\Gamma^* = \Gamma$.

It is interesting to illustrate this for several practical cases. First, since definitions do not have residuals, it does not matter for definitions whether they are specified in levels or in first differences. Second, in a non-stochastic forecast (standard at the CPB), all residuals are assumed zero within the forecasting period, so the only adjustment that has to be made to a first-difference model is to correct for the residuals of the associated levels model from the last period before the start of the forecasting period. Third, in a simulation with a first-difference model in which a shock is added to some equation in a certain period, minus this shock should be added to the same equation in the following period. Finally, if in a given simulation with a first-difference model a certain endogenous variable is fixed at an exogenous level, for instance because of government control, then in every period during this control, the implicit additive shocks that are applied to the corresponding equations should be calculated and subtracted in the following period. If the control continues the next period, a new shock should be calculated, etc. This leads to overlapping shocks, where shocks from one period are incorporated into the shocks for the next period, etc. This may, therefore, lead to a rather sizable jump in the first period after the controls have been lifted, but that is also what we would expect. Note that all of this is based on equation (42) which is easy to program.

6 Conclusion

In this paper we analyzed two possible frameworks for modeling dynamics and equilibrium within the same model, the autoregressive distributed lag model (ADLM) and the error-correction model (ECM). After showing that there is no essential difference between the two approaches, we concluded that the choice for one version or the other should be based on the relative advantages their structures provide in terms of insight, transparency, ease of incorporating economic theory and ease in model use.

With respect to these terms, the ECM appears to do very well at first sight. The basic building blocks of impact, feedback and equilibrium components fit neatly into our goal of integrating dynamics and equilibrium. In particular, the explicit modeling of feedback mechanisms has some major advantages. First, it allows or, in fact, forces the model builder to be explicit about the second phrase in the Granger quote cited in Section 1: "Thus, such variables may drift apart in the short-run ..., but if they continue to be too far apart in the long-run, then economic forces ... will begin to bring them together again." Modeling the feedback matrix forces us to be explicit about what these economic forces actually are.

The second advantage of the explicit modeling of the feedback mechanisms is that it allows for a neat analysis of some of the properties of the model that are directly related to the interplay of dynamics and equilibrium, such as unit roots and the lack of sufficient feedback mechanisms, stability of the error term and trend-neutrality.

A third advantage of the error-correction framework is that it is promising from an empirical point of view. Error-correction models are easily estimated and generally perform well under a variety of econometric tests with a relatively sparse specification.

However, we also showed that a rather mechanical implementation of error correction may lead to some serious problems in the interpretation of the short-run dynamics. For instance, part of the first-difference component of the model may only serve to correct the influence of the error-correction terms. We suggested that this problem of interpreting the short run in error-correction models is caused by the fact that the numerical value of the error-correction term may not be a sufficient statistic for the force it represents. We further suggested that the problem may be related to a lack of a clear economic interpretation of the error terms.

Our suggestion, then, is to use the error-correction framework only insofar as we can maintain a clear interpretation. Our working hypothesis is that this is accomplished by including those error terms (or linear combinations thereof) that have a clear economic interpretation. For the equations for which we cannot find such an error term, we propose to use the ADLM specification in the model (although we may still want to estimate it in error-correction or first-differences form to get around the multicollinearity problem). In that case we remain more agnostic about the forces behind the feedback mechanisms, but also, are less likely to be misled by a misguided structural interpretation.

References

Alogoskoufis, G. and R. Smith (1991), "On error correction models: specification, interpretation, estimation", *Journal of Economic Surveys*, **5**, 97–125.

Banerjee, A., J. Dolado, J.W. Galbraith, and D.F. Hendry (1993), *Co-integration and the econometric analysis of nonstationary data*, Oxford University Press, Oxford.

Campbell, J.Y. and P. Perron (1991), "Pitfalls and opportunities: what macroeconomists should know about unit roots", in NBER, editor, *NBER macroeconomics annual 1991*, MIT Press, Cambridge.

Central Planning Bureau (1992), *FKSEC a macroeconometric model for the Netherlands*, Stenfert Kroese, Leiden.

Davidson, J. (1984), "Error correction systems", Working Paper, London School of Economics, London.

Davidson, J. (1991), "The co-integration properties of vector autoregression models", *Journal of Time Series Analysis*, **12**, 41–62.

Davidson, J. and S. Hall (1991), "Co-integration in recursive systems", *The Economic Journal*, **101**, 239–251.

Gelauff, G.M.M. (1992), *Taxation, social security and the labour market: an applied general equilibrium model for the Netherlands.*, PhD thesis, Tilburg University, Tilburg.

Granger, C.W.J. (1986), "Developments in the study of co-integrated variables", *Oxford Bulletin of Economics and Statistics*, **48**, 213–228.

Kuh, E., J.W. Neese, and P. Hollinger (1985), *Structural sensitivity in econometric models*, John Wiley and Sons, New York.

Malgrange, P. (1989), "The structure of dynamic macroeconomic models", in B. Cornet and H. Tulkens, editors, *Contributions to operations research and economics: the 20th anniversary of CORE*, MIT Press, Cambridge.

Nickell, S. (1985), "Error correction, partial adjustment and all that: an expository note", *Oxford Bulletin of Economics and Statistics*, **47**, 119–129.

Schoonbeek, L. (1992), "Negative coefficients and eigenvalues of economic models", *Economic Modelling*, **9**, 111–120.

Methods and Applications of Economic Dynamics
L. Schoonbeek, E. Sterken and S.K. Kuipers (editors)

Chapter 3

Advances in the estimation and analysis of non-linear differential equation models in economics [1]

Clifford R. Wymer

1 Introduction

This paper reviews recent developments in the estimation of non-linear differential equation systems in economics and discusses the analysis of the dynamic properties of those models and their use for policy purposes. Previous work on the dynamic properties of non-linear models such as an analysis of its long-run properties, the stability of the model in the neighborhood of the steady state (if it exists), and the sensitivity of these properties to changes in the parameters of the model, was directed largely towards models which had a stable equilibrium or periodic orbit. This paper extends that work to investigate the properties of models which may have a strange attractor giving rise to aperiodic or chaotic long-run behavior. The paper also discusses the use of these models for policy purposes with the aim of obtaining results of a more qualitative nature as an option to extensive simulation.

Although much of this paper is applicable to general non-linear differential equation systems, this work has been developed in the context of continuous time macroeconomic models or models of financial or commodity markets. These models

1. I greatly appreciate discussions with William Barnett, Denis Richard and Kieran Donaghy on this work and wish to thank them as well as Herman Nieuwenhuis, Bert Schoonbeek and Elmer Sterken for their comments. I am also most grateful to Giancarlo Gandolfo for inviting me to the University of Rome, La Sapienza, to continue research in this field.

are generally relatively small and formulated as disequilibrium systems in continuous time. They are designed to be amenable to mathematical and statistical analysis so that they can be used for the investigation and analysis of macroeconomic behavior, or the behavior of financial and commodity markets, and for policy evaluation. The reasons for using continuous-time rather than discrete-time models in economics are discussed, e.g., in Bergstrom (1976), Wymer (1992a) and Gandolfo (1981), and these reasons are reviewed in Gandolfo (1992). A general overview of research into continuous time econometric models with extensive references to both theoretical and empirical work is given in Wymer (1992a, 1994).

Section 2 discusses the place of non-linear models in economics. Section 3 reviews the estimation of non-linear differential equation econometric models; such estimates will generally, but not necessarily, provide the basis for a study of the properties of the model and its policy implications. The core of the paper is Section 4. Previously, the steady-state or long-run properties of these models and the stability of those solutions have been studied by transforming the system to produce a non-linear model defined in terms of deviations about the steady state or particular solution. The stability of this system, and hence of the steady state, can be evaluated using the eigensystem of a linearization of that model, and the structural stability of the model can be examined using sensitivity analysis. Section 4 extends both the eigensystem analysis and the question of structural stability to take into account mathematical developments in the properties of non-linear dynamical systems; these developments allow an investigation of other forms of asymptotic behavior and, in particular, raise the possibility of these models having a strange attractor and chaotic behavior. Although this requires substantial mathematical groundwork, essentially the analysis is still based on a linearization of the non-linear model, the calculation of generalized eigenvalues and eigenvectors, and an investigation of structural stability based on sensitivity analysis. Finally, Section 5 discusses the use of non-linear systems for policy analysis and, specifically, the solution of non-linear models subject to constraint. From a mathematical point of view, this section considers the solution of boundary point problems subject to constraint; this includes the solution of both targeting problems and optimal control with inequality constraints on the control and state variables if required.

2 Non-linear continuous-time models in economics

The economic models being considered, whether macroeconomic or of a particular market or sector, are usually non-linear[2] owing to the economic theory and institutional structure underlying these models and the need to represent some features

2. Throughout this paper, a non-linear model means one that is non-linear in variables; the models discussed here will usually, but not necessarily, be non-linear in parameters.

of dynamic behavior observed in economic systems which are precluded by a linear model. Economic theory suggests that the basic structure underlying the economic system may give rise to behavioral functions which are highly non-linear while other equations may be linear or simple multiplicative functions of the variables. Institutional or market structures may also be non-linear, so the dynamic model must be able to incorporate such features and rigidities. These non-linearities may have significant implications both in the long run and in the adjustment from one state to another. In a dynamic adjustment model, for example, the rate of adjustment need not be constant but may vary according to the state of the economy or of the market; thus the model can allow for an acceleration in prices and wages or a rise in interest rates as the economy approaches full capacity or full employment and incorporate the conditions for a contraction better than a linear model.

From the point of view of estimation, these models are specified to incorporate theory and the institutional structure of the economy in a coherent manner throughout the model. Behavioral functions derived, implicitly or explicitly, by the optimization of some objective function subject to constraint, have a functional form determined by the underlying constrained objective function and are often subject to homogeneity, symmetry and curvature conditions. Institutional and market structures either may be embodied in these functions as constraints or these features superimposed on the more formal theoretical functions. Thus these models are likely to be heavily over-identified, with parameters often occurring non-linearly within and across equations. The aim in developing more sophisticated estimators is to allow these functional forms and restrictions on the parameters to be maintained during estimation so that the estimates of the model are consistent with its theoretical formulation.

Models of 15 to 25 equations have proved a reasonable representation of macroeconomic behavior, including both real and financial sectors, and these models are highly non-linear. The Knight and Wymer (1978) model of the United Kingdom, a mixed-order system with 21 equations, three of second order, includes the main national income aggregates, employment, prices, wages and interest rates, money, bonds, and bank advances, and net foreign assets of the private and public sectors. The number of variables can be reduced, however, if the banking system is consolidated with one of the other sectors of the economy, as in the UK model of Bergstrom and Wymer (1976) which has 11 equations; again that is a mixed-order stock/flow model with two second-order equations defining investment and the volume of money. The second-order model of Bergstrom *et al.* (1992) includes 14 endogenous variables. Many of the other macroeconomic models which have been developed are of a similar size; the Italian model of Gandolfo and Padoan (1990) has 24 equations and the US model of Donaghy (1992) has 21. In models of financial and commodity markets, the exchange and interest rate model in Richard (1980) and the related model in Armington and Wolford (1984) has as endogenous variables 11 interest rates and 10 exchange rates while the world copper market model of Richard (1978) has 16 equations, three of which are second order. Important feedbacks are likely to be omitted in macroeconomic models with fewer endogenous variables which could seriously affect the dynamic behavior of the system.

The purpose of these models is to contribute towards an understanding of economic behavior, to provide a basis for economic policy, and for forecasting. The role of these models is discussed in Wymer (1994). Often for policy purposes, whether for macroeconomic policy by a government or central bank or for decisions of a firm or some other economic agent, a model is required not so much for forecasting purposes but rather to provide a basis for analysis of an economy and the effects of different policies. Ideally, analytical results would be preferred, but these cannot be obtained except for very small and simple systems. The models discussed in this paper generally are too complex to allow short- to medium-term behavior to be studied analytically but it is possible to derive results which, although numerical, provide information of a more qualitative nature similar to that which can be obtained from small theoretical models. This is of direct use in considering the implications of the model for policy. For instance, if the model has a steady state, it may be possible to derive this analytically thus allowing a direct comparative study of long-run equilibria. Dynamic behavior can be investigated using sensitivity analysis to give the partial derivatives of the eigenvalues of a system with respect to its parameters as shown in Wymer (1992a). A nice feature of these results is that they are compact and can be obtained in a single calculation without the need for simulations or repeated calculations with different parameter values.

These models can also be used for solving targeting problems or for optimal control. Again, it is considered that the usefulness of optimal control is not that it will be used directly by policy makers, but that it helps to provide an understanding of the economic system and the extent to which it can be controled by various policies. A full optimal control solution would provide a baseline against which feedback rules can be evaluated. Given uncertainties in the economy, and of some parameter values, a relatively simple feedback rule which provides a satisfactory approximation to the optimal solution may be more useful than full optimal control. For example, Wymer (1982) provides a non-stochastic optimal control solution using the eigensystem for deterministic linear models; a useful feature of this approach is that it allows sensitivity analysis to be used to give the partial derivatives of the optimal control eigensystem with respect to the parameters of the whole optimal control eigensystem, including the parameters of the objective function. For non-linear models, a non-stochastic optimal control solution is given below, which permits non-linear inequality constraints to be imposed on the control variables. Following LaFrance and Barney (1991), this allows the partial derivative of the optimal value function with respect to the parameters of the economic model and the objective function to be derived. Again, these results may be obtained in a single calculation, thus providing information on the effect of changes in parameters in the model without the need for simulation.

It is assumed that the economic system can be represented by a mixed r-th order non-linear differential equation system but, with an appropriate definition of additional variables such that $Dy_i(t) = y_j(t)$, this can be written as a general first-order model of the form

$$\Psi\{Dy(t),\, y(t),\, z(t),\, \theta\} = \nu(t) \tag{1}$$

For the purposes of this paper, however, it is assumed that the economic system has a recursive representation which can be conveniently but imprecisely written as

$$Dy(t) = \psi\{y(t),\, z(t),\, \theta\} + u(t) \tag{2}$$

where $y(t)$ is a vector of m continuous endogenous variables, $z(t)$ is a vector of n continuous exogenous variables, θ a vector of p parameters, and $\psi\{y(t),\, z(t),\, \theta\}$ is a vector of continuous and differentiable functions of all variables and the set of parameters θ. D is the differential operator d/dt. It is assumed that the $u(t)$ are vectors of white noise disturbances so that the integral $\zeta(t) = \int_0^t u(s)ds$ is a homogeneous random process with uncorrelated increments. It can be shown that $\zeta(t)$ is non-differentiable so that the process $u(t)$ cannot be rigorously defined but for the purposes of this section, and as discussed in Wymer (1972), it may be viewed as if it were well defined. A precise definition of the model and the disturbances is given in Section 3. The variables $y(t)$ and $z(t)$ may be stocks or flows; this distinction becomes important for estimation.

Previous work has considered the steady-state equilibrium properties of these models and its stability. For example, if (1) has a steady state such that $y(t) = y^* e^{\rho t}$, assuming the exogenous variables are analytical functions of time, the system may be solved for y^* and ρ as functions of the parameters θ. Usually, owing to the nature of these models, a set of variables $x(t)$ may be defined as some transformation of the deviations of $y(t)$ about its steady state or other particular solution to produce an autonomous system

$$\dot{x} = f\{x(t),\, \theta\} \tag{3}$$

which is often highly non-linear. Usually (3) will have an equilibrium solution $\dot{x} = 0$ which may or may not be unique; if $x(t)$ is defined in terms of deviations of $y(t)$ about its steady state, the steady-state solution corresponds to a fixed point in phase space. The asymptotic stability properties of these models can then be investigated from a consideration of the linear terms of a Taylor series expansion of that model.

The dynamic behavior and asymptotic properties of (3) are considered from two points of view: first, the properties of the solutions for a given set of parameter values θ and, secondly, the structural stability of the model as one or more of these parameters vary. Although such analyses have been used routinely with many of the continuous time models developed in the past, as in Bergstrom and Wymer (1976), Jonson *et al.* (1982), Jonson and Taylor (1979), Knight and Wymer (1978), Richard (1978) and Gandolfo and Padoan (1990, 1992), relatively recent developments in the study of aperiodic dynamical systems and strange attractors has allowed this work to be extended to an investigation of more complex dynamical behavior. Thus the research discussed in this paper arises as a direct extension of previous work. In particular, some of the models developed over the past twenty years, such as that of the Australian economy in Jonson *et al.* (1976)[3] have eigenvalues which are either close to zero or are positive. While this may show that the economic system is simply unstable, it may be an indication of much more complex behavior, particularly given the nature of the non-linear structure of these models.

The work on deterministic chaos, or aperiodic solutions in strange attractors, shows that non-linear models are capable of producing deterministic solutions which have some of the characteristics of stochastic processes and thus provide observations similar to those seen in economic data. Thus endlessly varying solutions are derived without the need for exogenous shocks or assumptions of stochastic behavior, and these can exhibit the appearance of structural change although no such change has taken place.

In considering work on a-periodical behavior, a strict distinction must be made between discrete and continuous time models, i.e. between difference and differential equation systems. Chaotic behavior can arise in a single first-order difference equation, such as the logistic equation $x_{t+1} = kx_t(1 - x_t)$ for k in various intervals in the range $3.4 < k < 4.0$. In differential equation models, a minimum of three first-order equations are needed to produce chaotic behavior, such as the models of E.N. Lorenz (1963) or Rössler (1977)[4] discussed in Haken (1983), H-W. Lorenz

3. The RBA model of the Australian economy had an eigenvalue which was close to zero. At the time, it was considered that this was the result of a complex eigenvalue with a very small real part, as discussed in Wymer (1979). In retrospect, it is possible that the estimated parameters of that model are very close to a bifurcation point which could result in much more complex asymptotic behavior, but this has not yet been investigated.

4. The Rössler model, which is perhaps the simplest differential equation system known to have a strange attractor, is defined (see Zwillinger, 1992) as

$$\begin{aligned} \dot{x} &= -(y+z) \\ \dot{y} &= x + ay \\ \dot{z} &= b + xz - cz \end{aligned}$$

This model has a strange attractor called the Rössler band when $a = 0.2$, $b = 0.2$, $c = 5.7$, and another called the Rössler funnel when $a = 0.343$, $b = 1.82$, and $c = 9.75$.

(1989) or Zwillinger (1992) although, as noted in Stewart (1990), it has not yet been proved that the former has a strange attractor. This raises serious questions about the correct framework for these models in economics, especially as much of the economic literature in this field is in discrete terms, e.g. Benhabib and Day (1982), Grandmont (1985), Boldrin and Montrucchio (1986), and Grandmont and Malgrange (1986). If a difference equation model can be defined with the appropriate integral lags, as in some well-defined microeconomic behavior, that model could properly be used for an analysis of that behavior. Where economic behavior is essentially continuous, however, as in macroeconomics and in commodity and financial markets, it is necessary that this be represented by a differential equation system. An overlapping generations process, and almost any capital accumulation process, for example, will have a continuous lag structure, particularly at the aggregate level.

A discrete model which does not take into account the non-integral nature of the lag structure of the economic system may well exhibit chaotic properties when in fact none exist. For instance, if behavior given by two first-order differential equations is misrepresented by two difference equations that are not the discrete equivalents of a continuous model, the difference equation system may provide a chaotic solution although that is not a property of the differential equation system generating the data. This could lead to incorrect policy prescriptions.

Although from a stochastic point of view a linear differential equation system has a discrete VARMAX representation in that it is equivalent to a discrete autoregressive model in the endogenous and exogenous variables with moving average errors, this does not easily, if at all, carry over to non-linear systems. More importantly, however, the aperiodic dynamical properties of a model, and particularly those of strange attractors, may not carry over so it becomes essential to represent a continuous real system by a continuous model.

Research on chaos in economics has generally taken one of two forms. One approach involves the investigation of individual time series to determine whether they are the result of chaotic or stochastic behavior as in Brock and Dechert (1988), but the tests used to discriminate between these causes require a very large number of observations and the power of those tests is often low. At least partly for this reason, many of these studies have been inconclusive. If a series is considered to be chaotic, the question then arises of whether the system generating that behavior is conservative or dissipative; in the latter case, the non-integer or fractal dimension of the strange attractor in phase space can be estimated. Such studies provide little information on the source of the behavior, and although the attractor may be of low dimension, those dimensions will not be the same as those of observed economic variables but almost certainly a non-linear transformation of them.

Other research has been directed towards an economic interpretation of some classical models with strange attractors, particularly the Lorenz and Rössler models, such as that of Lorenz (1989) and Goodwin (1990). Although such models can produce behavior of a similar nature to that observed in economic systems, usually the parameter values are chosen such that the model exhibits dramatic behavior; these values may not be those found in the economic system. As the existence of strange attractors depends crucially on parameters assuming values lying within certain intervals, it is essential that the parameters be validated in order to decide whether the model has economic relevance. The approach discussed in this paper is that of specifying and estimating a structural model of the economic system and deriving its properties in the neighborhood of the parameter estimates.

It is a feature of most economic behavior that it is relatively stable in the sense that although the variables of the economic system may fluctuate, and these fluctuations may appear to be erratic, they seldom tend to become infinite; a counter example is hyper-inflation, especially of the form which occurred in Germany in the 1920's. Models of economic behavior must be able to reflect this feature, but this is essentially precluded by the use of a linear system. A linear model is either stable, in which case stochastic behavior or changes in exogenous variables are required in order to generate fluctuations, or it is unstable in which case the variables eventually become infinite. Linear models in which the real part of one or more eigenvalues of the system is zero can be ignored as unrealistic. It must be accepted, therefore, that economic behavior is essentially non-linear, and this must be represented by a non-linear model.

It is only relatively recently that the complexity of the properties of the dynamic behavior of non-linear systems is starting to be understood, although the study of such systems has a long history, dating back to Poincaré. A problem with theoretical work in this field is that many of the classical theorems on non-linear differential equation systems apply only to systems in $\mathbb{R}^2$ while chaotic behavior requires at least third-order systems. The solution of deterministic non-linear systems can be very sensitive to initial conditions, so that although the solution is fully deterministic it becomes unpredictable. Thus a deterministic system can generate a solution which appears to be stochastic. Moreover, the non-linearities in the system can prevent instabilities dominating the solution and ensure that these solutions remain bounded, and observable, for all time. An important feature from an economic point of view is that low dimension non-linear models can generate realistic aperiodic fluctuations endogenously. Such aperiodic or chaotic dynamical behavior is not generic. A model can have non-chaotic and stable solutions for one set of parameter values but exhibit chaotic behavior for another, and vary between chaotic and non-chaotic dynamical behavior as parameter values are slowly changed.

Nevertheless, there is considerable structure to deterministic chaos; in particular, many systems exhibit universal scaling properties in the transition to chaotic behavior so that it is possible to determine whether the solutions of system (3) are chaotic and to quantify the degree of that behavior. This involves calculating the Lyapunov exponents and the fractal dimension of the attractor.

The structure of many of the continuous time models mentioned in this paper has similarities with the structure of some simple mathematical models known to have strange attractors. In particular, the way in which the non-linearity enters the Rössler model resembles that which occurs, generically, in the continuous time models in price determination and its interaction with real and nominal variables. The macroeconomic models of Jonson *et al.* (1976), Knight and Wymer (1978), and Gandolfo and Padoan (1990) all contain this broad structural form in three or four highly interdependent sets of equations defining the interaction between (i) domestic supply, demand, money and prices, (ii) foreign trade, capital flows, exchange rate and monetary sector, (iii) fixed capital formation, output, interest rate and prices, and (iv) the labor market, domestic demand and supply, prices and wages. Commodity models, such as that of Richard (1978), have some of the same features. Moreover, in many of these models, linearization about the steady state produces a positive real eigenvalue, perhaps of the order of 0.04, and another one or two real or complex conjugate eigenvalues with a very small negative real part which is sometimes not significantly different from zero. Such eigenvalues show that the model is unstable. Sensitivity analysis of the eigenvalues shows that quite small changes perhaps in only one parameter, for example, could produce eigenvalues with a zero real part. This raises the possibility that with small variations in some parameters, these models could exhibit much more complex long-run behavior and, in particular, that they may have a strange attractor. None of these factors, other than the need for an eigenvalue with a zero real part, is either necessary or sufficient for the existence of a strange attractor, but these factors are consistent with such an attractor and with aperiodical behavior.

The economic system, almost certainly, will be subject to exogenous behavior or shocks which are not embodied in the model representing the system and, again almost certainly, will have a stochastic component. Thus, as in previous work, the asymptotic behavior of the model is a theoretical property of the model defined for given parameter values and for given exogenous variables and stochastic behavior. The question of whether or not chaotic behavior exists and, if so, the rapidity with which an economic system converges on the attractor will depend on the values of parameters of the system.

3 Non-linear estimators

The aim of much of the applied econometric research on continuous-time systems has been to develop models of the economic system, such as (1) or (2), and to use those models as directly as possible to estimate the parameters θ of the system. Owing to the difficulty of estimating the parameters of non-linear variables and as estimators of linear models are well-developed and their properties are well known, the non-linear model can be approximated by a Taylor series expansion about some appropriate point, such as the sample mean, or some path, such as the steady state, to give a linearized model which can then be estimated subject to all of the restrictions inherent in the non-linear model and in the linearization. This provides estimates of the parameters θ of the non-linear model and those estimates may be used with either the linearized or non-linear model for hypothesis testing, analysis and forecasting.

A problem with this approach is that the errors implicit in the linearization of (2) are generally not known, although they may be approximated by the second-order terms in the expansion. Moreover, even if the white noise innovations or their integrals in the non-linear model are Gaussian, this may not be true of the disturbances in the linearized model. In particular, the linearization of some identities may lead to those equations having residuals which are serially correlated, especially in linearization about sample means where the observations of the relevant variables have a strong trend. Thus linearization may bias the estimates of the parameters. Furthermore, some parameters may become poorly identified or even unidentified in the linearized model. These issues are discussed in Wymer (1992a, Part II).

While an approximate discrete estimator of the non-linear model (1) has been available for some time and is discussed in Wymer (1979) and Bailey *et al.* (1987)[5], an exact estimator was developed only recently and is presented in Wymer (1992b). This allows estimates of the parameters of the non-linear model to be obtained directly, but the properties of the exact estimator are not well known and have to be inferred heuristically and the costs of this estimator are high. Both estimators are reviewed in Wymer (1992a, Part II). Other non-linear differential equation estimators are those of Lo (1991) for a single equation asset pricing model and Chambers (1992) for fractional differential equation models.

For estimation purposes, the general non-linear model is assumed to be a recursive system of first-order stochastic differential equations of the form

$$dy(t) = \psi\{y(t),\, z(t),\, \theta\}\, dt + \zeta(dt) \tag{4}$$

where $y(t)$, $z(t)$, θ, and $\psi\{y(t),\, z(t),\, \theta\}$ are defined as in (2), $\zeta(dt)$ is a vector of white noise innovations such that $E[\zeta(dt)] = 0$, $E[\zeta(dt)\zeta'(dt)] = |\, dt\,| \Omega$ where Ω is a positive definite matrix of order m, and $E[\zeta_i(\Delta_1)\zeta_j'(\Delta_2)] = 0$ for any disjoint sets Δ_1 and Δ_2. A rigorous definition of these disturbances and their properties is given in Bergstrom (1983). Some equations may be identities with the corresponding elements of $\zeta(dt)$ and Ω zero; in this case the sub-matrix of Ω corresponding to stochastic equations will be positive definite.

5. This paper by Bailey *et al.* (1987) is essentially the same as an earlier version entitled *A Model of Output, Employment and Inflation in an Open Economy* which was presented at the 49th ANZAAS Congress in Auckland in January, 1979.

The linear, or linearized, model corresponding to (4) may be written

$$dy(t) = A(\theta)y(t)dt + B(\theta)z(t)dt + \zeta(dt) \tag{5}$$

where the elements of the matrices A and B are functions of θ, and in the linearized case, the point or path around which the system has been linearized. The solution to (5) is then

$$y(t) = e^{\delta A(\theta)}y(t-\delta) + \int_{t-\delta}^{t} e^{(t-s)A(\theta)}B(\theta)z(s)ds + \int_{t-\delta}^{t} e^{(t-s)A(\theta)}\zeta(ds) \tag{6}$$

Assume that the continuous variables are observed every δ time units (so that δ is the length of the observation interval in terms of the basic time unit of the model) and let x_τ be the discrete observation of the continuous variable at time t, so that $x_\tau = x(\tau\delta)$. The exact discrete model is then

$$\begin{aligned} y_\tau = \; & e^{\delta A(\theta)}y_{\tau-1} + \textstyle\int_{(\tau-1)\delta}^{\tau\delta} e^{(\tau\delta-s)A(\theta)}B(\theta)z(s)ds + \omega_\tau \\ & \text{where } \omega_\tau = \textstyle\int_{(\tau-1)\delta}^{\tau\delta} e^{(\tau\delta-s)A(\theta)}\zeta(ds) \end{aligned} \tag{7}$$

For the purposes of this paper, it will be assumed that the $z(t)$ are analytic functions of time so that the integral of the term involving exogenous variables can be evaluated exactly. Given the properties of the disturbances $\zeta(dt)$, it can be shown that

$$E[\omega_t] = 0,\; E[\omega_t\omega_t'] = \int_0^\delta e^{sA(\theta)}\Omega e^{sA'(\theta)}ds\;,\; E[\omega_t\omega_s'] = 0 \text{ for all } t,\; s,\; t \neq s \tag{8}$$

It must emphasized that even if Ω is a diagonal matrix this will not be true of the variance matrix of errors of the exact discrete model $E[\omega_t\omega_t']$ so that the ω_t are not independent but, given the properties of the innovation process $\zeta(dt)$, they will be serially uncorrelated.

Observations generated by the continuous model (5) will satisfy the exact discrete model (7) irrespective of the observation interval δ, so the sampling properties of the parameters θ may be derived from the sampling properties of (7). A full-information maximum-likelihood estimator of (7) allows all of the restrictions inherent in the underlying continuous model, and in any linearization of that model, to be imposed, and thus provides consistent and asymptotically efficient estimates. Moreover, following Bergstrom (1983), Gaussian estimators may be obtained under the assumption that the integral of the white noise innovation process is a Gaussian process although the innovations themselves are not assumed to have that property. Thus the innovations may be a mixture of Brownian motion and Poisson processes which provides a plausible representation of economic behavior in that the innovations may come as discrete jumps at random intervals.

It is assumed that the model is to be estimated using a sample of $T+1$ equispaced observations of the variables $y(t)$ and $z(t)$ with an observation length of δ; for estimation purposes the basic time unit is chosen such that $\delta = 1$. Although many parameters will be independent of the basic time unit, some parameters, such as rates of adjustment or their reciprocal, may vary in accordance with the basic time unit and must be defined in terms of this unit. In deriving some of the properties of these estimators the basic time unit will be fixed so that the limit as δ tends to zero can be considered. For simulation and prediction, δ may take on any value irrespective of the observation length used in estimation.

Exact estimators of mixed-order mixed stock/flow models may also be derived but are much more complex since flow variables, and derivatives of other variables, cannot be observed at a point but only as an integral over the observation period. Exact and approximate discrete estimators of the linear model (5) and their asymptotic properties are reviewed in Bergstrom (1990) and Wymer (1992a, Part II) both of which contain extensive references. Much of the empirical work on continuous time models has used samples of 50 to 300 observations, and for that sample size the estimates provided by the various estimators have been consistent with asymptotic theory. Although the approximate discrete estimators are biased, the bias is of $O(\delta^3)$ so that it decreases rapidly as the observation interval δ decreases; Monte Carlo studies suggest that the bias will be small and in empirical work the approximate estimator gives parameter estimates which are generally, but not always, close to those of the exact estimator. Moreover, Phillips (1991) has shown that the Gaussian estimators of the exact models are super-efficient in that the estimator of parameters and their asymptotic standard errors converges at a rate of $O(T^{-1})$ as $T \to \infty$ whereas the estimators of the approximate models converge at a rate of $O(T^{-1/2})$ as $T \to \infty$. In empirical work the estimates of the asymptotic standard errors of the exact estimators of linear or linearized models are much smaller than those of the approximate estimator. As these models are all estimated using full-information maximum-likelihood or Gaussian estimators, the estimates may be used both for testing the overall structure of the continuous model and specific hypotheses, as discussed in Bergstrom (1990).

One approach to the estimation of the non-linear model was that of Bailey *et al.* (1987) who used a non-linear discrete approximation to (4). Instead of linearizing (4) and using that model to estimate the parameters, the non-linear system is integrated over the observation interval and then approximated to give a system of non-linear functions of discrete variables which can be estimated by a quasi full-information maximum likelihood estimator; this estimator is described in Wymer (1977). This estimator is analogous to the approximate discrete estimator for linear models given in Wymer (1972); if (4) were linear the two estimators would be almost the same. Although the Bailey *et al.* approach removes the questions raised by linearization, the estimates will be asymptotically biased and the analogy with the approximate discrete estimator for linear systems suggests that they will not be as efficient as those of an exact non-linear discrete estimator.

An exact non-linear discrete estimator is described in Wymer (1992b). Although the exact discrete estimator for linear models is derived using the analytical solution to the differential equation system, for non-linear models the system must be solved by numerical integration, but the principle is the same in both cases. In the "pure" case, where all variables are observed at a point in time, the estimator will be consistent and efficient and is analogous to the exact discrete estimator for linear models which provides estimates which are super-efficient. If this estimator were applied to a linear model the estimates would be the same as the exact linear discrete estimator.

The derivation of the exact estimator of the non-linear model (4) is analogous to that of the linear estimator. Let $\omega(t)$ be the vector of errors in the trajectories of the system such that $\omega(t) = y(t) - \hat{y}(t)$ where $y(t)$ is the solution to (4) given initial conditions $y(t-\delta)$ and $\hat{y}(t)$ satisfies $D\hat{y}(t) = \psi\{\hat{y}(t), z(t), \theta\}$ given the same initial conditions. $E[\omega(t)\omega'(t)]$ is then the integral of an (unknown) function of the $\zeta(dt)$ over the interval $(0, \delta)$ and it follows from the properties of the error process $\zeta(dt)$ that the errors $\omega(t)$ are interdependent but serially uncorrelated. In the "pure" case, the endogenous variables $y(t)$ are assumed to be observable at a point in time, such as stocks, prices, interest and exchange rates, and the exogenous variables to be given analytic functions of time. For a given set of initial values of the parameters θ and a set of initial values for the variables at the point $t-1$, the solution trajectories of (4) can be found by a numerical integration procedure. Let the vector of solution trajectories at t given the observed $y(t-1)$ as initial values and the given set of θ be $\hat{y}(t;\, \theta)$. The residuals corresponding to $\omega(t)$ can then be calculated and used to form the likelihood function which can then be maximized to give full-information maximum-likelihood estimates of the parameters.

This "pure" exact non-linear discrete estimator requires the exogenous variables (or forcing functions) to be analytic functions of time so that the integration procedure is exact. Under those conditions the exact linear and non-linear discrete estimators are the same for linear models but this will not be true for more general exogenous variables. In most econometric models (Bergstrom and Wymer (1976), for example, is an exception) the exogenous variables are defined only by a series of discrete observations. As in the linear estimators, the continuous path of exogenous variables may be approximated using a polynomial fitted to nearby observations. In the linear case, the asymptotic bias of the approximate discrete estimator is of $O(\delta^2)$ as δ tends to zero, where δ is the length of the observation interval, while for the exact linear discrete estimator using a quadratic, Phillips (1974, 1976) has shown that providing the exogenous variables are sufficiently smooth non-random variables, or that they are stationary stochastic processes differentiable in the mean square, the asymptotic bias in the parameter estimates is of $O(\delta^3)$ as δ tends to zero.

Many economic models include flow variables such as production, consumption, and income which cannot be observed at a point in time but are measured only as an integral over some interval so that the "pure" case needs to be extended. Other variables such as implicit price deflators, which are usually defined as the ratio of two flows, are also measured as an integral over some interval. Moreover, the basic model underlying (2) may include higher-order variables so that the functions ψ in (4) would include derivatives of other variables in the model. The approximate non-linear discrete estimator of Bailey *et al.* (1987) incorporated stocks and flows using approximations similar to those of the linear approximate estimator. The exact non-linear estimator can also be extended to include stock/flow and higher-order models but, as with the "exact" estimator of linear stock/flow models, the estimator is no longer exact; it can, however, be expected to be a good approximation to an exact estimator. The analogy with the estimators of linear models suggests that the asymptotic bias of the "exact" estimator of such models will be less than that of the approximate estimator.

The numerical integration of the non-linear model requires initial values for the endogenous variables for the solution over each observation period. In the "pure" exact estimator, observations of the variables at the beginning of each observation period $(t-1,\ t)$ are available. Flow and averaged variables, however, are observed as integrals over time so that each observation $y^o(t) = \int_{t-1}^{t} y(s)ds$ for all t. Initial values of the flow variables at the point $t-1$ must be approximated from these observations.

The solution trajectories of the mixed stock/flow system are calculated numerically over the interval $(t-1,\ t)$, for $\delta = 1$, and the flow and averaged variables are simultaneously integrated. The errors for such variables are then

$$\omega(t) = y^o(t) - \int_{t-1}^{t} \hat{y}(t;\ \theta)ds \text{ for } t = 1, \ldots, T \tag{9}$$

where $\hat{y}(t;\ \theta)$ is the solution of the system given an initial value $y(t-1)$. Unlike the "pure" exact estimator, these values are unknown and must be approximated as a function of observed variables $y^o(t-1)$, $y^o(t-2)$ at least, so that $E[\omega(s)\,\omega'(t)]$, $s \neq t$, will contain the product of terms in the disturbances $\zeta(ds)$ where the $\zeta(ds)$ are not disjoint, and thus the $\omega(t)$ will be serially correlated.

For linear flow models, Phillips (1978) has shown that the asymptotic bias of the "exact" discrete estimator is of $O(\delta)$ as $\delta \to 0$, but the approximate discrete estimator is asymptotically biased even in the limit as the observation interval tends to zero. This suggests that the asymptotic bias in the estimator being considered here would also be of $O(\delta)$ but, since it is the approximation of the initial values which introduces serial correlation into the residuals, it may be possible to reduce this bias. It may be noted that in the linear estimators the serial correlation may be eliminated, at least to an approximation, by transforming the data; such a transformation is precluded by a non-linear system.

The exact non-linear estimator was used by Donaghy and Richard (1992) to estimate and test highly constrained, and highly non-linear, currency substitution models involving homogeneity, symmetry and curvature conditions. It is also being used to estimate the non-linear Italian model of Gandolfo and Padoan (1990); these results are presented in Gandolfo *et al.* (1994). A comparison of the linear and non-linear estimators shows that while many parameter estimates are not significantly different, some estimates are quite different; this occurs particularly with parameters which appear to be poorly identified in the linearized model. Although the costs can be high in terms of computing time, especially if the model is defined in the implicit form (1) rather than the recursive form (2), the estimates suggest that there are substantial benefits in using the non-linear estimator in that the asymptotic standard errors are very small relative to the estimators of the linearized model and to the approximate discrete estimator of the non-linear model. The mean square residuals are also smaller. It is considered that these results are due partly to the use of an "exact" rather than approximate estimator, which would be consistent with the estimators of linear models, but also because the specified relationships, and especially identities, are estimated directly without introducing errors of linearization and, perhaps more importantly, eliminating any serial correlation arising from linearization.

4 Long-run properties

The non-linear model (1) or (4), or the linearized model (5), may be used for analysis and forecasting, irrespective of the estimator of the parameters. In some cases, as in the UK model in Bergstrom and Wymer (1976) and related models, the theoretical model (1) may be solved analytically for the steady state, if it exists, but often for other purposes the parameter estimates are required. In very small models the dynamic behavior can also be derived analytically, but for most of the models considered here this will not be possible. While simulation can always be used to investigate the properties of a model, more sophisticated techniques provide results which, although numerical and hence dependent on parameter estimates, are more qualitative in nature.

The aim of this investigation is first to determine the dynamic properties of the system and secondly to consider the implications of its behavior for policy purposes. This need not be only government policy but could involve a study of market behavior and the implications for forecasting. A study of the properties of the system includes not only determining its stability for the estimated or given parameter values, but also the question of whether it is structurally stable over some relevant range of parameter values such as the confidence intervals of the parameter estimates. Essentially, a model is structurally stable if small changes in parameters do not produce a qualitative change in its dynamic properties; points at which parameter changes do have a qualitative effect are bifurcation points. In very simple models with few parameters, bifurcation points can be found by an increasingly fine grid search of the relevant intervals for the parameter set. In larger models, sensitivity analysis can be used to determine the parameters which crucially affect the dynamics of the system and which are likely to be relevant. If the model is structurally unstable for some parameter values, and if this can lead to some behavior of the system which is undesirable, it may be possible to introduce policies which will shift the relevant parameters away from critical values. These policies may need to be of a distributional nature.

In previous work the asymptotic properties of the non-linear system (1) have been studied by deriving some transformation of the variables, such as deviations about the steady state, which allows the model (1) to be written as the autonomous system (3). Differentiation of the equilibrium point $x^*(\theta)$ with respect to the parameters θ allows an analysis of the steady state, and dynamical behavior in the neighborhood of the steady state may be investigated using the eigenvalues and eigenvectors of the system. The structural stability of the model, i.e. the effect on the dynamic properties of changes in the parameter values, may be studied using sensitivity analysis by differentiating the eigenvalues (and eigenvectors if required) with respect to the parameters as discussed in Wymer (1987, 1992a). These techniques can be extended directly to a study of more general dynamical behavior in non-linear systems.

The definition and properties of attractors, and particularly of strange attractors, is considered in Subsection 4.1 while Subsection 4.2 discusses the use of Lyapunov exponents and other measures to determine and classify these asymptotic properties. Lyapunov exponents, which are based on a generalized eigensystem analysis, may be used to determine the nature of the attractor of a given model, with given parameter values, and thus to distinguish between classical and strange attractors. Other measures such as the correlation dimension may be used to find the dimension of an attractor of an economic system from a sequence of observations generated by that system; this provides a lower bound for the dimension of any model representing that system and helps to distinguish between classical and strange attractors but gives little information on the structure of the model. Finally, the structural stability of a model, i.e. the extent to which it is qualitatively robust to changes in parameters, can be investigated as shown in Subsection 4.3; this is analogous to the use of sensitivity analysis of linear systems which have a steady state.

4.1 Attractors

In considering more complex properties of non-linear systems it is necessary to define an attractor in phase space; a stable equilibrium solution or fixed point is a special case. For these purposes, assume that the system is the set of autonomous, first-order, non-linear differential equations, as in (3),

$$\dot{x} = f\{x(t),\ \theta\},\ x \in \mathbb{R}^n \tag{10}$$

where $x(t)$ is a vector of n variables, f a vector function, and θ a vector of p parameters. In the following, the solution path or orbit of the system with initial point $x(t_0)$ will be denoted $\phi\{x(t_0),\ t\}$ or, where necessary, $\phi\{x(t_0),\ t,\ \theta\}$; usually, $t_0 = 0$. The parameters θ will be omitted where they are fixed. Although this paper considers only autonomous systems specifically, a non-autonomous system can be written as an autonomous system with little loss in generality, but with some change in interpretation. Specifically, if an $(n-1)$ dimensional non-autonomous system is $\dot{x} = g\{x(t),\ \theta,\ t\}$, defining $\dot{x}_n = 1$ allows this to be written as

$$\begin{aligned} \dot{x} &= g\{x(t),\ \theta,\ x_n(t)\} \\ \dot{x}_n &= 1 \end{aligned} \tag{11}$$

which has the same form as the n-dimensional autonomous system (10).

The system (10) is assumed to be coupled in that it is not separable into two independent systems. Since the system is autonomous, it describes a vector field in $\mathbb{R}^n$ so that given an initial point $x(t_0)$ the system determines a set of solution curves $x(t) = \phi\{x(t_0), t\}$ in phase space (called the flow in the mathematical literature) such that $x(t_0) = \phi\{x(t_0), t_0\}$; in effect, this is a mapping of the trajectories in time-state space onto phase space where t can be considered a parameter in phase space. As the vector field is invariant with respect to t, solutions based at $t_0 \neq 0$ can be translated to $t_0 = 0$. The trajectory is tangent to the vector field at all points.

An attractor and an attracting set are defined as in Guckenheimer and Holmes (1986). A closed invariant set $A \subset \mathbb{R}^n$ is an attracting set if there exists an invariant n-dimensional neighborhood U of A such that if $x(0) \in U$, then $\phi\{x(0), t\} \in U$ for $t > 0$ and $\phi\{x(0), t\} \to A$ as $t \to \infty$. Thus if $x(0)$ is an initial point in the neighborhood of the attractor the trajectory will remain in that neighborhood and will converge on the attractor. The trajectory from $x(0) \in U$, i.e. $\phi\{x(0), t\}$, which is not yet on the attractor is called the transient. The basin of attraction or domain of A is the set of all points for which A is the attracting set. A repelling set is defined analogously but with t replaced by $-t$. An attractor can then be defined as an attracting set with a dense orbit; the requirement of a dense orbit, i.e. an orbit which covers the whole of the attractor, ensures that the attractor is not the union of two or more smaller attractors.[6] Since an attractor is a surface it has zero volume in phase space.

Classical attractors, such as fixed points, limit cycles and tori, lie on manifolds, which are topological spaces locally resembling an open set in $\mathbb{R}^n$ and are the analog of a surface. The dimension of these attractors can be seen by a suitable mapping of the attractor, so that a fixed point is of dimension 0, while a limit cycle, which can be mapped onto a line, has dimension 1 and is thus a T^1 torus, and a T^2 torus has dimension 2 as it can be mapped onto a plane. These attractors have integer dimensions. Whether a trajectory is dense on a torus depends on the frequencies of its orbit; a trajectory on a T^2 torus, for example, will be dense if the ratio of its frequencies is irrational, so that the trajectory will eventually become arbitrarily close to any given point in which case it will have a quasi-periodic cycle; if its frequencies are rational, it has a periodic cycle and only lines on the torus are covered.

A strange attractor, which belongs to a class of attractors which do not lie on manifolds, is defined as an attractor which has a sensitive dependence on initial conditions $x(0)$ in an invariant neighborhood U of the attractor, and which is indecomposable in that it does not degenerate into two (or more) distinct attractors. Thus for an initial point in some neighborhood of the attractor, the trajectory $\phi\{x(0), t\}$ approaches and remains arbitrarily close to the attractor for sufficiently large t, while small variations in the initial value of $x(0)$ lead to essentially different time paths of the system after some time interval. While a strange attractor is strictly not a surface, it can be visualized as a "surface" consisting of a folded structure with an infinite number of very close layers with a finite volume of phase space between the layers. The attractors are not a closed curve (even of a complicated form) but consist of an aperiodic trajectory. Strange attractors have non-integer or fractal dimensions[7]; the dimension of such attractors must be less than that of the

6. A less restrictive definition given in Guckenheimer and Holmes (1986, p. 256) states that an attractor is an indecomposable closed invariant set A with the property that, given $\varepsilon > 0$, there is a set U of positive Lebesque measure in the ε-neighborhood of A such that $x \in U$ implies that $\lim_{t\to\infty} \phi(x,t)$ is contained in A, and that the forward orbit $\phi(x,t)$ is contained in U. This definition is provided as an idealization of the statement that there is a positive probability that computed trajectories beginning with a randomly chosen point will tend to A. An attractor is strange if it contains a transversal homoclinic orbit, i.e. an orbit connecting a point to itself where the stable and unstable manifolds intersect transversely, not tangentially.

7. The economic literature is not clear on this point. Lorenz (1989, p. 183) states that a fractal dimension is neither necessary nor sufficient for the existence of a strange attractor, but (p. 138) that a dynamical system is chaotic if it possesses a strange attractor as defined above. Barnett and Chen (1988, p. 208) define an attractor to be strange when it has a fractal dimension, and state (p. 206) that the existence of a strange attractor is neither necessary nor sufficient for chaos. In the physics and mathematical literature De Souza-Machado *et al.* (1990, p. 322) define a chaotic or strange attractor as a folded, layered structure with a fractional dimension while Zwillinger (1992, p. 28) states that the trajectories of a chaotic system asymptotically approach a strange

phase space but greater than two, as shown in Schuster (1988). For given parameter values, a dynamical system will exhibit aperiodic or chaotic behavior if it possesses a strange attractor, providing that the trajectory passes through the neighborhood U of the attractor as defined above. As Stewart (1990) states, almost all initial conditions lead to such a trajectory and hence lead to chaotic solutions. Although the system is deterministic and hence given initial conditions leads to uniquely defined trajectories, the sensitivity of the system to those initial conditions means that the behavior of the system is apparently random.

Analysis of the stability of fixed point attractors, and conditions for the existence and stability of other attractors, are based on a Taylor series expansion of the system about an appropriate point or path. Assume that the system has an equilibrium or fixed point x^*, so that $\dot{x} = f\{\phi(x^*, t), \theta\} = 0$. Let $\tilde{x} = x - x^*$, and expand (10) to give

$$D\tilde{x} = J(x,\theta)|_{x=x^*}\tilde{x} + h(\tilde{x},\, x^*\,,\theta) \text{ where } J(x,\theta) = (\frac{\partial f_i}{\partial x_j}) \qquad (12)$$

and h contains higher-order terms in $\tilde{x}$. The study of fixed point attractors is based on the Hartman-Grobman theorem (see Guckenheimer and Holmes, 1986) which states that if x^* is a fixed point of the system (10) and the Jacobian $J(x,\theta)|_{x=x^*}$ has no purely imaginary or zero eigenvalues, then the linearized flow near x^* is topologically equivalent to the actual flow; in this case, the fixed point is said to be hyperbolic or non-degenerate. Thus the non-linear system will be asymptotically stable[8] in the neighborhood of x^* if $\dfrac{h(\tilde{x}, x^*, \theta)}{|\tilde{x}|}$ is uniformly convergent in t and the eigenvalues of the linear term in the expansion (12), i.e. the Jacobian $J(x,\theta)|_{x=x^*}$, have negative real parts. Since the system is assumed to be autonomous, h is independent of t so the question of uniformity of convergence does not arise. An analogous technique using Poincaré sections can be used to determine the stability of periodic orbits, at least for systems of low dimension, as discussed e.g. in Stewart (1990).

In considering the properties of solutions of non-linear systems it is useful to define the concept of stable and unstable manifolds. For each fixed point of a non-linear system there is a stable manifold along which the flow tends towards the fixed

---

attractor defined as an attractor with a fractional dimension. It can be accepted, therefore, that a strange attractor has a fractal dimension and almost all trajectories with initial point in the neighborhood of that attractor, i.e. in the basin of attraction, will be chaotic. As noted in footnote 9, chaotic behavior may also occur when Hamiltonian systems, which do not have an attractor, are perturbed.

8. A solution $\phi(x_0,\, t)$ is locally stable if, for any $\varepsilon > 0$, there exists a $\delta > 0$ such that for all x_1 for which the system (10) is defined and for which $|x_1 - x_0| < \delta$, $|\phi(x_1,\, t) - \phi(x_0,\, t)| < \varepsilon$. A solution is asymptotically stable if it is stable and $\lim_{t\to\infty} |\phi(x_1,\, t) - \phi(x_0,\, t)| = 0$.

point and an unstable manifold along which it tends away from the point. Let a linear system on $\mathbb{R}^n$ be

$$\dot{x} = Ax \tag{13}$$

where A is a matrix of order n, and let λ_i, $i = 1, \ldots, n$, be the eigenvalues of A. Let the generalized eigenspace of the system (13) be $\{v \in \mathbb{R}^n : (A - \lambda)^n v = 0\}$ and let E^s, E^c and E^u be the stable, center and unstable eigenspaces of (13) corresponding to $\mathbb{R}(\lambda_i) < 0$, $\mathbb{R}(\lambda_i) = 0$ and $\mathbb{R}(\lambda_i) > 0$, respectively. The linear flow preserves these spaces and is towards the origin on E^s and away from the origin on E^u. As noted in Stewart (1990), on E^c the form of the linear flow is more complicated and can have a center on E^c when E^c is of dimension 2 but other possibilities arise.

For general non-linear systems with a fixed point x^*, local stable and unstable manifolds W^s, W^u may be defined (see Guckenheimer and Holmes, 1986) such that

$$\begin{aligned} W^s(x^*) &= \{x \in U : \phi(x, t) \to x^* \text{ as } t \to \infty \text{ and } \phi(x, t) \in U \text{ for all } t \geq 0\} \\ W^u(x^*) &= \{x \in U : \phi(x, t) \to x^* \text{ as } t \to -\infty \text{ and } \phi(x, t) \in U \text{ for all } t \leq 0\} \end{aligned} \tag{14}$$

where $U \subset \mathbb{R}^n$ is a neighborhood of x^*. These manifolds are non-linear analogues of the stable and unstable eigenspaces of the linear system. The stable manifold theorem (see Guckenheimer and Holmes, 1986), which is a generalization of the Hartman-Grobman theorem, then states that if the system (10) has a hyperbolic fixed point, there exist local stable and unstable manifolds $W^s(x^*)$, $W^u(x^*)$ of the same dimension as the eigenspaces E^s, E^u of the linearized system and tangent to E^s, E^u at x^*. $W^s(x^*)$ and $W^u(x^*)$ are as smooth as the functions $f(x, \theta)$. Hence, at such a hyperbolic fixed point the stable and unstable manifolds for the linearized flow are a close approximation to those of the actual flow. As discussed in Guckenheimer and Holmes (1986), if the fixed point is non-hyperbolic a center manifold tangent to E^c must be introduced but such manifolds may not be unique and may not be smooth.

Economic models may not have a fixed point solution, and even in models for which a steady-state solution does exist, corresponding to a fixed point in phase space, as in the model of the United Kingdom of Bergstrom and Wymer (1976) and related models, that fixed point may not be stable. Moreover, the fixed point may not be hyperbolic so that its stability becomes a more difficult question. This raises the question of whether other attractors exist for the system, and if so, what are their properties.

4.2 Lyapunov exponents and the dimension and nature of attractors

A distinction must be made between conservative and dissipative systems; the latter always possess attractors or repellers, such as fixed points, tori or strange attractors, while conservative or Hamiltonian systems do not but have an infinity of closed orbits so that any initial point will always lie on one of these orbits. The two types of systems can be distinguished using the generalized divergence of f. Let a set of initial conditions be contained in a vanishingly small hyper-ellipsoid V in $\mathbb{R}^n$. This volume will change as a function of t as $x(t)$ changes, so that

$$\frac{dV}{dt} = \int_V \int \dots \int \left(\sum_{i=1}^{n} \frac{\partial f_i}{\partial x_i} \right) dx_1 \dots dx_n \tag{15}$$

The summation term is the generalized divergence or Lie derivative of f; dissipative systems are characterized by contracting volumes, i.e. $dV/dt < 0$, while in conservative or Hamiltonian systems V is constant. This term, which is the trace of the Jacobian, is thus equal to the sum of the eigenvalues of $J(x,\ \theta)$. The Jacobian of a Hamiltonian system can be written as a block diagonal matrix with one block being the negative of another.

Any trajectory of a dissipative system will approach an attractor as $t \to \infty$. For systems exhibiting chaos in the neighborhood of a strange attractor, the trajectories have a sensitive dependence on the initial conditions, so that the separation of two nearby trajectories increases exponentially with time. This means that there is a stretching of the hyper-ellipsoid V in one direction which is more than compensated by a contraction in other directions, so that the volume defined by the arbitrary initial conditions decreases with time. The hyper-ellipsoid cannot always be stretched in the same direction but must be folded such that it is located in the specified neighborhood of the initial conditions.

The Lyapunov exponents provide information on the relative rates of expansion or contraction of this hyper-ellipsoid in each dimension and hence on the asymptotic properties of a system. Let an initial point be x_0. Consider the solution of the system

$$\dot{\phi}(x_0,\ t) = f\{\phi(x_0,\ t),\ t\} \quad \text{with } \phi(x_0,\ t_0) = x_0 \tag{16}$$

and differentiate with respect to x_0 to give the variational (matrix) equation

$$\begin{aligned} &\dot{\Phi}(x_0,\ t) = J\{\phi(x_0,\ t)\}\Phi(x_0,\ t) \\ &\text{where } \Phi(x_0,\ t) = \tfrac{\partial \phi(x_0,\, t)}{\partial x_0} \text{ and } \Phi(x_0,\ t_0) = I \end{aligned} \tag{17}$$

which is the linearization of the vector field along the orbit $\phi(x_0, t)$. Thus if δx_0 is a small perturbation about x_0, $\delta x(t) = \Phi(x_0,\ t)\delta x_0$. Let the eigenvalues of $\Phi(x_0,\ t)$ be $\mu_1(t), \dots, \mu_n(t)$. The Lyapunov exponents can then be defined as $\lambda_i = \limsup_{t\to\infty} \frac{1}{t} \log |\mu_i(t)|$, for $i = 1, \dots, n$. For simplicity, it will be assumed that the exponents are arranged in descending order such that $\lambda_1 \geq \lambda_2 \geq \dots \geq \lambda_n$. Let the corresponding generalized eigenvectors be $\eta_1, \dots, \eta_n$.

The Lyapunov exponents are a generalization of the eigenvalues at an equilibrium point. Let x_0 be an equilibrium point so that $J\{\phi(x_0,\ t)\}$ is time-invariant and (17) becomes $\Phi(x_0, t) = e^{J\{\Phi(x_0, t)\}t}$. If λ_i^* are the eigenvalues of $J(x^*)$, then $\frac{1}{t}\log|\mu_i(t)| = \mathbb{R}(\lambda_i^*)$ so that the Lyapunov exponents of the equilibrium point are $\lambda_i = \mathbb{R}(\lambda_i^*)$. Thus the Lyapunov exponents indicate the rate of expansion or contraction of the hyper-ellipsoid in the neighborhood of the equilibrium point, or the average rate where $x_0 \neq x^*$, and the subspace within which this occurs is defined by the corresponding eigenvectors. Every point in the basin of attraction of an attractor (or almost every point in the case of a strange attractor) has the same Lyapunov exponents as the attractor.

Corresponding to the n ordered generalized eigenvalues λ_i of the linearized system (17) there is a set of n nested subspaces W_i such that $W_1 \supset W_2 \supset \ldots \supset W_n$ where dim $(W_i) = n - i + 1$. These subspaces are spanned by the generalized eigenvectors such that $W_i = \text{span}\ \{\eta_i, \ldots, \eta_n\}$. Each of the columns of $\Phi(x_0, t)$ will tend to lie in the largest perturbation subspace W_1 and hence all the columns of $\Phi(x_0, t)$ will become aligned with η_1.

Calculation of the Lyapunov exponents is by no means trivial owing to the numerical properties of the solution $\phi(x, t)$ in (16) and the variational equation (17). As at least one Lyapunov exponent is positive in chaotic systems, the solutions $\Phi(x_0, t)$ are unbounded as $t \to \infty$ and the matrix is ill-conditioned. Thus some form of orthonormalization of these solutions is necessary in order to maintain precision for calculating all Lyapunov exponents.

The Lyapunov exponents λ_i may be used to classify and help determine the form of the attractor.[9] In order for an attractor to exist the volume of the hyper-ellipsoid defined by the generalized divergence must contract so that $\sum_{i=1}^{n} \lambda_i < 0$. Haken (1983) has shown that for attractors other than an equilibrium point, at least one Lyapunov exponent must be zero. Thus, for non-chaotic attractors, for an asymptotically stable equilibrium point $\lambda_i < 0$ for all i, while for an asymptotically stable k-torus, k exponents must be zero and the remainder negative; thus, a limit cycle or T^1 torus has only one zero exponent and the rest negative. A non-chaotic attractor is non-degenerate or hyperbolic if its dimension equals the number of zero Lyapunov exponents. For chaotic attractors, at least one of the Lyapunov

9. Only dissipative systems are considered here. Hamiltonian or conservative systems with m state variables (and hence m degrees of freedom or co-state variables, so that the system as defined above has dimension $2m$) have Lyapunov exponents such that $\sum_{i=1}^{2m} \lambda_i = 0$, at least two exponents are zero, and $\lambda_i = -\lambda_{2m-i+1}$ for $i = 1, \ldots, m$. All conservative systems are structurally unstable and do not possess attractors but chaotic behavior with positive Kolmogorov entropy can arise in the neighborhood of the Hamiltonian orbit when the system is perturbed. The trajectories can then bifurcate into a sequence of tori, distorting the original orbit and producing resonances which can lead to zones of chaotic behavior in phase space previously separated by non-resonant tori. Such systems are discussed e.g. in Guckenheimer and Holmes (1986), Schuster (1988) and Tabor (1989).

exponents must be positive and at least one zero. In addition, the dimension of a chaotic attractor must be a non-integer.

Lyapunov exponents and other measures such as the Hausdorff dimension (which is also called the Kolmogorov capacity) and the correlation dimension may be used to determine the dimension of the attractor. Let the set of points defining a surface in n-dimensional space be covered with n-dimensional hypercubes of length ε. The Hausdorff dimension of the object can then be defined as

$$D^H = \liminf_{\varepsilon \to 0} \frac{\log N(\varepsilon)}{-\log \varepsilon} \tag{18}$$

where $N(\varepsilon)$ be the number of hypercubes necessary to cover all points; a more precise definition is given in Guckenheimer and Holmes (1986, p. 285). The Hausdorff dimension is identical to the Euclidian dimension for surfaces in Euclidean space. This dimension is also of relevance to objects with a non-integer dimension associated with Cantor sets as discussed in Lorenz (1989) who identifies the Hausdorff dimension with the fractal dimension.

The correlation dimension is defined for a single time series. Let x_t, $t = 1, \ldots, T$ be an observed time series of a variable generated by the dynamical system but possibly observed with measurement error, and define its m-history to be $x(m, i) = (x_i, x_{i-1}, \ldots, x_{i-m+1})$ for $i = m, \ldots, T$. As each m-history is a point in m-dimensional space defining the delayed observed values of x_t in $x(m, i)$, m is called the embedding dimension. Takens (1981) showed that (i) if the variables of the true dynamical system are located on an attractor, i.e. there are no transients, (ii) if the dynamical system and measurement function are smooth, and (iii) if $m > 2n - 1$ where n is the dimension of the system, then the behavior of the dynamical system may be identified from the series.

Let $C^m(\varepsilon)$ be the correlation integral of the time series with embedding dimension m defined such that for a small positive number ε,

$$C^m(\varepsilon) = \lim_{T_m \to \infty} \frac{1}{T_m^2} \sum_{i,j=1}^{T_m} H(\varepsilon - ||x(m,i) - x(m,j)||) \tag{19}$$

where $T_m = T - m + 1$ is the number of m-histories, $||\ ||$ is the Euclidean norm, and H is the Heaviside function $H(y) = 1$ if $y > 0$, $H(0) = \frac{1}{2}$, and 0 otherwise. The correlation dimension in embedding dimension m is then defined (see Eckmann and Ruelle, 1985) as $D^C(m) = \lim_{\varepsilon \to 0} \frac{\log C^m(\varepsilon)}{\log \varepsilon}$ and the correlation dimension as $D^C = \lim_{m \to \infty} D^c(m)$.

Bergé *et al.* (1984) show that the calculated values of the correlation dimension are a close approximation to the Hausdorff dimension and is such that $D^C \leq D^H$, so that it provides a lower bound to the Hausdorff dimension. If required, the structural model can be used to generate long series of observations which can then be used to calculate the correlation integral and correlation dimension. Following Eckmann and Ruelle (1985), the correlation dimension can be estimated by finding a constant ratio of $\frac{\log C^m(\varepsilon)}{\log \varepsilon}$ that is independent of m when m is large. The correlation integral and correlation dimension form the link between time series analysis and the structural approach discussed in this paper.

The Lyapunov dimension is defined as $D^L = k + \frac{\sum_{i=1}^{k} \lambda_i}{|\lambda_{k+1}|}$ where k is the largest number of eigenvalues such that the sum is positive, i.e. k is such that $\sum_{i=1}^{k} \lambda_i > 0$ and $\sum_{i=1}^{k+1} \lambda_i < 0$. As positive Lyapunov exponents indicate the expansion of an initial hyper-ellipse in one or more directions while Kolmogorov entropy measures the average expansion in all directions, the Kolmogorov entropy $K \leq \sum_i \lambda_i$ for $\lambda_i > 0$. A good approximation to Kolmogorov entropy proposed by Grassberger and Procaccia (1983) and discussed in Eckmann and Ruelle (1985) is $K_2 = \lim_{m\to\infty} \lim_{\varepsilon\to 0} \frac{1}{\delta} \log \frac{C^m(\varepsilon)}{C^{m+1}(\varepsilon)}$ where δ is the observation period of a continuous series $x(t)$. As $K_2 \leq K$, these two measures provide an upper and lower bound for Kolmogorov entropy. The extreme cases are limit cycles where $C^m(\varepsilon) = C^{m+1}(\varepsilon)$ and hence K_2 is zero while if the series is purely random, K is infinite. As noted in Lorenz (1989), a chaotic system has finite entropy so that $0 < K_2 < \infty$; in terms of the correlation integral, K_2 approaches a finite, positive value from above as the embedding dimension is increased.

The Lyapunov exponents and associated measures, the correlation integral, correlation dimension and Kolmogorov entropy all provide information on the nature of the attractor of the system and on its asymptotic behavior. It must be emphasized, however, that the question of whether an orbit is dense can be extremely difficult. Guckenheimer and Holmes (1986) suggest that many of the "strange attractors" found numerically may not be attractors but merely attracting sets as they may not be dense but contain stable periodic orbits.

4.3 Structural stability

The second question of interest is the structural stability of the solution of the differential system (10), i.e. whether the asymptotic properties of the system change qualitatively for different values of the parameters. For example, for some parameter values the system may have a stable fixed point while for others it may have some form of torus as an attractor or perhaps a strange attractor, while for others still it may be unstable. Such structural stability is of crucial importance when considering the policy implications of a system. A system is structurally stable when small perturbations produce topologically equivalent systems. Heuristically, the system will be structurally stable if there is a one-to-one mapping of the flow of the system for small changes in parameter values; if not, the system is structurally unstable. The asymptotic properties of the logistic function, for example, can change dramatically even for very small changes in its parameter, as shown in Haken (1983).

The analysis of such structural stability in the context of strange attractors is an extension of sensitivity analysis as discussed in Wymer (1987, 1992a). If the eigenvalues of $A(\theta) = J(x, \theta)$ are λ_i, some of which may be complex conjugate, the partial derivatives $\partial\lambda_i/\partial\theta_\ell$ and $\partial\lambda_i/\partial a_{jk}$ may be found, where a_{jk} are elements of A. These partial derivatives give an indication of which parameters or coefficients in the model are critical to its stability; often the number of these parameters is quite small, as shown e.g. in Knight and Wymer (1978). This has policy implications if those parameters are policy parameters or are such that they could be affected by policy. Secondly, if $\partial\lambda_i/\partial\theta_\ell$ is large it may be useful to examine the effects on the dynamics of the model of allowing θ_ℓ to vary within its asymptotic confidence interval; this gives an indication of whether effort should be made to get more precise estimates of that parameter. Thirdly, knowledge of these partial derivatives often allows certain parameters and variables, or certain feedbacks, to be associated with particular cyclical behavior within the system, thus giving information on the overall dynamic properties of the system. Sensitivity analysis has been used in a number of studies such as Bergstrom and Wymer (1976), Jonson *et al.* (1982), Knight and Wymer (1978) and Gandolfo and Padoan (1990).

In the dynamical system $\dot{x} = f\{x(t), \theta\}$, as the set of parameters θ varies the phase portrait of the system usually changes gradually so that the system is topologically unchanged, but at some values of θ, called bifurcation points, the topology may change, perhaps with a change in the number of fixed points or periodic orbits, or with a change in the nature of a strange attractor; thus the system becomes structurally unstable at that point. Specifically, a point $\theta = \theta_0$ is a bifurcation point if there exists a θ_1 arbitrarily close to θ_0 such that $f(x, \theta_0)$ and $f(x, \theta_1)$ are topologically different. Such bifurcation points are characterized by a change in the number of eigenvalues of the system with zero real parts at that point so that the conditions for a point to be a bifurcation point can be defined in terms of the Jacobian of $f(x, \theta)$ or its eigenvalues.

The simplest bifurcations at a fixed point x_0 are the limit point bifurcation when one eigenvalue of the Jacobian becomes zero and the Hopf bifurcation when the real part of a complex conjugate eigenvalue becomes zero. Conditions for these and some other types of bifurcations are given, e.g. in Guckenheimer and Holmes (1986), Haken (1983), Lorenz (1989) and Stewart (1990). Let $f(x_0, \theta_0) = 0$ and let the Jacobian $J(x_0, \theta)$ at some point θ near θ_0 have eigenvalues λ with negative real parts so that the system is stable. Assume for simplicity that only one parameter in the system is relevant for structural stability. The simplest steady-state bifurcation occurs when one real negative eigenvalue becomes zero at θ_0, with the eigenvalue crossing and non-degeneracy conditions $\dfrac{\partial\lambda_1}{\partial\theta} \neq 0$ at θ_0 and $\dfrac{\partial J(x_0, \theta_0)}{\partial x} \neq 0$. If more real eigenvalues are zero at θ_0, or if the non-degeneracy conditions do not hold, further types of more complex bifurcations are possible.

The Hopf bifurcation which produces periodic orbits has an equivalent set of conditions. Assume that for some θ near θ_0 the Jacobian $J(x_0, \theta)$ has a complex conjugate pair of eigenvalues with non-zero real part. At the point $\theta = \theta_0$ assume these eigenvalues are the purely imaginary pair $\pm i\omega$ and that $J(x_0, \theta_0)$ has no other purely imaginary eigenvalues that are integer multiples of $i\omega$. Then providing $\frac{\partial \mathbb{R}(\lambda)}{\partial \theta} \neq 0$ at θ_0 the system bifurcates at (x_0, θ_0) to produce a continuous branch of limit cycles in the neighborhood of that point with period tending to $2\pi/\omega$ as $\theta \to \theta_0$. A further increase in λ may generate a second Hopf bifurcation so that the limit cycle bifurcates into a T^2 torus. The problem which arises analytically is that in order for the T^2 torus to be invariant the second set of purely imaginary eigenvalues must be independent of time, but the Jacobian is being evaluated on the limit cycle so that it is time-dependent; thus analytically, the system must be transformed about the center manifold on the torus to produce a system of dimension $n - 1$. The stable and unstable manifolds, W^s and W^u, are given by the eigenspaces corresponding to eigenvalues with negative and positive real parts, but the center manifold may be neither unique nor smooth, as discussed in Guckenheimer and Holmes (1986, p. 123ff).

A succession of bifurcations can lead to a strange attractor and aperiodic or chaotic dynamical behavior.[10] In particular, Newhouse *et al.* (1978) showed that if x is a constant vector field on a torus T^m, then if $m = 3$ there exists an open vector field with a strange attractor in every twice differentiable neighborhood of x, and if $m \geq 4$ there exists an open vector field with a strange attractor in every infinitely differentiable neighborhood of x. Thus for a system of sufficiently high dimension with the flow being on at least a three-dimensional torus, perhaps arising after three Hopf bifurcations, then there is a strange attractor in the neighborhood of the torus so that if the system is perturbed the trajectory may move towards that attractor.

Although successive bifurcations may arise as the parameter set θ is slowly changed within $\mathbb{R}^p$ and chaotic behavior may occur within some sub-intervals, yet within these sub-intervals there may be embedded a secondary set of sub-intervals

10. A classical example is the discrete logistic equation $x_{t+1} = kx_t(1-x_t)$ in which increases in the parameter k through the interval (3.4, 4.0) lead to bifurcations which produce an orbit of period 2, while further increases in k may lead to bifurcations producing orbits of 4, 8, ... in what is known as the Feigenbaum period doubling cascade as k is slowly increased. Within this are points where orbits of period 3 arise, again leading to another Feigenbaum cascade. The limit of these cascades produces chaotic behavior when the period has doubled infinitely often. The successive critical values of k satisfy a limiting universal property, at least for many simple systems. Feigenbaum (1978a, 1978b) showed that for the discrete logistic equation, if successive bifurcation values of k which led to period doubling are $\ldots k_{n-1}, k_n, k_{n+1} \ldots$ then $\lim_{n\to\infty} \frac{k_n - k_{n-1}}{k_{n+1} - k_n} = \delta \approx 4.6692\ldots$.

which produce windows of regular behavior. Such behavior arises in very simple models; examples of such features are provided in Lorenz (1989) and Stewart (1990).

The study of bifurcations involves an analysis of the successive terms in the Taylor series expansion of (10) or (12), and particularly any degeneracy of those terms. The behavior of the system in the neighborhood of a bifurcation point can become even more complex when more than one parameter can lead to bifurcations or if other "secondary" parameters take on certain values affecting the nature of the bifurcation. Golubitsky and Schaeffer (1985) and Golubitsky *et al.* (1988) present an extensive analysis of singularities and bifurcations.

The derivation of the steady state of economic models provides some information on the equilibrium properties and structural stability of the model. For example, the economic models discussed in this paper often have multiple steady-state equilibria. This is true of the UK model in Knight and Wymer (1978) but these equilibria collapse to a unique equilibrium if certain constraints are imposed on some parameters. If these constraints are removed, the model would become structurally unstable as those parameters assumed different values. Sensitivity analysis can then be used to help determine which parameters may have bifurcation points in the neighborhood of the equilibrium point of (10). As indicated above, sensitivity analysis of existing models suggests that only a limited number of parameters, perhaps only 5 in a model with 60 parameters, will be strong candidates for further investigation but, of course, this may change in the neighborhood of a degenerate solution. The asymptotic confidence interval of the parameter estimates provides the relevant range of variation of the parameters for this purpose. Many of the techniques and facilities required for the investigation of the properties of non-linear systems discussed above are already implemented in Apredic (see Wymer, 1993); the remaining procedures will be implemented shortly.

As the asymptotic properties of these models are not generic but depend crucially on its parameter values, it is necessary to estimate these parameters and their standard errors. The dynamic properties of a system and, for dissipative systems, the nature of its attractor, can then be derived using the techniques discussed above and used for policy purposes. This is analogous to the use of sensitivity analysis in the study of the policy implications of linear models which have a steady state, but the asymptotic behavior of non-linear models may be far more complex. For example, if the estimated parameter values are such that the system apparently has aperiodic behavior and a strange attractor or attracting set, the nature and magnitude of that attractor becomes relevant. Moreover, if changes in these parameters result in a stable fixed point with desirable properties, it may be possible and appropriate to undertake policy measures to change the system such that it converges on that fixed point.

5 Policy analysis - solutions subject to constraint

The properties of the model and their implications for policy can also be examined by solving the model subject to boundary point constraints. These issues, and the special case of optimal control, have been discussed in Wymer (1994) and used in a number of studies. The solution of general deterministic boundary point problems with linear, or linearized, models using the eigensystem is given in Wymer (1982) and was used by Gandolfo and Petit (1987). A rigorous derivation of stochastic optimal control within the context of linear differential equation systems is given in Bergstrom (1987).

Stochastic optimal control is used in Bergstrom *et al.* (1994) to derive the feedback equations for optimal monetary and fiscal policy within the linearized second-order model of the United Kingdom given in Bergstrom *et al.* (1992). One of the difficulties of optimal control shown by this study, however, is that although a range of plausible weights in the objective function give satisfactory smoothing of the path of the target variables for given initial conditions of the state variables, the initial values of the paths of the control variables are extreme. This suggests that either quite different weights in the objective function are required, or that inequality constraints should be imposed on the control variables. This would almost certainly result in more cyclical paths of the target and control variables and may decrease the overall rate of convergence of the system to its long-run equilibrium. An alternative possibility, however, is that the non-linearities in the model are important and that taking these into account explicitly may reduce the extreme initial values of the control variables.

The solution of boundary point problems in non-linear differential equation systems is a much more complex problem; techniques to solve such problems for non-stochastic continuous time models have been implemented by Wymer (1993) within a general framework. These allow the solution of non-linear optimal control problems, targeting problems where some target defined by $F(Dx(t),\, x(t),\, z(t))|_T = 0$ is to be achieved at $t = T$ (such as the Maastricht problem), the solution of models involving rational expectations, and the solution of differential Nash and Stackelberg games over some interval $(0, T)$.

Let a differential equation model, which may be non-linear, be defined as the set of first- and zero-order equations

$$Dx_1(t) = g_1\{x(t),\, z(t),\, \theta\} \tag{20}$$

$$g_2\{x(t),\, z(t),\, \theta\} = 0 \tag{21}$$

or, more generally,

$$G\{Dx(t),\, x(t),\, z(t),\, \theta\} = 0 \tag{22}$$

where x_1 is a vector of m_1 first-order endogenous or state or co-state variables, and x_2 a vector of m_2 zero-order endogenous variables, with $x = (x_1\, x_2)'$, $z(t)$ is a vector of known exogenous variables or forcing functions, and θ a vector of parameters. $g = (g_1\, g_2)'$ is the vector of functions defining the system, with the first-order variables being defined by g_1 and the zero-order variables by g_2.

The boundary point problem is that, given the systems (20) and (21), or (22), a solution is to be found which satisfies a set of functions $F_k\{Dx(t),\, x(t),\, z(t)\}|_{t=t_k} = 0$ representing the constraints on the variables at given points $t_k \in (0, T)$ along their path. Generally, but not necessarily, the F_k will refer to extreme points only, so that, for some $x_i(0)$ given, a solution is to be found which satisfies a set of functions $F\{Dx(t),\, x(t),\, z(t)\}|_{t=T} = 0$. The functions F allow the boundary points to be defined, e.g. in terms of ratios of levels of variables or differences between their rates of growth. optimal control is a special case.

A general non-linear optimal control problem may be defined as the maximization of the integral of some point or instantaneous objective function $f\{x(t), u(t), t, \theta\}$ over some interval $(0, T)$, where T may be infinite, subject to constraints imposed by the economic system as in (20) and (21), and subject to any equality or inequality constraints on the control variables. Formally, the optimal control problem is to

$$\text{maximize } Q = \int_{s=0}^{T} f\{x(s),\, u(s),\, z(s),\, \theta\} ds + F\{x(T),\, z(T)\} \tag{23}$$

subject to

$$Dx(t) = g\{x(t),\, u(t),\, z(t),\, \theta\} \quad \text{for all } t \in \{0,\, T\} \tag{24}$$
$$\text{with } x(0) = x_o \text{ and } z(t) \text{ given}$$
$$h\{x(t),\, u(t),\, z(t),\, \theta\} = 0 \quad \text{for all } t \in \{0, T\} \tag{25}$$
$$a\{x(t),\, u(t),\, z(t),\, \theta\} \geq 0 \quad \text{for all } t \in \{0, T\} \tag{26}$$

where $x(t)$ is a vector of m endogenous or state variables, with given initial state $x(0) = x_o$, $z(t)$ is a vector of n exogenous variables or forcing functions, and $u(t)$ is a vector of control variables. The vectors $x(t)$ and $z(t)$ may contain derivatives defining a higher-order system as in (2). As the forcing functions are assumed to be known functions of time, or can be approximated by such functions, the vector $z(t)$ will be replaced in the discussion below, without loss of generality, by the scalar t, and the functions f, g, h and a and parameters θ assumed to be defined accordingly. The point objective function f may contain a discount factor so that the intertemporal objective function Q may be defined as the discounted present value of f. Equation (24) is the dynamic model defining the system with g being a vector of non-linear functions, corresponding to ψ in (2). Equality constraints on the control variables $u(t)$ are given by the set of equations (25), and (26) represents a set of inequality constraints on the $u(t)$. A constraint of the form $a \leq u(t) \leq b$ merely corresponds to defining two inequality constraints of the form (26).

Necessary and sufficient conditions for the solution of (23) may be derived using the dynamic envelope theorem, under appropriate conditions on the functions f, g, h, and a, from the Lagrangian

$$\begin{aligned} L\{x, u, \lambda, \mu, \nu, t, \theta\} = f\{x(t),\, u(t),\, t,\, \theta\} + \lambda'(t) g\{x(t),\, u(t),\, t,\, \theta\} \\ + \mu'(t) h\{x(t),\, u(t),\, t,\, \theta\} + \nu'(t)\, a\{x(t),\, u(t),\, t,\, \theta\} \end{aligned} \tag{27}$$

where $\lambda(t)$ is the vector of Hamiltonian multipliers corresponding to the system (24), and $\mu(t)$ and $\nu(t)$ are the vectors of Lagrangian multipliers corresponding to the equality constraints (25) and inequality constraints (26). In the unconstrained case, $\mu(t)$ and $\nu(t)$ are zero so that the Lagrangian collapses to the Hamiltonian given by the first two terms only. The difficulty which arises with inequality constraints such as (26) is that some of these constraints may be binding over only part of the interval $(0, T)$, and the set of binding constraints may change along the optimal path, but this can be handled by a set of switch functions.

The sensitivity of the objective function to the parameters of the system may be derived from these results. If Q^* is the optimal value function of (23), LaFrance and Barney (1991) show that under the conditions derived from (27), the partial derivative $\partial Q^* / \partial \theta$ is continuous and twice differentiable in θ and

$$\frac{\partial Q^*}{\partial \theta} = \int_{s=0}^{T} \frac{\partial L(x^*,\, u^*,\, \lambda^*,\, \mu^*,\, \nu^*,\, s,\, \theta)}{\partial \theta}\, ds \tag{28}$$

Thus the partial derivative of Q^* may be obtained easily since the partial derivative of L may be calculated analytically, even for very general systems, and the integral calculated at the same time as the optimal path.[11] The matrix of second-order partial derivatives $\dfrac{\partial^2 Q^*}{\partial \theta\, \partial \theta'}$ may be calculated in a similar way; $\dfrac{\partial^2 Q^*}{\partial \theta\, \partial \theta'}$ is symmetric but this holds only in the integral form and not at a given point in time. These partial derivatives, which may be calculated from (28) even for very complex models, provide a useful tool for determining the properties of a model and evaluating its policy implications.

The solution of the optimal control problem (27), with extensions as discussed in Wymer (1994), has been implemented by Wymer (1993) within the more general framework of the solution of boundary point problems. This program is currently being used for the solution of non-linear optimal control problems in emissions control

11. As emphasized by LaFrance and Barney (1991), the Lagrangian must be differentiated prior to substitution of the optimal path of state, co-state and control variables, and the partial derivative then integrated. This is not the same as substituting the optimal solutions into the Lagrangian, differentiating with respect to the parameters, and then integrating.

(see Donaghy and Mukherjee, 1992), traffic planning and pollution (see Donaghy and Schintler, 1993, 1994), investment (see Thimann, 1993), and the solution of continuous Nash and Stackelberg games. These techniques are applicable to such questions as target zones for exchange rates and the EMS problem as well as to models with such features as lumpy investment.

6 Conclusions

This paper has reviewed recent developments in the estimation and dynamic analysis of non-linear differential equation models in economics. Although the complexity of this work is much greater than that for linear models, and allows for a much richer interpretation, nevertheless it is essentially an extension of previous research. Many of the models already developed in the continuous time literature are non-linear, and although most have been estimated using a linearized form derived from the non-linear system and subject to all of the constraints inherent in that system, some have been estimated by recently developed non-linear techniques.

The steady-state conditions of many of these models are known, and eigensystem and sensitivity analysis has been used to determine the properties of these models under the assumption that a steady state exists. Under these assumptions, some of these models are unstable given the estimated parameters. The highly non-linear nature of the models, and the broad similarity between some aspects of these models and some small mathematical models which are known to exhibit chaotic behavior and have strange attractors suggests that these estimated models may also have similar properties in the neighborhood of the estimated parameter values. An important question is whether such properties do exist, especially within some plausible confidence interval around the parameter estimates.

The long-run properties of economic models have important implications for economic policy. These models may also be used, however, to provide an assessment of policy by solving them to achieve given targets or for optimal control. Although the optimal control solution would not be used directly for policy making, it can be used to investigate the effect of various policy objectives on economic behavior.

The use of the continuous time models discussed in this paper highlights two problems which have arisen in investigations of chaotic behavior in economics. First, many economic models are specified as difference equations and hence may seriously misrepresent the behavior of the economy if in fact the economy is essentially continuous. Secondly, the long-run properties of non-linear models are crucially dependant on the parameter values. Policy discussions based on an economic interpretation of mathematical models which are known to exhibit chaotic behavior are relevant only if the parameter values are realistic; these parameters need to be estimated. The models and techniques discussed in this paper are designed to develop economic theory and its implications for policy and should help to determine whether or not economic systems are chaotic.

References

Armington, P. and C. Wolford (1984), *Exchange rate dynamics and economic policy*, Armington Wolford Associates, Washington DC.

Bailey, P.W., V.B. Hall, and P.C.B. Phillips (1987), "A model of output, employment, capital formation and inflation", in G. Gandolfo and F. Marzano, editors, *Keynesian theory, planning models and quantitative economics: essays in memory of Vittorio Marrama, Volume 2*, Giuffrè, Milano, 703–768.

Barnett, W.A. and P. Chen (1988), "The aggregation-theoretic monetary aggregates are chaotic and have strange attractors: an econometric application of mathematical chaos", in W.A. Barnett, E.R. Berndt, and H. White, editors, *Dynamic econometric modelling*, Cambridge University Press, Cambridge.

Benhabib, J. and R.H. Day (1982), "A characterization of erratic dynamics in the overlapping generations model", *Journal of Economic Dynamics and Control*, **4**, 37–55.

Bergé, P., Y. Pomeua, and C. Vidal (1984), *Order within chaos*, John Wiley, New York.

Bergstrom, A.R. (1976), *Statistical inference in continuous time economic models*, North-Holland, Amsterdam.

Bergstrom, A.R. (1983), "Gaussian estimation of structural parameters in higher order continuous time dynamic models", *Econometrica*, **51**, 117–152.

Bergstrom, A.R. (1983), "Optimal control in wide-sense stationary continuous time stochastic models", *Journal of Economic Dynamics and Control*, **11**, 425–443.

Bergstrom, A.R. (1990), *Continuous time econometric modelling*, Oxford University Press, Oxford.

Bergstrom, A.R., K.B. Nowman, and S. Wandasiewicz (1994), "Monetary and fiscal policy in a second order continuous time macroeconometric model of the United Kingdom", *Journal of Economic Dynamics and Control*, **22**, forthcoming.

Bergstrom, A.R., K.B. Nowman, and C.R. Wymer (1992), "Gaussian estimation of a second order continuous time macroeconometric model of the United Kingdom", *Economic Modelling*, **9**, 313–351.

Bergstrom, A.R. and C.R. Wymer (1976), "A model of disequilibrium neoclassical growth and its application to the United Kingdom", in A.R. Bergstrom, editor, *Statistical inference in continuous time economic models*, North-Holland, Amsterdam.

Boldrin, M. and L. Montrucchio (1986), "On the indeterminacy of capital accumulation paths", *Journal of Economic Theory*, **40**, 26–39.

Brock, W. and W.D. Dechert (1988), "Theorems on distinguishing deterministic and random systems", in W.A. Barnett, E.R. Berndt, and H. White, editors, *Dynamic econometric modelling*, Cambridge University Press, Cambridge.

Chambers, M.J. (1992), "The estimation of continuous time long-memory time series models", Discussion Paper Series 410, University of Essex, Essex.

Coddington, E.A. and N. Levinson (1955), *Theory of ordinary differential equations*, McGraw-Hill, New York.

De Souza-Machado, S., R.W. Rollins, D.T. Jacobs, and J.L. Hartman (1990), "Studying chaotic systems using micro-computer simulations and Lyapunov exponents", *American Journal of Physics*, **58**, 321–329.

Donaghy, K.P.F. (1992), "A continuous time model of the Unites States economy", in G. Gandolfo, editor, *Continuous time econometrics: theory and applications*, Chapman-Hall, London, 151–193.

Donaghy, K.P.F. and J. Mukherjee (1992), "Multilateral policy responses to global warming: a differential game analysis", unpublished manuscript [Conference Paper: Conference of the International Society of Dynamic Games, Grimementz].

Donaghy, K.P.F. and L.A. Schintler (1993), "Managing congestion, pollution, and infrastructure: a dynamic transportation network model", unpublished manuscript [Conference Paper: North American Meetings of the Regional Science Association International, Houston].

Donaghy, K.P.F. and L.A. Schintler (1994), "Optimal policies for reducing congestion of major commuting arteries in a growing urbanized area", *Journal of Planning Education and Research*, **13**, 189–198.

Eckmann, J-P. and D. Ruelle (1985), "Ergodic theory of chaos and strange attractors", *Reviews of Modern Physics*, **57**, 617–656.

Feigenbaum, M.J. (1978a), "Quantitative universality for a class of non-linear transformations", *Journal of Statistical Physics*, **19**, 25–52.

Feigenbaum, M.J. (1978b), "Quantitative universality for a class of non-linear transformations", *Journal of Statistical Physics*, **21**, 669–706.

Gandolfo, G. (1981), *Qualitative analysis and econometric estimation of continuous time dynamic models*, North-Holland, Amsterdam.

Gandolfo, G. (1992), "Continuous time econometrics has come of age", in G. Gandolfo, editor, *Continuous time econometrics: theory and applications*, Chapman-Hall, London, 1–11.

Gandolfo, G. and P.C. Padoan (1990), "The Italian continuous time model: theory and empirical results", *Economic Modelling*, **7**, 91–132.

Gandolfo, G. and P.C. Padoan (1992), "Continuous time econometric modelling and the issue of capital liberalization", in P.C.B. Phillips, editor, *Models, methods and applications of econometrics*, Blackwell, London.

Gandolfo, G., P.C. Padoan, G. de Arcangelis, and C.R. Wymer (1994), "Non-linear estimation of a non-linear continuous time model", in W.A. Barnett, G. Gandolfo, and C. Hillinger, editors, *Dynamic disequilibrium modelling*, Cambridge University Press, Cambridge.

Gandolfo, G. and M.L. Petit (1987), "Dynamic optimization in continuous time and optimal policy design in the Italian economy", *Annales d'Economie et de Statistique*, **6/7**, 311–333.

Golubitsky, M. and D.G. Schaeffer (1985), *Singularities and groups in bifurcation theory I*, Springer-Verlag, Berlin.

Golubitsky, M., I.N. Stewart, and D.G. Schaeffer (1988), *Singularities and groups in bifurcation theory II*, Springer-Verlag, Berlin.

Goodwin, R.M. (1990), *Chaotic economic dynamics*, Clarendon Press, Oxford.

Grandmont, J-M. (1985), "On endogenous competitive business cycles", *Econometrica*, **53**, 995–1045.

Grandmont, J-M. and P. Malgrange (1986), "Non-linear economic dynamics: introduction", *Journal of Economic Theory*, **40**, 3–12.

Grassberger, P. and I. Procaccia (1983), "Estimation of Kolmogorov entropy from a chaotic signal", *Physical Review A*, **28**, 2591–2593.

Guckenheimer, J. and P. Holmes (1986), *Non-linear oscillations, dynamical systems, and bifurcations of vector fields*, Springer-Verlag, Berlin.

Haken, H. (1983), *Advanced synergetics*, Springer-Verlag, Berlin.

Jonson, P.D., W.J. McKibbin, and R.G. Trevor (1982), "Exchange rates and capital flows: a sensitivity analysis", *Canadian Journal of Economics*, **15**, 669–692.

Jonson, P.D., E.R. Moses, and C.R. Wymer (1976), "A minimal model of the Australian economy", in W.E. Norton, editor, *Conference in applied economic research*, Reserve Bank of Australia, Sydney.

Jonson, P.D. and J.C. Taylor (1979), "Inflation and economic stability in a small open economy: a systems approach", *Carnegie-Rochester Conference Series on Public Policy*, **4**, 289–323.

Kamien, M.I. and N.L. Schwartz (1981), *Dynamic optimization: the calculus of variations and optimal control in economics and management*, North-Holland, Amsterdam.

Knight, M.D. and C.R. Wymer (1978), "A macroeconomic model of the United Kingdom", *IMF Staff Papers*, **25**, 742–778.

LaFrance, J.T. and L.D. Barney (1991), "The envelope theorem in dynamic optimization", *Journal of Economic Dynamics and Control*, **16**, 355–385.

Lo, A.W. (1991), "Long-term memory in stock market prices", *Econometrica*, **59**, 1279–1313.

Lorenz, E.N. (1963), "Deterministic non-periodic flow", *Journal of Atmospheric Sciences*, **20**, 130–141.

Lorenz, H-W. (1989), *Non-linear dynamical economics and chaotic motion*, Springer-Verlag, Berlin.

Newhouse, S., D. Ruelle, and F. Takens (1978), "Occurrence of strange axiom A attractors near quasi-periodic flows on t^m, $m > 3$", *Communications in Mathematical Physics*, **64**, 35–40.

Phillips, P.C.B. (1974), "The estimation of some continuous-time models", *Econometrica*, **42**, 803–824.

Phillips, P.C.B. (1976), "The estimation of linear stochastic differential equations with exogenous variables", in A.R. Bergstrom, editor, *Statistical inference in continuous time economic models*, North-Holland, Amsterdam, 135–174.

Phillips, P.C.B. (1978), "The treatment of flow data in the estimation of continuous-time systems", in A.R. Bergstrom, A.J.L. Catt, M.H. Preston, and B.D.J. Silverstone, editors, *Stability and inflation*, John Wiley, New York, 257–274.

Phillips, P.C.B. (1991), "Error correction and long-run equilibrium in continuous time", *Econometrica*, **59**, 967–980.

Richard, D.M. (1978), "A dynamic model of the world copper industry", *IMF Staff Papers*, **25**, 779–833.

Richard, D.M. (1980), "A global adjustment model of exchange and interest rates", in D. Bigman and T. Taya, editors, *The functioning of floating exchange rates: theory, evidence and policy implications*, Ballinger, Cambridge, 243–276.

Rössler, O.E. (1977), "Continuous chaos", in H. Haken, editor, *Synergetics - a workshop*, Springer-Verlag, Berlin.

Schuster, H.G. (1988), *Deterministic chaos - an introduction*, Physik Verlag, Weinheim.

Seierstad, A. and K. Sydsaeter (1977), "Sufficient conditions in optimal control theory", *International Economic Review*, **18**, 367–391.

Stewart, I.N. (1990), "Dynamical systems", in W. Lederman, E. Lloyd, S. Vajda, and C. Alexander, editors, *Handbook of applicable mathematics (supplement)*, John Wiley, New York.

Tabor, M. (1989), *Chaos and integrability in non-linear dynamics*, John Wiley, New York.

Takens, F. (1981), "Detecting strange attractors in turbulence", in D. Rand and L. Young, editors, *Dynamical systems and turbulence*, Springer-Verlag, Berlin.

Thimann, C. (1993), "Sudden jump or gradual climb? An extended model of investment response in Eastern Germany", Discussion Paper, University of Munich, Munich.

Wymer, C.R. (1972), "Econometric estimation of stochastic differential equation systems", *Econometrica*, **40**, 81–95.

Wymer, C.R. (1977), "Program manual: Asimul (and supplements)", Mimeo, International Monetary Fund, Washington DC.

Wymer, C.R. (1979), "The use of continuous time models in economics", Mimeo, International Monetary Fund, Washington DC.

Wymer, C.R. (1982), "Program manual: Contines (and supplements)", Mimeo, International Monetary Fund, Washington DC.

Wymer, C.R. (1987), "Sensitivity analysis of economic policy", in G. Gandolfo and F. Marzano, editors, *Keynesian theory, planning models and quantitative economics: essays in memory of Vittorio Marrama, Volume 2*, Giuffrè, Milano.

Wymer, C.R. (1992a), "Continuous time models in macroeconomics: specification and estimation", in G. Gandolfo, editor, *Continuous time econometrics: theory and applications*, Chapman-Hall, London.

Wymer, C.R. (1992b), "Estimation of non-linear differential equation systems", in P.C.B. Phillips, editor, *Models, methods and applications of econometrics*, Blackwell, London.

Wymer, C.R. (1993), "Program manual: Apredic (and supplements)", unpublished manuscript.

Wymer, C.R. (1994), "The role of continuous time disequilibrium models in macroeconomics", in W.A. Barnett, G. Gandolfo, and C. Hillinger, editors, *Dynamic disequilibrium modelling*, Cambridge University Press, Cambridge.

Zwillinger, D. (1992), *Handbook of differential equations*, Academic Press, Boston.

Methods and Applications of Economic Dynamics
L. Schoonbeek, E. Sterken and S.K. Kuipers (editors)

Chapter 4

Evaluating the dynamic properties of macroeconometric models [1]

Anton P. Barten

1 Introduction

In the early beginning of empirical macroeconomic model building considerable attention was given to the evaluation of the dynamic properties of such models – e.g. Frisch (1933) and Tinbergen (1939). These models were seen as business cycle models. It was then only natural to try to find out whether they implied indeed cyclical behavior for the endogenous variables. Questions of the periodicity of eventual cycles and the damped or explosive nature of the reactions to shifts in the initial conditions drew quite some interest.

As far as these macroeconomic models were systems of linear difference equations these questions can be answered by deriving the eigenvalues of a certain coefficient matrix. If some of these are pairs of conjugate complex numbers cyclical behavior is built in and one can easily establish periodicity and the convergent or divergent nature of the cycles.

Most macroeconomic models are not fully linear but are mixtures of linear, log-linear and generally non-linear equations. It is then virtually impossible to read off the dynamic properties from the coefficients of the model. A possibility is to

---

1. Support by the Interuniversity Attraction Poles programme (project nr. 26) of the Belgian Department of Science Policy is gratefully acknowledged. The present version has benefitted from the comments of Luc Lauwers, of other members of the Econometrics Unit of the Economics Department of the University of Louvain, of Bert Schoonbeek, Elmer Sterken and other participants of the Groningen workshop.

linearize the model and study the dynamics of the linearized version. It is not clear to what extent one eliminates then interesting dynamic features.

Another problem arises. As the models grow larger and larger one can expect the number of non-zero eigenvalues to increase also although not necessarily at the same rate. In that case it becomes virtually impossible to determine the eigenvalues. Also linearization is becoming more and more difficult as the number of deviations from linearity increases.

Given the size of modern macroeconomic models and the variety of functional forms for the structural equations the traditional approach to evaluating dynamic properties is not attractive. There is another possibility, however, which we plan to explore in this paper. Simulation of a model generates time paths for the endogenous variables which reflect the dynamic properties of the model. How can one deduce from these time paths the counterpart of the eigenvalues of the traditional approach? The following section presents the traditional approach for fully linear models. Section 3 will look into the matter of the extent to which one can extract the eigenvalues from the analysis of the simulated time path. The case of the full linear model serves as a benchmark. If one cannot handle that case there is hardly any hope to assess the dynamic properties of non-linear models. There is little one can say in general about the dynamics of such models. One can, however, study some cases to see to what extent the technique of analyzing the simulated time path of linear models can also be applied to that of non-linear models. In Section 4 the case of an almost-linear model is taken up. Many real-world models could be considered to fall in this category. In that section also the use of non-linear characterization is considered. In Section 5 the focus is on a more strongly non-linear model.

Given the exploratory nature of this paper the models used are small and simple. There is no pretense to let them be empirically useful. Their only purpose is to illustrate the methodological point and to prepare the way for more realistic application. If you cannot handle the small and simple there is little hope for success in mastering the large and complex.

Some of the issues dealt with in this paper might remind one of certain topics in time series analysis. Here, however, no stochastics are involved. A technique like least squares is purely used as a curve fitting device. As far as standard errors are given these should be only seen as measures to gauge the quality of the curve fitting exercise.

2 The case of linear models[2]

Without loss of generality one can write the reduced form of a system of linear difference equation as

$$x(t) = A\,x(t-1) + B\,z(t) \tag{1}$$

where $x(t)$ is an m-vector of values of endogenous variables at (discrete) time t, while $z(t)$ is a k-vector of values of exogenous variables, including possibly disturbance terms. A is an $(m \times m)$ matrix of constant coefficients, while B is an $(m \times k)$ matrix of such coefficients. We assume that A cannot be rearranged in block-triangular form. If such a form would be possible system (1) could be decomposed in the basic constituant blocks and the analysis of the dynamics would be specific for each block.

The presence of a single lag on the right-hand side of (1) is not really restrictive. System (1) can be seen as a compressed version of a system with any finite number of lags in the endogenous and exogenous variables.

The eigenvalues of the matrix A are of special interest for the purpose of analyzing the dynamics of a system like (1). These eigenvalues solve the characteristic equation

$$|A - \lambda I| = \lambda^g + c_1\,\lambda^{g-1} + \cdots + c_{g-1}\,\lambda + c_g = 0 \tag{2}$$

where $g \leq m$ is the rank of matrix A, which provides the upperbound of the number of non-zero eigenvalues of A. Eigenvalues can be real or complex. In case of real eigenvalues larger than unity a shift in initial conditions will steadily increase the difference between the new time path and the original one. One has divergence. Convergence occurs when the eigenvalue is in between -1 and $+1$. The negative eigenvalues correspond with a 2-period cycle. If the eigenvalue is less than -1 one has a divergent 2-period cycle. Complex eigenvalues come in conjugate pairs like

$$\lambda_1 = \rho(\cos\,\varphi + i\sin\,\varphi) \qquad \lambda_2 = \rho(\cos\,\varphi - i\sin\,\varphi) \tag{3}$$

where $\rho > 0$ is the modulus or amplitude parameter and φ is the frequency parameter. If φ is expressed in degrees it takes $360/\varphi$ periods to complete a cycle, i.e. to move from one maximum to the next one. A shift in initial conditions will generate fluctuations around the original time path. If $\rho < 1$ these will be shrinking in amplitude. There is convergence. Increasing amplitude corresponds with the modulus to be larger than one.

The case of $\rho = 1$ corresponds with a constant cyclical component or with convergence to a cycle. This is rare for linear difference equations but can occur under

2. This and the next section is based on Barten (1987). See also Schoonbeek (1989) and Wallis (1977).

more general conditions in non-linear systems.

Example 2.1: Consider the following simple macroeconomic model

$$
\begin{aligned}
&(\text{A.1}) \quad C(t) = 50 + 0.6\,Y(t) + 0.25\,C(t-1) \\
&(\text{A.2}) \quad I(t) = 0.2747\,(Y(t) - 0.9\,Y(t-1)) + 0.75\,I(t-1) \\
&(\text{A.3}) \quad Y(t) = 0.6\,(C(t) + I(t) + G(t))
\end{aligned}
$$

with C, I, Y being consumption, gross investment, and domestic production, respectively, all endogenous, while G, autonomous (government) expenditure, is exogenous. There is no pretense about the empirical validity of this model. Error terms have been omitted because the focus is on deterministic dynamics. The reduced form is

$$
\begin{pmatrix} C(t) \\ I(t) \\ Y(t) \end{pmatrix} = \begin{pmatrix} 0.439 & 0.568 & -0.187 \\ 0.087 & 1.010 & -0.333 \\ 0.316 & 0.947 & -0.312 \end{pmatrix} \begin{pmatrix} C(t-1) \\ I(t-1) \\ Y(t-1) \end{pmatrix} + \begin{pmatrix} 87.88 & 0.758 \\ 17.34 & 0.347 \\ 63.13 & 1.263 \end{pmatrix} \begin{pmatrix} 1 \\ G(t) \end{pmatrix}
$$

The matrix A turns out to be of rank 2. Its characteristic equation is

$$\lambda^2 - 1.137\,\lambda + 0.316 = 0$$

The non-zero eigenvalues are then 0.653 and 0.484, both real, positive and less than unity. The system is obviously damped. □

To derive the characteristic equation of matrix A is not necessarily a simple matter. Moreover, current solution techniques bypass the reduced form, so that usually no direct information about A is available. The next section looks at an alternative which better fits current practice.

3 Estimating the separated form of a linear model

Use will be made of a theorem that puts forward the existence of a matrix polynomial lag operator, $H(L)$, of order g (= rank of matrix A), with $H_0 = I$, and of a scalar polynomial lag operator, $c(L)$, also of order g, with $c_0 = 1$, such that

$$H(L)(I - AL) = c(L)I$$

with the c_i of $c(L)$ being the coefficients of the characteristic equation of the matrix A. The H_i can be obtained from the recursive equation $H_i = c_i I + H_{i-1}A$.

Write (1) as

$$(I - AL)x(t) = B\,z(t)$$

and premultiply both sides by $H(L)$. According to the theorem one then has

$$c(L)I\,x(t) = H(L)\,B\,z(t) \tag{4}$$

or

$$\begin{aligned} x(t) &= -c_1 x(t-1) - \cdots - c_g x(t-g) + Bz(t) + H_1 Bz(t-1) + \cdots \\ &\quad + H_g Bz(t-g) \end{aligned}$$

Note that the c_i are scalars by which the $x(t-i)$-vectors are multiplied. Tinbergen (1939) names (4) (the system of) "final equations". Marschak (1950) proposes the name of "separated form".

Example 3.1: Using the coefficients of the characteristic equation of Example 2.1 we can write

$$\begin{pmatrix} C(t) \\ I(t) \\ Y(t) \end{pmatrix} = 1.137 \begin{pmatrix} C(t-1) \\ I(t-1) \\ Y(t-1) \end{pmatrix} - 0.316 \begin{pmatrix} C(t-2) \\ I(t-2) \\ Y(t-2) \end{pmatrix} + \text{ terms in } \begin{pmatrix} 1 \\ G(t-j) \end{pmatrix}$$

for $j = 0, 1, 2$. For our purpose the coefficients of the $(1,\, G(t-j))$ vectors are not really needed. □

The idea is to use the structural form to generate a time path for the endogenous variables and then to estimate the c_i-coefficients of the separated form by the method of least squares. For the analysis of endogenous dynamics the interest is primarily in the autoregressive c_i-coefficients and not so much in the coefficient matrices of the $z(t-j)$. In the simulation experiment one can just as well set the z variables at zero. Only initial conditions have to be specified.

Example 3.2: The model of Example 2.1 has been used for the simulation experiment. Time series for $C(t)$, $I(t)$ and $Y(t)$ were generated with $G(t) = 0$ for all $t = 1, \ldots, 30$ and $C(0) = 3000, I(0) = 500, Y(0) = 2100$. Next, a regression was run of $C(t)$ on a constant, $C(t-1)$ and $C(t-2)$. It resulted in

$$C(t) = 24.62 + 1.137\,C(t-1) - 0.316\,C(t-2)$$

The R^2 is 1.000000. The standard errors are 0.01 for the intercept, 0.0001 for the coefficient of $C(t-1)$ and 0.0001 for that of $C(t-2)$, respectively. The outcome for the regression coefficients agrees well with the coefficients of the characteristic equation of Example 2.1. Running similar regressions for $I(t)$ and $Y(t)$ gives the same autoregressive coefficients, but different intercepts, as is to be expected. Using different initial values produced basically the same numerical results for the autoregressive equation. □

The longest lag in the regression corresponds with the rank of matrix A. In practice, matrix A is usually not available and even if it is available its rank is not so easy to establish. Again here, the simulation regressions can be helpful. If the R^2 is not equal to one, one or more lags should be added until perfect fit is obtained.

Example 3.3: Regressing simulated $C(t)$ on a constant and $C(t-1)$ yields

$$C(t) = 72.02 + 4.67\,C(t-1) \qquad R^2 : 0.999867$$

The R^2 is close but not equal to one. Also the standard error of regression is considerably larger than the one obtained for the regression of the previous example. The necessity to add another lag is clearly indicated. □

It may also happen that the rank is less than *a priori* guessed. One is running an overfitted regression. Of course, the R^2 will be equal to one, but the standard errors are not equal to zero. Another symptom of overfitting is the difference in the autoregressive coefficients for the different endogenous variables. Overfitting may also lead to insufficient rank of the regression matrix. A reduction in the longest lag is clearly indicated.

Example 3.4: The simulated $C(t)$ was regressed on a constant, $C(t-1)$, $C(t-2)$ and $C(t-3)$. The result is

$$C(t) = 22.85 + 1.209\,C(t-1) - 0.399\,C(t-2) + 0.023\,C(t-3)$$

The $R^2 = 1.000000$ as expected. The standard errors of the autoregressive coefficients are 0.196, 0.223 and 0.062, respectively. Running a similar regression for $I(t)$ gave

$$I(t) = 1.47 + 1.291\,I(t-1) - 0.492\,I(t-2) + 0.049\,I(t-3)$$

which is clearly a different set of values for the autoregressive coefficients. The standard error of the coefficient of $I(t-3)$ is 0.061. Performing regressions with $C(t-4)$ or $I(t-4)$ added failed because of multicollinearity. It is of some interest to note that the first two roots of the $C(t)$ and $I(t)$ regressions are pairwise virtually the same, *viz.* 0.658/0.650 and 0.488/0.492 and also close to the ones obtained earlier in Examples 2.1 and 3.2, and that the additional roots are relatively small: 0.073 for C and 0.155 for I. Overfitting appears not to be misleading for the more important characteristics of endogenous dynamics. □

The linear case appears to be manageable. What about the autoregressive representations for the endogenous variables of systems of non-linear difference equations?

4 Almost-linear systems

Once one leaves the safety of the shore of linearity one gets into murky waters, partly uncharted and full of surprises. Instinctly one keeps as close as possible to the shore. Quite a few non-linear systems are hybrids of many linear difference equations and some non-linear ones. One would expect that what is valid for linear systems is also valid, but only to a certain extent, for those almost-linear models.

Example 4.1: In the model of Example 2.1 equation (A.1) is being replaced by a log-linear expression, which was fitted to the simulated data in order to represent roughly the same time shape as (A.1)

$$\text{(B.1)} \quad \ln C(t) = 1.356 + 0.249 \ln Y(t) + 0.500 \ln C(t-1)$$

Equations (A.2) and (A.3) have been retained. One would not expect the new system to imply totally different dynamics. □

The separated form of linear systems can also be obtained by a process of elimination and substitution, i.e. by replacing in the equation for, say, $x_1(t)$ all the values of $x_i(t-j)$, $i > 1$, $j \geq 0$, by lagged x_1-values. It can be assumed that under fairly general conditions also non-linear systems allow such a process of elimination and substitution resulting in a non-linear separated form, which is, however, not necessarily unique.

Example 4.2: The system consisting of (B.1), (A.2) and (A.3) was simulated. The resulting time path for C was fitted to an autoregressive pattern

$$C(t) = 11.13 + 1.260\,C(t-1) - 0.343\,C(t-2)$$

The $R^2 = 0.989$. The standard errors of the coefficients of $C(t-1)$ and $C(t-2)$ are 0.11 and 0.04, respectively, which is not really small. Similar results were obtained for regressions of $I(t)$ and $Y(t)$:

$$\begin{aligned} I(t) &= 1.84 + 1.079\,I(t-1) - 0.213\,I(t-2) \quad R^2 : 0.998 \\ Y(t) &= 11.00 + 1.086\,Y(t-1) - 0.226\,Y(t-2) \quad R^2 : 0.975 \end{aligned}$$

The eigenvalues for the C-equation are 0.862 and 0.398, respectively. Those for the I-equation are somewhat smaller: 0.819 and 0.260, respectively. It seems as if the introduced log-linearity has increased the dominant eigenvalue, i.e. has reduced somewhat the damped nature of the model. Adding another lagged term in the C and I regression improved the fit considerably. The leading eigenvalues remained roughly the same. Adding more lagged terms did not improve the fit much more. □

It appears that a linear approximation to the non-linear autoregressive structure can already give some information. Another possibility is to use quadratic or cubic approximations.

Example 4.3 : The simulated time path for $C(t)$ has been regressed on $C(t-1)$ and $C(t-2)$ and on the squares of these variables:

$$\begin{aligned} C(t) &= 24.67 + 1.194\,C(t-1) - 0.456\,C(t-2) + 0.0064\,C(t-1) \\ &\quad - 0.00019\,C(t-2) \end{aligned}$$

The $R^2 = 0.999997$. Adding cubic terms gives

$$\begin{aligned} C(t) &= 18.59 + 1.348\,C(t-1) - 0.527\,C(t-2) + 3.098\,.\,10^{-4}\,C(t-1)^2 \\ &\quad + 1.918\,.\,10^{-4}\,C(t-2)^2 - 1.062\,.\,10^{-4}\,C(t-1)^3 \\ &\quad - 5.071\,.\,10^{-9}\,C(t-2)^3 \end{aligned}$$

with $R^2 = 0.999999$. In terms of fit there is a clear improvement over adding more lags. One can relate these results to the ones of the previous example by linearizing the derivatives of $C(t)$ with respect to $C(t-1)$ and $C(t-2)$, respectively. For $C = 140$, the stationary value of the simulation, the "cubic" case gave 1.372 and -0.474 for these derivatives. The linear terms obviously dominate. The values obtained imply a complex pair of eigenvalues $0.686 \pm 0.058\,i$. Given the very small size of the imaginary part it can be ignored for the interpretation. One may conclude that the non-linear separated form does not give another picture of the dynamics then the linear one of Example 4.2. □

Example 4.4: One can argue that in non-linear separated forms the time path of the exogenous values matters. Indeed, when simulating the model with a non-zero time path for G, and estimating the "cubic" version of the previous example with linear, quadratic and cubic terms for G added, the regression coefficients are quite different from those of the "cubic" equation of Example 4.3. However, the derivatives of $C(t)$ with respect to $C(t-1)$ and $C(t-2)$ are 0.997 and -0.283 when evaluated at the stationary value of $C = 675$. These derivatives are close to the regression coefficients of Example 4.2, in particular those for I. □

Quadratic and cubic approximations may capture some of the non-linearities better than increasing the number of lags of the linear form. The latter has the advantage of a direct interpretation of the results in terms of characteristics of the time path. There is the presumption that for almost-linear models the linear autoregressive form may capture at least the dominant characteristics.

5 A non-linear case

Since it is difficult to be general for non-linear difference equations we will use in this section a non-linear model which, following Puu (1993), has a third degree term in the structural form. We will generate the time path for the endogenous variables. This will be used to fit a linear autoregressive form to find out what can be learned about the system dynamics.

Example 5.1: The model used in this section consists of equation (B.1) of Example 4.1, with the intercept adjusted to 2.2, equation (A.3) of Example 2.1 and two other equations replacing equation (A.2), namely

(C.2a) $\ln K(t) = \ln K(t-1) + 750\,(Y(t-1)/K(t-1) - 0.85)^3$

(C.2b) $I(t) = K(t) - 0.9\,K(t-1)$

The intercept of (B.1) and the value of 750 in (C.2a) were obtained after some calibration to obtain a feasible time path for the variables. One can interpret (C.2a) as an adjustment of capital, K, towards a degree of utilization of capacity of 85 percent. □

Example 5.2: The model of the previous example was used to simulate a time path for the four endogenous variables C, K, I and Y. Results will be given for the autoregressions for C and I. It appears that only a rather high-order lag pattern can adequately fit the generated time series. For I six lags were needed resulting in an R^2 of 0.999863. We will not give the detail of the regressions, but focus on the roots. There are two real roots: 0.655 and -0.131, the latter one being of not too great interest. There are two pairs of complex roots. One pair is $-0.056 \pm 0.549\,i$ with a modulus of 0.552 and a periodicity of 4 periods. The second pair is $0.424 \pm 0.367\,i$ with a modulus of 0.561 and a periodicity of 9 periods. The dynamics are clearly damped. An attempt to estimate a similar autoregressive pattern for C failed because of multicollinearity. The 5-th order pattern had, however, a quite satisfactory fit with $R^2 = 0.999959$. The estimated coefficients are very roughly of the same order as those of the estimated 6-th order pattern for I. There is one real root: 0.574 and there are two pairs of complex roots. The first one is $-0.053 \pm 0.567\,i$ with modulus 0.569 and periodicity 4. The second one is $0.395 \pm 0.332\,i$ with modulus 0.516 and periodicity 9. Comparing these results with those for I one is struck by their similarity. They are surely not identical, as they should have been for a linear model, but they basically give the same impression of the dynamics: one substantial real root of about 0.6 and two cycles both with a modules of about 0.55 and periodicity of 9 and 4, respectively. □

To draw lessons from a simple example is a hazardous undertaking. Still, it is encouraging to see that (i) the linear autoregressive pattern appears to fit the simulated time path and (ii) the dynamic characteristics are rather similar across variables.

One could view the fitting of a linear autoregressive pattern as a kind of implicit linearization of the structural form. Does this yield the same results as working with the linear(ized) structural form?

Example 5.3: To answer that question equation (B.5) has been replaced by a linear one fitted to the generated data of the previous example:

$$\text{(D.1)} \quad C(t) = 1016.60 + 0.388\, Y(t) + 0.505\, C(t-1)$$

Equation (C.2a) is linearized by

$$\text{(D.2a)} \quad K(t) = 0.281\,(Y(t-1) - 0.85\, K(t-1)) + K(t-1)$$

Also equations (C.2b) and (A.3) are linear. The whole structural model is then linear. It has been simulated and a linear autoregressive pattern of order 6 has been fitted to the resulting time series. The order has been set at 6 to make comparison with the results of the previous example easier. The outcomes are, of course, the same for all four variables, so that only those for I are given here. There are also now two real roots, both of them small: 0.192 and -0.036 respectively. The two pairs of complex roots are (i) $-0.546 \pm 0.490\, i$ with modulus 0.733 and periodicity 3, (ii) $0.721 \pm 0.121\, i$ with modulus 0.731 and periodicity 37. The two sine components have a relatively high modulus as compared to the case of the previous example. The wave with the long periodicity is surely a feature which distinguishes the results for the linearized model with those for the linear autoregressive form of a non-linear model. □

The example shows that indeed there is a difference. The time path generated by the non-linear model is a different one from that generated by the linearized model. It is then only natural to find different autoregressive patterns with different implied dynamic characteristics. Otherwise said, linearizing the structural form of the model and then evaluating its dynamic properties, may fail to establish the dynamic properties of the original model, a conclusion also reached by Malgrange (1981).

6 Summary and conclusions

The major point of this paper is to deduce the dynamic properties of a model from the coefficients of an autoregressive form fitted to the simulated time path of the endogenous variables as generated by the model. Theory suggests that for linear models, i.e. linear systems of difference equations, the coefficients should reveal indeed the dynamic properties. An example confirms this proposition.

In the case of non-linear models one may argue that some kind of non-linear autoregressive pattern should be able to explain a simulated time series. An example shows that when adding quadratic and cubic lag patterns one obtains a reasonably good fit. When evaluating the relevant autoregressive derivatives it appears that the results are qualitatively not really different from those of the linear autoregressive form of the model. Therefore, it is suggested to employ the latter form as an approximation.

This approach works also for a rather strong non-linear dynamic model. It fits the generated time series well and the dynamics are roughly the same across endogenous variables.

The approach proposed here is similar to that of Cooper and Fisher (1975). These authors, working with a non-linear model, generate the time path for the endogenous variables in the usual way. They next run regressions on the time path for the instruments (controls) to obtain an idea of the time path for the multipliers. The contribution of Cooper and Fisher appears to have been lost out of sight.

The exploratory nature of this paper implied working with small models, but the approach is really only meaningful for larger models. There will be a problem of identifying the length of the lag pattern. Some overfitting cannot do too much harm. There is no degrees of freedom problem because the length of the simulation period can be choosen at will. The number of roots may be large. Computer programs are available for their solution. The analysis can limit itself to the more important components: the ones with a long half-time, for example, or the ones with absolute value larger than one. Still, the issue of numerical precision of the determination of the eigenvalues does not become less of a problem with the increase in the number of roots. For the characterization of the dynamics of a model one needs perhaps more the order of magnitude than exact values.

The approach of this paper amounts to some kind of linearization. This means a perhaps rough approximation to fundamental non-linearities. One should remain aware of the possibility of failure to capture one or more of these.

References

Barten, A.P. (1987), *Methodological aspects of macroeconomic model construction*, Academia, Louvain-la-Neuve.

Cooper, J.P. and S. Fischer (1975), "A method for stochastic control of nonlinear econometric models and an application", *Econometrica*, **43**, 147–162.

Frisch, R. (1933), "Propagation problems and impulse problems in dynamic economics", in *Economic essays in honour of Gustav Cassel*, Allen and Unwin, London.

Malgrange, P. (1981), "Note sur le calcul des valeurs propres d'un modèle macroéconométrique", *Annales de l'INSEE*, **41**, 67–77.

Marschak, J.A. (1950), "Statistical inference in economics: an introduction", in T.C. Koopmans, editor, *Statistical inference in dynamic economic models*, Wiley and Sons, New York.

Puu, T. (1993), *Nonlinear economic dynamics*, Springer-Verlag, Berlin.

Schoonbeek, L. (1989), *Eigenvalues and eigenvectors of macroeconometric models*, PhD thesis, University of Groningen, Groningen.

Tinbergen, J. (1939), *Statistical testing of business-cycle theories, vol. II: business cycles in the United States of America, 1919-1932*, League of Nations, Geneva.

Wallis, K.F. (1977), "Multiple time series analysis and the final form of econometric models", *Econometrica*, **45**, 1481–1497.

Methods and Applications of Economic Dynamics
L. Schoonbeek, E. Sterken and S.K. Kuipers (editors)

Chapter 5

Graph-theory based tools in the practice of macroeconometric modeling [1]

Manfred Gilli

1 Introduction

Even though already Tinbergen used graphs to depict the structure of the very first macroeconometric model, these did not, surprisingly, become part of a model builder's standard toolbox. Of course, every modern modeling software will first put a model's Jacobian matrix into its blocktriangular form, but, its aim is, in general, only to obtain the recursive sequence of indecomposable subproblems for an efficient numerical solution of the model. The blockrecursive structure is then not further analyzed and little attention is given to display this information in a clarifying way.

Moreover, the knowledge of the blockrecursive pattern of the Jacobian matrix in itself is not sufficient to describe completely a model's logical structure and does not contain any information in the case of a dynamic model.

Macroeconometric models are characterized by a large number of equations, the complexity of which, i.e. the number of variables in a particular equation, does not, in general, depend on the model's size. Hence, the Jacobian matrix and the other matrices of derivatives, with respect to lagged endogenous and exogenous variables, become more and more sparse as the number of equations increases. The more a system is sparse, the more some particular behaviors are exclusively driven

1. Some of the results given draw on joint research with Myriam Garbely and Giorgio Pauletto. They also contributed to the preparation of this paper, for which I would like to thank them sincerely. Financial support from the Swiss National Science Fund (grant 12–31072.91) is gratefully acknowledged.

by its structure. Graphs have been invented to handle structures, which makes it very natural to use them for the investigation of the structural properties of macroeconometric models.

Resorting to a graph-theory based methodology for such a task gives access to a large set of theoretical results, which contribute to deal more efficiently with the complex structure representing macroeconometric models. In general, efficient algorithms are also available, providing the tools for practical real-world applications.

The paper is divided into two main sections. First, in Section 2 so-called techniques for causal ordering are presented. Such techniques were first discussed by Simon (1953), Ando and Fisher (1963) and Lindbeck (1966). More recently, questions about causal ordering were presented in McElroy (1978), Gilli (1978, 1992), Boutillier (1983) and Houtman and Sterken (1989), among others. The analysis is extended in order to identify links in the model which are essential to preserve the dependencies of the system in the static and in the dynamic cases. This section deals mainly with concepts represented by oriented graphs.

Next, Section 3 is concerned with nonoriented structural characteristics of a model, i.e. concepts represented by nonoriented graphs. Relying only on the structure of the incidence matrix of a matrix, an upper bound for its rank is identified. It is then shown how this problem is linked to the normalization of the equations, and some issues in connection with the choice of the normalization are discussed. We conclude in Section 4 with some final remarks.

2 Hierarchical structures

The hierarchical or logical structure of a model is not connected to a particular quantification. Hence, this kind of analysis provides fundamental insight into the functioning of a model, revealing important properties without resorting to the numerical solution of the model. In this section, tools are presented to describe the connections between the interdependent mechanisms of a macroeconometric model. These causal chains are first investigated for the static model (or the current period of a dynamic model). After the presentation of classical and well-known concepts, original tools are presented, which give more information about the type of causal connections allowing to identify links which are essential to preserve the dependencies in the model. The analysis is then extended to the successive periods of a dynamic model.

2.1 Blocktriangular decomposition of the Jacobian matrix

Let us start with the problem where we seek the blocktriangular form of a model's Jacobian matrix. We therefore consider the deterministic part of a structural model, formally represented by the set of n equations

$$y_i = g_i(y_j, z_k) \quad \Longleftrightarrow$$

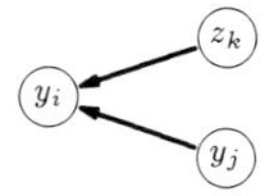

Figure 1: Equation g_i and corresponding partial subgraph

$$y = g(y, z) \tag{1}$$

where $y \in R^n$ are the endogenous variables and $z \in R^m$ the exogenous ones including also, if present, lagged endogenous variables. We also suppose that the set of equations has been normalized, i.e. a different left-hand side variable has been assigned to each equation, so that the i-th equation is of the form

$$y_i = g_i(y_1 \dots, y_{i-1}, y_{i+1} \dots, y_n, z) \quad i = 1, \dots, n \tag{2}$$

We then say that there exists a causal link going from the variables in the right-hand side of the equation to the variable on the left-hand side. Such causal links can be very naturally represented by a graph where the vertices or nodes represent the variables and the arcs represent the causal links. Figure 1 shows an equation and the partial subgraph corresponding to that equation.

The graph of the complete model could be obtained by simply putting together all partial graphs corresponding to all the single equations. Yet it is preferable to formalize this in the way which follows.

The structure is already defined, if we know which variables occur in the different equations. It is therefore convenient to consider the linearized form of model (1), which is

$$y = Dy + Fz \qquad \text{with} \qquad D = \frac{\partial g}{\partial y'}, \; F = \frac{\partial g}{\partial z'} \tag{3}$$

and we are interested in the incidence matrices of matrix D and F. An incidence matrix of a given matrix consists of 1's for nonzero elements and zero otherwise. Throughout the paper we use the same notation for a matrix and its incidence matrix. The (incidence) matrices D and F then contain all the information about the causal links existing between the variables in all equations. They define the *causal structure* of the model.

We now consider the set of all variables $X = Z \cup Y$ with Y the set of endogenous variables and Z the set of exogenous variables, as well as a matrix A partitioned so that the first rows and columns correspond to the variables in set Z and the remaining rows and columns to the variables of set Y. Matrix A is the adjacency matrix which defines the graph G corresponding to the causal structure of model (1).

$$
\begin{aligned}
x_1 &= g_1(x_2, x_3, x_4, x_7) \\
x_2 &= g_2(x_7, x_{9_{-1}}) \\
x_3 &= g_3(x_6, x_9, x_{8_{-1}}) \\
x_4 &= g_4(x_7, x_{1_{-1}}) \\
x_6 &= g_6(x_1, x_3, x_4) \\
x_7 &= g_7(x_2, x_5, x_{8_{-2}}) \\
x_8 &= g_8(x_5, x_7, x_9)
\end{aligned}
\qquad
A = \begin{pmatrix} 0 & 0 \\ F & D \end{pmatrix} =
\begin{array}{c|cc|ccccccc|}
 & x_5 & x_9 & x_1 & x_2 & x_3 & x_4 & x_6 & x_7 & x_8 \\
\hline
x_5 & . & . & . & . & . & . & . & . & . \\
x_9 & . & . & . & . & . & . & . & . & . \\
\hline
x_1 & . & . & . & 1 & 1 & 1 & . & 1 & . \\
x_2 & . & . & . & . & . & . & . & 1 & . \\
x_3 & . & 1 & . & . & . & . & 1 & . & . \\
x_4 & . & . & . & . & . & . & . & 1 & . \\
x_6 & . & . & 1 & . & 1 & 1 & . & . & . \\
x_7 & 1 & . & . & 1 & . & . & . & . & . \\
x_8 & 1 & 1 & . & . & . & . & . & 1 & . \\
\hline
\end{array}
$$

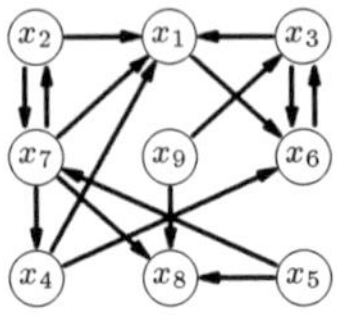

$G = (X, U)$

Figure 2: Model with corresponding adjacency matrix and graph

Hereafter, the partitioned matrix A and the corresponding graph G read

$$A = \begin{pmatrix} 0 & 0 \\ F & D \end{pmatrix}, \qquad G = (X, U) \tag{4}$$

The set of vertices $X = Z \cup Y$ in the graph represents the endogenous and exogenous variables and the set U is the set of all arcs $x_i \to x_j$ so that the corresponding element in the adjacency matrix A verifies $a_{x_j x_i} \not\equiv 0$.

The following steps may be best introduced by means of a simple example consisting of a model of 7 equations, the causal structure of which is given on the left side in Figure 2. Considering the current variables only, Figure 2 shows the adjacency matrix A defining the graph of the causal structure and the picture of the graph.

The *arcs* in the graph correspond to the causal links in the model. A sequence of arcs from a vertex i to a vertex j is a *path*, which corresponds to an indirect causal link in the model, i.e. a variable i which has an effect on a variable j through the interaction of a set of equations. Paths are therefore equivalent to the existence of nonzero multipliers in the model.

A first task consists now of finding the sets of simultaneous equations of the model, which correspond to the irreducible diagonal matrices in the blockrecursive decomposition. In the graph this corresponds to the strong components. A *strong component* is the largest possible set of interdependent vertices, i.e. the set where any ordered pair of vertices (i, j) verifies a path from i to j and a path from j to i. The strong components define a unique partition among the equations of the model into sets of simultaneous equations.

Algorithms to find the strong components of a graph are standard and can be found in textbooks about algorithmic graph theory or computer algorithms, see e.g., Sedgewick (1989, p. 482) or Aho *et al.* (1974, p. 193).

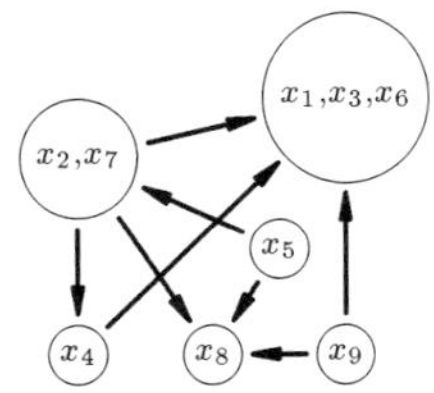

Figure 3: Reduced graph of model in Figure 2

For our graph in Figure 2, the strong components are formed by the sets of vertices: $\{2,7\}$, $\{1,3,6\}$, $\{4\}$, $\{5\}$, $\{8\}$ and $\{9\}$ and we see that a single vertex can also correspond to a strong component.

After having identified the interdependent portions of the model, we wish to know the causal links between these blocks. Therefore, we define a new graph whose vertices are the strong components of the previous graph and where there will be an arc between the new vertices, if there is at least one arc between the vertices corresponding to the two strong components considered. This new graph is called a *reduced graph* and it will be used to analyze causal links existing between the sets of simultaneous equations. In the case of our example the reduced graph is given in Figure 3.

Since, by construction, the reduced graph is without circuits, i.e. there do not exist interdependencies, it will be possible to draw the vertices in a hierarchical order where arcs will go only from top to bottom. At level zero we draw the vertices with no ingoing arcs (5 and 9 in our case). By dropping these vertices in the original graph, we generate new vertices with no ingoing arcs, which then form level one. The vertex corresponding to the strong component {2,7} forms level one for our example. Continuing this procedure until all vertices have been explored, we get the ordered reduced graph shown in Figure 4. In order to keep notation simpler the variables are only labeled with their subscript.

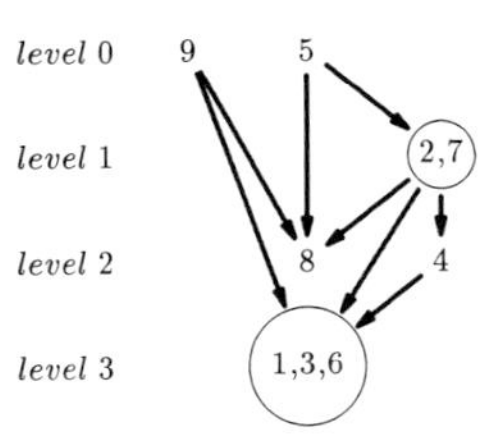

	5	9	2,7	4	8	1,3,6
9	·	·	·	·	·	·
5	·	·	·	·	·	·
{2,7}	·	1	·	·	·	·
4	·	·	1	·	·	·
8	1	1	1	·	·	·
{1,3,6}	1	·	1	1	1	·

Figure 4: Ordered reduced graph and adjacency matrix

$D =$

	x_2	x_7	x_4	x_8	x_1	x_3	x_6
x_2	.	1					
x_7	1	.					
x_4	.	1	.				
x_8	.	1	.	.			
x_1	1	1	1	.	.	1	.
x_3	.	.	.	.	.	.	1
x_6	.	.	1	.	1	1	.

Figure 5: Blocktriangular decomposition of matrix D

Level zero of such a graph always contains the exogenous variables of the model; indeed exogenous variables do not receive any causal link and are therefore independent. The rest of the graph clearly describes how blocks in higher numbered levels depend upon blocks in lower numbered levels.

Rearranging the variables of the rows and columns of the incidence matrix D according to the order they appear in the levels of the ordered reduced graph, we obtain its blocktriangular decomposition shown in Figure 5, which gives the sequence in which the interdependent subsystems can be solved recursively.

2.2 Reachability matrix and minimal graph

As already mentioned in the introduction, the blocktriangular decomposition which, up to permutations of blocks within a same level, is unique, can also be obtained by resorting to row and column permutations of matrix D, see e.g. Duff (1981). The graph-theory based approach we suggest, however, has the advantage that we can immediately use our reduced graph to further investigate interesting properties of the model's structure.

We therefore construct the *reachability matrix* (see Figure 6) of the reduced graph. An entry in row i and column j of the reachability matrix will exist if there is a path in the reduced graph going from vertex j to vertex i. The adjacency matrix already contains the paths of length one and we complete this matrix by setting all entries corresponding to paths longer than one to "i". For the model this indicates the existence of an *indirect causal link*. The dots corresponds to

	5	9	2 7	4	8	1 3 6
{2,7}	1	·				
4	i	·	1			
8	1	1	1	·		
{1,3,6}	i	1	1	1	·	

Figure 6: Reachability matrix

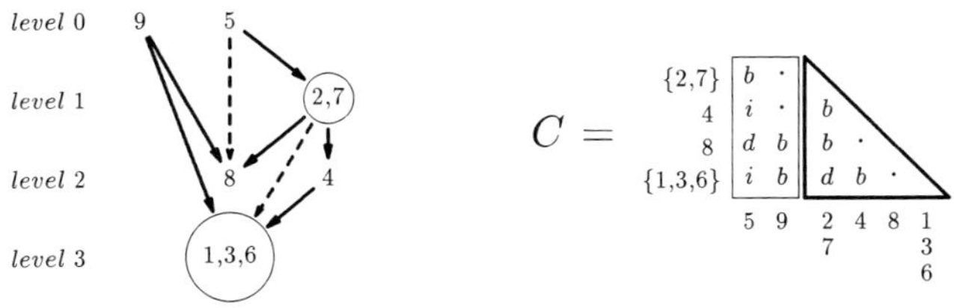

Figure 7: Minimal graph (solid arcs) and matrix C

zero entries. The rows forming level zero and which correspond to the exogenous variables, are dropped, as they must always be empty, as well as the upper triangle of the reachability matrix.

It might also be interesting to point out those causal links in a model which are essential. In the case of the reduced graph, this consists of finding the *minimal graph* which is the smallest possible subgraph with the same reachability matrix as the original graph. Such a minimal graph is the more interesting as it is unique.

The minimal graph is found by removing those arcs $i \to j$ for which there exists a path from i to j of length greater that one. Figure 7 shows the reduced graph of our example in which the arcs forming the minimal graph are drawn in solid lines and the arcs which may be removed are drawn in dotted lines. The reachability matrix introduced in Figure 6 has been modified and is now called matrix C. The entries in matrix C corresponding to the arcs forming the minimal graph are set to "*b*", which stands for basic link, and the entries corresponding to the other arcs are set to "*d*", which stands for direct link.

The rectangular submatrix of matrix C corresponds to the incidence matrix of the multiplier matrix $(I - D)^{-1}F$. The lower triangular submatrix of matrix C corresponds to the incidence matrix of the shift multiplier matrix $(I - D)^{-1}$. The reachability matrix already shows the overall logic of the model in a very clear way. For instance, the possibility of simulations of a particular policy can be checked according to whether a multiplier exists or not. The incidence matrix of the shift multiplier matrix shows the causal links existing among the endogenous variables.

The modified reachability matrix then gives us additional information about the nature of the causal links. For instance, if one wants to remove a causal link in the model, it can only be done by removing arcs from the minimal graph, i.e. the arcs labelled with a "*b*" in matrix C. Removing a link characterized by a "*d*" entry in matrix C will leave an indirect causal link between the corresponding blocks. If, on the contrary, one wants to create a causal link, one has to add an arc in a location in matrix C which previously had a zero entry. A new link between two blocks, which in the corresponding entry in matrix C showed an "*i*", will only strengthen an existing causal link, i.e. the incidence matrix of the multiplier matrix will remain unchanged.

In many circumstances, it is interesting to deal with only parts of a model. The question we raise is how to find submodels which, if treated separately, lead to the same conclusions as the complete model. The idea behind this is very simple and consists of dropping the variables which are not connected by causal links to a particular variable. This is known as the problem of *model separability*.

The reachability matrix C, which we already defined, contains all the information necessary for answering the following three questions, which will most frequently occur in the context of analyzing a model's separability:
1) Given a block i, find the smallest set of blocks containing block i that may be solved independently from the rest of the model. This set of the variables corresponds to the set of blocks whose entries in row i of matrix C are nonzero. In the reduced graph it corresponds to all the vertices which are ascendants of vertex i which represents block i. When solving the model for variable 1 in the example we carry on, the set of ascendants is $\{1, 3, 6, 4, 2, 7, 5, 9\}$.
2) What is the set of variables affected by a perturbation of a variable in block i? This set is given by the descendents of vertex i in the reduced graph and corresponds in matrix C to the set of blocks defined by the nonzero entries in column i. For variable 9 this set of reachable vertices is $\{9, 8, 1, 3, 6\}$.
3) What is the set to be considered, if we study the effect of a perturbation of block i on a particular block j only? This set is given by the vertices which are situated along every path going from block i to block j, that is to say by the intersection of the set of descendants of vertex i with the set of ascendants of vertex j. Going from variable 9 to variable 1, the set of variables we seek is given by the intersection of the set of all ascendants to vertex 1 with the set of all reachable vertices from vertex 9, which is $\{1, 3, 6, 9\}$.

2.3 Dynamic models

The presence of lagged endogenous variables creates causal links among variables at different periods. In order to analyze the causal relations existing between variables related to past periods and current variables, or the causal relations between current variables and variables related to future periods, we can proceed in a similar way as we did for the static case. Formally, we simply define a new enlarged static model corresponding to the dynamic model.

In order to illustrate our ideas, let us consider a model containing endogenous variables lagged over r periods

$$y_t = g(y_t, y_{t-1}, \dots, y_{t-r}; z_t) \tag{5}$$

and for which we want to analyze the dynamic causal links for s future periods. Stacking the equations (5) for $s+1$ successive periods we obtain the system

$$\begin{aligned} y_{t+o} &= g(y_{t+o}; z_{t+o}) \\ y_{t+1} &= g(y_{t+1}, y_{t+o}; z_{t+1}) \\ &\vdots \\ y_{t+s} &= g(y_{t+s}, y_{t+s-1}, \ldots, y_{t+o}; z_{t+s}) \end{aligned}$$

where y_{t+i} and z_{t+i} are the vectors of endogenous, respectively exogenous variables related to period $t+i$. The functions g have no indices as they are, in general, invariant over time. By defining the partitioned vector $y^* = (y'_{t+o}\ y'_{t+1} \cdots y'_{t+s})'$ and the partitioned vector $z^* = (z'_{t+o}\ z'_{t+1} \ldots z'_{t+s})'$, these $s+1$ stacked systems of equations can be considered as the static model

$$y^* = g^*(y^*; z^*) \tag{6}$$

Hence, the dynamic causal relations we want to analyze have been transformed into causal relations between variables y_{t+p} and variables y_{t+q}, $p > 0$ and $p \neq q$ in the static model g^*. From now on, we proceed as before, by associating a graph G^* with this model, seeking its strong components and constructing the modified reachability matrix C^* which describes the causal links between these strong components. Matrix C^* has the following form

$$C^* = \begin{matrix} t+o \\ t+1 \\ \vdots \\ t+s \end{matrix} \begin{pmatrix} C & & & \\ C_1 & C & & \\ \vdots & \vdots & \ddots & \\ C_s & \cdots & C_1 & C \end{pmatrix} \tag{7}$$

Submatrix C of C^* is the modified reachability matrix of the static model, already introduced in the previous section, which shows the causal links between variables of a same period. Submatrix C_i, $i = 1, \ldots, s$, shows the causal links between variables related to period $t+p$ and variables related to period $t+p+i$. At this point, it is interesting to mention that the choice of $s > r$ periods for the dynamic analysis can be meaningful. This can be seen in the illustration which follows.

As an illustration, let us analyze the dynamic structure of our model, the equations of which are given in Figure 2. The model contains endogenous variables lagged over one and two periods as well as an exogenous variable lagged over one period. In its linearized form the model is then

$$y_t = Dy_t + E_1 y_{t-1} + E_2 y_{t-2} + F z_t + F_1 z_{t-1} \tag{8}$$

where matrices D and F are already defined in (3). The incidence matrices of D and F are given in Figure 2. The remaining matrices are defined as $E_1 = \frac{\partial g}{\partial y'_{t-1}}$,

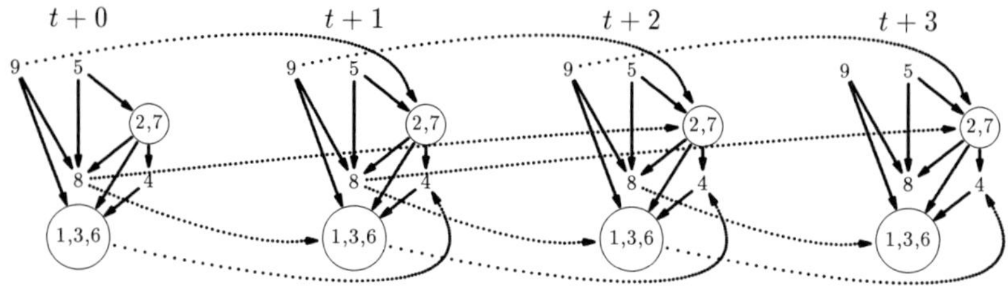

$$C_1 = \begin{array}{r|cc||cccc|} \{2,7\} & \cdot & b & \cdot & \cdot & \cdot & \cdot \\ 4 & i & i & i & i & \cdot & b \\ 8 & \cdot & i & \cdot & \cdot & \cdot & \cdot \\ \{1,3,6\} & i & i & i & i & b & i \\ \hline & 5 & 9 & 2,7 & 4 & 8 & 1,3,6 \end{array} \qquad C_2 = \begin{array}{r|cc||cccc|} \{2,7\} & i & i & i & \cdot & b & \cdot \\ 4 & i & i & i & i & i & i \\ 8 & i & i & i & \cdot & i & \cdot \\ \{1,3,6\} & i & i & i & i & i & i \\ \hline & 5 & 9 & 2,7 & 4 & 8 & 1,3,6 \end{array} \qquad C_3 = \begin{array}{r|cc||cccc|} \{2,7\} & \cdot & i & \cdot & \cdot & \cdot & \cdot \\ 4 & i & i & i & i & i & i \\ 8 & \cdot & i & \cdot & \cdot & \cdot & \cdot \\ \{1,3,6\} & i & i & i & i & i & i \\ \hline & 5 & 9 & 2,7 & 4 & 8 & 1,3,6 \end{array}$$

Figure 8: Matrices C_1, C_2, C_3 and graph of dynamic causal links

$E_2 = \frac{\partial g}{\partial y'_{t-2}}$ and $F_1 = \frac{\partial g}{\partial z'_{t-1}}$. The incidence matrices of these matrices, which can be immediately established by inspection of the model's equations, are not reproduced here. Setting $K = (I - D)^{-1}$, we can write the reduced form of the model as

$$y_t = KE_1 y_{t-1} + KE_2 y_{t-2} + KFz_t + KF_1 z_{t-1} \tag{9}$$

We then see that matrix C_1 corresponds to the incidence matrix of the partitioned multiplier matrix $(KF_1 \ : \ KE_1)$. Substituting y_{t-1} in (9) we find that C_2 corresponds to the incidence matrix of $(KE_1KF_1 \ : \ (KE_1)^2 + KE_2)$. Matrices C_1, C_2 and C_3 are reproduced in Figure 8, where we also give the picture of the reduced graph of the dynamic causal relations (dotted arcs) between four consecutive periods.

By inspection of the matrices C_1, C_2 and C_3 (or by inspecting the picture of the graph) we observe, for instance, that the dynamic effect of a shock in variable 5 at period $t + 0$ reaches variables 2, 7 and 8 only in period $t + 2$. For the periods $t + 1$ and $t + 3$ these variables are not affected by the shock. A shock to variable 8 at period $t + 0$ will affect in period $t + 1$ only the variables 1, 3 and 6; in period $t + 2$ all endogenous variables are affected and in period $t + 3$ only the variables 1, 3, 4 and 6 are affected.

Thus, we notice that the dynamic effect of variable 8 in the model is different for all three periods and that matrix C_3 provides information not contained in matrix C_1 and C_2, even though the highest lag in the model is two.

We see that these matrices provide important insight into a model's dynamic relations, showing where strategic links are located. This is because, in general,

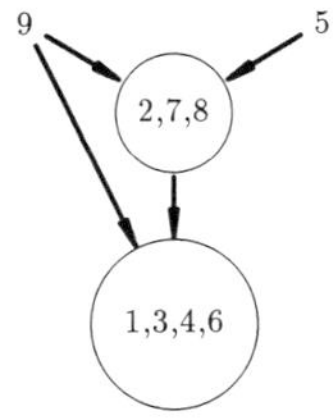

Figure 9: Logical structure in the long term

for real-world macroeconometric models, only a few of the many lagged variables generate feedbacks (corresponding to "b" entries in the matrices C_i). Moreover, the matrix C^* enables us to investigate the problem of model separability in the dynamic case.

Another important question for dynamic models is to know the structure of the cumulated multiplier matrices and the structure of the equilibrium multiplier matrix. This would correspond to the sum of the matrices C_i. We obtain this structure by defining a new graph where present as well as lagged causal links are considered simultaneously. The corresponding reduced graph then represents the logical structure of the model in the long term. Figure 9 shows the logical structure in the long term, i.e. corresponding to the graph where all lags of the endogenous and exogenous variables have been removed. For this example we see, for instance, that for a numerical analysis the problem can be decomposed into two smaller recursive problems.

3 Nonoriented structures

This section deals with certain properties of a matrix which are essentially nonoriented but again rely on the structure of the corresponding incidence matrix. The edges of the graphs used in this investigation are nonoriented as they represent binary relations which have no directional character. In particular, the connections existing between the structure of a matrix and its rank are explored and it is shown how the normalization of the equations of a model is linked to this problem.

3.1 Structural rank of a matrix

In the practice of macroeconometric modeling, one often has to verify the rank of a particular matrix. For a dense matrix, this is, of course, exclusively a numerical problem. In the case of a sparse matrix, however, it is meaningful to investigate its structure in order to get an upper bound for the rank of the matrix. We call this the *structural rank* of a matrix. Prior to any numerical investigation, we will then be

$$M = \begin{array}{c|c|c|c|c|c|} & \multicolumn{5}{c}{} \\ h_1 & 1 & 1 & . & 1 & 1 \\ h_2 & 1 & 1 & 1 & 1 & . \\ h_3 & . & . & 1 & . & 1 \\ h_4 & 1 & . & . & 1 & . \\ h_5 & 1 & . & 1 & . & . \\ & y_1 & y_2 & y_3 & y_4 & y_5 \end{array} \qquad \begin{array}{c|c|c|} & H & Y \\ H & 0 & M \\ Y & M' & 0 \end{array}$$

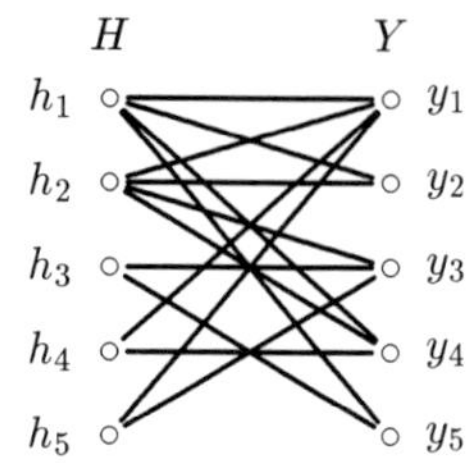

Figure 10: Matrix M and associated bipartite graph $G = (H, Y, E)$

able to check for necessary conditions in a variety of problems, such as, for instance local uniqueness of the solution or identification in the case of linear models.

Let us consider a matrix M with $H = \{h_1, \dots, h_n\}$ the set of rows and $Y = \{y_1, \dots, y_n\}$ the set of columns. The structure of such a matrix can be conveniently represented by a graph

$$G = (H, Y, E) \tag{10}$$

where H is the set of vertices representing the rows and Y the set of vertices representing the columns of matrix M. E is the set of edges defined so that $[h_i, y_j] \in E$ iff $m_{h_i y_j} \neq 0$.

We illustrate this in Figure 10, where we give the incidence matrix of a square matrix M of order 5, the corresponding adjacency matrix defining the graph, as well as its picture. One verifies that the set of vertices in the graph is partitioned into two subsets H and Y, in a way that all edges have one vertex in set H and the other vertex in set Y. Such a graph is defined as a *bipartite graph*.

In the following, we use the bipartite graph G defined in (10) to establish an upper bound for the rank of matrix M. By definition, the determinant of matrix $M \in \mathbb{R}^{n \times n}$ is given by the expression

$$\det(M) = \sum_{\pi} \operatorname{sign}(\pi)\, m_{1\pi_1}\, m_{2\pi_2} \cdots m_{n\pi_n} \tag{11}$$

where the summation extends over all $n!$ permutations π of the set $\{1, \dots, n\}$, π_i is the i-th component of permutation π and $\operatorname{sign}(\pi)$ is the sign of the permutation π. We then immediately conclude that an upper bound for the rank of matrix M is given by the size p of the largest submatrix of matrix M, for which there exists at least one permutation π such that all elements in the product $m_{1\pi_1} \cdots m_{p\pi_p}$ in (11) are nonzero.

A set of p nonzero entries $m_{i\pi_i}$, $i = 1, \dots, p$, corresponds in the bipartite graph to a set of p non-adjacent edges. By definition, a set of non-adjacent edges in a graph is called a matching, denoted by W. The cardinality of W, card(W), is equal to the number of edges in the matching.

Theorem 1. The maximum cardinality of a matching in the bipartite graph G representing the structure of a matrix M constitutes an upper bound for its rank.

The proof of Theorem 1 is contained in the explanation that follows relation (11).

A matching of cardinality n, i.e. saturating all the vertices of the bipartite graph, is called a *perfect matching*. As a corollary we have that a necessary condition for a matrix $M \in \mathbb{R}^{n \times n}$ being nonsingular is the existence of a perfect matching W, i.e. verifying card$(W) = n$, in the bipartite graph G representing the structure of the matrix. If a perfect matching does not exist, the matrix is said to be *structurally singular*, which *a fortiori* implies numerical singularity. This problem has been first discussed by Dulmage and Mendelsohn (1963).

Whereas the identification of the permutation π, verifying the largest number of nonzero elements in the product in (11), is a very hard task, it is easy to establish the maximum cardinality of the matchings in graph G. To do this, we start with an arbitrary matching $W \subseteq E$ for the bipartite graph $G = (H, Y, E)$. The matching W generates a partition $H' \cup H''$ and $Y' \cup Y''$ of the set of vertices; H' and Y' are the sets of *saturated vertices*, i.e. the end vertices of the edges W; H'' and Y'' are the sets of *unsaturated vertices*, i.e. all other vertices.

An *alternating path* in G is then an elementary path, i.e. a path not going twice over a same vertex, whose edges alternatively belong to W and $E - W$. We denote by μ_W the set of edges in the alternating path belonging to W and by $\mu_{\overline{W}}$ those not belonging to W. An *augmenting path* with respect to W is an alternating path between two unsaturated vertices (one belonging to H'' and the other to Y''). An augmenting path obviously verifies card$(\mu_{\overline{W}}) =$ card$(\mu_W) + 1$ and therefore the edges $\mu_{\overline{W}}$ can be considered as defining a new matching W', the cardinality of which is increased by one.

As an illustration, let us consider the bipartite graph given in Figure 10, for which we consider the matching $W = \{[h_1, y_2], [h_2, y_3], [h_3, y_5], [h_4, y_1]\}$. This is represented on the left side in Figure 11, where the edges belonging to the matching are drawn in dotted lines. The sets of unsaturated vertices are then $H'' = \{h_5\}$ and $Y'' = \{y_4\}$ and an augmenting path, among other existing ones, is given by

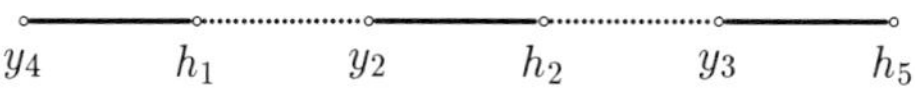

where $\mu_{\overline{W}} = \{[y_4, h_1], [y_2, h_2], [y_3, h_5]\}$ and $\mu_W = \{[h_1, y_2], [h_2, y_3]\}$. Exchanging the edges in the augmenting path gives

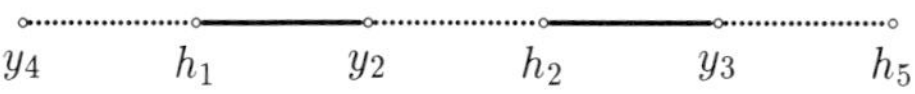

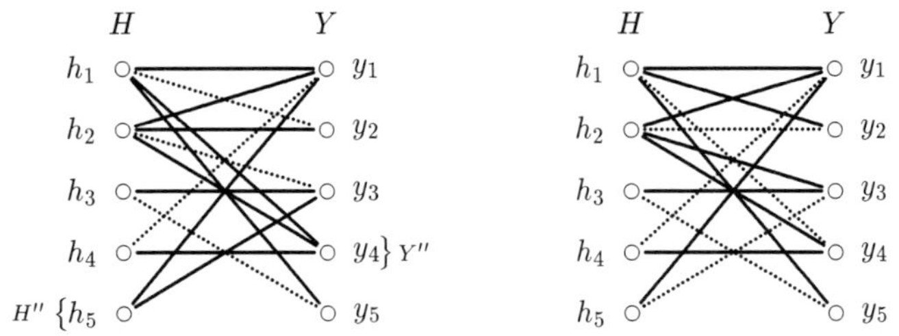

Figure 11: Matching W and W' in bipartite graph $G = (H, Y, E)$

which then defines a new matching W', shown on the right side in Figure 11, the cardinality of which is augmented by one.

An efficient algorithm for finding a maximum-cardinality matching then builds on the following theorem, see e.g. Berge (1957; 1973, p. 119) or Thulasiraman and Swamy (1992, p. 225):

Theorem 2. (Berge, 1957) In a bipartite graph a matching is of maximum cardinality if and only if there does not exist an augmenting path.

Theorem 2 then suggests immediately the following algorithm to find a maximum-cardinality matching in a bipartite graph.

Algorithm 1. Maximum-cardinality matching in a bipartite graph $G = (H, Y, E)$.

1. Select an arbitrary matching W
2. **repeat** Construct H'' and Y'' according to W
3.   **while** $\exists i \in Y''$ and i not marked, **do**
4.   seek an augmenting path μ from $i \in Y''$ to $j \in H''$
        if $\mu = \emptyset$, **then** mark vertex i, **else** goto 6
    enddo
5.   card(W) is maximum, $\nexists$ augmenting path in G, stop
6.   Construct new W (permutation of edges in μ)

end

The algorithm's time complexity is polynomial; the best known algorithm is $O(n^{2.5})$, see Hopcroft and Karp (1975). Statement 2 is executed at most n times (the cardinality of the matching increases by 1 at each loop) and, in statement 3, one explores at most card(E) edges.

In order to facilitate the search of the augmenting path, it is convenient to orient the edges of a bipartite graph verifying a matching W as follows: (a) edges $e_i \in W$ are oriented so that the starting vertex is in H' and the ending vertex is in Y'; (b) edges $e_i \notin W$ are oriented in the opposite direction (starting vertex in Y and ending vertex in H). In an oriented graph, a path corresponds to a sequence of oriented edges, where the final vertex of an edge is the initial vertex of the next edge. An augmenting path in the bipartite graph G corresponds then in the oriented version of G, to a path going from a vertex of set Y'' to a vertex of set H''.

3.2 Rank deficient matrices

The following discussion is closely linked to the problem of determining the structural rank of a matrix. A model builder has sometimes to cope with the situation where, in the process of model construction, a particular matrix does not fulfill a given rank condition. The challenge is then how to identify where changes in the structure of the matrix should take place in order to meet this condition.

This problem can be efficiently approached by introducing the notion of cover in the bipartite graph corresponding to the particular matrix. We will be interested in a *minimum (cardinality) cover*, sometimes also called a transversal, i.e. the smallest set of vertices which meets every edge in G. An interesting relation between matching and covers is then given by the following theorem, see e.g. Thulasiraman and Swamy (1992, p. 223):

Theorem 3. (König-Egervary, 1931) In a bipartite graph $G = (H, Y, E)$ a maximum-cardinality matching W and a minimum cover C always verify card(W) = card(C).

This means that the maximum number of edges in a matching equals the minimum number of vertices in a cover.

Given a bipartite graph $G = (H, Y, E)$, corresponding to a given matrix $M \in \mathbb{R}^{n \times n}$, verifying a maximum-cardinality matching W, with $\text{card}(W) = p$, $p < n$, we use a minimum cover C to reorder the rows and columns of matrix M. We denote by H_C the set of vertices in the minimum cover belonging to H and by Y_C the set of those vertices in the cover belonging to Y. Let $v_1 = \text{card}(H_C)$ and $v_2 = \text{card}(Y_C)$, with obviously $v_1 + v_2 = p$. We now reorder the rows of the matrix M by taking first the $n - v_1$ equations from set $\overline{H_C}$ and then the remaining v_1 equations from set H_C. The columns are reordered taking first the v_2 vertices from set Y_C and then the $n - v_2$ vertices from set $\overline{Y_C}$. As a consequence, matrix M shows the following pattern

$$M = \begin{array}{c} \\ \overline{H_C} \\ H_C \end{array} \begin{array}{c} \begin{array}{cc} \quad Y_C \quad & \quad \overline{Y_C} \quad \end{array} \\ \begin{pmatrix} M_{n-v_1,v_2} & O_{n-v_1,n-v_2} \\ M_{v_1,v_2} & M_{v_1,n-v_2} \end{pmatrix} \end{array} \tag{12}$$

where the dimension of the zero matrix O verifies $n - v_1 + n - v_2 > n$. Such a characterization of a structurally singular matrix is also known as the Frobenius-König theorem. The partition of the rows and columns of a matrix as presented in (12) is then extremely useful in the situation where we want to modify the structural rank of a matrix. Introducing nonzero elements in the rows and columns defining the zero matrix $O_{n-v_1,n-v_2}$ will clearly modify the structural rank of matrix M.

Before presenting the procedure for finding a minimum-cardinality cover in a bipartite graph, we need to introduce a few definitions. We start with the bipartite graph $G = (H, Y, E)$ and $W \subseteq E$ a matching of maximum cardinality supposed not to be a perfect matching, i.e. $\text{card}(W) < \text{card}(H)$. Again, we consider the partitions $H = H' \cup H''$ and $Y = Y' \cup Y''$ generated by the matching W, with H' and Y' as the sets of saturated vertices and H'' and Y'' as the sets of unsaturated vertices.

We now need to define $R(h_i)$ as the set of *proper descendants* of h_i, i.e. the set of all vertices reachable along all alternating paths starting from vertex h_i. By definition, the starting vertex h_i does not belong to $R(h_i)$. We then have

$$R(H'') = \bigcup_{h_i \in H''} R(h_i) \tag{13}$$

as the set of proper descendants from the set H'' of unsaturated vertices. We also need the set of edges $W_{H''} \subset W$, which belong to the different alternating paths starting from H''. We then have the subsets $T_H \subset H'$ and $T_Y \subset Y'$ of vertices saturated by $W_{H''}$ and, of course, $\text{card}(T_H) = \text{card}(T_Y)$.

The set $R(H'')$ then verifies the following property

$$R(H'') \cap Y'' = \varnothing \quad \text{and} \quad R(H'') \cap H'' = \varnothing$$

as there are no unsaturated vertices in $R(H'')$ and because W is of maximum cardinality. It then follows that

$$R(H'') = T_H \cup T_Y \tag{14}$$

To find minimum-cardinality covers we then use the following theorem:

Theorem 4. (Roy, 1969) In a bipartite graph $G = (H, Y, E)$, with a maximum-cardinality matching W and the corresponding partition $H = H' \cup H''$ into saturated and unsaturated vertices, a minimum-cardinality cover C is given by

$$C = \{H' - R(H'')\} \cup \{R(H'') - H'\}$$

where $R(H'')$ is the set of proper descendants of H'' as defined in (13).

Substituting in the theorem the set of proper descendants $R(H'')$ by the expression given in (14), a minimum-cardinality cover is also defined by

$$C = \{H' - T_H\} \cup T_Y$$

This then defines the sets H_C and Y_C of the partition of matrix M given in (12), i.e.

$$H_C = H' - T_H \quad \text{and} \quad Y_C = T_Y$$

We then derive the following algorithm to find a minimum-cardinality cover and to compute the sets H_C and Y_C which define the partition given in (12).

Algorithm 2. Minimum-cardinality cover in a bipartite graph $G = (H, Y, E)$.

1. Select maximum-cardinality matching W
2. Compute H', H''
3. Compute $R(H'')$ the set of proper descendants
4. $T_H = R(H'') \cap H$; $T_Y = R(H'') \cap Y$;
5. $H_C = H' - T_H$; $Y_C = T_Y$; $C = \{H' - T_H\} \cup T_Y$;

In order to facilitate the exploration of the alternating paths in the bipartite graph $G = (H, Y, E)$ with matching W, it is again convenient to orient the edges in the same way we suggested for the Algorithm 1.

An example

An important property one expects from a macroeconometric model is local uniqueness of the solution in the neighborhood defined by the exogenous variables. We know from the implicit function theorem, that a necessary and sufficient condition for local uniqueness is that the Jacobian matrix of the model must be nonsingular. From the corollary of Theorem 1, we know that a necessary condition for this nonsingularity consists of the existence of a perfect matching, or, which is equivalent, a normalization of the equations. For a model written as in (2), the Jacobian matrix is of the form $I - D$ and the existence of the matching is immediately verified as it corresponds to the entries on the diagonal. However, as it will be discussed in the next section, macroeconometric models are constituted by a set of explicit and implicit equations so that a normalization is not immediately apparent. Prior to the choice of a particular normalization, one has to check whether the system admits any normalization, since, in the opposite case the Jacobian matrix is structurally singular. In such a situation, one has to make a decision on how to modify the system of equations, in order to remove this singularity and to achieve the uniqueness of the solution the model should provide.

To illustrate this, let us consider the system of $n = 8$ equations presented in Figure 12, which is supposed to represent the mix of explicit and implicit relations one frequently encounters in real macroeconometric models. One can verify that the maximum cardinality of a matching in the bipartite graph, corresponding to the Jacobian matrix D, is $p = 6$. In other words, there does not exist a permutation that allows more then six nonzero entries to lie on the diagonal. We can find 252 different matchings with cardinality 6 from which we select: $W = \{[h_1, y_1], [h_3, y_3], [h_4, y_4], [h_5, y_5], [h_6, y_6], [h_7, y_7]\}$.

$$
\begin{aligned}
&h_1 : f_1(y_1, y_2, y_3, y_4, y_5) = 0 \\
&h_2 : y_6 = f_2(y_3) \\
&h_3 : y_3 = f_3(y_7) \\
&h_4 : f_4(y_1, y_2, y_4, y_6, y_7, y_8) = 0 \\
&h_5 : f_5(y_5, y_6) = 0 \\
&h_6 : y_6 = f_6(y_7) \\
&h_7 : y_7 = f_7(y_3) \\
&h_8 : f_8(y_3, y_5) = 0
\end{aligned}
\qquad
D = \begin{array}{c|cccccccc|}
h_1 & 1 & 1 & 1 & 1 & 1 & . & . & . \\
h_2 & . & . & 1 & . & . & 1 & . & . \\
h_3 & . & . & 1 & . & . & . & 1 & . \\
h_4 & 1 & 1 & . & 1 & . & 1 & 1 & 1 \\
h_5 & . & . & . & . & 1 & 1 & . & . \\
h_6 & . & . & . & . & . & 1 & 1 & . \\
h_7 & . & . & 1 & . & . & . & 1 & . \\
h_8 & . & . & 1 & . & 1 & . & . & . \\
\hline
 & y_1 & y_2 & y_3 & y_4 & y_5 & y_6 & y_7 & y_8
\end{array}
$$

Figure 12: Model equations and incidence matrix D of Jacobian matrix $\frac{\partial h}{\partial y'}$

In order to remove the singularity of the system of equations, a simple strategy would consist of dropping the $n-p=2$ equations which are not in the matching, i.e. equations h_2 and h_8 for our example. However, the resulting model will depend on the particular matching we selected before and which is, as indicated, not unique. Moreover, one might not wish to exogenize some of the $n-p$ variables that are not in the matching, i.e. the variables y_2 and y_8.

According to what has been suggested in the previous section, we seek a minimum cover and partition the Jacobian matrix as shown in (12). Figure 13 shows the bipartite graph representing our Jacobian matrix. The edges drawn in dotted lines belong to the matching W and the vertices in the boxes form the minimum cover $C = H_C \cup Y_C$. We have $H_C = \{h_1, h_4\}$ and $Y_C = \{y_3, y_5, y_6, y_7\}$. On the left side we have the reordered incidence matrix of the Jacobian matrix.

The sets $\overline{H_C}$ and $\overline{Y_C}$ then clearly indicate where the modifications of the structure of the equations should occur. More precisely, the $n-p$ equations which have to be modified must be chosen among the set $\overline{H_C}$, and the variables which have to be added to these equations have to be in set $\overline{Y_C}$. In case one is willing to exogenize the $n-p$ variables not saturated by the matching, once again, the set $\overline{H_C}$ indicates where to choose the $n-p$ equations one has to drop. In the case of the example, without the information given by the cover, one would automatically drop equations h_2 and h_8, whereas the set $\overline{H_C}$ allows us to choose two equations among a set of six equations.

Hereafter, we also trace the several steps in Algorithm 2 when seeking the minimum cover for our example. $W = \{[h_1, y_1], [h_3, y_3], [h_4, y_4], [h_5, y_5], [h_6, y_6], [h_7, y_7]\}$ is the maximum-cardinality matching defining the partition $H' = \{h_1, h_3, h_4, h_5, h_6, h_7\}$ and $H'' = \{h_2, h_8\}$. We then explore all the alternating paths starting from vertex h_2 and vertex h_8 and we get the sets of proper descendants $R(h_2) = \{y_3, h_3, y_7, h_7, y_6, h_6\}$ and $R(h_8) = \{y_5, h_5, y_6, h_6, y_7, h_7, y_3, h_3\}$. The union of the

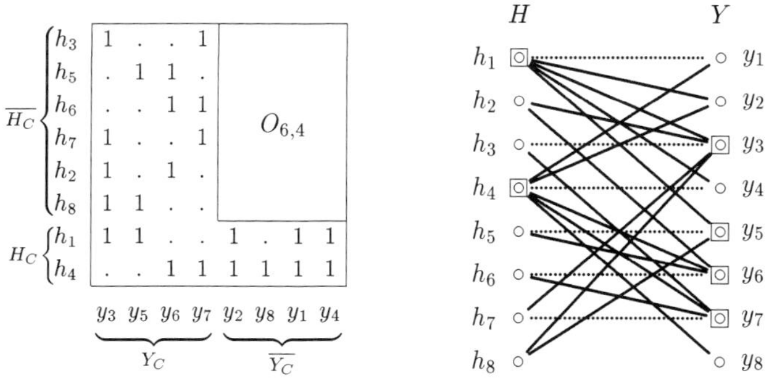

Figure 13: Partitioned Jacobian matrix and bipartite graph of example

sets $R(h_2)$ and $R(h_8)$ gives $R(H'') = \{y_5, h_5, y_6, h_6, y_7, h_7, y_3, h_3\}$ and we easily verify that $R(H'')$ partitions into $T_H = \{h_3, h_5, h_6, h_7\}$ and $T_Y = \{y_3, y_5, y_6, y_7\}$. Thus we have $H_C = H' - T_H = \{h_1, h_4\}$ and $Y_C = T_Y = \{y_3, y_5, y_6, y_7\}$, which defines our minimum cover $C = H_C \cup Y_C$.

3.3 Choice of the normalization of the equations

The model we introduced in (2) is written in its explicit form, i.e. each equation shows a different left-hand side variable. This is called a *normalization of the equations* and we know that it corresponds to a perfect matching in the bipartite graph corresponding to the Jacobian matrix, which precisely constitutes a necessary condition for the local uniqueness of the model's solution. Except for recursive models, there exist many different normalizations for a same model and we will see that some properties of the model are invariant with respect to the normalization chosen and others are not.

Modeling generally proceeds in specifying a set $H = \{h_1, \ldots, h_n\}$ of functional relations, involving a set $X = \{x_1, \ldots, x_p\}$ of variables. This set of functional relations then constitutes a system of explicit and implicit equations

$$h_i(x_1, \ldots, x_p) = 0 \qquad i = 1, \ldots, n \tag{15}$$

The behavioral equations are in general explicit and the normalization for these equations can therefore be considered as given. Some of the variables involved in the behavioral equations verify the relations of the System of National Accounts which have to be included in the model together with other definitional equations and/or equilibrium conditions. For these equations, the choice of a normalization is in general chosen arbitrarily.

First, we will show that the logical structure of the model, i.e. the reduced graph, is invariant with respect to the choice of a normalization.

We therefore represent the structure of the system (15) with a bipartite graph

$$G^o = (H, X, E^o) \tag{16}$$

where the sets of vertices H and X represent the equations, respectively the variables of the system, and $E^o = \{[h_i, x_j] \mid \frac{\partial h_i}{\partial x_j} \neq 0\}$ is the set of edges.

At this point, the model builder specifies the set of endogenous variables, which defines the partition $X = Y \cup Z$ among the set of variables X with Y the set of endogenous variables and Z the set of exogenous variables. We then suppose that the model satisfies the necessary condition for the local uniqueness of the solution, i.e. that there exists a matching W in G^o which saturates the vertices of set H and the vertices of set Y.

The matching W enables the definition of a particular orientation of the edges of G^o and we get an oriented version

$$G^o_W = (H, X, U^o) \tag{17}$$

of our bipartite graph G^o. The set of arcs U^o is constituted by U', the set of edges belonging to W which are oriented from H to X, and by the set of arcs U, i.e. all other edges which are oriented from X to H. Formally we have

$$U^o = U' \cup U$$

with

$$U' = \{(h_i, x_j) \mid [h_i, x_j] \in W\} \quad \text{and} \quad U = \{(x_j, h_i) \mid [h_i, x_j] \in E^o - W\}$$

In the oriented bipartite graph G^o_W, the set of arcs U' define a biunivoque correspondence, i.e. a one-to-one mapping, between the sets of vertices H and Y. It is then possible to obtain a condensed oriented graph

$$G_W = (X, U) \tag{18}$$

involving the set of vertices X and the set of arcs U only, by contracting all vertices from set H into set Y according to the correspondence given by the arcs of set U'.

Theorem 5. Graph G^o_W and the corresponding condensed graph G_W verify the same reachability matrix for the vertices of set X.

Proof. By definition, every vertex h_i in G^o_W has only one outgoing arc, which then is an ingoing arc for just one y_j. Thus, every path in the oriented bipartite graph G^o_W, that reaches a vertex y_j, goes over the arc $h_i \to y_j$ defined by the matching W;

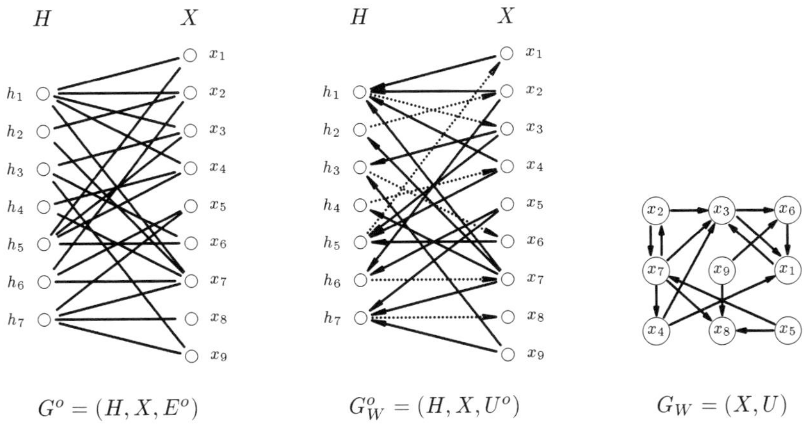

Figure 14: Graph G^o, G^o_W and G_W

therefore the contraction of vertex h_i into vertex y_j cannot create any new paths. ■

This condensed graph corresponds then to the graph we already defined in (4) for the normalized model.

The several steps which lead from a model written in its implicit form to the oriented graph are illustrated with the set of equations given in Figure 2 considered in their implicit form, i.e. $g_i(x_1, \ldots, x_{i-1}, x_{i+1}, \ldots, x_n) - x_i = 0$.

A fundamental property of the reduced graph is its invariance with respect to the matching W, on which the particular orientation of G_W relies. We can verify that the reduced graph of the graph in Figure 14 corresponds to the reduced graph given in Figure 3.

Theorem 6. For any perfect matching W in a bipartite graph G, the corresponding condensed oriented graph G_W verifies the same strong components and the same reduced graph.

If, instead of considering the bipartite graph G, we reason with the corresponding Jacobian matrix D, proofs for Theorem 6 can be found in Brualdi and Ryser (1991, p. 57) or Duff (1977, p. 341). However, if we want to investigate the incidence of a particular matching on the graph G_W, it becomes useful to discuss Theorem 6 using the bipartite graph G. For this discussion, we will consider a particular perfect matching in the bipartite graph G corresponding to the Jacobian matrix D, and show that different perfect matchings in G can only be generated by a permutation of the edges along a circuit within a same strong component.

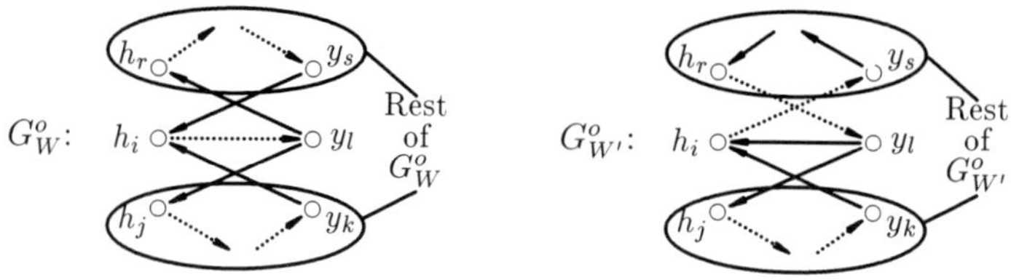

Figure 15: Permutation of edges along an alternating circuit in G^o_W

Given a perfect matching W in a bipartite graph, we know from Theorem 2 that there cannot exist any augmenting path in the bipartite graph and that, by definition, all vertices are saturated by the matching. It is therefore impossible to obtain a different perfect matching W' by a permutation of the edges along an alternating chain.

The only way to generate a different perfect matching W' consists of a permutation of the edges along an alternating circuit. This is evident if the alternating circuit has no common edges with other alternating circuits. In fact, such a permutation is always possible. This can be immediately seen from the graphs G^o_W and $G^o_{W'}$ in Figure 15, where the dotted arcs represent the matching. For G^o_W let us consider the alternating circuit $\cdots \to y_s \to h_i \to y_\ell \to h_r \to \cdots$ and the alternating circuit $\cdots \to y_k \to h_i \to y_\ell \to h_j \to \cdots$, which have edge $h_i \to y_\ell$ in common. A permutation of the edges of the first alternating circuit produces a new matching W' which is perfect, as all vertices remain saturated by the new matching.

Let us then show that the new perfect matching W' will not modify the strong components in $G^o_{W'}$. By definition, two vertices in G^o_W belong to the same strong component, if and only if they are in at least one common circuit. In other words, this means that each vertex in a same strong component is reachable from each other vertex in the same strong component. It is easy to verify in Figure 15 that the reachability in G^o_W and $G^o_{W'}$ is the same. Indeed, for the first circuit, the permutation implies a reversion only of the orientation; for the vertices on the second circuit, the reachability is the same, but simply using different paths. We verify that, in G^o_W, we have a path $y_k \to h_i \to y_\ell \to h_j$ and a path $h_j \to \cdots \to y_k$. In $G^o_{W'}$ the path $h_j \to \cdots \to y_k$ remains unchanged and the path $y_k \to \cdots \to h_j$ has been modified as it goes over $y_k \to h_i \to y_s \to \cdots \to h_r \to y_\ell \to h_j$.

Finally, if the strong components in G^o_W and $G^o_{W'}$ are identical, we conclude from Theorem 5 that the corresponding condensed graphs G_W and $G_{W'}$ also verify the same strong components.

The invariance of the reduced graph is then due to the fact that an edge between different strong components in G^o_W, or an edge connecting an exogenous variable, can by definition not belong to an alternating circuit. Therefore, such edges will remain unchanged for all different matchings.

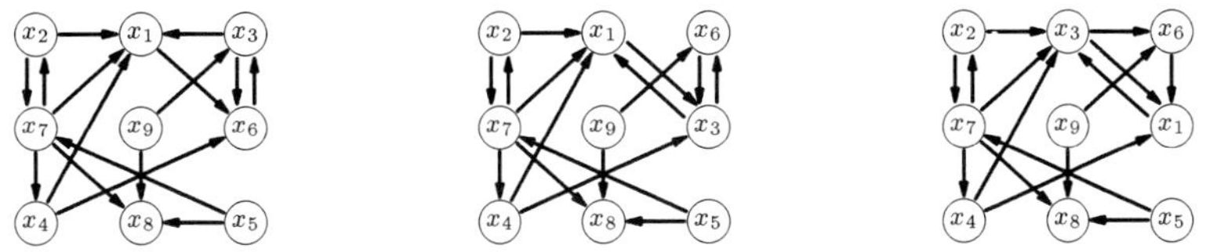

$[h_1,x_1],[h_3,x_3],[h_5,x_6]$ $[h_1,x_1],[h_3,x_6],[h_5,x_3]$ $[h_1,x_3],[h_3,x_6],[h_5,x_1]$

Figure 16: Graphs corresponding to three different matchings for block $\{x_1, x_3, x_6\}$

Incidence of a particular normalization

As already mentioned before, models verify many different normalizations, except recursive models, for which the normalization is unique. Recursive models contain no interdependent blocks, i.e. strong components of a cardinality greater than one.

In the preceding section, we already showed that the composition of the interdependent blocks of the causal structure does not depend on the choice of a normalization. In the proof of Theorem 6, we have seen how different matchings define different circuits within a strong component. For the example in Figure 14, we verify six perfect matchings. There are two possibilities of assigning a variable in equations h_2 and h_6 of the first interdependent block $\{x_2, x_7\}$ and three possibilities for the equations h_1, h_3 and h_5 of the second interdependent block $\{x_1, x_3, x_6\}$. In Figure 16, we show the oriented graphs G_W, corresponding to three different matchings, where the matching for the first block is always $[h_2, x_2]$, $[h_6, x_7]$ and the matching for the second block is indicated with each graph. It can be clearly seen that the structure differs from one graph to another. For instance, variable x_3 has a different position in all three graphs. Moreover the arcs will also be valued differently in each graph. For real world models, where the interdependent block is of much greater size, the number of different matchings becomes very large and the following question then arises: How can we describe the structural characteristics of this very large set of graphs? One could think that it might be possible to classify the different oriented graphs corresponding to the matchings into a much smaller number of classes of isomorphic graphs and then analyze the structure of the graphs of each class.

The choice of a particular normalization can also become relevant when we come to the numerical solution of the model. Two types of methods are commonly used for the solution: Newton-like methods and first-order iterative techniques such as Gauss-Seidel.

If a Newton-like method is chosen, one is faced with the problem of repeated solutions of a linear system involving the Jacobian matrix. This solution is in general achieved by using the Gaussian-elimination and the crucial point is then the condition number of the Jacobian matrix. In this situation, it does not seem important to pay attention to a particular choice of the normalization. Nevertheless, one could think of improving the scaling of the Jacobian matrix by means of a normalization, that maximizes the diagonal element of lowest weight in the Jacobian matrix.

For first-order iterative solution techniques, it is absolutely necessary to specify the normalization, which then defines the variable for which each equation has to be solved, either explicitly or implicitly. In this context, it then becomes important to discuss the impact of different causal structures on the behavior of the solution algorithm.

For instance, it is well known that the convergence of the Gauss-Seidel algorithm depends on the eigenvalues of a matrix $B = (L + \text{diag}(D))^{-1}U$, defined by splitting the Jacobian matrix D into $L + \text{diag}(D) + U$, where L is lower triangular, $\text{diag}(D)$ is the diagonal of matrix D and U is upper triangular.

The eigenvalues of B depend of course on the ordering of the equations, yielding different splittings of the Jacobian matrix. This corresponds to simultaneous row and column permutations. Different matchings correspond to independent permutations of the rows and columns of the Jacobian matrix and therefore also influence the eigenvalues of matrix B. However, if one wants to evaluate the impact of a particular matching on the numerical behavior of the solution algorithms, one certainly needs to take also into consideration the quantitative structure of the Jacobian matrix.

Moreover, it might be worthwhile to mention that the different decompositions of the Jacobian matrix into the matrices L and U, mentioned above, are relevant when first-order iterative algorithms are executed on a computer with a parallel architecture, see for instance Gilli and Pauletto (1993).

4 Concluding remarks

There are many reasons to believe that the tools presented in this paper can prove useful in many steps of the process of building, solving and simulating macroeconometric models. A sound knowledge of the logical structure of a model largely contributes to the understanding of the logical implications of its specification. For instance, it can be easily seen which are the control variables for a particular target or which are the targets for a particular control variable. From an economic point of view, it tells the user of a model about the behavior a model may be able to track or not to track. This whole methodology has been programmed in Gilli (1984) and is available upon request. The program has also been implemented in the TROLL software and an interface from TSP is in the process of being released.

For the very sparse matrices encountered while doing numerical computations with macroeconometric models, it becomes very interesting to be able to determine the necessary conditions the structure of such matrices have to fulfill, so that they verify a certain rank. In case such conditions fail to be verified, an analyst is usually bound to explore more or less randomly modifications of the structure of the problem until he finds some alternatives. An original approach is presented in this paper to cope with this challenging problem.

Finally, some unresolved problems concerning the choice of a normalization of the equations are mentioned together with some hints on how they could be approached.

The material presented in this paper does not, of course, completely cover the potential use of graphs in macroeconometric modeling. Many interesting extensions of the use of graph-theory based tools exist and are worthwhile being developed. For instance, the problem of qualitative solvability of economic systems can be efficiently approached with graph theory, see e.g. Fontaine *et al.* (1991). Another application of the use of graphs when investigating the structure of matrices is given in Garbely and Gilli (1991), where un upper bound for the number of nonzero eigenvalues is found for the dynamic multiplier matrix.

References

Aho, A.V., J.E. Hopcroft, and J.D. Ullman (1974), *The design and analysis of computer algorithms*, Addison-Wesley, Reading MA.

Ando, A. and F.M. Fisher (1963), “Near-decomposability, partition and aggregation, and the relevance of stability discussions”, *International Economic Review*, **4**, 53–67.

Berge, C. (1957), “Two theorems in graph theory”, *Proceedings of the Academy of Sciences of the United States of America*, **43**, 842–844.

Berge, C. (1973), *Graphes et hypergraphes*, Dunod, Paris.

Boutillier, M. (1983), “The concept of reading as analysis of macroeconomic models”, in T. Baser, editor, *Fourth IFAC/IFORS/IIAAS conference on the modeling and control of national economies and the 1983 SEDC conference*, McGregor and Werner, Washington DC.

Brualdi, R.A. and H.J. Ryser (1991), *Combinatorial matrix theory*, Cambridge University Press, Cambridge.

Duff, I.S. (1977), “On permutations to block triangular forms”, *Journal of the Institute of Mathematics and its Applications*, **19**, 339–342.

Duff, I.S. (1981), “On algorithms for obtaining a maximum transversal”, *ACM Transactions on Mathematical Software*, **7**, 315–330.

Dulmage, A.L. and N.S. Mendelsohn (1963), “Two algorithms for bipartite graphs”, *Journal of the Society for Industrial and Applied Mathematics*, **7**, 183–194.

Fontaine, P., M. Garbely, and M. Gilli (1991), "Qualitative solvability in economic models", *Computer Science in Economics and Management*, **4**, 285–301.

Garbely, M. and M. Gilli (1991), "Qualitative decomposition of the eigenvalue problem in a dynamic system", *Journal of Economic Dynamics and Control*, **15**, 539–548.

Gilli, M. (1978), *Etude et analyse des structures causales dans les modèles économiques*, Peter Lang, Bern.

Gilli, M. (1984), "Causor, a program for the analysis of recursive and interdependent causal structures", Cahiers du Département d'Econométrie 84.03, Université de Genève, Genève.

Gilli, M. (1992), "Causal ordering and beyond", *International Economic Review*, **33**, 957–971.

Gilli, M. and M. Garbely (1993), "Matchings, covers, and Jacobian matrices", Cahiers du Département d'Econométrie 93.08, Université de Genève, Genève.

Gilli, M. and G. Pauletto (1993), "Econometric model simulation on parallel computers", *International Journal of Supercomputer Applications*, **7**, 254–264.

Gilli, M., G. Pauletto, and M. Garbely (1992), "Equation reordering for iterative processes - a comment", *Computer Science in Economics and Management*, **5**, 147–153.

Hopcroft, J.E. and R.M. Karp (1975), "An $n^{5/2}$ algorithm for maximum matching in bipartite graphs", *SIAM Journal on Computing*, **2**, 225–231.

Houtman, M. and E. Sterken (1989), "The structure of macroeconomic models", in IFAC, editor, *Dynamic modelling and control of national economies, preprints of the IFAC Symposium, Edinburgh, UK, 27-29 June 1989*, Institute of Measurement and Control, London, 629–634.

Lindbeck, A. (1966), "The method of isolation in economic statics - a pedagogical note", *Swedish Journal of Economics*, **68**, 148–165.

McElroy, F.W. (1978), "A simple method of causal ordering", *International Economic Review*, **19**, 1–23.

Roy, B. (1969), *Algèbre moderne et théorie des graphes*, Dunod, Paris.

Sedgewick, R. (1989), *Algorithms*, Addison-Wesley, Reading MA.

Simon, H.A. (1953), "Causal ordering and identifiability", in W.C. Hood and T.C. Koopmans, editors, *Studies in econometric methods, (Cowles Foundation Monograph 14)*, John Wiley and Sons, New York.

Thulasiraman, K. and N.S. Swamy (1992), *Graphs: theory and algorithms*, John Wiley, New York.

Methods and Applications of Economic Dynamics
L. Schoonbeek, E. Sterken and S.K. Kuipers (editors)

Chapter 6

Causality and dynamic analysis of MEFISTO: the monetary and financial model of the Banque de France[1]

Michel Boutillier and Pascal Jacquinot

1 Introduction

The usual macroeconometric modeling process includes a thorough analysis of the model in order to verify the model's behavior and a check on its economic consistency. The analysis usually breaks down into two steps. The first is an external analysis, which mainly involves elementary technical simulations. The second is usually referred to as internal analysis. It combines a study of hierarchies or interdependences within the model and an assessment of its dynamics. The pros and cons of internal analysis have already been widely discussed by numerous authors: see Deleau and Malgrange (1975a), Rossier (1979), Gandolfo (1981) and Kuh *et al.* (1985), for instance.

MEFISTO (Model of the Evolutions of FInancial STOcks) is a quarterly model of the French monetary and financial system that provides a detailed description of the evolution of interest rates, financial flows and, above all, stocks of assets and liabilities. This type of model is a novelty in France. It was made possible by an exhaustive database recently constructed at the Banque de France. An earlier

---

1. The views expressed herein are those of the authors and not necessarily those of the Banque de France. The authors would like to express particular gratitude to all their colleagues of the MEFISTO team and to the careful readers who greatly improved this paper by their criticisms: Bert Schoonbeek, Elmer Sterken, Jarig van Sinderen, Manfred Gilli, Rahim Loufir and Pierre Malgrange. The usual disclaimer applies.

version of MEFISTO has been published in MEFISTO (1992). Corrections of the database and many improvements – concerning the completion of financial flow variables, foreign direct investments and the behavior of financial intermediaries such as insurance companies and credit institutions – have lead to the publication of a second model version in MEFISTO (1993). For this version, the estimation period is mostly, but not invariably, from the mid-seventies to the last quarter of 1989.

As usual, an external analysis of the second version has been carried out, see Brossard (1993). The present paper deals with the internal analysis and, more specifically, the two aspects suggested above. Section 2 gives a brief presentation of the main features of the second version of MEFISTO, which will hereinafter be referred to as MEFISTO, with a view towards the subsequent analysis. Section 3 examines the causality structure, next breaks the model down into blocks and examines the loop variables within these blocks. Section 4 assesses the model through its dynamic properties, computing the eigenvalues and using sensitivity analysis to assign them to economic behavior patterns. Section 5 concludes with some remarks about monetary and financial modeling.

2 A brief economic description of MEFISTO

There is no need to discuss the relevance of having a self-constructed model of the French monetary and financial system at the Banque de France. It is more important to point out why such a model is constructed as a comprehensive flow-of-funds model. Much theoretical and applied research gives sharp criticism on the textbook IS/LM-model and illustrates the significant drawbacks of single aggregate money demand functions and/or term structure equations. The modeling in MEFISTO (1993), as well as in MEFISTO (1992), stems from three strands of theoretical work. First, the assumption of perfect substitutability between bank loans and bonds has been criticized. Therefore, the modeling covers credit, as well as money and bonds, to create a more complete flow-of-funds. Second, the assumption of exogenous money supply appeared often dubious, also in France. Therefore, a credit divider was stressed instead of the classical money multiplier. Finally, a recent line of research based on microeconomic theory emphasizing the asymmetry of information in financial markets has renewed the criticism of the unbalanced treatment of bank liabilities (money) and assets (loans and bonds). All these strands of theoretical work are seen as significantly and the LM-curve, which results from money supply and demand only, seems insufficient to encompass the complexity of the financial sphere.

The system of accounts implied by the former theoretical foundations is a flow-of-funds table with eight categories of agents: households; ICC's[2]; insurance companies; UCITS[3]; Banque de France; credit institutions; public sector; and the rest of the world. There are ten types of assets: sight deposits, banknotes and bank reserves, often referred to as cash; assets bearing interest at regulated rates; assets bearing interest at money market rates; interbank market assets; French bonds; French equities; actuarial reserves of insurance companies; bank loans; other advances in francs; and foreign currency assets.

As assets holdings and issues are to be distinguished for every investor, the flow-of-funds table is a matrix with 160 entries. Some of these entries are set to zero by definition and some others are netted out. Thus, nearly 90 stocks of assets and liabilities, and their associated flows, are described. Exogenous variables are reflecting the "real" economic activity and financial surpluses or deficits, for instance. The variables also include various interest rates or yields, three of which are endogenous.

The model begins by determining the non-financial agents' demand for financing and next their demand for financial investments. Subsequently, financial agents (insurance companies, UCITS, banks and the central bank) determine some residual balance-sheet items and, more important, the interest rates. The theoretical causality thus goes from credit to money and from money demand to money supply (or central money). In turn, interest rates affect funding and portfolio composition.

The three interest rates endogenous in the model are:

- the money market interest rate (*TMMF*[4]), which is determined by a reaction function of the central bank. In France, this rate is influenced mainly by exchange rate considerations, driven by the real interest rate differential between France and Germany and the ratio of foreign currency held by the Banque de France to foreign trade flows (*BETR2R*). The latter variable stems from the behavior and budget constraints of all agents, as well as from all market equilibria, and thus from the whole flow-of-funds system.
- the bond market interest rate (*TOFR*), which is determined by the term structure of interest rates. In addition to the usual factors, this rate is influenced by the share (*M3P*) of money (*M3* aggregate) in liquid assets held by residents (*M3* plus bonds). An increase in *M3P*, i.e. a greater liquidity preference, implies a rise in the bond interest rate paid by borrowers.
- the lending rate (*TDES*), which is modeled as the money market interest rate plus a risk premium derived from the corporate default risk. This premium expresses the asymmetry of information in the credit market. The default

2. Industrial and Commercial Companies.
3. Undertakings for Collective Investment in Transferable Securities or mutual funds (or OPCVM in French).
4. A comprehensive list of symbols and variables is given in the Appendix.

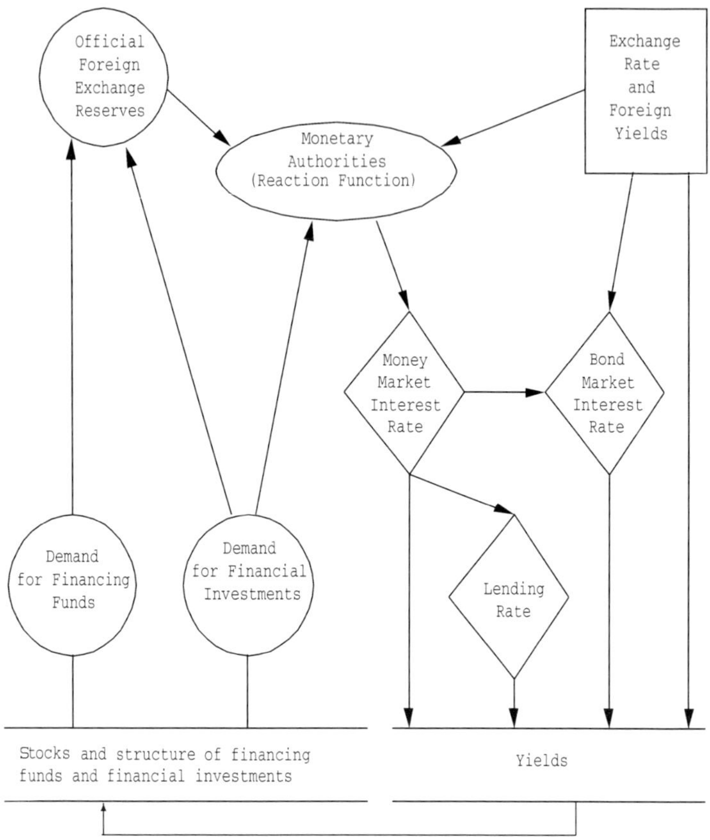

Figure 1: Global view of MEFISTO's causality

risk varies with the business cycle and with the ratio of the corporate debt to output (*SDETVA*). This indebtedness is also endogenous in the model.

The model as a whole is a description of the interaction between the behavior of non-financial agents, i.e. households and firms, and the behavior of financial intermediaries, i.e. credit institutions which manage portfolios and, more generally, manage interest rates on various assets. Figure 1 provides a useful overview.

We present an assessment of this interaction, from a qualitative and causality point of view in Section 3 and from a quantitative and dynamic point of view in Section 4. Section 3 provides an insight into the overall structure and lays down some guidelines for an assessment of the model's dynamics. This help is very valuable as numerical problems make the eigenvalue sensitivity analysis for the whole model impracticable. Therefore, the eigenvalues are assigned to economic mechanisms using a stepwise addition of the loops which are suggested in the next section.

In this context, it should be noted that the project team has tried to distinguish between long-run (permanent) and short-run (temporary) effects and that almost all of the equations are specified as error-correction mechanisms (ECM's). These were systematically validated with cointegration techniques developed since the second half of the eighties. See Engle and Granger (1987) and Johansen (1988) for a justification of this approach. An advantage lies in setting a clear time horizon for every causal link, which facilitates the economic interpretation as well as the causality analysis as we shall see below.

Among the 440 equations in the model, 31 are behavioral ones, and 29 of those are ECM's. The other two econometric equations concern households' demand for credit (housing and other loans denominated in French francs). Ten of the ECM's were estimated directly, while the others were estimated under constraint using a two-step procedure.[5] One-step or two-step procedures have no consequences for the results of the causality analysis, whereas coefficients and eigenvalues may depend on the choice of the procedure.[6] The fact that for two ECM's the error-correction term is lagged over two periods, and not over one period as for all other ECM's, is also important for the dynamic analysis. The two-period lags concern the share of high-risk assets in the households' total portfolio and the share of French equities in these high-risk assets.

The distinction between the short and the long run made with the ECM's and the central role of interest rate equations in the following analyses make it necessary to point out that flow-of-funds variables have only temporary effects on the money market interest rate equation (*BETR2R* on *TMMF*) and on the bond market interest rate equation (*M3P* on *TOFR*), whereas the indebtedness ratio (*SDETVA*) has only a long-run effect on the lending rate (*TDES*).

3 A causality description of MEFISTO

The causality concept used here was introduced by Simon (1953). It differs basically from the Granger-causality concept as used for ECM's. The Simon-causality concept refers to a specific model and not to a real world where relationships between some phenomena are tested. According to Simon, the method is not intended for testing the causality between variables but rather for studying *a posteriori* properties of a

5. ECM specifications may be scrutinized in MEFISTO (1992, 1993). For English readers, it should be noticed that the first version of MEFISTO is not very different from the second, with regard to our use of ECM methodology.

6. As long as the short-run dynamics estimation is conditioned by the long-run constraint.

particular model. More specifically, it is used when the econometrician or theorist (or both) have already distinguished endogenous and exogenous variables, whereas the purpose of Granger tests is to make this distinction.

Considering the causal structure of a model, if variable A occurs in the equation explaining variable B, then A is said to cause B. Such a link can be represented in a graph by an arc from vertex A to vertex B or by a "1" at the intersection of row B and column A in a Boolean matrix; see e.g. Hénin (1974), Rossier (1979), Gilli (1979), or Chapter 6 by Gilli in this book. The Boolean matrix is the incidence matrix derived from the Jacobian matrix of the model. With the help of algorithms, cf. Jacquinot *et al.* (1991), the set of vertices of the graph can be partitioned into strongly connected components (SCC's), which correspond to the sets of interdependent equations. According to the SCC's, the incidence matrix can be reordered into a blocktriangular form showing the hierarchy existing among the interdependent parts of the model. In most econometric models, the top and bottom of hierarchies are filled with many trivial SCC's or blocks (constituted by a single element). We call the cluster of trivial blocks at the top the "prologue" and the cluster at the bottom the "epilogue". We next determine a set of loop variables in every non-trivial block or SCC. The tearing of these variables produces a graph without circuits or a fully triangular incidence matrix, or equivalently a fully recursive system of equations. According to usual practice, we only consider the sets of loop variables with minimal cardinality, called essential sets or feedback node sets. Generally, essential sets are far from being unique. Instead of giving numerous essential sets without economic relevance, we limit our discussion only to the essential sets selected by us, i.e. the sets of large economic relevance. Most econometric models contain only one non-trivial SCC or block, which in general is quite large.

In the following analysis, MEFISTO is evaluated for its economic consistency by means of the interpretation of causal structures, hierarchies and interdependences. An important byproduct of this analysis turned out to be a better reordering of the model's equations, which optimized its solving, especially on a personal computer. This kind of procedure is frequently used with respect to "real" models in France, cf. Jacquinot (1992) for an application and a recent survey, but it is rarely used with respect to financial models, except in the case of the financial part of the OFCE annual model, see Boutillier and Durand (1986).

As noted earlier, one of the original features of MEFISTO is the use of ECM's throughout practically the whole model. The ease of distinguishing between the long run and the short run has led to the analysis of a short-term version of MEFISTO, called MEFISTO-ST, which was obtained by eliminating error-correction terms, and a long-term version, called MEFISTO-LT, which combines the identities with the long-run (or cointegration) relationships. We refer to Boutillier and Jacquinot (1994) for the full causality analysis of MEFISTO.

Two remarks are relevant here. The first is that MEFISTO has the same instantaneous (static) causality as MEFISTO-ST because every error-correction term is obviously lagged by at least one period. The second remark notes a small distinction between our (econometric) long run and the one often used in such internal analyses, which is associated with a steady-growth solution and requires a rewriting of the model. See Deleau *et al.* (1990) and, for a recent application, Chapter 10, by Loufir and Malgrange, of this book. Our method keeps the model intact and points out how the transitory behavior of the agents in the financial markets differs from their permanent behavior. In other words, we observe changes in loop variables induced by a change in the time horizon. This method stresses the importance of temporal aggregation because it can take into account both instantaneous causalities and lagged influences, for instance of error-correction mechanisms.

These arguments give rise to three subsections. The first (Subsection 3.1) deals with the instantaneous causality of MEFISTO-ST (or MEFISTO). The second (Subsection 3.2) is devoted to the causality within MEFISTO-LT. In the third (Subsection 3.3), temporal aggregation is performed upon MEFISTO, resulting in a version called MEFISTO-MT, in order to identify a sort of causal dynamics (or dynamic causality).

All the computations were performed using the CAUSOR program, see Gilli (1984), in the version included in TROLL software. Furthermore, we kept the normalization as fixed by the modelers in the estimation stage, recalling that the cardinality of the essential set depends on the normalization retained for every equation, see Boutillier (1982).

3.1 Instantaneous causality in MEFISTO-ST

Two non-trivial SCC's were obtained: a large one with 159 variables and an essential set of cardinality eight, and a small one with only five variables and an essential set of cardinality one. Therefore, MEFISTO as a whole has the nine loop variables listed below:

- *NSOM2T*, total portfolio held by households;
- *SAHO3T*, net corporate equity liability;
- *SSOMHA*, total portfolio held by ICC's (excluding equities);
- *ASOMHD*, total portfolio held by insurance companies (excluding assets in foreign currencies);
- *RACT1T*, total holding of French equities;
- *RMMF1T*, total holding of assets bearing interest at money market interest rates;
- *LOFR2T*, French-bonds portfolio of credit institutions;
- *LRBD1T*, sight deposits in credit institutions; this variable is in the small SCC;

– *M3P*, share of *M3* aggregate in money and securities held by non-financial residents; this variable has already been discussed as a "cause" of the bond market interest rate.

In order to overcome an opacity of results, we start with homogeneous subparts of MEFISTO and their essential sets, which are easy to understand. Then, through successive aggregation, we re-build the above mentioned essential set for the whole model. This Cartesian procedure has been used successfully in our previous work, cf. Boutillier and Durand (1986) and Jacquinot (1992), and it reveals the loops within and between the subparts.

But this procedure raises the problem of choosing the subparts. The lack of a solid tradition in financial modeling, and above all, in financial model analysis, means that no *a priori* break-down is available, except the *ex ante* reference structure given by the modelers and embedded in the system of accounts and the econometric specification. Two decompositions of MEFISTO can be chosen: by agents or by markets (i.e. by columns or by rows in the flow-of-funds matrix, see MEFISTO (1993)). The choice is clearly in favor of the agent approach with respect to the foreign sector, the personal sector (households), the corporate sector (ICC's), the insurance companies and the UCITS, because the behavior of these agents is quite autonomous in the model. It is more ambiguous for the public sector, whose behavior is exogenous and which is therefore largely excluded. Market balancers, such as credit institutions and the central bank, are also excluded by this approach (in a rigorous approach, foreign financial institutions and the Treasury are also market balancers). Therefore, we put them into the same subpart for our purposes. Interest rate equations form the last subpart.

Foreign sector subpart

This subpart is fully recursive and there is no loop variable. This is due to its exogenous character. Especially there is an exogenous proxy for the foreign portfolio.

Personal sector subpart

Within this subpart, we obtain a 24-variable SCC with an essential set that only includes gross wealth (*NSOM2T*). This SCC concerns portfolio behavior while the prologue of the subpart concerns households' demand for credit. In a graph-theoretical framework, it means that borrowing is a "cause" of portfolio decisions. More generally, indebtedness, rather than the cumulative sum of net financial surpluses or deficits, provides the major basis for a portfolio.

Figure 2 gives the detailed relationships within this SCC. These relationships may be summarized as follows. The portfolio choice in the personal sector is a two-step procedure. First, there is the allocation of gross wealth between high-risk assets incurring capital risk (*NNRXP*), i.e equities and foreign assets, and low-risk assets

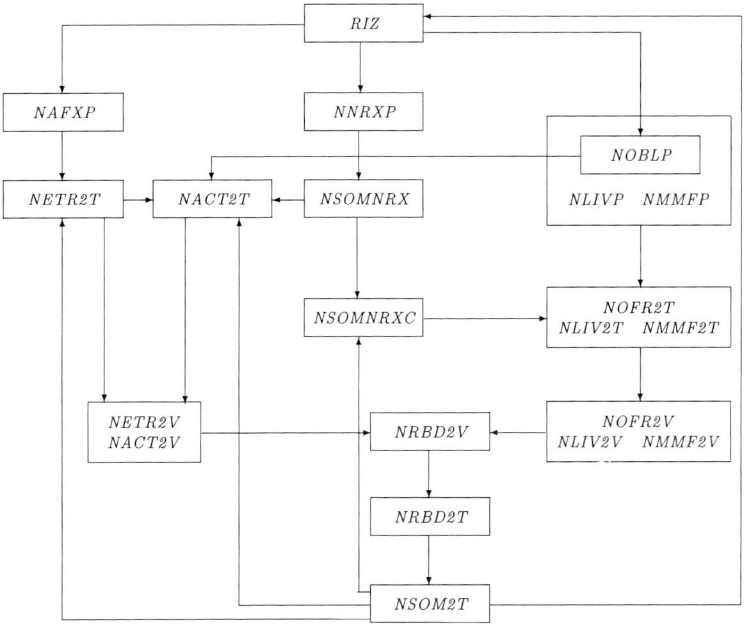

Figure 2: Personal sector portfolio choice SCC

such as cash, passbooks, bills and bonds. The second step (*NAFXP, NLIVP, NMMFP* and *NOFRP*) is the allocation within both categories. Both steps are carried out in accordance with net real wealth (*RIZ*), which is defined as the difference between households' assets (*NSOM2T*) and liabilities. Because the endogenous variables in the five behavioral equations are shares of gross wealth (*NSOM2T*) or a fraction of it, we have to multiply these five shares by *NSOM2T* (or a fraction of it) in order to obtain holdings of the five assets (*NETR2T, NACT2T, NLIV2T, NMMF2T* and *NOFR2T*) and the associated flows. The households' budget constraint, according to which the financial surplus equates the net flow of assets and liabilities, provides the sixth asset flow (*NRBD2V*) and, by capitalization, the sixth asset stock (*NRBD2T*). By adding the six assets stocks, *NSOM2T* can be computed. It is a stock variable that appears as a natural loop variable.

Figure 3 gives a more simple view of these relationships that will also be relevant for portfolio choices of other institutional sectors: the corporate sector and the insurance companies.

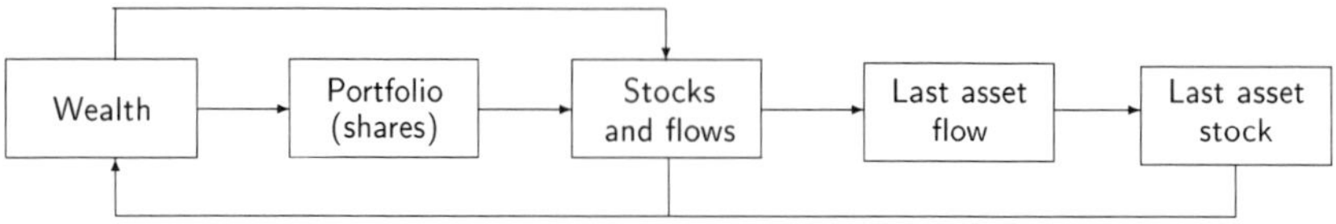

Figure 3: Portfolio choice SCC pattern

Corporate sector subpart

As in the previous subpart, liabilities are determined before assets but SCC's are obtained in both sides. The first SCC has only three variables and deals with net corporate capital issues (*SAHO3T*). These are determined by a smoothed ratio of corporate indebtedness to issued equities (*SAHO3T*). Consequently, the single loop variable is *SAHO3T* itself. In the second SCC, portfolio variables are combined in the same way as in the personal sector and the only loop variable is gross wealth again. The differences are that the relevant gross wealth variable *SSOMHA* excludes equities and is split using a single-step procedure.

Insurance companies subpart

Like households, insurance companies have a two-step procedure in their portfolio choice. In the first step, liquid assets are separated from long-term investments in gross wealth excluding foreign currencies (*ASOMHD*). This gives rise to a SCC with loop variable *ASOMHD* and with the same structure as in Figure 3.

UCITS subpart

Two SCC's arise which are linked to the markets on which UCITS shares are traded: the money market for the short-term UCITS and the equity market for the long-term UCITS. On both markets, UCITS have exogenous market shares of the total holdings (*RMMF1T* and *RACT1T*). This market share configuration provides the two loop variables. On the one hand, the total holding in the equity market *RACT1T* sums all issuers' liabilities, UCITS included, and provides the first loop variable. On the other hand, the total holding in the money market (*RMMF1T*) sums all holders' assets. UCITS have an exogenous portfolio choice. The total amount of UCITS shares is invested in various assets, particularly in money market assets. Finally, money-market assets held by UCITS become a part of *RMMF1T* which then becomes the loop variable of the second SCC.

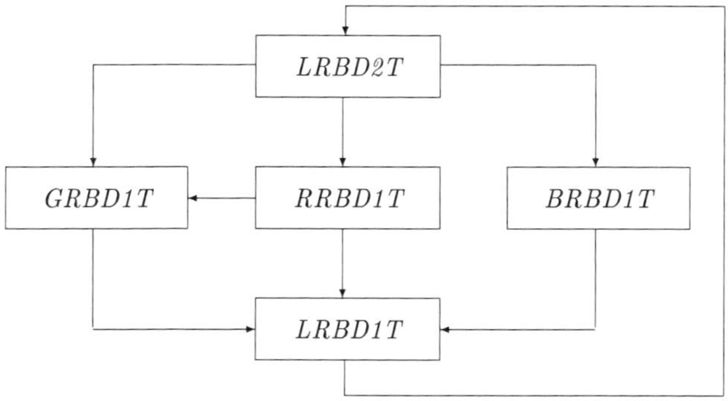

Figure 4: Cash market SCC

Credit institutions and central bank subpart

Once again, there are two SCC's with a single loop variable each, i.e. *LOFR2T* and *LRBD1T*. The bonds held by credit institutions (*LOFR2T*) are involved in two circuits in the first SCC. The most relevant circuit is worth describing. Long-term bank resources, including net equity and bond issues, are motivated by investments in credits as well as in securities, so that bonds held (*LOFR2T*) determine bonds issued (*LOFR1T*). Conversely, the credit institutions' bond issues determine *LOFR2T*, because the bond market is balanced by the credit institutions' gross position (*LOFR2T*). The other circuit involves the second range of behavior of credit institutions, which manage a ratio of held equities to their balance sheet size (including *LOFR2T*).

The second SCC in the credit institutions' subpart turns out to correspond exactly to the second SCC for the whole model (see Figure 4). This SCC represents the cash market and the distribution of money balances between the public sector, the banking sector and the Banque de France. The banks' holdings in this market are solely their required reserves (*LRBD2T*) which are a part of the total holding of the cash (*RRBD1T*). Reserve requirements are obviously a liability for the central bank (a part of *BRBD1T*), whereas some sight deposits are assigned to the public sector (Treasury and Giro accounts, *GRBD1T*) in proportion to an exogenous market share. The remaining sight deposits are assigned to credit institutions (*LRBD1T*) and used to compute reserve requirements (*LRBD2T*) according to the ratio set by the central bank (an exogenous monetary policy variable).

Interest rate and yields subpart

This large subpart is yet fully recursive owing to the number of exogenous variables involved: regulated or foreign interest rates, stock market indices, and real variables such as inflation. The latter variables are exogenous because a non-linked version of MEFISTO is analyzed here.

Aggregation of the subparts

Our previous analysis, subpart by subpart, has given us eight from the nine loop variables of the whole model. They are explained, respectively, by portfolio choices (*NSOM2T, SSOMHA* and *ASOMHD*), by corporate equity issue behavior (*SAHO3T*), by market share mechanisms (*RACT1T, RMMF1T* and *LRBD1T*) and by the portfolio management of credit institutions (*LOFR2T*). The last loop variable, still unexplained, is *M3P*. It can only appear in case we aggregate the subparts. *M3P* determines the bond market interest rate (*TOFR*), which heavily influences financial behavior and explains many elements of the flow-of-funds table. In turn, *M3P* results from various elements of the latter table.

This general loop is sufficient to give rise to the broad SCC obtained with the complete MEFISTO model. Nevertheless, this general loop as well as the loops described above are not the only interactions existing after the overall aggregation. This can simply be observed by tearing *M3P* away from the model. It turns out that then almost each small (or local) SCC previously analyzed reappears. This result shows the relevance of our procedure to assess the working of MEFISTO. The only exception appears to be the larger credit institutions' SCC which becomes even larger by adding the securities held by the foreign sector. As we have seen, credit institutions' holdings of bonds (*LOFR2T*) are related to those in equities. Furthermore, whereas credit institutions clear the bond market, the foreign sector is assumed to be rationed on the French-equity market and accordingly to balance this market. French equities and French bonds are substitutes in the long-term holdings of the foreign sector. Because this long-term portfolio as a whole is endogenous, the bonds the foreign sector holds are deduced from the equities it holds. So an interdependence between credit institutions and the rest of the world appears, involving a new loop, which modifies the credit institutions' SCC and gives more strength to *LOFR2T* as a loop variable. As in the market of sight deposits, banknotes and bank reserves, a market logic again works and concerns more than one institutional sector.

As it can be seen from the sparse incidence matrix of Figure 5, MEFISTO has the following causal structure. Since interest rates, except the bond market interest rate (*TOFR*), are explained by exogenous variables, these variables lie at the top of the incidence matrix. So, given the interest rates, blocks are solved in the following order, while considering first sectors and after that markets: the foreign

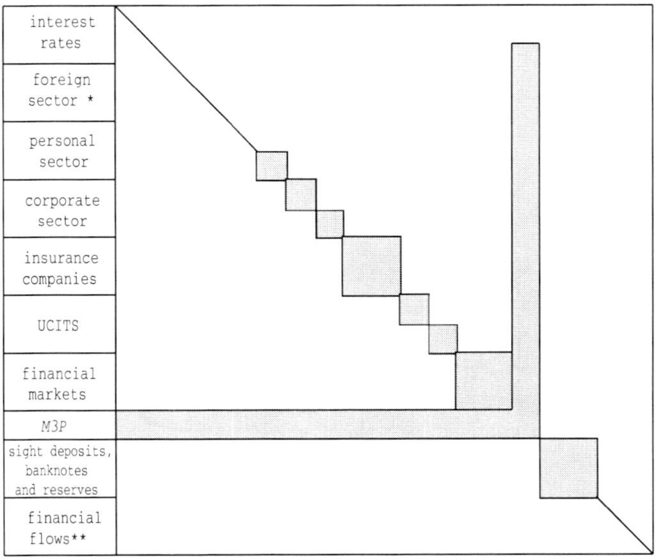

Figure 5: MEFISTO or MEFISTO-ST incidence matrix
Just the shape of the matrix is drawn here; blank parts are filled with zeros; grey parts contain nonzero coefficients and cannot be reduced in size by any reordering of rows and columns.

$*$ excluding stocks in French bond and equity markets
$**$ excluding financial flows of households, ICC's and insurance companies

sector (excluding holdings in French bond and equity markets); the personal sector; the corporate sector (including two SCC's); insurance companies; UCITS (including two SCC's); long-term security markets (bonds and equities) with credit institutions and, partly, the foreign sector; the cash market involving credit institutions, the public sector and the Banque de France. To complete the flow-of-funds table: the French interbank market and the foreign currency market which are balanced by the central bank.

It is useful to notice that, apart from five direct investment equations located in the prologue, almost each econometric equation and, therefore, almost each behavioral equation is contained in the large SCC. Finally, we can notice that the spike represents the single feedback of *M3P* on the bond market interest rate (*TOFR*) and underlines the quasi-recursive structure of MEFISTO, at least in case we only take into account instantaneous links.

3.2 Long-run causality in MEFISTO-LT

Generally, the ECM's of MEFISTO include the same variables in the short run and in the long run. Therefore, from a structural point of view, MEFISTO-LT might be close to MEFISTO (or MEFISTO-ST). In fact, because of the lack of influence of *M3P* on *TOFR* in the long run, MEFISTO-LT is close to MEFISTO if *M3P* is torn. Eight non-trivial SCC's are found again as well as nine loop variables.

Elementary SCC's associated with UCITS and the cash market remain unchanged according to their accounting nature. To the elementary SCC associated with respectively the personal sector's and insurance companies' portfolio choices, only one variable is added and the logic as well as the loop variables remain unchanged. In the case of the corporate sector's portfolio choice, four variables disappear, mainly because portfolio wealth has only a short-run effect. The financial market SCC is increased with three variables due to weighted interest rates. The main features do not vary but the essential set of the financial market SCC becomes larger with the presence of both bond issues (*LOFR1T*) and bond holdings (*LOFR2T*) of credit institutions. The reason is that long-term resources of credit institutions, including bonds, depend in the long run on interest rates weighted by *LOFR1T* and *LOFR2T*.

On the other hand, changes are more important for the corporate sector's liabilities. As the smoothed ratio of indebtedness to issued equities works only in the short run, the net capital issue SCC (with *SAHO3T*) disappears. Instead, a mutual causation of the corporate indebtedness and the lending rate is introduced through the ratio of indebtedness to added value (*SDETVA*). Both influences only exist in the long run.

Concluding, we can say that feedbacks are the same in MEFISTO-LT as in MEFISTO-ST, except that *SDETVA* is substituted for *SAHO3T*, *M3P* is deleted and *LOFR1T* appears as a loop variable.

All these elements justify the even sparser incidence matrix of Figure 6, where several blocks correspond to various agents or markets and where the new location of the lending rate (*TDES*) reflects its long-run status. Other interest rates are again influenced by foreign or non-financial variables and are part of the prologue.

3.3 Temporal aggregation and MEFISTO-MT

After the analysis of instantaneous causal relations in MEFISTO (or MEFISTO-ST) and MEFISTO-LT, lagged influences should also be taken into account. Because a variable is lagged by no more than two periods at most, we just need to consider, on the one hand the aggregation of one-period lagged influences to instantaneous influences and on the other the aggregation of two-period lagged influences (or more) to one-period lagged and instantaneous influences. The combination of both operations provides a sort of medium-run version of the model, MEFISTO-MT,

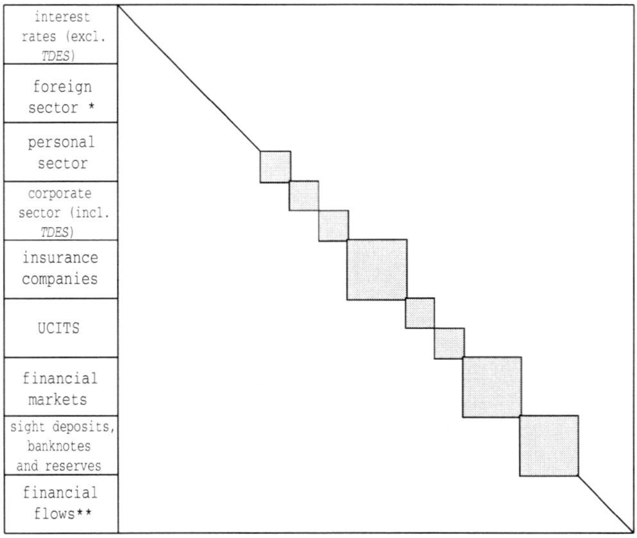

Figure 6: MEFISTO-LT incidence matrix
Just the shape of the matrix is drawn here; blank parts are filled with zeros; grey parts contain nonzero coefficients and cannot be reduced in size by any reordering of rows and columns.

* excluding stocks in French bond and eqnity markets
** excluding financial flows of households, ICC's and insurance companies

where short-run effects still exist and long-run effects have begun to work. This MEFISTO-MT will be a natural tool in the dynamic analysis because it gathers all interdependent dynamics.

One-period lagged influence aggregation

In addition to the nine loop variables analyzed in Subsection 3.1, four new loop variables appear in the essential set corresponding to the whole model:

- *SDETVA*, stressed above as influencing the lending rate (*TDES*) and found as a loop variable in MEFISTO-LT;
- *LOFR1T*, which appeared already as a loop variable in MEFISTO-LT;
- *AMMFP*, the share of money-market assets in the insurance companies' portfolio;

- *BETR2R*, which determines the money market interest rate (*TMMF*) only in the short run (see Section 2).

The first two additional variables illustrate that the aggregation of one-period lagged influences gives rise to a mixture of loop variables of instantaneous MEFISTO-ST (or MEFISTO) and instantaneous MEFISTO-LT. This is not the case for the last two variables. *AMMFP* has a long-run and lagged influence, while *BETR2R* has a short-run and lagged influence. First, *AMMFP* reflects the complexity in the local SCC of insurance companies' portfolio choice through endogenous weighted yield of liquid assets.[7] Second, we note (Figure 1) that the ratio of central-bank's reserves to foreign trade (*BETR2R*) comes from the complete chain of market equilibria in the flow-of-funds. Furthermore, *BETR2R* has a one-period lagged feedback to the money market interest rate (*TMMF*). In turn, *TMMF* influences almost every component of the flow-of-funds table, i.e. almost every agent (foreign sector, personal sector, corporate sector, insurance companies, credit institutions) in its portfolio or funding behavior. Other interest rates as *TOFR* and *TDES* are influenced by *TMMF*: that gives rise to a very large SCC.

Further temporal aggregation

The aggregation of all lagged influences to instantaneous influences provides the MEFISTO-MT model. This model has a large SCC of 190 variables containing 13 loop variables. The small SCC associated with the cash market remains unchanged with five variables and one loop variable.

The additional loop variable is *NNRXP*, the share of low-risk assets in the households' portfolio. Like *AMMFP* in the previous temporal aggregation, *NNRXP* reflects an increased complexity in the small SCC of the personal sector's portfolio choice through the endogenous weighted yield of low-risk assets. It only appears with this temporal aggregation because the weighted yield is an argument of a two-period lagged error-correction term in the behavioral equation determining *NNRXP*.

After the complete temporal aggregation, it is interesting to observe the new incidence matrix related to MEFISTO-MT and reported in Figure 7. With regard to instantaneous causality (see Figure 7), the order and the shape of the small (or local) SCC's and of the large SCC remain unchanged. Global interdependences nevertheless have become more important because of the influences of *BETR2R* and *M3P* on two endogenous interest rates (*TMMF* and *TOFR*). Thus we can derive a dynamic description of the causal relations. Only *M3P* is a general instantaneous feedback. Progressively, interdependence is increasing due to *BETR2R*. However, in the long run, each interdependence disappears and leaves a hierarchy of small or

7. A different writing of the model corresponding to the same economic logic and the same mathematical solving would have lead to the presence of *AMMFP* in an essential set only after further temporal aggregation. This formal point does not deserve further discussion.

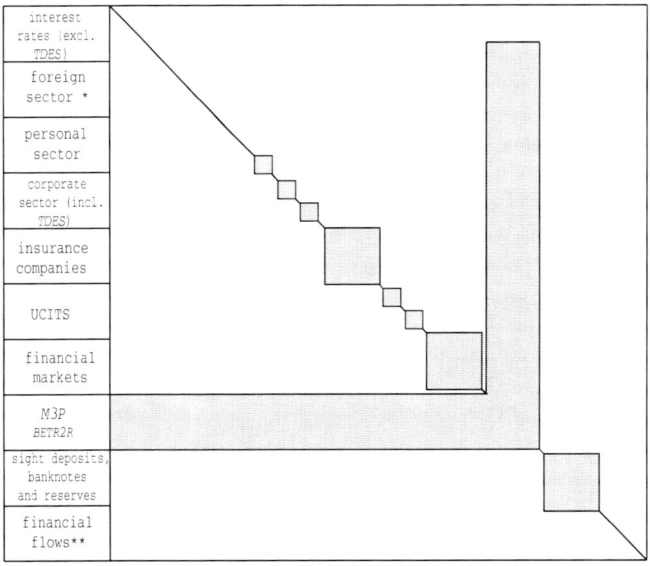

Figure 7: MEFISTO-MT incidence matrix
Just the shape of the matrix is drawn here; blank parts are filled with zeros; grey parts contain nonzero coefficients and cannot be reduced in size by any reordering of rows and columns.

$*$ excluding stocks in French bond and equity markets
$**$ excluding financial flows of rest of the world, households, ICC's and insurance companies

trivial SCC's, with interest rates at the top[8] (particularly, the money market interest rate *TMMF*, i.e. the monetary policy instrument).

All these results lead to distinguish two levels of interdependences. The first one is an overall interdependence (large SCC) going through interest rate determination and only of short-run relevance. The second one is concerned with local interdependences and works in the short run as well as in the long run; it involves small SCC's related to corporate liabilities, portfolio choices of households, ICC's and insurance companies, UCITS market shares and financial market interactions. Because the long-run structure is left almost hierarchical, MEFISTO seems to be opposed to previous French financial models, cf. Boutillier and Durand (1986), where the

8. A noticeable exception is the lending rate (*TDES*) which belongs to the "corporate indebtedness SCC".

lending rate plays a permanent regulation role. An explanation of this interesting feature lies in the new specifications for interest rate equations (MEFISTO, 1992), especially in the new lending rate specification due to financial innovation in the eighties, see Boutillier and Derangère (1992). All parts of the credit institutions' balance sheet previously had an influence on the lending rate while now it is only influenced by ICC's credits.

To sum up, MEFISTO would appear as a rather hierarchical model, at least in the long run. This means that, at such a time horizon, the money market interest rate depends no longer on intermediary targets, i.e. strictly financial variables (like foreign currency reserves, monetary aggregates, and so on), but only on final targets such as the real interest-rate spread between Germany and France. It also means that the bond market interest rate is determined by a pure term structure (inflation and short-term interest rates) without any supply or demand effect. On the contrary, the lending rate is clearly linked to relationships of banks and firms as France is now endowed with a deregulated financial intermediation.

4 A dynamic description of MEFISTO

4.1 Procedures for eigenvalue computations and encountered difficulties

A drawback of external analysis of econometric models is the difficulty of identifying variables at the origin of some behavior. The model works like a black box. A way to go further inside and to control intellectually the dynamics of the model is to compute eigenvalues in order to match eigenvalues and endogenous variables, cf. Kuh *et al.* (1984), Kuh *et al.* (1985) and Jacquinot (1992). For instance, in the macroeconomic models of the French real economy which were built in the seventies, it turns out that the indexation of wages on prices implied a non-converging dynamic movement, which became stabilized when it interacted with other blocks of the model. This common feature of many models was explained by a consensus about specification choices, or a conservatism, on which the core model of Deleau *et al.* (1984) sheds some light.

Because, at least in France, such a tradition does not exist for financial models, it is worth looking out for some typical dynamics. Simulations with MEFISTO do not show any surprising or dubious feature, apart from a large sensitivity of equity issues to the lending rate, see Brossard (1993), and a cyclical reaction to a disturbance of the money market interest rate. So we find it useful to study relations between variables or specifications and dynamic peculiarities such as this cyclical reaction. Moreover, what is implied by the portfolio choice mechanism used for various agents? Which sort of role is played by interest rates in the general dynamics?

What can be said about specific features of financial models such as the numerous derivations from stock variables to flow variables and conversely? This problem is quite unknown in major "real" models. Finally, what are the consequences of error-correction mechanisms in case the latter are two-period lagged?

Another word of introduction to this section concerns the links between causality and sensitivity analysis. Their closeness is restricted by the qualitative character of the former and the quantitative character of the latter. The former confuses a great number of loops with a strong interdependence. According to the latter, some strongly connected components (SCC's) simply place side by side the single eigenvalues without really disturbing them (that means that feedbacks are very close to zero).

At first glance, a large model implies eigenvalues that are difficult to interpret. In other words, assigning eigenvalues to variables becomes hard as the model size increases. Numerous variables can affect the same eigenvalue or the eigenvalue related to a single equation dynamics can be affected by interactions of this dynamics with the rest of the model.

In the particular case of MEFISTO, the former difficulty is increased by numerical problems. When performed on the whole model or on the large SCC obtained by temporal aggregation, the eigenvalue computation is possible (see the overview in Table 1) but the eigenvalue sensitivity analysis is quite impossible. Because of too high condition numbers, eigenvectors are only obtained for the first two unit roots and it is possible to analyze only two eigenvalues among about the seventy which are interesting.

Facing these difficulties, the procedure already used in the causality analysis can be used once again in the dynamic analysis. Starting with computations restricted to single equations or small blocks one obtains guidelines to assess eigenvalue perturbations introduced by interdependences. In other words, the procedure consists of following the evolution of eigenvalues with even wider aggregation. Fortunately, it is facilitated by small variations of some eigenvalues in the aggregation process (especially with regard to the complex eigenvalues). Furthermore, small sets of equations are numerically more accurate so that eigenvectors and sensitivity elasticities can be found. But, after multiple aggregation, the problem becomes difficult and somewhat tedious again and the process has to be deductive. When the assignment becomes quite impossible, one or more variables are discarded in order to assess which eigenvalues are perturbated by this operation. When variables set exogenous are the global loop variables, the procedure is equivalent with the computation of eigenvalues of the small SCC's and the assessment of how they are changed by the aggregation of these SCC's (see Subsection 4.3). What we draw from our causality analysis is the unique block decomposition. The non-uniqueness of essential sets does not matter; the aim is to cut the loops, whatever the vertices chosen to cut these loops. When *M3P* and *BETR2R* are torn, we drop the overall loops involving

Table 1: LIMO output with eigenvalues for the whole MEFISTO model

index	real part	imaginary part	magnitude	periodicity
1	1.	0.	1.	0.
2	1.	0.	1.	0.
3	1.	0.	1.	0.
4	1.	0.	1.	0.
5	1.	0.	1.	0.
6	1.	0.	1.	0.
7	1.	0.	1.	0.
8	1.	0.	1.	9.999999E+29
9	1.	0.	1.	0.
10	1.	0.	1.	0.
11	1.	0.	1.	0.
12	1.	0.	1.	0.
13	1.	0.	1.	0.
14	1.	0.	1.	0.
15	1.	0.	1.	0.
16	1.	0.	1.	0.
17	1.	0.	1.	0.
18	1.	0.	1.	0.
19	1.	0.	1.	0.
20	1.	0.	1.	0.
21	1.	0.	1.	0.
22	1.	0.	1.	0.
23	1.	0.	1.	0.
24	1.	0.	1.	0.
25	1.	0.	1.	0.
26	1.	0.	1.	0.
27	1.	0.	1.	82141.5
28	0.909	0.	0.909	0.
29	0.9	0.	0.9	0.
30	0.892	0.001	0.892	9602.81
31	0.882	0.	0.882	0.
32	0.857	0.	0.857	0.

Table 1 (continued)

33	0.819	0.244	0.854	21.657
34	0.853	0.	0.853	0.
35	0.843	0.	0.843	0.
36	0.838	0.	0.838	0.
37	0.8	0.	0.8	0.
38	0.738	0.309	0.8	15.855
39	0.8	0.	0.8	0.
40	0.796	0.023	0.796	216.445
41	0.773	0.	0.773	0.
42	0.752	0.	0.752	0.
43	0.749	0.	0.749	0.
44	0.21	0.719	0.749	4.882
45	0.737	0.	0.737	0.
46	0.72	0.	0.72	0.
47	−0.719	0.	0.719	0.
48	−0.435	0.563	0.711	2.819
49	0.702	0.	0.702	0.
50	0.668	0.015	0.668	277.062
51	0.655	0.	0.655	0.
52	0.64	0.	0.64	0.
53	0.62	0.	0.62	0.
54	0.571	0.	0.571	0.
55	0.561	0.	0.561	0.
56	0.5	0.	0.5	0.
57	0.5	0.	0.5	0.
58	0.411	0.	0.411	0.
59	0.386	0.	0.386	0.
60	0.355	0.	0.355	0.
61	−0.017	0.332	0.332	3.874
62	0.307	0.	0.307	0.
63	0.037	0.298	0.301	4.337
64	0.265	0.	0.265	0.
65	−0.183	0.	0.183	0.
66	−0.128	0.079	0.151	2.427
67	0.119	0.	0.119	0.
68	0.08	0.027	0.084	19.418

interest rate determination. Moreover, this procedure is consistent with our initial views because there are links between blocks (or SCC's) and economic logic.

Another procedure would have been to build a small core model reproducing the main properties of the large model and to use this core model in the sensitivity analysis, see Kuh *et al.* (1984) and Jacquinot (1992). But it is difficult to assess the reliability of the correspondence between the core model and the original one, at least because this procedure assumes the problem we have to solve is already solved! Furthermore, the size and complexity of MEFISTO, as seen above, do not justify such a questionable procedure.

In order to discard the time dependence of the eigenvalue solution, see Malgrange (1981), the model has been linearized around a reference path. According to Ando's methodology, see Ando and Loufir (1990), and before any eigenvalue computation, a baseline was obtained by simulating MEFISTO over one century from the first quarter of 1990 (1990Q1) to the last quarter of 2089 (2089Q4). Such a long simulation has been particularly motivated by the great sluggishness of households' portfolio choices and the need to reach constant growth rate trajectories for each endogenous variable. Constant growth rate trajectories have been assumed for exogenous variables, with a growth rate associated with each class of variables: 0.5% per quarter for volumes and 1% per quarter for prices.[9] ECM equations have been corrected in order to obtain consistencies between growth rates in the short as well as in the long run, see Hall and Henry (1988): in the short run, intercepts have been corrected and, in the long run, trends have been corrected in their slopes or, if necessary, introduced. Simulations were difficult to maintain on a realistic path and exogenous variables difficult to calibrate; the only exogenous variables were growth rates and initial conditions (i.e. in 1990Q1).[10] These difficulties could be explained by numerous unit roots as it will be stressed below.

The model was linearized around the 2089Q4 point of the baseline where the steady state was practically reached. We then computed its state-space representation and the eigenvalues of the associated dynamic matrix A:

$$X_t = AX_{t-1} + BZ_t \tag{1}$$

where X_t is the endogenous variable vector and Z_t the exogenous variable vector at time t. The methodology of the eigenvalue assignment, cf. Schoonbeek (1984), consists of obtaining the derivative, or the elasticity, of the eigenvalue of interest with respect to each element of the dynamic matrix A. Next, elasticities are added up for each row, or column, in such a way that the sensitivity of a root according to

9. For our monetary and financial model, there is no need to make any assumption about population growth and technical progress.

10. The only exception to this rule was made for the corporate equity issue equation. It was forced to follow a constant growth rate path until the whole model gets a smoothed path, i.e. during the first thirty years of simulation. This is to be related to the cyclical behavior already mentioned.

a variable is obtained. This method is very close to the one of Deleau and Malgrange (1975b) who propose to set to zero all elements of a row, or of a column, in order to examine the more affected roots. Kuh *et al.* (1985) give all details about the mathematical foundations of the procedure as well as about LIMO, the program included in TROLL that we used for this task.[11]

With the whole model, the full results concerning the eigenvalues are in Table 1. We observe that 67 eigenvalues have a modulus greater than 0.1, or 79 if we take into account every complex eigenvalue. Among these 79 roots, 29 are unit roots whereas others are converging. The periodicity of the five pairs of complex eigenvalues is less than two years. Among the eigenvalues with a modulus smaller than unity, almost a half (index 28 to index 49 in Table 1) have a modulus greater than 0.7.

As a result of the intractability of the sensitivity analysis, it is useful to consider smaller systems. A good starting point is to eliminate the prologue and epilogue, and to consider only the strongly connected components: this leads to keep the larger SCC of MEFISTO-MT, obtained after the complete temporal aggregation. As it can be read in the second column of Table 2, tearing the prologue eliminates four eigenvalues related to exponential smoothing of exogenous variables (0.9, 0.8, 0.5 and 0.5), six eigenvalues linked to direct investment ECM's and thirteen unit roots. With the tearing of the epilogue, nine unit roots disappear. Thus the number of roots in the large SCC, and especially of the unit roots (only seven in the fourth column of Table 2), strikingly decreases, although the larger SCC contains almost each behavioral equation. Nevertheless, with regard to the sensitivity calculation the numerical inaccuracy remains. To go further we propose to use the method suggested by the causality analysis: we begin with single equations (Subsection 4.2), aggregate them in small (or local) SCC's and finally rebuild the large SCC (Subsection 4.3).

4.2 Single eigenvalues

The analysis of single equations is split into the analysis of stock-flow equations, which are deterministic, and the analysis of ECM's, which are stochastic.

Stock-flow equations

The simultaneous presence of stock and flow variables is a main characteristic of MEFISTO. Stock-flow equations are not restricted to the prologue or to the epilogue, as the causality analysis shows, but also appear in the large SCC's obtained above after temporal aggregation. The main reason is that much behavior – portfolio as well as borrowing behavior – and market equilibria involve stocks, whereas budget constraints derive from net financial surpluses or deficits and concern flows. This structural reason justifies the presence of equations to compute stocks from flows, and conversely, within the SCC's or the whole model. Such equations imply

11. In this study, we consider no longer elasticities which are smaller than 0.1 (our cutoff was 0.1).

Table 2: Eigenvalue assignments in various aggregation stages

SECTORS	SINGLE EQUATIONS			SMALL SCCS		LARGE SCC (with all feedbacks)
	smoothing of		0.9			
	exogenous		0.8			
	variables		0.5			
			0.5			
	stocks as		12			
	cumulative sums		times			
	of exogenous flows		1.0			
PROLOGUE		AN	0.756			
	direct investment	CE	0.615			
	in france	RO	0.904			
			0.306			
	stock/flow eq.		1.0			
	direct investment	RO	0.697			
	abroad	CE	0.556			
INTEREST	money market rate		0.697			0.734+0.091i
RATES AND YIELDS	bond market rate		0.775			0.831+0.220i
REST	FRF share		0.426			0.544
OF THE	short term share		0.415			0.411
WORLD	stock/flow eq.	ETR	1.0			1.0
	credits		1.0			1.0
			1.0			1.0
	low-risk share		0.735		0.736	0.736
	in whole portfolio		0.265		0.263	0.266
HOUSEHOLDS	equity share		0.839		0.838	0.833
	in risky portfolio		0.386	portfolio	0.386	0.391
	low-risk shares	LIV	0.858	SCC	0.863	0.858
	in low-risk	OFR	0.853		0.855	0.852
	portfolio	MMF	0.892		0.905	0.892+εi
	stock/flow eq.	RBD	1.0		1.0	1.0
	lending rate		0.372	indebtedness	0.454	0.356
	indebtedness		0.890	SCC	0.813	0.892−εi
	credits		0.605			0.831−0.220i
	net capital issues		0.310	net	0.735±0.317i	0.687±0.315i
				capital issue	0.217±0.717i	0.222±0.732i
				SCC	−0.421±0.578i	−0.425±0.570i
ICCS					−0.704	−0.715
		RBD	0.785		0.785	0.799+εi
	portfolio	MMF	0.753	portfolio	0.753	0.752
	shares	OFR	0.664	SCC	0.664	0.639+εi
		ETR	0.816		0.816	0.799−εi
	stock/flow eq.	OPA	1.0		1.0	1.0
	portfolio	LIQ	0.640		0.640	0.639−εi
INSURANCE	shares	MMF	0.749	portfolio	0.749	0.749
COMPANIES		OFR	0.800	SCC	0.800	0.800
	stock/flow eq.	ACT	1.0		1.0	1.0
PRIVATE SECTOR	short term share		0.655			0.655
INVESTMENT	direct investment	AN	0.877			0.882
ABROAD	stock/flow eq.		1.0			1.0
CREDIT	permanent			financial		
INSTITUTIONS	capital ratio		0.825	market	0.825	0.841
	equities share		0.770	SCC	0.770	0.734−0.091i
	stock/flow equations		1.0			
	for UCITS, government		1.0			
	and credit institutions		1.0			
EPILOGUE	output		1.0			
	equations		1.0			
	(capitalization		1.0			
	indices for the		1.0			
	balances in		1.0			
	every market)		1.0			

Abbreviations used in Table 2:

Direct investments:

AN	North America
CE	EEC
RO	rest of OECD

Assets:

ACT	equities
ETR	foreign assets
LIQ	liquidity
LIV	passbooks
MMF	money market assets
OFR	bonds
OPA	shares of long-term UCITS
RBD	cash

unit roots. Table 1 and the second column of Table 2, which gathers the main results of Section 4, show the seven unit roots in the large SCC (obtained after the complete temporal aggregation). The others are in the prologue and in the epilogue.

Such results force us to examine the reasons for the existence of unit roots (or more generally eigenvalues of a modulus greater than or equal to one). Four steps are to be distinguished in an ideal chain of macroeconometric model building: theory, estimation, simulation and dynamic analysis. As d'Autume (1992) states for the first step, it is difficult to have theoretical arguments in favor of non-converging or unit roots associated with economic processes. According to Engle and Granger (1987) or Johansen (1988), the estimation step, as far as it concerns ECM's, explicitly eliminates unit roots because they indicate specification errors. The (deterministic) simulation step supposes the writing of a complete model, i.e. the gathering of the behavioral equations, estimated with univariate or multivariate procedures, and the accounting equations. In this step roots of modulus greater than or equal to one could arise from accounting identities or from perturbations of ECM roots due to interdependences. The latter occurrence may be related to simultaneity biases that have not been corrected by the relevant methodology. In the last step, the eigenvalue problem remains in the perspective of the simulation step. This problem involves the study of how each eigenvalue contributes to model responses as a result of perturbations of the exogenous variables or the parameters. We remark here that the magnitude of an eigenvalue is not the sole explanation of its contribution.

Thus, our present investigations, focused on deterministic simulations and related to eigenvalue calculations and analyses, ignore whether the origins of roots are stochastic, as in the case of behavioral equations, or deterministic, as in the case of accounting equations. In this sense, it is possible to say that this section deals with a sort of "Simon-dynamics", recalling that the previous section has dealt with the Simon-causality that ignores stochastic properties of economic variables and the estimation step in the model-building process. On the other hand, the simultaneous presence of stock and flow variables in financial models shows that there could be good (theoretical ?) reasons for observing unit roots in econometric models, even if simultaneity biases have been avoided. Such importance of stock and flow variables has also been stressed in the continuous-time literature with a view towards the model dynamics, see e.g. Gandolfo (1981).

As explained by Amable *et al.* (1993), these unit roots may not at all be confused with hysteresis or remanence. They imply, on the one hand, persistence or permanent effects of transitory shocks[12] and, on the other hand, a multiplicity of equilibria (a "continuum" and not a single point). With such a multiplicity, the equilibrium effectively reached depends on initial conditions and adjustment speed parameters. Two conclusions may be drawn. First, it is essential that the latter equilibria reachable by a complete deterministic model are not to be confused with equilibria of single ECM's, i.e. long-run or cointegration relationships. Second, the sluggishness of trajectories and the non-uniqueness of equilibria, observed during the calibration phase of the century baseline, depend not only on the large or unit roots but also on the eigenvalue hierarchy. The latter is studied in Subsection 4.3.

ECM's

Our almost systematic choice in favor of ECM's simplifies our work. In most cases, speed adjustment parameters quickly provide roots for the single mechanisms which are the starting points for our dynamic analysis of the whole model. In the most simple ECM specification, the more widely used in MEFISTO, there is a one-period lagged error-correction term and no autoregressive term

$$\Delta X_t = -\alpha X_{t-1} + \dots \tag{2}$$

where X_t is either the level or the logarithm of an endogenous variable, and $\Delta X_t = X_t - X_{t-1}$. It is easy to make a correspondence between the adjustment speed parameter α and the eigenvalue λ

$$\lambda = 1 - \alpha \tag{3}$$

It means that the error-correction coefficient α directly gives the eigenvalue $1 - \alpha$ for 26 behavioral equations in the second column of Table 2.

Beside this general case, three special cases arise within MEFISTO. First, keeping the one-period lagged error-correction term, an autoregressive term can be added

12. Persistence does not mean remanence as far as, in the terms of Amable *et al.* (1993, p. 128), "a first shock, followed by a second one of the same intensity in the opposite direction, takes the (system with persistence) back to its initial level, whatever the intensity of the shock", whereas "a system with hysteresis would exhibit remanence when subject to this kind of impulse."

$$\Delta X_t = \beta \Delta X_{t-1} - \alpha X_{t-1} + ... \tag{4}$$

and the eigenvalues are the solutions of the following second-order characteristic equation

$$\lambda^2 - (1 - \alpha + \beta)\lambda + \beta = 0 \tag{5}$$

This justifies both eigenvalues (0.904 and 0.306) associated with the single ECM explaining direct investments from the rest of the OECD (see Table 2). Second, the error-correction term can be two-period lagged and, even without an autoregressive term, we obtain a second-order difference equation

$$\Delta X_t = -\alpha X_{t-2} + ... \tag{6}$$

and the eigenvalues are the solutions of the following second-order characteristic equation

$$\lambda^2 - \lambda + \alpha = 0 \tag{7}$$

This justifies both eigenvalues (0.735 and 0.265) associated with the single ECM linked to the low-risk share in the whole households' portfolio (see Table 2). Now, mixing the two previous cases, we obtain the third special case

$$\Delta X_t = \beta \Delta X_{t-1} - \alpha X_{t-2} + ... \tag{8}$$

and the eigenvalues are the solutions of the following second-order characteristic equation

$$\lambda^2 - (1 + \beta)\lambda + (\alpha + \beta) = 0 \tag{9}$$

This justifies both eigenvalues (0.839 and 0.386) associated with the single ECM linked to the French equity share in the high-risk households' portfolio (see Table 2).

As a conclusion of this subsection devoted to single equation dynamics, it is worth indicating the hierarchy of eigenvalues, as we have stressed above its importance in the derivation of the effective baseline. On the liability side for non-financial agents, unit roots for both equations of households' credit demand are striking. The ratio of net borrowing requirements (flows) to households' disposable income, modeled in first differences and without an error-correction term, and the total loans (stocks), derived from cumulative sums of the former flows, produce both unit roots. The dynamics of corporate liabilities are more contrasted, i.e. the total indebtedness adjusts very slowly (with a root equal in modulus to 0.890), whereas bank indebtedness (or credit) and equities adjust faster (root magnitudes of, respectively, 0.605

and 0.310). As far as indebtedness is a cause of portfolio for the personal and corporate sectors, as stressed in Subsection 3.1, it is important to observe that liability dynamics drive the whole behavior of the non-financial private sector.

About the asset side, the major asset holder, i.e. the personal sector, is particularly slow with regard to the portfolio adjustment. Other sectors, especially the foreign sector, have more speed and this can be related to their more professional portfolio management. It is worthwhile to observe that in the incidence matrix (see Figure 7) households are above insurance companies and credit institutions.[13] Then the households' sluggishness could influence the financial intermediation dynamics.

According to the causality analysis of MEFISTO-MT (Subsection 3.3), interest rates are responsible for the general interdependences. Adjustment speeds are diverse. The lending rate responsiveness is as great as it is in the daily practice (root of 0.372), whereas the central bank seems to smooth shocks as much as possible (the root associated with *TMMF* equals 0.697). With regard to a Modigliani-Shiller scheme, the term structure contains smoothing expectations (the root associated with *TOFR* equals 0.775).

4.3 Submodels and eigenvalues

Small blocks (or SCC's)

Now attention must be paid to the eigenvalues corresponding to the small (or local) SCC's stressed in the causality analysis of MEFISTO-MT (see Figure 7). They are displayed in the third column of Table 2. The "accounting" SCC's related to UCITS or the cash market are not concerned. For portfolio SCC's as well as for the financial market SCC, eigenvalues are easily assigned by sensitivity analysis. We find that these eigenvalues are very similar to the eigenvalues associated with the single dynamic equations.

The only two exceptions to this close relation concern both SCC's of corporate liabilities. In the net capital issue SCC, corporate equity issues depend on the smoothed ratio of corporate debt to these issues. The smoothing by a seventh-order Almon polynomial implies a seventh-order characteristic equation, the solutions of which are three pairs of conjugated complex eigenvalues and one real but negative eigenvalue. With their outstanding periodicities of about sixteen quarters (approximately four years), five quarters and three quarters, respectively, it will be very easy to trace them in further aggregation. The second SCC is the interaction between the lending rate and the corporate indebtedness. It weakens the eigenvalue linked to the debt (from 0.890 to 0.813) and it strengthens the eigenvalue linked to the

13. And before UCITS, but this sector is not modeled explicitly and thus is adjusting instantaneously because of exogenous portfolio or market shares.

lending rate (from 0.372 to 0.454). Once again, it is worthwhile to use causality analysis results. Indeed, corporate issues cause corporate portfolio and, by transitivity, financial intermediation and markets (see Figure 7).

Large block (or SCC)

The global loop variables (*BETR2R* and *M3P*) are now included and the very large SCC of MEFISTO-MT (obtained after the complete temporal aggregation, see Figure 7) is found again. The eigenvalues in the fourth column are obtained by LIMO but, as discussed above, the sensitivity analysis is no longer possible. A "tâtonnement" must be implemented, considering for instance intermediate and tractable cases like the large SCC with one or two torn feedbacks. A difficulty arises with close eigenvalues for which a numerical artefact builds a pair of complex eigenvalues. But usually their periodicity allows us to recognize them. Fortunately, the task is not too difficult for a lot of endogenous variables because interdependences are not so strong. This process has lead us to propose a possible assignment in the last column of Table 2. This assignment remains a one-to-one matching, although it could be more complicated. Indeed, some eigenvalues are influenced by a lot of behavioral equations but we prefer to make all columns of Table 2 consistent with each other.

Seven dynamic relations are very affected, most of them forced towards more slowness. They concern interest rates, corporate liabilities, credit institutions and the foreign sector. Money market and bond market interest rates are revealed to be very influenced by feedbacks from the flow-of-funds table. In this manner, overall loops, which seem to be very tenuous in the causality analysis because they are restricted to the short run, have a full influence in the transitory dynamics. With respect to this dynamic analysis, the MEFISTO-MT model seems to be the more relevant, as a result of the role played by the feedbacks related to *TMMF* and *TOFR*. It is worthwhile to recall that the money market interest rate (or *BETR2R*) represents the main integration channel of MEFISTO because this rate influences the bond-market and the lending rates. More specifically, the money market interest rate interacts with foreign sector behavior which plays an important role in determining the foreign reserves (and *BETR2R*).

Although the sensitivity results are too long to be reproduced here, analysis of them sheds more light about the previous assumptions. For instance, the importance of credit institutions' behavior for many eigenvalues clearly appears, even while the eigenvalues more related to this behavior have not changed dramatically. It must be noticed that the debt to equity ratio explains credit institutions' equity holdings as well as corporate equity issues, whereas the market is balanced by the foreign sector. In turn, the credit institutions fix the lending rate according to the corporate indebtedness. Actually, the SCC's denominated in Table 2 as "ICCs' indebtedness SCC", "ICCs' net capital issue SCC" and "financial market SCC" are mixed together through the interest rates.

In other respects, although the causality analysis has greatly focused on portfolio choices as sources of interactions, the dynamic analysis shows that the households' portfolio SCC is not "strongly connected in a dynamic sense" and very isolated from other parts of the model. The dynamic analysis emphasizes the interdependence of interest rates, corporate liabilities, the financial intermediation and the foreign sector. All these factors may be summed up as the "credit side".

Finally, the interaction between money-market and bond-market interest rates and quantity choices (financial investments as well as financing funds) leads to a variety of small eigenvalues (in magnitude) that are sometimes complex (with a short periodicity like 3 or 4 quarters). These eigenvalues do not appear in Table 2, but appear with indices 61, 63, 65, and so on, in Table 1. All these eigenvalues disappear in case interest-rate smoothing as well as lags on feedbacks (*BETR2R* and *M3P*) are torn.

It is not possible to complete this study without mentioning the views of Ando, Fisher and Simon about the near-decomposability of macroeconomic models, see Ando and Fisher (1963) and Simon and Ando (1961). These views cannot be fully tested in the present analysis because only the magnitude or periodicity of an eigenvalue are considered and because numerical problems make it impossible to perform an analysis of eigenvector-eigenvalue contributions to the dynamics of every variable. In spite of this restriction, it is possible though to make some assertions about a hierarchical type of dynamics within MEFISTO.

Due to their high modulus, many eigenvalues do not see their effect rapidly weakening. This applies in particular to the eigenvalues associated with corporate equity issues, which become cyclical and large within the associated small SCC. Thus the pattern of dynamic influences is not very different in the short and long run. The graphics in Figure 8 show that the cycle introduced by corporate equity issues drives the full model dynamics through the interest rates. In the case of a 1% shock on the money market interest rate, Figure 8 exhibits the responses for corporate equity issues, *M3* monetary aggregate and the bond market interest rate. It suggests that the overall feedbacks from the flow-of-funds table variables towards interest rates (through *BETR2R* and *M3P*) are strong and that we really do not observe a propagation of the dynamics within an almost hierarchical model.

5 Concluding remarks

With regard to the methods applied in this study while using the programs CAUSOR and LIMO, the conclusion deals with their complementarity: although causality analysis gives an imperfect description of MEFISTO, it does give results and a

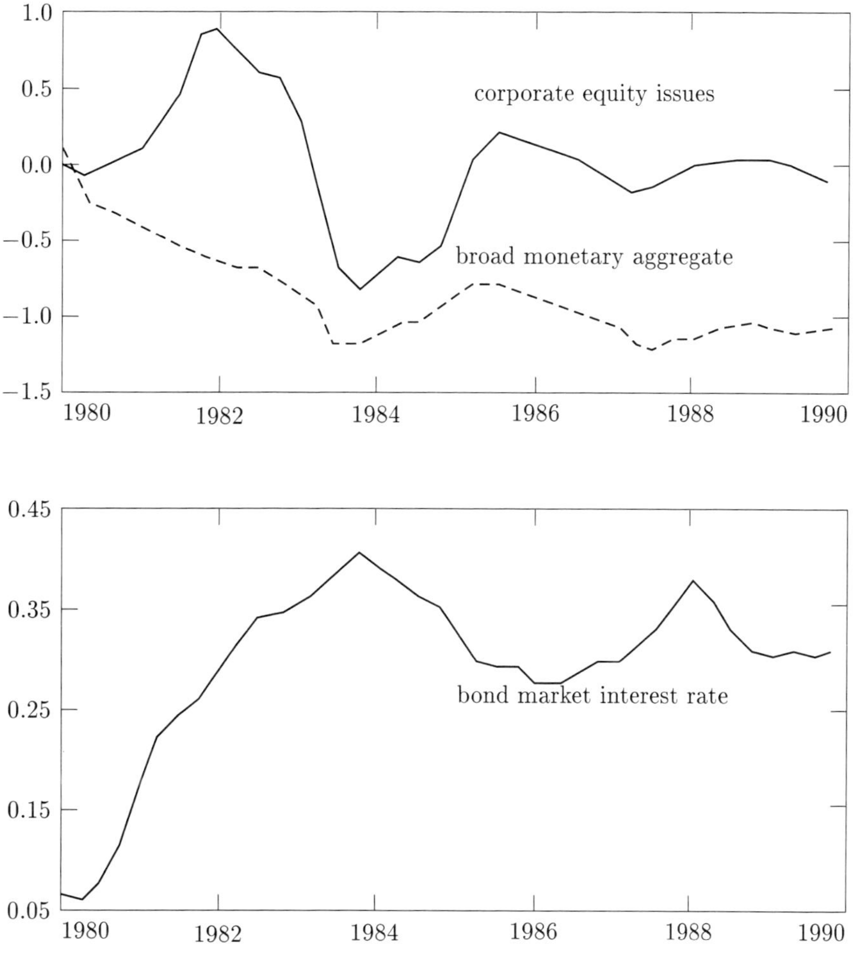

Figure 8: Responses to 1% shock on the money market interest rate for corporate equity issues, *M3* monetary aggregate and bond market interest rate (deviations from the baseline)

frame for dynamic analysis. This frame is especially valuable because of problems in the dynamic analysis which arise from numerical inaccuracy. Furthermore, the obtained results allow a firm assessment of important features of MEFISTO and increase the controllability of the model more quickly and rationally than with usual external methods. Finally, some advantages of ECM's have also been emphasized: a clear long run and dynamic structure. The latter advantage is lost in general systems because the dynamics are mainly altered through interactions.

As a whole, MEFISTO has noteworthy features. The causal structure contains two levels of interdependences. The first level, restricted to the short run, is overall and arises due to interest rate determination. The second level is permanent and only associated with local interdependences: i.e. corporate liabilities, portfolio choices of households, ICC's and insurance companies, UCITS market shares and financial market interactions. Thus the long run is organized in a hierarchical manner with the money and bond market interest rates at the top. Because of numerous unit roots, long-run equilibria reached by deterministic simulations are not unique but depend on the initial conditions and adjustment speed parameters, i.e. the transitory dynamics. Moreover, eigenvalues are generally large in modulus.

In the dynamic analysis, it appears that a lot of feedbacks, within the small (or local) blocks, are not so strong apart from the corporate equity issue SCC – where periodic and persistent behavior is observed – and from the corporate indebtedness SCC. Another noticeable exception is the overall interaction which affects the dynamics of interest rates, the corporate liabilities and the foreign sector behavior. Because of the overall interaction, i.e. through the interest rates, cyclical dynamics diffuse within the whole model, as the graphics in Figure 8 confirm.

It is worth noting that some of the previous features are not restricted to MEFISTO, in particular the interaction of both stocks and flows which implies unit roots. Moreover, from an economists' point of view, the whole dynamics appear to originate not from the personal sector, despite its large portfolio, but from the interaction between corporate indebtedness, the foreign sector, the interest rates and the balance sheet management of financial intermediation.

A strong core of interactions emerges which gathers interest rates, financial intermediation and ICC's. This core is rather on the money supply side (i.e. the central bank and commercial banks), than on the money demand side (i.e. the portfolio choices, for instance by households). Our model can therefore not be characterized as a sophisticated money demand function. It is more consistent with a "credit view". This interaction, although fragile from a causality point of view, is strong according to the dynamic analysis.

APPENDIX: Symbols used throughout the paper

The rules used to derive the symbols in the flow-of-funds matrix are as follows. The symbols consist of six alphanumerical characters.
– A first letter is related to the institutional sector:

A : insurance companies
B : Banque de France
F : UCITS
G : public sector
L : credit institutions
N : personal sector (households)
R : total
S : corporate sector (ICC's)
U : foreign sector (rest of the world)

– The three following letters are related to assets:

ACT : French equities
ETR : foreign assets
LIV : passbooks
MMF : assets at money market interest rates
OFR : French bonds
OPA : shares of long-term UCITS
RBD : sight deposits and reserve requirements
RTA : actuarial reserves of insurance companies
SOM : total

– The figure in fifth position points out whether it concerns:

1 : liabilities
2 : assets
3 : net liabilities
4 : net assets

– The last letter shows whether it concerns a stock variable (T), a flow variable (V), or a share variable (P).

In Table 2, the following abbreviations are also used to characterize areas of foreign direct investments:

AN : North America
CE : EEC
RO : rest of OECD

Alphabetical listing of the symbols used throughout the paper

AMMFP	Share of assets at money market interest rates in *ASOMHD* – Insurance companies
ASOMHD	Total portfolio (excluding foreign assets) – Assets – Insurance companies (stock)
BETR2R	Ratio of currency assets to foreign trade flows – Banque de France
BRBD1T	Sight deposits and reserve requirements – Liabilities – Banque de France (stock)
GRBD1T	Sight deposits – Liabilities – Public sector (stock)
LOFR1T	French bonds – Liabilities – Credit institutions (stock)
LOFR2T	French bonds – Assets – Credit institutions (stock)
LRBD1T	Sight deposits – Liabilities – Credit institutions (stock)
LRBD2T	Reserve requirements – Assets – Credit institutions (stock)
M3P	Share of *M3* monetary aggregate in liquid assets held by residents
NACT2T	French equities – Assets – Households (stock)
NACT2V	French equities – Assets – Households (flow)
NAFXP	Share of French equities in the high-risk assets – Households
NETR2T	Currency assets – Assets – Households (stock)
NETR2V	Currency assets – Assets – Households (flow)
NLIVP	Share of passbooks in *NSOMNRXC* – Households
NLIV2T	Passbooks – Assets – Households (stock)
NLIV2V	Passbooks – Assets – Households (flow)
NMMFP	Share of assets at money market interest rates in *NSOMNRXC* – Households
NMMF2T	Assets at money market interest rates – Assets – Households (stock)
NMMF2V	Assets at money market interest rates – Assets – Households (flow)
NNRXP	Share of high-risk assets in *NSOM2T* – Households
NOBLP	Share of French bonds in *NSOMNRXC* – Households
NOFR2T	French bonds – Assets – Households (stock)
NOFR2V	French bonds – Assets – Households (flow)
NRBD2T	Sight deposits – Assets – Households (stock)
NRBD2V	Sight deposits – Assets – Households (flow)
NRTA2T	Actuarial reserves of insurance companies – Assets – Households (stock)
NSOMNRX	Low-risk asset portfolio (included *NRTA2T*) – Households (stock)
NSOMNRXC	Low-risk asset portfolio (except *NRTA2T*) – Households (stock)
NSOM2T	Total assets – Households (stock)
RACT1T	French equities – Liabilities – Total (stock)

RIZ	Net real wealth – Assets – Households
RMMF1T	Assets at money market interest rates – Liabilities – Total (stock)
RRBD1T	Sight deposits and reserve requirements – Liabilities – Total (stock)
SAHO3T	Net capitalization – Liabilities – Industrial and Commercial Companies (stock)
SDETVA	Ratio of indebtedness to net output – Industrial and Commercial Companies
SSOMHA	Total portfolio (excluding equities) – Industrial and Commercial Companies (stock)
TDES	Lending rate – Industrial and Commercial Companies
TMMF	Money market interest rate
TOFR	Bond market interest rate

References

Amable, B., J. Henry, F. Lordon, and R. Topol (1993), "Unit-root in the wage-price spiral is not hysteresis in unemployment", *Journal of Economic Studies*, **20**, 123–135.

Ando, A. and F.M. Fisher (1963), "Near-decomposability, partition and aggregation, and the relevance of stability discussions", *International Economic Review*, **4**, 53–67.

Ando, A. and R. Loufir (1990), "Rules and optimal control in econometric models", Mimeo, University of Pennsylvania.

Autume, A. d' (1992), "Coïntegration et modèles dynamiques", *Economie et Prévision*, **106**, 71–83.

Boutillier, M. (1982), *Lecture des modèles macroéconomiques, recherche des bouclages*, PhD thesis, Université de Paris I, Paris.

Boutillier, M. and S. Derangère (1992), "Le taux du crédit accordé aux entreprises françaises: coûts opératoires des banques et prime de risque de défaut", *Revue Economique*, **43**, 363–382.

Boutillier, M. and B. Durand (1986), "Investigations in the causal structure of the yearly OFCE model", *Journal of Economic Dynamics and Control*, **10**, 131–137.

Boutillier, M. and P. Jacquinot (1994), "Structure hiérarchique du modèle financier MEFISTO-2", SEMEF, Working Paper 1994-2, Banque de France, Paris.

Brossard, O. (1993), "Propriétés variantielles de MEFISTO-2", SEMEF, Working Paper, Banque de France, Paris.

Deleau, M., C. Le Van, and P. Malgrange (1990), "The long run of macroeconometric models", in Champsaur, P. *et al.*, editors, *Essays in honor of Edmond Malinvaud, volume II, macroeconomics*, MIT Press, Cambridge.

Deleau, M. and P. Malgrange (1975a), "Méthodes d'analyse des modèles empiriques", *Annales de l'INSEE*, **20**, 3–34.

Deleau, M. and P. Malgrange (1975b), "L'étude des mécanismes du modèle STAR", *Annales de l'INSEE*, **20**, 35–93.

Deleau, M., P. Malgrange, and P-A. Muet (1984), "A study of short-run and long-run properties of macroeconometric models by means of an aggregative core model", in P. Malgrange and P-A. Muet, editors, *Contemporary macroeconomic modelling*, Basil Blackwell, Oxford.

Engle, R.F. and C.W.J. Granger (1987), "Co-integration and error correction: representation, estimation, and testing", *Econometrica*, **55**, 251–276.

Gandolfo, G. (1981), *Qualitative analysis and econometric estimation of continuous time dynamic models*, North-Holland, Amsterdam.

Gilli, M. (1979), *Etude et analyse des structures causales dans les modèles économiques*, PhD thesis, Université de Genève, Genève.

Gilli, M. (1984), "Causor, a program for the analysis of recursive and interdependent causal structures", Cahiers du Département d'Econométrie 84.03, Université de Genève, Genève.

Gilli, M. (1995), "Graph-theory based tools in the practice of macroeconometric modeling", This volume.

Hall, S.G. and S.G.B. Henry (1988), *Macroeconomic modelling*, North-Holland, Amsterdam.

Hénin, P.Y. (1974), "Sur la définition des structures causales en économétrie", *Cahiers du Séminaire d'Econométrie*, **15**, 9–26.

Jacquinot, P. (1992), *Evaluation des propriétés internes d'un modèle économétrique: application au modèle MUSCAT*, PhD thesis, Université de Paris I, Paris.

Jacquinot, P., R. Loufir, and F. Mihoubi (1991), *MUSCADET et MUSCADINE. Deux outils pour la micro-informatique appliquée à la macro-économie*, Economica, Paris.

Johansen, S. (1988), "Statistical analysis of cointegration vectors", *Journal of Economic Dynamics and Control*, **12**, 231–254.

Kuh, E., C. Le Van, and P. Malgrange (1984), "Une étude de la dynamique structurelle des modèles macroéconomiques", Technical Report, CEPREMAP, Paris.

Kuh, E., J.W. Neese, and P. Hollinger (1985), *Structural sensitivity in econometric models*, John Wiley and Sons, New York.

Loufir, R. and P. Malgrange (1995), "The long run of macroeconometric models: the case of MULTIMOD", This volume.

Malgrange, P. (1981), "Note sur le calcul des valeurs propres d'un modèle macroéconométrique", *Annales de l'INSEE*, **41**, 67–77.

MEFISTO (1992), "A model of the French financial system at the Bank of France: MEFISTO I", *Economic Modelling*, **9**, 211–252.

MEFISTO (1993), "La maquette du système financier français de la Banque de France (MEFISTO version 2)", *Cahiers Economiques et Monétaires de la Banque de France*, **42**, 41–95.

Rossier, E. (1979), *Economie structurale*, Economica, Paris.

Schoonbeek, L. (1984), "Coefficient values and the dynamic properties of econometric models", *Economics Letters*, **16**, 303–308.

Simon, H.A. (1953), "Causal ordering and identifiability", in W.C. Hood and T.C. Koopmans, editors, *Studies in econometric methods, (Cowles Foundation Monograph 14)*, John Wiley and Sons, New York.

Simon, H.A. and A. Ando (1984), "Aggregation of variables in dynamic systems", *Econometrica*, **29**, 111–138.

Methods and Applications of Economic Dynamics
L. Schoonbeek, E. Sterken and S.K. Kuipers (editors)

Chapter 7

Shock resilience in macroeconometric models under error correction and consistent expectations [1]

Andries Brandsma and Alexander Italianer

1 Introduction

Dynamic macroeconometric models seldom support every conceivable shock or combination of shocks to their exogenous variables. For some shocks they break down, and they typically do so either early in the simulation period or very late. Even for the model proprietors it can be a tedious task to find out what causes a particular problem in a large and complicated system. There is a clear need for systematic testing procedures of complete models.

Two approaches are combined in this paper. The first is to slim a large model to its bare essentials by constructing a maquette. The second approach is to apply stochastic simulation as a complement to deterministic analysis to investigate the properties, and the possible deficiencies, of the model. This follows a suggestion made by Fair (1993), with one important proviso. Fair predicts that, even for large models involving forward-looking behavior and model-consistent expectations, stochastic simulation will become a routine matter. At present, there are still limitations to the size and complexity of the model which can be subjected to an exercise such as that. This is one reason for using a maquette of the Commission's Quest model for the applications in this paper. A major difficulty with this approach is

1. The views and opinions expressed in this paper are those of the authors and cannot be attributed to the European Commission. We would like to thank Nanne Brunia, Henk Don, Ken Wallis and the editors of this volume for their comments.

that the stochastic properties of the original model have to be transformed into a stochastic environment for the smaller model. For that purpose, some analytical tools for extracting information from the distribution of forecast errors are put forward.

For several reasons, multiplier analysis alone cannot give a complete answer to the question why a model breaks down in a simulation. In the first place, the multipliers depend on a linearization of the model around some steady state. Most macroeconometric models are fairly linear in this respect and eigenvalues can be computed to analyze their stability. Nevertheless, economists such as Waelbroeck in his discussion of Kuh and Neese (1982) have expressed some uneasiness with the interpretation of the eigensystem. Schoonbeek (1989) has advanced the method in a practical direction by relating the eigenvalues and eigenvectors to properties of the structural form of the model. Linearization remains a serious restriction if the stability of the system in long-run simulations is to be analyzed, however. One reason is that, if the model is linearized, the error-correction mechanisms which make sure that the economy returns to the steady state are overridden.

A second reason why the economy can be stable, even if its representation in the form of a model is not, is that the feedbacks for the policy variables may be missing from the structural form. In simulations, this is recognized when a shock to a noncontrollable variable is combined with the policy reactions to such a shock. Optimal control is an efficient method for computing the required policy adjustments, see Brandsma (1989). Stochastic simulations can help to identify the type and combination of shocks for which stabilization is needed.

This paper is organized as follows. In Section 2 an analytical framework is developed which allows us to make a distinction between shocks which move the economy away from the steady state in the short run, including the front-loaded effect of rational expectations, and the mechanisms which ensure a return to the steady state in the long run. Stability tests should be concerned with both aspects. Section 3 contains a concise description of the Quest model. It is shown that its stability depends on the monetary and exchange rate regime under which the model is simulated. The core mechanisms are then brought together in a maquette of the model. In Section 4 the main stochastic influences in the original model are analyzed and converted into a stochastic profile for the maquette. This forms the basis for the stochastic simulations in Section 5. In the final section we discuss some general lessons to be drawn from these experiments.

2 The analytical framework

2.1 The deterministic structure of the model

Model structures may be cast in many different forms, depending on the feature which is highlighted. Hughes Hallett and Rees (1983) discuss the advantages and disadvantages of many of these forms. We follow their notation and terminology and start with a model which is linearized to

$$Y_t = A(L)Y_t + CX_t + V_t \tag{1}$$

where $A(L) = A_0 + A_1 L + A_2 L^2 + \ldots$ denotes a polynomial in the lag operator L, Y_t is the vector of endogenous variables and X_t the vector of variables which are exogenous to the model. The matrix C contains the impact multipliers, and the model is calibrated upon its data with the help of the vector V_t. Any model can be transformed into its reduced form (1) by the proper linearizations and the dimensions can be kept to a minimum by substituting out redundant definitions and non-feedback equations. The dynamic multipliers follow from the distributed lag expansion of $(I - A(L))^{-1}C$ and the stability of the linearized system can be analyzed by computing the eigenvalues of $(I - A_0)^{-1}(A(L) - A_0)$.

Eigenvalues which are larger than one in absolute value do not necessarily imply that the underlying model, as it is used in simulations, is unstable. Some complications which are typical for today's approach to economic modeling are discussed below: the correction of deviations from the long-run solution, the feedback of policy responses to target failures and the treatment of expectational errors. These interventions affect the simulation performance of the model, but their implications are usually discarded in multiplier analyses.

2.2 Error-correction mechanisms

Models can be linearized analytically or numerically, and the results are only locally valid. A common way of linearizing a model is by expressing the equations in terms of the rates of change and first differences of the variables. The experience with models which are formulated in growth rates is that the slightest inconsistencies in model or data can cause the solution to go off track in the long run. Hendry (1979) shows that incorporating the levels of the variables in the equations which are expressed in rates of change implies that the model solution will ultimately return to the steady state described by the relation imposed upon the levels. Denoting the first differences of the (logarithms of the) variables by lower case characters, the model can be transformed into

$$y_t = A_1(L)y_t + C_1 x_t + F_1(Y_{t-1} - C_2 X_{t-1}) + v_t \tag{2}$$

where $A_1(L)$ and C_1 are evaluated in the process of linearization and C_2 should be consistent with the long-run behavior implied by (1). The speed of adjustment towards the steady state is determined by the parameters in the matrix F_1, and v_t is used to calibrate the model after its transformation.

The inclusion of the error-correction term ($F_1 \neq O$) in (2) has consequences for the distribution of the residuals. Hendry (1979) points out that the main reason why equations are specified in rates of change is that, the residuals, in terms of levels, exhibit substantial autocorrelation. If the model is linearized around the steady state implied by the relation in levels, the error-correction terms are dropped from the model and the projection of v_t over time should be adjusted accordingly. Apart from performing stochastic simulations on the basis of the non-linear model, there appears to be no obvious way around this problem. In fact, (1) and (2) can only be reconciled by definitions of the form

$$Y_t = Y_{t-1} + y_t \tag{3}$$

and this is just the type of equation which, as Schoonbeek (1989) shows, tends to produce roots which are close to one for the system as a whole.

In practice, error-correction mechanisms are more important for the long-run stability of the model. In their absence, stochastic shocks which change the rate of growth would cause a permanent deviation from the steady state in the level of a variable. The error-correction terms do not have much effect on the short-run behavior of the model, unless the mechanism is so strong that it requires adjustments which are not feasible in either a technical or an economic sense.

2.3 Policy feedbacks

Among the exogenous variables of the model, a distinction should be made between the variables which are beyond the control of policy makers and those which are not. The noncontrollables N_t are purely stochastic. The policy variables, on the other hand, can be assumed to respond to changes in the state of the economy and to counteract undesired present and future developments. If the policy responses are cast in the form of a feedback rule

$$X_t = G(L)Y_t + KN_t \tag{4}$$

the model can be turned into a vector-autoregressive (VAR) system, of which the stability can be analyzed by standard methods.

Sims (1980) started a line of research in which such systems, which contain no exogenous variables, are put forward as an alternative to structural models. VAR models are a frame of reference against which the forecasting performance can be measured. Sims shows that they can also be used for policy analysis. The exogeneity of a policy variable is not imposed *a priori*, as in structural models, but by analyzing the system's response to typical random shocks and by computing the contributions of such innovations to the forecast error variances.

The VAR approach avoids the pitfalls of introducing policy reaction functions in the structural form of an econometric model. Hughes Hallett and Rees (1983) point out that, to eliminate the deviation of the current state from its desired value, the order of the difference equations determining the controls should be larger than the order of the system which is controled. For that reason, the state-space form is a popular representation of the model for applications of control theory in engineering. It describes how the current state develops from the previous state plus any influences since that state was formed.

The state-space form is much less popular in economic applications because of the artificiality of the state variables and the sparsity of the matrices. But, if the dynamics of economic systems are so complicated that it is difficult to design a stable control system, and if the uncertainty surrounding economic variables is so great that it pays off to update both the model and the information set conditioning the policy decisions at frequent intervals, it must also be difficult to identify a feedback control rule for economic policies which can be included in the structural form of the model. We agree with Fair (1993) that it will become a standard practice to design policy adjustments by optimal control using large-scale economic models. Hughes Hallett and Rees (1983) state that the reduced form stacked over the planning period could serve this purpose equally well as the state-space form. Kendrick (1982) acknowledges that, even to engineers, Theil's certainty equivalence approach has a great appeal.

The applications of optimal control to economic problems in Brandsma (1989) and Hughes Hallett and Rees (1983) show, for quite a broad selection of the parameters in the objective function, that the optimal policy responses to deviations from the desired state are big in the early part of the planning period when the failures tend to increase. Later on, the policy adjustments become much smoother, as the economy returns to the steady state. It is unlikely that simple feedback rules of the type (4) can be found which stabilize the model for every conceivable shock to N_t. On the other hand, feedback rules may exist which make the system more robust to the most frequent shocks. This can be investigated by stochastic simulations with a model in which alternative rules can be inserted.

2.4 Rational and model-consistent expectations

A typical feature of economic models is that monetary variables are volatile and respond almost instantaneously to news and innovations, while the real side of the economy adjusts only slowly. If policy makers are allowed to adjust their policies to anticipated future deviations in the state of the economy, as described in the previous subsection, it cannot be maintained that financial markets would not take this information into account. Exchange rates are a typical variable about which expectations are formed which should play a role in the decisions of market participants and policy makers. The reduced form of the model should therefore be amended to

$$Y_t = A(L)Y_t + E_tB(L^{-1})Y_t + CX_t + V_t \tag{5}$$

where $E_tB(L^{-1})Y_t = B_0Y_{t,t}+B_1Y_{t+1,t}+B_2Y_{t+2,t}+\ldots$ denotes a distributed lead over the expectations about future values of Y_t, formed on the basis of the information available at the start of period t.

The inclusion of forward-looking expectations enriches the simulation possibilities enormously. For instance, the anticipation of a future change in economic policy will have an immediate effect on the current state of the economy. Moreover, the immediate effect of a policy shock will differ according to whether the adjustment is perceived to be temporary or permanent. The price to pay is a complication of the dynamic structure of the model, which can no longer be solved sequentially forwards in time. Terminal conditions have to be specified, and the model has to be solved forwards, starting from the initial conditions, by some form of multiple shooting. Thanks to the algorithm of Fair and Taylor (1983), and later refinements, there are little technical impediments to the simulation of forward-looking models. The forward iterations stop when a steady state is reached in which the variables about which expectations are formed do no longer change from one period to the next. In order to avoid sudden jumps when the initial deviations from the steady state are not very large, the convergence criterion for the forward iterations is usually not set too tightly, but substantial shocks are amplified or dampened immediately through jumps in the expectational variables.

The application of optimal control to forward-looking models raises a conceptual issue of some importance, related to the subtle difference between model-consistent expectations and rational expectations. Both concepts are used more or less interchangeably in the literature. Model consistency emphasizes the requirement that the expectations on which decisions are based should be reproducible as the forecast of the model conditioned on the information available at the time when the expectations are formed. Rationality, in addition, requires that the information is also used to determine the responses to be expected in terms of the policy variables of the model. Both concepts obviously coincide in closed-loop systems, but without optimal control the inclusion of consistent expectations can easily destabilize the model. Fisher (1988) shows that the solution cannot stabilize upon the terminal conditions before the controls have fully worked out.

This has consequences for any stochastic simulations with a forward-looking model. In the model-consistent concept, the expectational terms should not be changed, since they reflect the mean over all possible drawings. Contrarily, in the rational expectations concept, the forward-looking variables must change because a particular realization prompts the reaction of economic agents. Nevertheless, unless this realization is treated as news about the distribution of the stochastic shocks, the expectation of future drawings should not change.

2.5 The stochastic profile of the model

In several instances above it has been stressed that the proper way to analyze incomplete models involves a careful study of their stochastic complement. Major elements of such an analysis are the variances and covariances of the residuals and the noncontrollables of the model. They build up the forecast error variances. Let the forecast error be denoted as

$$\hat{y}_t = Y_t - Y_{t,t-1} = Y_t - E_{t-1}L^{-1}Y_{t-1} \tag{6}$$

the difference between the realization of the endogenous variables in period t and its projection at $t-1$, given the model and the expected values of the exogenous variables. Don (1993) shows that the noncontrollables and the error terms are the most important contributors to the forecast error variances. In the linearized model, the contribution of each exogenous variable to the forecast error is

$$\hat{y}_t^i = (I - A_0)^{-1}C^i\hat{x}_t^i = C_0^i(X_t^i - E_{t-1}L^{-1}X_{t-1}^i) \tag{7}$$

where C^i is the i-th column of the matrix C in (1), $i = 1, \ldots, p$, with p the number of exogenous variables, and $C_0^i = (I - A_0)^{-1}C^i$. Similarly, using obvious notation,

$$\hat{y}_t^j = ((I - A_0)^{-1})^j(V_t^j - E_{t-1}L^{-1}V_{t-1}^j) \tag{8}$$

for $j = p+1, \ldots, q$, is the contribution of the j-th stochastic disturbance.

In non-linear models, the contributions in terms of the first differences of the variables can be computed by performing simulations at time $t-1$ in which only the value of the exogenous variable concerned is replaced by its value at time t. This can also be done for a group of variables, for instance to reduce the impact of the feedbacks which may exist between them. Finally, the impact which remains from past shocks can be computed by deducting all the other contributions from the observed first difference at time t. It should be noted that to carry out the analysis in terms of first differences and one period ahead projections is rather restrictive with regard to the assumptions about the stochastic distributions. Don (1993) shows how a proper analysis in terms of forecast errors can be approached. Expert interference with the forecast remains a major problem for the evaluation, however.

The linearized form (1) shows that the first difference of Y_t may be attributed to $\hat{y}_t^i$ and $\hat{y}_t^j$ and a distributed lag of the form

$$\hat{y}_t^l = (I - A_0)^{-1}(A(L) - A_0)y_t = (I - A_0)^{-1}(A_1 + A_2L + A_3L^2 + \ldots)y_{t-1} \tag{9}$$

which is a lagged distribution of first differences observed in the past. If the model is transformed so that y_t is the deviation from a steady state, then $\hat{y}_t^l$ accumulates the differences which cannot be accounted for by the (presumably stochastic) shocks in the other variables.

The decomposition is used below to show which shocks are important and also to determine the variance-covariance matrix on the basis of which the shocks are generated in the stochastic simulations. The contribution corresponding with (9) is interpreted as a measure of the inertia of the system with respect to a particular endogenous variable. It proves to be difficult to find a grouping of variables for which the contribution of the "inertia" term is relatively unimportant. This implies that the dynamic responses to exogenous shocks are rather different. The analysis can perhaps be improved by extending the period over which the model is simulated in response to single or grouped shocks.

3 The Quest model

3.1 General properties

Quest is a quarterly model of the world economy, constructed and maintained by the European Commission. Its main purpose is to serve as an empirical frame of reference for macroeconomic policy analysis and international policy coordination. A secondary use of the model is to provide a consistency check on macroeconomic forecasts. The present version of the system contains structural models for all twelve Member States of the European Union and for the United States and Japan. They are tied together by a trade linkage model and (optionally) by a portfolio balance model of the monetary relations which renders interest rates and exchange rates endogenous.

The Quest model has been well documented in its various stages of development, see Italianer (1987), Bekx *et al.* (1988), Commission of the European Communities (1991) and Brandsma (1994). This section focuses on three features which characterize the responses of the system to shocks: a steep wage-price spiral, a strong accelerator and sudden jumps in the exchange rates. That the model has been given rather volatile dynamic properties in the short run is deliberate, because of its signalling function for policy adjustment. For all practical purposes, the solution of the model should return to a steady state in the long run, even without policy responses which are not endogenous to the model. The model therefore includes several stabilization devices.

In the description below, these mechanisms are more or less associated with each of the three features of the model which are highlighted. Their importance for the stability of the system as a whole, in which there are all sorts of interlinkages, both between the different mechanisms in one country and between the countries, is later

Table 1: Some selected parameters of the maquette of the Quest model

Eq.	wage-price		supply block			exports	
	a_2	b_2	ρ	κ	100π	ξ_2	*open*
BL	0.09	0.27	1.0	4.1	0.6	0.7	0.41
DK	−0.01	0.12	0.3	0.8	0.5	1.0	0.25
DE	0.02	0.09	0.6	0.5	0.6	1.0	0.23
GR	0.00	0.13	0.6	2.7	0.8	2.8	0.23
SP	0.02	0.10	0.8	4.5	1.0	1.0	0.17
FR	0.03	0.13	1.4	0.7	0.6	1.0	0.19
IR	0.01	0.35	1.8	1.2	1.0	0.2	0.38
IT	0.04	0.22	0.3	1.5	0.7	1.0	0.16
NL	0.04	0.07	0.7	1.7	0.7	1.0	0.37
PO	0.02	0.10	2.7	3.7	1.0	1.0	0.26
UK	0.09	0.11	2.2	0.0	0.5	1.0	0.23
US	0.05	0.22	0.5	0.8	0.2	1.0	0.12
JA	0.05	1.04	0.4	6.8	1.2	0.3	0.11

Note: Belgium (BL), Denmark (DK), Germany (DE), Greece (GR), Spain (SP), France (FR), Ireland (IR), Italy (IT), the Netherlands (NL), Portugal (PO), the United Kingdom (UK), the United States (US) and Japan (JA)

illustrated by the results of some stochastic simulations on a maquette of the Quest system. This maquette reduces the size of the model from a several thousands of equations to a few hundred without losing the key long-run properties described below. Its main parameters are presented in Table 1.

3.2 The core of the model

The wage-price block

The basic equations of this block are a standard mark-up on wage cost determining value-added pricing and an augmented Phillips curve for wage setting. In percentage changes, the wage-price block for each country consists of

$$\begin{aligned} p &= wc + a_0 - a_1(yq - ld) + a_2 \ln(WC.LD/(YQ.P))_{-1} \\ pcp &= (open)pm + (1 - open)p \\ wr &= pcp + b_0 + b_1(1 - open)(yq - ld) - b_2\, LUR \\ wc &= wr \end{aligned} \tag{10}$$

where p is the inflation in the value-added price level P, YQ the level of output and LD the level of employment. The change in wage cost wc is equal to the change in the wage rate wr. The consumption price PCP is the average of import prices PM and domestic prices. They are weighted by the degree of *open*ness, which is defined as the ratio of imports to total demand. LUR is the unemployment rate.

The uncommon features of (10) in the Quest model are the speed of mark-up and indexation and the rigidity of nominal wages with respect to productivity improvements $(yq - ld)$. The median time lags involved are shorter than one year, except for indexation in the United States, where wage contracts cover a longer period. Statistical tests of this simultaneous system of wage and price equations per country also confirmed that the restriction $a_1 = b_1$ could not be rejected. The restriction implies full rigidity of nominal wages to short-run productivity changes.

In the long run, real wages fully reflect labor productivity improvements. This is ensured by the error-correction term in the price equation, which implies that real unit labor costs (i.e. the share of wages in total value-added) return to some steady-state level. A trading nation cannot sustain a permanent loss in competitiveness and the labor share in income in industrialized countries is observed to remain within the range of 60 to 90%.

It can easily be seen that, with the error correction towards a constant labor share in income, the long-run relationship between wages and prices can be described by

$$\begin{aligned} p &= pm - (yq - ld) + (b_0 - b_2\, LUR)/open \\ wr &= pm + (b_0 - b_2\, LUR)/open \end{aligned} \tag{11}$$

This subsystem of the model shows that, for each country, there exists a long-run equilibrium rate of unemployment in which wages develop in line with import prices. The adjustment towards this level is relatively stronger in the least open economies. This is of course a partial analysis. The adjustment also depends on relative price movements generated by international differences in the development of labor productivity. This paper proposes the use of simulations to investigate the properties of the system as a whole.

The supply block

The standard version of the Quest model contains a hybrid investment equation, which combines the Keynesian accelerator with terms expressing the cost of internal and external funding. Capital and labor are joined in a CES-type production function. Röger (1992) has made amendments for the age of the capital stock and thereby obtained more reliable estimates which allow for a consistent specification of investment and labor demand. They are included in the maquette in the form

$$\begin{aligned} POT &= \alpha[0.30(K/AGE^{\kappa})^{-\rho} + (1-0.30)(e^{\pi t}LD)^{-\rho}]^{-(1/\rho)} \\ ld &= \lambda_1 ld_{-1} + (1-\lambda_1)[yq - (wc-p)/(1+\rho)] + \lambda_0 \\ IQ/K &= \iota_1(IQ/K)_{-1} + 0.30\iota_2(\alpha/AGE^{\kappa})_{-1}^{-\rho}(YQ/K)_{-1}^{1+\rho} - \iota_2(RL-p) + \iota_0 \end{aligned} \tag{12}$$

where POT is potential output, $AGE = 1 + (1-\delta)AGE_{-1}K_{-1}/K$ is an index of the age of the capital stock, IQ is real investment and RL is the nominal long-term interest rate.

Since the average age of the capital stock decreases when new investments are larger than the depreciation δK_{-1}, the adjustment towards a normal level of capacity utilization is faster than in a model without the age component. The formulation of the investment equation in levels, consistent with the production function, ensures that the utilization rate returns to its steady-state level. The labor demand equation does not need such a level adjustment term, since a constant labor income share in the long run is already implied by the error-correction mechanism in the value-added price equation. In the model, the effect of changes in the utilization rate on inflation provides a further link between the wage-price block and the production block.

The monetary sector

The volatility of prices in the Quest model may cause problems in simulations in which monetary instruments are not used. Figure 1 provides an example, using the Quest model for Denmark.[2] A flat extrapolation in which all the exogenous variables, including the residuals, are held constant leads to a break-down of the simulation within a period of 40 quarters. This period can be extended by setting the residuals of those equations which are expressed in terms of growth rates to zero, but the instability can only be removed by fixing the price level. Figure 1 shows that dampened oscillations would occur when the price level is fixed by controlling the money supply.

The results on the Danish model suggest that endogenizing the monetary reactions may be essential for the stability of the model. In an international setting, characterized by capital mobility, full control of the domestic money supply can only be achieved if exchange rates are flexible. For that reason, linked simulations of the national models in Quest incorporate the use of a portfolio balance model in which interest rates and exchange rates solve for equilibrium in the asset and currency markets. Assets are assumed to be denominated in US dollars, Japanese yen or a single European currency, and the exchange rates are modeled in a forward-looking

2. The figure is inspired by the results of experiments with the Quest model reported in Kristensen *et al.* (1993). The results are slightly affected by the wrong sign of the error-correction coefficient in (10), but they also experimented with the models for Germany and the United States and found similar divergencies.

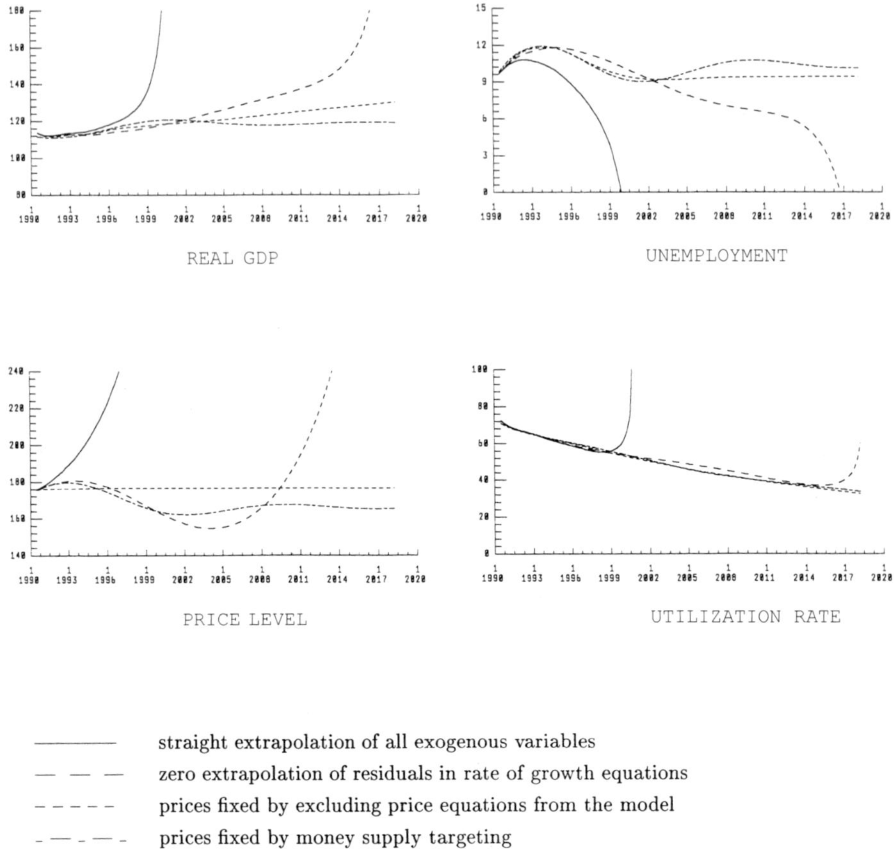

Figure 1: Some simulation experiments on the Quest model for Denmark

mode. Exchange rates and interest rates within the Community differ according to interest premia which are either fixed or only slightly affected by inflation. Although the European Monetary System is not modeled explicitly, this generates a rather tight grid for the EMS currencies. Since the substitution between different assets is completed fairly rapidly, the portfolio balance model can be represented by just two equations per country in the maquette which is built to focus on the long-run behavior of the system as a whole. The two equations describe the uncovered (open) interest parity condition and the effect of the current balance on the money supply

$$\begin{aligned} e_{t+1,t} &= RL_t - RLUS_t + \varepsilon_0 \\ ms &= \mu_1(X - M)/Y + \mu_0 \end{aligned} \tag{13}$$

where $e_{t+1,t}, t = 0, \ldots, T$, is the expected depreciation against the US dollar, $RLUS$ is the US interest rate and ms is the growth in the money supply. The parameter μ_1 is a measure of the degree in which current account balances $(X - M)$ are sterilized. The long-term interest rate, RL_t, depends on the money market rate which is determined by the equilibrium condition that money supply equals money demand.

Equation (13) is the only place in the model where forward-looking expectations play a role. The spot exchange rate enters the model via the import prices and the competitors' export prices. In simulations, the model is solved for a horizon T which is extended until, within a preset margin of tolerance, the exchange rate stabilizes at a certain level. Policy changes, even if they are announced for the future, will in general induce immediate jumps in the exchange rate. The model is not guaranteed to solve in this mode, but, if it does, it produces a stable solution. This property makes the use of a forward-looking solution algorithm in stochastic simulations very attractive, since unstable solutions are automatically excluded from the sample. Unsuccessful simulations are reflected in the failure rate but do not distort the results which are reported. Ideally, they should be replaced by additional simulations if the standard errors are to be estimated and compared. This paper is more concerned with trouble shooting in the sense of identifying simulations which deserve a thorough further analysis.

The closure of the maquette

In the full-size Quest system, exports are determined by market growth and relative prices in the trade linkage block. Adding-up constraints ensure trade consistency on a world level, see Italianer (1986). The maquette retains only the latter aspect in the form

$$ONE = \Sigma MQ/\Sigma XQ \tag{14}$$

where the summation Σ is over all the countries and ONE is an auxiliary variable which in equilibrium should be equal to 1. The constraint may be repeated for any subset of the countries concerned.

The aggregate export equations include a spreader of the discrepancies appearing on the world level during a simulation

$$\ln(XQ/\Sigma MQ) = \xi_1 \ln(XQ/\Sigma MQ)_{-1} - (1-\xi_1)\xi_2 \ln(PCP/E) + \ln(ONE) \quad (15)$$

where ξ_2 is the long-run price elasticity. Because of the strong price responses in Quest, price movements are fairly homogeneous except for exchange rate movements (PCP/E is the price in dollars). That is the reason why a detailed international pricing system is not included in the maquette.

The labor supply is exogenous to the Quest model and is the only variable to remain so in the maquette. As in the model proper, a provision is made for the important migration flows between Ireland and the UK. This virtually invalidates the working of the Phillips curve for Ireland.

A final amendment to the standard version of Quest is that government deficits in each country are endogenously adjusted to produce a stable debt ratio in the long run.

4 The composition of shocks in the Quest model

The next step is to reproduce the stochastic structure of the Quest system in such a form that it may be applied to the maquette. Our point of departure is an analysis of the variances of the endogenous variables of the full-size model, which are attributed to the variances of the exogenous variables organized by country and group. Per country, seven groups are considered:

X. Foreign sector (shocks to the country's export share in world markets, competitors' prices, factor income residuals and transfer payments received from abroad)

M. Monetary policy (changes in interest rates and exchange rates)

F. Fiscal policy (changes in tax rates, social security contributions and real government expenditure components, with the exception of automatic stabilizers)

S. Supply side (population growth, shifts in the participation rate, and autonomous factors in the decisions of firms with regard to investment, labor demand and the utilization of capital)

D. Demand side (shifts in the household savings rate, autonomous components of residential investment decisions, and the residuals of the import equations)

P. Prices (shocks to domestic prices and wages)

I. Inertia (forecast errors remaining after accounting for all the other contributions).

The decomposition of the variances on the basis of this grouping, applying the method of Subsection 2.5 to the country modules of the Quest model, produces a great variety of results. Table 2 contains the variances of the contributions to the forecast errors of the form (7) and (8) for each group of exogenous variables in the larger countries. Table 3 summarizes, for all the countries, the main contributors for the same selection of endogenous variables. The variances are expressed as a percentage of their total for each variable. In all cases, this total is larger than the variance of the endogenous variable observed over the sample period (1988Q1–1992Q4), and in some cases it is much larger, which may reflect that short-run responses are over-emphasized in the Quest model and that important feedback mechanisms are missing.

At first sight, it seems counter-intuitive that inertia accounts for such a large proportion of the forecast error variance. For almost one half of the cases listed in Table 3, the remainder of the forecast error after all the contemporaneous contributions have been deducted is itself the largest contributor to the total variance. This concerns unemployment and real unit labor costs, but also GDP growth in real or nominal terms. A more careful interpretation of (9), however, suggests that inertia reflects shocks from the past which could not be fully neutralized. In this sense, the missing feedbacks and the lags involved in the adjustment mechanisms are responsible for the rigidity of the system in the short run. To put the same in other words: the one-period ahead horizon of the forecasts is shorter than the memory of the system. This connects the issue to our discussion of the state-space form in Subsection 2.3. A proper analysis of the forecast error variances would require a lengthening of either the state vector or the forecast horizon. Both approaches would complicate the analysis; the first because the intertemporal covariances implied by the extended state vector would have to be taken into account, the second because the same has to be done for the development of forecast errors over time. In this paper, it is assumed that the model is formulated in such a way that these intertemporal covariances are small. At the same time, some allowance is made below for the fact that the adjustment process takes time.

Policy shocks, in general, do not feature as important sources of variance in Table 3, except for the impact of fiscal changes on the government deficit. This suggests that, if anything, policy adjustments have been used to neutralize the effect of stochastic shocks in other exogenous variables. Monetary policy only appears as a major source of variance for real GDP growth in Germany and Belgium and the current balance of Ireland and the United Kingdom during the past five years. It can be tentatively concluded that German and Belgian monetary policies must have been directed at other targets than the stabilization of real GDP growth. Likewise, it can be surmized that the preoccupation of Irish monetary policy with exchange rate

Table 2: Percentage contributions to the shocks in terms of variances

	External	Monetary	Fiscal	Supply	Demand	Prices	Inertia
Germany							
Current balance (1)	40.7	14.3	15.0	0.1	6.3	18.7	4.8
Government deficit (1)	4.8	0.0	76.6	7.3	0.5	0.5	10.4
Nominal GDP	15.8	1.4	1.9	2.2	3.5	27.1	48.2
GDP deflator	21.9	19.5	0.6	1.5	0.3	28.5	27.7
Real GDP	20.1	24.1	2.7	1.0	10.4	1.4	40.4
Unemployment (2)	0.2	0.1	2.1	50.1	0.1	0.2	47.2
Real unit labor costs	9.4	2.0	0.9	34.9	1.3	12.2	39.2
France							
Current balance (1)	53.0	27.1	0.8	0.8	0.3	16.4	1.6
Government deficit (1)	6.8	0.1	36.4	4.4	0.2	0.9	51.2
Nominal GDP	12.6	3.7	2.6	6.7	0.6	9.7	64.0
GDP deflator	30.2	22.2	7.8	2.3	0.3	20.0	17.2
Real GDP	4.9	5.4	1.6	10.0	2.8	1.1	74.2
Unemployment (2)	0.0	0.0	13.1	15.9	0.0	0.0	70.9
Real unit labor costs	12.1	2.1	19.5	9.3	1.4	7.2	48.4
Italy							
Current balance (1)	43.3	15.8	1.4	0.6	0.5	32.5	5.9
Government deficit (1)	6.5	0.9	34.4	15.9	1.2	3.3	38.0
Nominal GDP	22.6	6.5	12.9	2.7	1.3	28.7	25.3
GDP deflator	31.9	15.9	9.3	1.3	1.6	28.8	11.1
Real GDP	25.9	17.5	0.8	4.1	15.0	3.4	33.3
Unemployment (2)	0.1	0.0	32.7	27.8	0.1	0.0	39.3
Real unit labor costs	3.8	0.3	11.3	28.1	3.5	16.3	36.9
United Kingdom							
Current balance (1)	18.1	24.3	17.1	1.0	0.9	20.5	18.1
Government deficit (1)	3.1	2.2	36.2	3.3	2.8	1.7	50.7
Nominal GDP	4.4	5.4	24.1	2.3	3.4	12.0	48.4
GDP deflator	6.0	8.0	45.4	0.4	0.1	32.2	7.8
Real GDP	2.7	2.8	27.2	2.4	7.5	24.4	33.0
Unemployment (2)	0.0	0.0	3.3	13.3	0.2	0.0	83.1
Real unit labor costs	8.7	10.6	8.9	10.9	6.4	33.5	21.1
United States							
Current balance (1)	44.2	0.0	0.4	1.5	2.2	19.4	32.4
Government deficit (1)	4.8	0.3	7.1	5.0	4.6	5.4	72.6
Nominal GDP	6.2	0.1	1.4	4.4	5.2	23.7	59.1
GDP deflator	1.4	0.0	0.0	0.0	0.0	48.5	50.0
Real GDP	1.7	0.1	1.9	6.8	6.4	25.4	57.8
Unemployment (2)	1.9	0.0	0.6	14.5	2.4	5.7	74.9
Real unit labor costs	3.9	0.0	0.4	1.7	1.8	47.3	44.7

Table 2: continued

	External	Monetary	Fiscal	Supply	Demand	Prices	Inertia
Japan							
Current balance (1)	22.5	0.3	0.1	0.2	4.5	19.4	53.1
Government deficit (1)	5.5	2.0	14.6	1.6	4.9	12.9	58.4
Nominal GDP	9.3	6.2	6.7	10.9	16.4	4.8	45.7
GDP deflator	3.0	5.7	0.8	3.9	12.0	32.2	42.4
Real GDP	7.6	8.7	4.6	10.3	20.8	8.8	39.1
Unemployment (2)	0.0	0.0	0.0	36.6	0.0	0.0	63.4
Real unit labor costs	4.3	0.9	1.9	12.8	3.6	44.9	31.4

Note: Growth rates except for (1) % GDP (2) % labor force
Source: Simulations on the Quest model

stability has led to the neglect of balance of payments equilibrium (in fact, Ireland ended up with a large surplus on the current account). The United Kingdom, on the other hand, has undergone a regime switch towards full participation in the exchange rate mechanism of the European Monetary System during the period concerned. The UK policy stance is particularly interesting since, apparently, fiscal policy has not been used for stabilization purposes either. Fiscal policy changes are the main source of variance for GDP growth and inflation in the United Kingdom.

Shocks which are truly stochastic, in the sense that no structural relations with other variables exist which could be included in the model, should turn up rather arbitrarily as the main source of variance in different countries. This appears to be the case among the entries for nominal and real GDP growth in Table 3. It is not the case for the current balance, for which external shocks are the main source of variance, and the deficit of the government, for which fiscal policy is the dominant source. Moreover, the link from supply-side shocks to changes in unemployment appears to be a feature of the model which can be improved. As to the external sector, it should be noted that the properties of the model can only be properly examined in simulations in which the individual country models are linked. In such simulations the external shocks can be consistently associated with shifts in the preferences for the goods and services of the different countries.

In the following way, the variance contributions of the 6 groups of exogenous variables (excluding inertia) are assigned to single error shocks in the maquette of the Quest model. First, the effects of unit shocks in the candidate error terms are simulated with the help of the maquette. The maximum effects (R^{ik}, where i denotes the parameter and k the selected endogenous variable) are reached after

Table 3: Groups of exogenous variables which contribute most to the forecast error variances in each country

	BPC/Y	$DEFG/Y$	Y	PY	YQ	LUR	$RULC$
BL	X	F	X	X	M	I/S	I/P
DK	I/X	F	F	X	I/X	I/F	I/S
DE	X	F	I/P	P	I/M	S	I/S
GR	X	F	I/P	I/P	I/X	S	I/F
SP	X	F	P	P	F	I/F	I/X
FR	X	I/F	I/X	X	I/S	I/S	I/F
IR	M	F	I/X	I/X	I/X	S	I/S
IT	X	I/F	P	X	I/X	S	I/S
NL	F	F	P	P	D	S	P
PO	X	F	X	I/P	D	I/S	X
UK	M	I/F	I/F	F	I/F	I/S	P
US	X	I/F	I/P	I/P	I/P	I/S	P
JA	I/X	I/F	I/D	I/P	I/D	I/S	P

Note: Current balance (BPC), government deficit ($DEFG$), nominal GDP (Y), GDP deflator (PY), real GDP (YQ), unemployment rate (LUR) and real unit labor costs ($RULC$). For the meaning of the abbreviations of the countries, see Table 1.

an unspecified period, which depends on the lags and the speed of adjustment implied by the model. This maximum effect, in absolute terms, is used to scale the variance-covariance matrix (Ω^k) of each endogenous variable, giving

$$\Omega = (1/n) \sum_{k=1}^{n} (R^k)^{-1} \Omega^k (R^k)^{-1}.\text{var}(Y^k)/\text{trace}(\Omega^k) \tag{16}$$

where R^k is a diagonal matrix with the scaling factors $|R^{ik}|$, $i = 1, \ldots, 6$, corresponding with the groups associated with the 6 error terms in the maquette, on the diagonal. Ω^k can be derived from the variances in Table 2. The summation can be over all the endogenous variables of the model or over a subset. The variance-covariance matrix of each variable is scaled to its observed variance to avoid the over-estimation which is due to the incompleteness of the model.

Table 4 reproduces the standardized shocks which result from applying the above procedure for each of the countries represented in the Quest model and its maquette. The computations involve the six endogenous variables listed in the table, and the maximum effects which the standardized error shocks would have on each variable are also shown. The presented size of the individual shocks depends on a

Table 4: Effects of standardized error shocks in the maquette of the Quest model

	Export market share	Money supply growth	Governm. deficit (%GDP)	Potent. output growth	Household savings rate	Inflation rate
Belgium						
Standard shock	0.5	0.4	0.5	0.1	0.2	0.2
Real GDP growth	0.1	0.1	0.0	0.1	0.0	0.1
Inflation	0.4	0.3	0.1	0.1	0.1	0.4
Unemployment rate	0.4	0.3	0.1	0.6	0.1	1.3
Current balance (%GDP)	0.9	0.9	0.1	0.2	0.3	0.8
Government deficit (%GDP)	0.7	0.4	0.5	0.7	0.4	0.9
Real unit labor costs	0.3	0.2	0.1	0.6	0.1	0.5
Denmark						
Standard shock	1.9	0.8	1.3	0.3	0.1	0.7
Real GDP growth	0.5	0.4	0.1	0.5	0.1	0.4
Inflation	0.1	0.3	0.1	0.3	0.0	0.4
Unemployment rate	0.6	0.4	0.1	3.0	0.0	9.7
Current balance (%GDP)	0.5	1.6	0.2	0.4	0.1	0.7
Government deficit (%GDP)	0.3	0.1	1.3	1.2	0.1	2.1
Real unit labor costs	0.5	0.3	0.1	4.2	0.0	3.3
Germany						
Standard shock	0.8	1.0	1.9	0.2	0.2	0.2
Real GDP growth	0.1	0.3	0.0	0.2	0.0	0.2
Inflation	0.4	0.8	0.1	0.1	0.2	0.3
Unemployment rate	0.7	1.1	0.2	1.6	0.2	3.5
Current balance (%GDP)	0.9	2.2	0.3	0.1	0.4	0.4
Government deficit (%GDP)	0.4	0.5	1.9	0.4	0.4	0.4
Real unit labor costs	0.3	0.5	0.1	1.3	0.2	0.7
Greece						
Standard shock	2.4	1.3	4.0	1.0	0.1	1.9
Real GDP growth	0.9	0.4	0.3	1.5	0.2	1.7
Inflation	0.4	0.7	0.3	0.6	0.2	1.0
Unemployment rate	0.8	0.6	0.2	8.2	0.2	25.2
Current balance (%GDP)	1.5	2.8	0.6	1.2	0.4	3.5
Government deficit (%GDP)	2.6	2.0	8.7	6.1	1.0	10.8
Real unit labor costs	0.7	0.4	0.3	10.7	0.2	8.3

Table 4: continued

	Export market share	Money supply growth	Governm. deficit (%GDP)	Potent. output growth	Household savings rate	Inflation rate
Spain						
Standard shock	0.4	0.3	2.7	0.1	0.1	0.4
Real GDP growth	0.1	0.2	0.2	0.1	0.0	0.3
Inflation	0.0	0.2	0.1	0.1	0.0	0.2
Unemployment rate	0.1	0.3	0.1	0.9	0.0	6.8
Current balance (%GDP)	0.1	0.6	0.1	0.1	0.0	0.2
Government deficit (%GDP)	0.1	0.2	2.8	0.5	0.1	1.5
Real unit labor costs	0.1	0.2	0.2	1.1	0.0	2.4
France						
Standard shock	0.9	0.9	3.3	0.1	0.7	0.1
Real GDP growth	0.0	0.1	0.0	0.1	0.0	0.1
Inflation	0.3	0.7	0.2	0.0	0.3	0.1
Unemployment rate	0.3	0.5	0.1	1.0	0.1	1.6
Current balance (%GDP)	0.7	1.8	0.4	0.1	0.6	0.1
Government deficit (%GDP)	0.4	0.5	3.3	0.2	0.5	0.1
Real unit labor costs	0.2	0.3	0.2	1.0	0.2	0.5
Ireland						
Standard shock	0.5	1.0	1.7	0.2	0.1	0.6
Real GDP growth	0.6	0.5	0.4	0.6	0.1	1.2
Inflation	0.1	0.8	0.1	0.2	0.0	0.4
Unemployment rate	0.3	0.7	0.1	1.0	0.0	1.8
Current balance (%GDP)	0.4	1.7	0.3	0.4	0.1	1.5
Government deficit (%GDP)	0.6	1.6	1.7	0.9	0.1	2.9
Real unit labor costs	0.5	0.7	0.4	1.9	0.1	1.7
Italy						
Standard shock	0.7	0.4	1.3	0.3	0.1	0.2
Real GDP growth	0.0	0.1	0.0	0.2	0.0	0.2
Inflation	0.2	0.4	0.1	0.2	0.1	0.2
Unemployment rate	0.2	0.2	0.1	1.9	0.0	1.8
Current balance (%GDP)	0.6	0.9	0.1	0.2	0.1	0.3
Government deficit (%GDP)	0.6	0.5	1.3	2.1	0.4	0.9
Real unit labor costs	0.3	0.3	0.1	4.1	0.1	1.0

Table 4: continued

	Export market share	Money supply growth	Governm. deficit (%GDP)	Potent. output growth	Household savings rate	Inflation rate
Netherlands						
Standard shock	0.8	1.5	3.0	0.4	2.9	0.4
Real GDP growth	0.1	0.3	0.0	0.3	0.2	0.4
Inflation	0.4	1.0	0.3	0.4	1.6	0.4
Unemployment rate	0.3	0.7	0.1	6.2	0.5	9.1
Current balance (%GDP)	0.8	3.1	0.5	0.8	3.1	0.8
Government deficit (%GDP)	0.5	0.7	3.0	1.2	3.3	0.9
Real unit labor costs	0.2	0.4	0.2	0.9	0.7	0.7
Portugal						
Standard shock	0.5	1.1	1.3	0.4	0.7	0.7
Real GDP growth	0.2	0.4	0.1	0.6	0.2	0.4
Inflation	0.2	0.3	0.1	0.4	0.2	0.5
Unemployment rate	0.2	0.5	0.0	6.3	0.1	12.9
Current balance (%GDP)	0.4	2.2	0.2	0.6	0.4	1.0
Government deficit (%GDP)	0.6	0.4	2.1	3.8	0.7	3.8
Real unit labor costs	0.2	0.4	0.1	4.4	0.1	2.9
United Kingdom						
Standard shock	0.6	1.0	18.1	0.2	0.6	0.5
Real GDP growth	0.0	0.2	0.1	0.2	0.1	0.3
Inflation	0.3	0.9	1.3	0.1	0.4	0.5
Unemployment rate	0.3	0.7	0.7	2.9	0.2	7.7
Current balance (%GDP)	0.8	2.1	2.6	0.2	0.8	0.8
Government deficit (%GDP)	0.3	0.5	18.1	0.4	0.9	0.5
Real unit labor costs	0.2	0.3	0.8	1.2	0.2	1.3
European Community						
Standard shock	0.7	0.8	4.8	0.2	0.5	0.3
Real GDP growth	0.1	0.2	0.1	0.2	0.0	0.2
Inflation	0.3	0.6	0.3	0.1	0.3	0.3
Unemployment rate	0.4	0.6	0.2	2.1	0.2	4.6
Current balance (%GDP)	0.7	1.7	0.7	0.2	0.5	0.5
Government deficit (%GDP)	0.5	0.5	4.9	0.9	0.6	0.8
Real unit labor costs	0.3	0.3	0.3	1.9	0.2	1.2

Table 4: continued

	Export market share	Money supply growth	Governm. deficit (%GDP)	Potent. output growth	Household savings rate	Inflation rate
United States						
Standard shock	0.8	0.2	8.9	0.2	1.8	0.5
Real GDP growth	0.0	0.0	0.0	0.2	0.0	0.6
Inflation	0.2	0.2	0.2	0.1	0.2	0.5
Unemployment rate	0.2	0.1	0.2	0.7	0.3	3.6
Current balance (%GDP)	0.4	0.4	0.4	0.1	0.5	0.4
Government deficit (%GDP)	0.1	0.1	8.9	0.1	0.9	0.5
Real unit labor costs	0.1	0.0	0.1	0.6	0.1	0.8
Japan						
Standard shock	4.2	1.6	0.6	0.1	0.8	0.8
Real GDP growth	0.1	0.2	0.0	0.2	0.1	0.5
Inflation	0.9	1.4	0.0	0.2	0.2	0.5
Unemployment rate	0.1	0.2	0.0	0.2	0.0	1.2
Current balance (%GDP)	1.9	3.2	0.0	0.1	0.3	0.5
Government deficit (%GDP)	1.4	1.4	0.6	0.5	0.4	0.9
Real unit labor costs	0.8	1.1	0.1	1.0	0.4	1.5

particular triangularization of the error structure in the order given by the columns of Table 4. Highly correlated variables make the result sensitive to the chosen order and in some cases this seems to have somewhat distorted the standardization. It should also be noted that the computations are based on a mixture of simulation results obtained from the model and the maquette. The monetary loop described in (13), for instance, is not operational as such in the model itself. The results show that changes in the growth of the money supply have substantial effects on the current balance. The unemployment rate, on the other hand, is more affected by supply conditions and permanent changes in the inflation rate.

5 Stochastic simulations with the maquette

Emerson *et al.* (1992) present simulations with the MULTIMOD model which suggest that establishing an economic and monetary union (EMU) could help to reduce the variability in inflation and growth rates within the Member States of the European Union. The same study contained a decomposition of the forecast error variances, which has been repeated above for the countries in the Quest model. We are now able to combine these two approaches by performing stochastic simulations on a maquette of this model, which includes forward-looking and model-consistent expectations with regard to exchange rates. In contrast with the MULTIMOD simulations of Masson and Symansky (1990) and Emerson *et al.* (1992), the exchange rates themselves are only subject to stochastic shocks via the policy reactions to those shocks. For that purpose, the maquette includes equations in which the interest rate is determined by equilibrium on the money market and in which the deficit of the government is adjusted so that the debt/GDP ratio remains stable in the long run, but shocks to these policy reaction functions themselves are not excluded.

It should be made clear from the outset that the repetition of the exercise here is not meant to shed a different light on the costs and benefits of EMU. The benefits in terms of a reduction in the variability of output growth and inflation when bilateral exchange rates within the Community are irrevocably fixed become almost a truism as soon as it is recognized that fiscal and monetary policies cannot respond fast enough and with sufficient power to remedy the negative impacts of all stochastic shocks. On the other hand, these benefits would not be reaped without greater fiscal and monetary discipline. In as far as the policy responses observed in the past cannot be captured by structural relations in the model, the effects of a greater discipline can only be simulated by restricting the variance of error terms in the model. This can be done in stochastic simulations. The purpose of the exercises below is mainly to illustrate how stochastic simulations can be used for model diagnosis under different policy regimes.

The set-up chosen for the exercise on the maquette of the Quest model is as follows. As a starting point, a steady-state baseline is constructed for each of the countries. The models are calibrated on the levels at the start of the simulation period, given the behavioral parameters which have been taken over from the full-size model. Inflation is assumed to be zero and real GDP and wage rates are growing with the speed of labor augmenting technical progress. Unemployment and real unit labor costs remain at their pre-simulation levels, among other things due to the error-correction mechanisms which are present in the model. Since the supply side conditions differ between countries, as was shown in Table 1, the linkage initiates an adjustment process in terms of real exchange rates. The stochastic shocks may amend the pattern of adjustment.

Figures 2 to 4 show a selection of the results of two simulations. No particular significance should be attached to the choice of the countries, although Germany and Italy are more representative for the results in the countries for which the results are not reproduced than Denmark and Greece. In the "non-EMU" simulation, the exchange rates of the currencies of all EC countries against the US dollar are generated by the open interest-parity condition for the country itself. Fiscal shocks are a major source of stochastic shocks, although they may be dampened by the covariances with other error terms. These covariances have been estimated

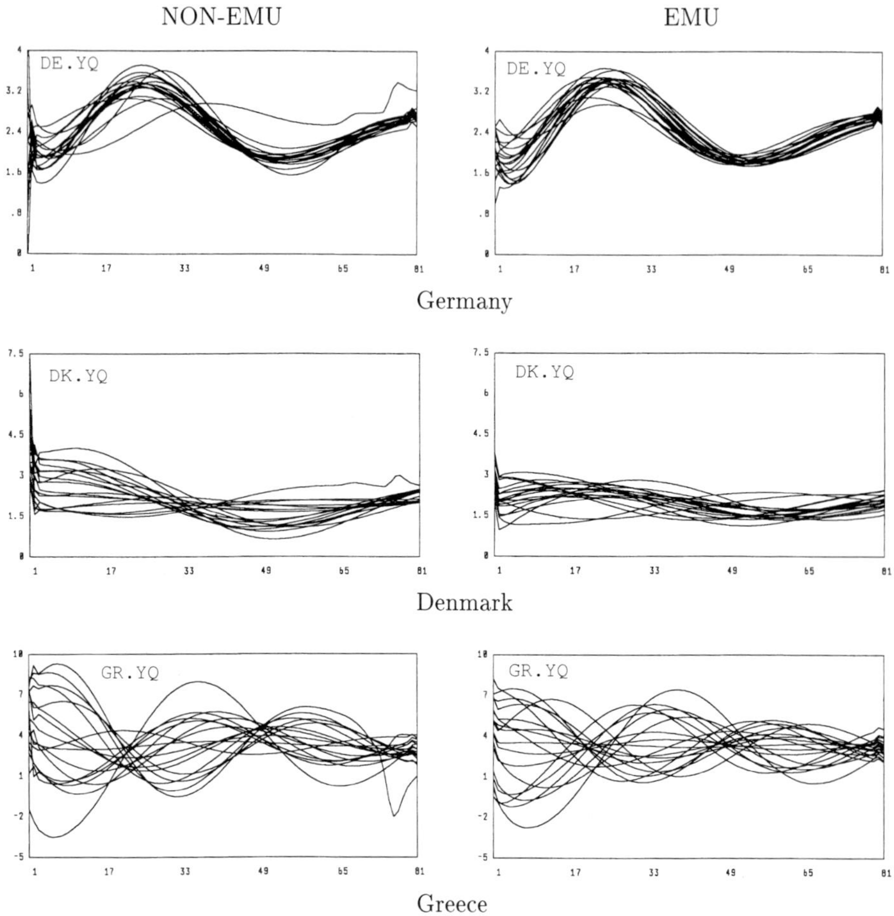

Figure 2: The results for GDP growth in Germany, Denmark and Greece in stochastic simulations over a period of 20 years, with and without an EMU regime for exchange rate determination

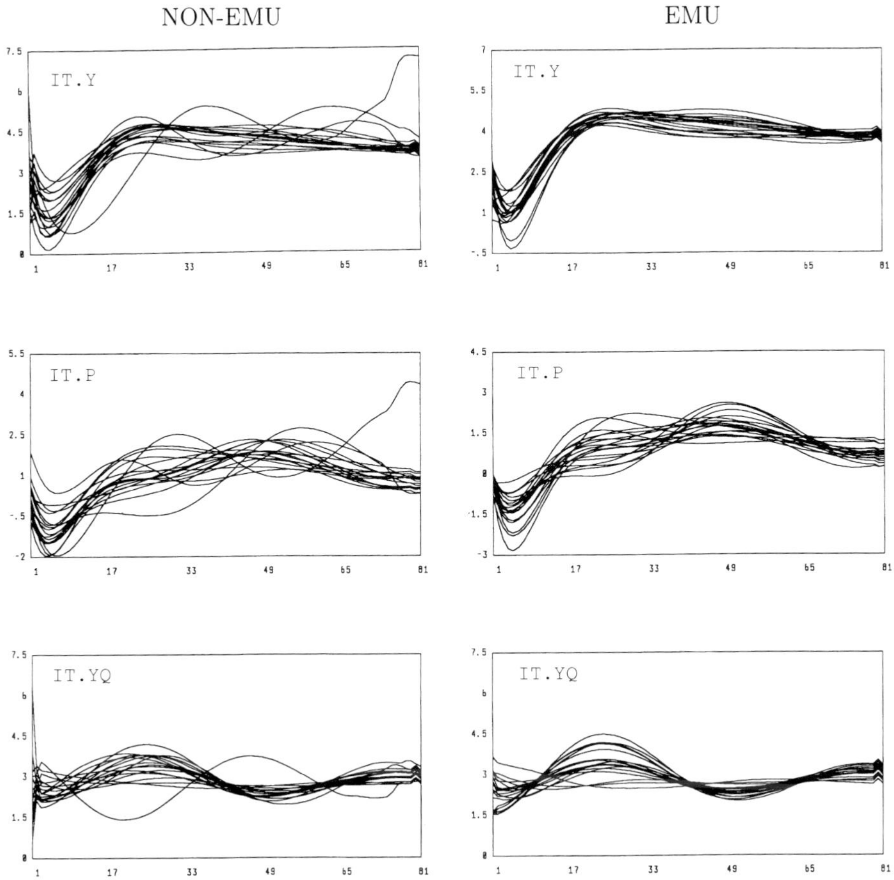

Figure 3: The results for nominal GDP growth, inflation and real GDP growth in Italy in stochastic simulations over a period of 20 years, with and without an EMU regime for exchange rate determination

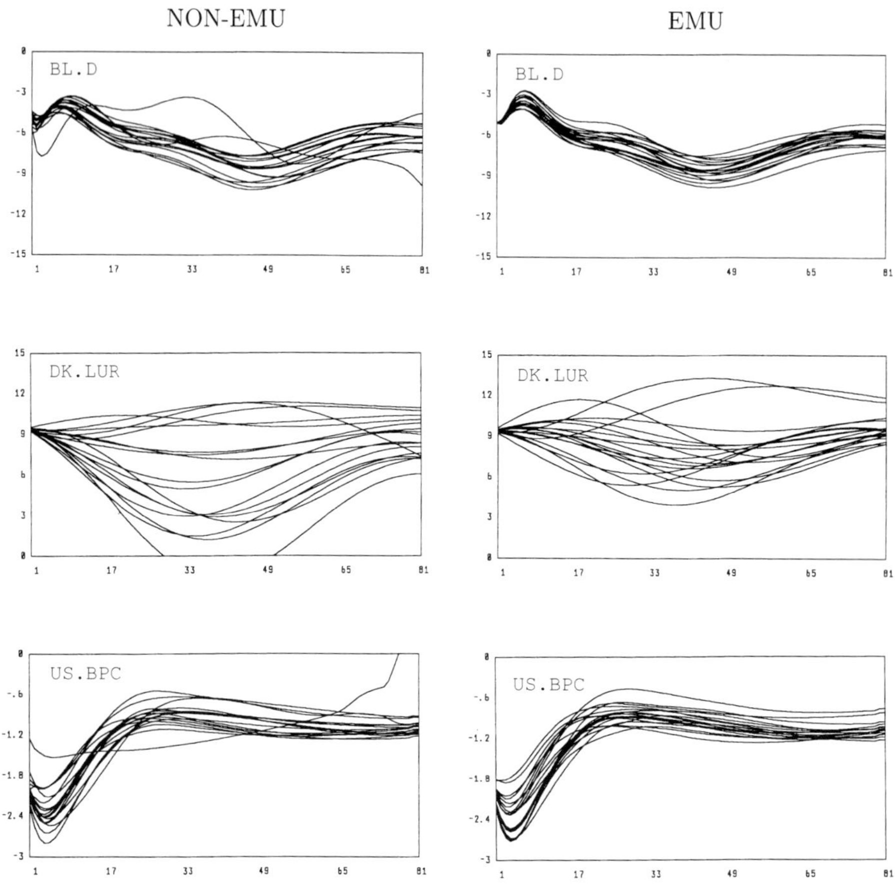

BL.D: Primary budget deficit of the Belgian government (% GDP)
DK.LUR: Danish unemployment rate (% labor force)
US.BPC: Current balance of the United States (% GDP)

Figure 4: Some miscellaneous results of the stochastic simulations with and without an EMU regime for exchange rate determination

by the procedure described in Section 4. It is assumed that there is no correlation between the error terms belonging to different countries. The transmission of the effects runs through the trade linkages expressed by equations (14) and (15) and the relative price changes induced by exchange rate movements. In the "EMU" simulation, the exchange rate responses for all European currencies are generated by the open interest-parity condition for Germany. In addition, it is assumed that the policy discipline in each member state is such that no stochastic shocks occur in the government deficits which are targeted by fiscal policy.

Figure 2 illustrates that the pattern emerging for different countries is rather diverse. Damped oscillations are the result of the differences in the initial conditions in all countries. The figure shows that the impact of stochastic shocks in the "non-EMU" case can be large early in the simulation period, but that does not necessarily affect the dynamic pattern resulting from the initial shock. For Germany the model captures the dynamics of the adjustment process in terms of GDP growth within a margin of error of 1.5% point, after the stochastic disturbance has worked out, and this margin decreases with time. For Denmark, and even stronger for Greece, the girations caused by the stochastic shocks continue to blur the original pattern of adjustment.

Under EMU, the model produces more robust solutions.[3] It would still be unwarranted to present the dynamic responses to an initial shock simulated for Greece and Denmark, but GDP growth rates resulting from the adjustment process are within a tighter band. Figure 3 illustrates that for larger countries, such as Italy, the results of policy analysis may also become more reliable. Some simulations for the "non-EMU" case fail to pick up the feature that nominal GDP is stabilized when stochastic shocks, other than those attributed to fiscal policy, are taken into account. This becomes apparent in the EMU simulations, which show that the variation in nominal GDP growth rates over time is much less than that of real GDP growth and inflation. The combinations of the residuals drawn in the stochastic simulations must be responsible for this pattern. Since fiscal shocks are excluded under EMU, there is a strong presumption that monetary policy is used for nominal GDP targeting in Italy.

The results for some miscellaneous variables for different countries are displayed in Figure 4. The first part of the figure, for instance, shows that in simulations under EMU, the required adjustment of the primary deficit in Belgium receives a more uniform profile. The last part suggests that the current balance of the United States would be little affected by EMU. Finally, Figure 5 contains an arbitrary sample of the exchange rate movements in different member states of the Community in the

3. What is not shown in the figure (except for one curious drawing of parameters which escaped the steady-state requirement of the forward-looking solution algorithm), is the failure rate of the stochastic simulations. In the "non-EMU" case, 17 out of a hundred drawings of the parameters failed to produce a solution, against 3 in the "EMU" case.

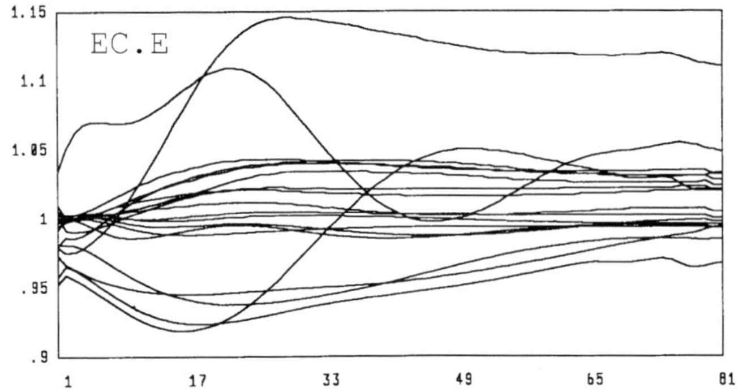

Figure 5: Exchange rate movements in EMS currencies in response to stochastic shocks (non-EMU)

"non-EMU" simulation. The figure suggests that the recent widening of the EMS bandwidths to 30 per cent may not have been too far off the mark, if the objective was to avoid realignments which are solely due to stochastic shocks.

6 Conclusion

Perfect and complete models of the world economy do not exist, but the analysis of existing models can be improved by using the available information on the part which is not modeled in a deterministic sense. In this paper, we have applied stochastic simulations to a maquette of the Quest model. The construction of a maquette helps to distinguish the basic features of the model and to develop a more consistent and practical tool for long-run simulations. We found that the simultaneity in the wage-price block and its interaction with the labor demand function included in the supply block are essential for the dynamic properties of Quest. This becomes even more apparent when the country models are linked in simulation so that supply conditions become important for the competitive position of a country on the world market.

The construction of a maquette has the disadvantage that the stochastic information about the error structure of the model has to be compressed. Some information is inevitably lost. This is perhaps less of a disadvantage when the difficulties in presenting this bulk of information in a somewhat intelligible and accessible manner are recognized. In this paper we have developed and applied a decomposition method, which produces "standardized" shocks for the error terms of the maquette. The results are not entirely satisfactory, but they do seem to indicate that fiscal policy shocks are important and are next in line to external shocks as a source of change.

The differences in the results of the stochastic simulations with and without EMU suggest that, in spite of the relatively low contribution of fiscal shocks to the variation in GDP growth in most of the countries, it can be important to constrain fiscal surprises in some of the countries. In fact, the exchange rate jumps may result to a large extent from fiscal policy shocks. Macroeconomic modeling should pay the highest attention to the determination of policy responses and how they are coordinated internationally between countries and policy makers.

References

Bekx, P., A. Bucher, A. Italianer, and M. Mors (1989), "The Quest model (1988 version)", Economic Papers 75, European Commission, Brussels.

Brandsma, A.S (1989), *Ambition and risk aversion in the design of economic policies*, PhD thesis, Erasmus University, Rotterdam.

Brandsma, A.S. (1994), "The Quest model of the European Community", in S. Ichimura, editor, *Econometric models of Asian-Pacific countries*, Springer-Verlag, Tokyo.

Commission of the European Communities (1991), "Quest: a macroeconometric model for the countries of the European Community as part of the world economy", *European Economy*, **47**, 163–236.

Don, F.J.H. (1993), "Forecast uncertainty in economics", Mimeo, Central Planning Bureau, The Hague.

Emerson, M., D. Gros, A. Italianer, J. Pisany-Ferry, and H. Reichenbach (1992), *One market, one money*, Oxford University Press, Oxford.

Fair, R.C. (1993), "What happened to macroeconometric models?: Testing macroeconometric models", *American Economic Review, Papers and Proceedings*, **83**, 287–293.

Fair, R.C. and J.B. Taylor (1983), "Solution and maximum likelihood estimation of a dynamic nonlinear rational expectations models", *Econometrica*, **51**, 1169–1186.

Fisher, P.G. (1988), "Rational expectations in empirical macroeconomic models", Mimeo, ESRC Macroeconomic Modelling Bureau, Warwick.

Hendry, D.F. (1979), "Predictive failure and econometric modelling in macroeconomics: the transactions demand for money", in P. Ormerod, editor, *Economic Modelling*, Heinemann, London.

Hughes Hallett, A.J. and H. Rees (1983), *Quantitative economic policies and interactive planning: a reconstruction of the theory of economic policy*, Cambridge University Press, Cambridge.

Italianer, A. (1986), *Theory and practice of international trade linkage models*, PhD thesis, University of Groningen, Groningen.

Italianer, A. (1987), "Estimation and simulation of international trade linkages in the Quest model", *European Economy*, **31**, 61–130.

Kendrick, D. (1982), "Stochastic control and uncertainty in dynamic economic systems", in M. Hazewinkel and A.H.G. Rinnooy Kan, editors, *Current developments in the interface: economics, econometrics, mathematics*, D. Reidel Publishing Company, Dordrecht.

Kristensen, K., M. Petersen, and J.S. Sörensen (1993), "On the stability of macroeconomic models", Mimeo, University of Århus, Århus.

Kuh, E. and J. Neese (1982), "Econometric model diagnostics", in G.C. Chow and P. Corsi, editors, *Evaluating the reliability of macro-economic models*, John Wiley, New York; with a discussion by J. Waelbroeck.

Masson, P.R. and S.A. Symansky (1990), "Stochastic simulation results for MULTIMOD", Technical report, Paper presented at the Brookings conference on the empirical evaluation of alternative policy regimes, March 1990.

Röger, W. (1992), "Productivity and the age of the capital stock", Mimeo, Commission of the European Communities, DGII.

Schoonbeek, L. (1989), *Eigenvalues and eigenvectors of macroeconometric models*, PhD thesis, University of Groningen, Groningen.

Sims, C.A. (1980), "Macroeconomics and reality", *Econometrica*, **48**, 1–48.

Methods and Applications of Economic Dynamics
L. Schoonbeek, E. Sterken and S.K. Kuipers (editors)

Chapter 8

Model-consistent learning: some recent developments

Stephen G. Hall and Anthony Garratt

1 Introduction

This paper focuses on the development of adaptive learning mechanisms in large-scale macroeconomic models. Expectations have been a central area of research over the last twenty years both in large empirical models and in analytical work where the main focus has been on rational expectations (RE). However, it is only recently that we have begun to appreciate that whilst the approach of rational expectations may yield important insights into the long-run behavior of an economy it does not accurately characterize the short to medium run. In particular, the expected jumps in expectations variables under RE are not empirically observed and the tendency is for these variables to change more gradually over time. However, the short or medium term is precisely the time horizon which is of most relevance to the policy maker or forecaster. As a result interest has switched towards the adoption of learning as a basis for expectations formation, as potentially this may account for the observed short- to medium-term dynamics of key variables. This has lead to the adoption, in a number of applications, of adaptive learning as a basis for expectations formation.

In the theoretical literature on expectations formation learning has remained an area of relatively minor interest, a number of studies (see below) have addressed the problem of how learning might operate and when it will converge on the rational expectations equilibria. In this literature learning is viewed mainly as a route to achieving RE and as such it is seen as being of only minor interest in the long run.

In this paper we will argue, however, that when our primary concern is with the medium to short run, learning becomes of paramount importance. It may be that in the long run the same equilibrium is reached, but if that long run is decades in the future the adjustment path towards that equilibrium may be very important. Moreover, evidence is mounting that learning can give a very different adjustment path to that given by the RE assumption.

In Section 2 we outline the formal framework for the implementation of learning in the models. For a recent survey of the more general learning literature, see Evans and Honkapohja (1994). Next, we focus, in turn, on some applications of learning in a number of existing models (Section 3), the effects of using alternative learning rules (Section 4), testing procedures for the rational expectations assumption (Section 5), and the use of rules that combine learning with rational expectations (Section 6). We conclude in Section 7.

2 Learning and non-linear models

Learning can be modeled on the basis of a number of assumptions about the underlying knowledge which agents possess. The earlier theoretical literature which used rational learning models is the most demanding in terms of informational requirements, see e.g. Friedman (1975), Townsend (1978, 1983), Frydman (1982), Bray (1983) or Bray and Kreps (1984). The assumption made in this literature is that agents know the true structure of the model but that some of the parameters of the system are unknown. As the true structural equations are known the agents' learning problem is essentially one of estimating the parameters of the system. As long as a consistent estimation procedure is used we would expect the system to converge on a full rational expectations equilibrium (REE), and indeed most of the theoretical investigations of small analytical models have shown this to be the case. Rational learning models, however, still make very stringent assumptions about the degree of knowledge which agents have of the structure of the system. Agents are still assumed to process all available information in an optimal fashion and the degree of sophistication on the part of economic agents is still considerable. The only departure from the strong form of RE is that agents are not assumed to have full information. So they are likely to make mistakes in the short run although they may well not make systematic errors over an extended period and hence the learning model may fulfill the criteria for weak RE.

A weaker informational assumption gives rise to the boundedly rational learning models. Here the general assumption is that agents use some "reasonable" rule of learning to form expectations and that the form of the rule remains constant over time. In fact choosing a rule which all agents regard as reasonable is rather difficult and almost always the choice has been the reduced form of the whole system, see e.g. DeCanio (1979), Radner (1982) and Bray and Savin (1986). Thus it is assumed that agents know the reduced form of the whole system as it would exist under RE but again do not know some or all of the parameters. The move to bounded rationality in this form may seem to be a rather small one and yet it has important consequences for the behavior of the system. The reason for this is that even in the absence of regime changes the reduced form of the model is a combination of the stable structural equations and the changing parameters of the expectations rule, so that it is time varying. The boundedly rational agent is usually assumed to be attempting to parameterize a stable reduced form system and so is actually trying to estimate a misspecified model. Under this assumption Bray and Savin (1986) are able to show that, for a simple cobweb model, the model sometimes converges to the RE equilibrium and sometimes cycles or diverges from the RE equilibrium.

The behavior of the parameters in the learning rule gives an important insight into the form of equilibria which may emerge from the system. Evans (1989), Evans and Honkapohja (1990, 1992a, 1992b, 1992c, 1994) introduce the concept of E-stability, defining a set of conditions for stability across a range of linear and non-linear models which include the adaptive learning rule. Marcet and Sargent (1988) summarize the main results. The concept of learning is characterized as a mapping of the parameters of the agents' expectations rule. A fixed point of that mapping is then a situation where the parameters of the expectations rule cease changing. So suppose an agent has a rule which is a linear function of a set of parameters D and the learning process – assumed to be some form of least-squares learning – is represented by a mapping S, such that $D_{t+1} = S(D_t)$. Hence the learning process produces a sequence of parameters of the expectations rule. Then the concept of E-stability is defined in terms of the mapping S, of the perceived law of motion (the expectations rule) to the actual law of motion, where a solution is said to be E-stable if the difference equation above is locally asymptotically stable. A fixed point of the mapping is represented by convergence of this sequence to some fixed value. This point is sometimes referred to as an expectations equilibrium or an E-equilibrium. Marcet and Sargent (1989a) demonstrate that this fixed point is also a full rational expectations equilibrium. Furthermore, Evans (1983, 1986a, 1986b), Marcet and Sargent (1989a, 1989b) and Woodford (1990) demonstrate that the least-squares learning procedure actually rules out many of the undesirable equilibria which can arise among the conventional rational expectations equilibria. When a fixed point of the mapping is found we not only have a RE solution but we also have one which is not dependent on an arbitrary terminal condition.

E-stability conditions can resolve or at least aid in the problem of choosing a solution where a multiplicity of solutions exist, see Evans (1986b). For example, in the case where two solutions exist it may be possible to classify one as not satisfying the criteria for E-stability, and therefore to identify the other solution as the form to be adopted. The degree to which the use of adaptive learning schemes aids in the choice of an appropriate equilibrium, in case multiple equilibria are possible, depends on the form of the learning scheme adopted. It may be the case that all solutions satisfy E-stability criteria, in that case the choice is not narrowed. In addition, Evans (1989) and Evans and Honkapohja (1990, 1992a, 1992b, 1992c, 1994) make a distinction between weak and strong E-stability. For example, take the case where the solution to a structural model, which has multiple equilibria, is classified as having an AR(1) representation. Where the perceived law of motion is an AR(1) process this may imply that one of say two possible solutions is unstable, and therefore aid in the selection. If this result can be shown to hold when the perceived law of motion is overparameterized (e.g. as an AR(4) or more general ARIMA model where E-stability still holds) then the solution is said to be strongly E-stable. Hence a variation on the perceived law of motion around an AR(1) still enables the learning model to converge on an E-stable solution.

2.1 Model-consistent learning

Below we outline the framework adopted in this paper which involves the combination of a large-scale non-linear macroeconomic model and adaptive learning. Let the model which incorporates expectations be described by the following set of n structural equations

$$Y_{it} = F_i(Y, X, Y^e_{t,t+1}) \qquad i = 1, \ldots, n; \;\; t = 1, \ldots, T \tag{1}$$

where Y is a vector of current and lagged values of the n endogenous variables, X is a vector of exogenous variables over all time periods (periods $1, \ldots, T$) and $Y^e_{t,t+1}$ is the expectation based on information available at time t of Y in period $t+1$.[1] Over the period of the simulation Y_{it} represents the model solution of the i-th endogenous variable at moment t and the lagged values are previous model solutions.

In our application we assume that agents, at time t, have the perceived law of motion or expectations rule of the following form

$$Y^e_{t,t+1} = D'_t Z_t + e_{1t} \quad \text{where} \quad e_{1t} \sim (0, W) \tag{2}$$

which they use to form current period's expectations of the next period's value of Y, or by leading the equation to form expectations with a longer lead time. The vector Z is the information set which can consist of a subset of the matrices Y and X over all current and lagged time periods, and D is a time-varying matrix of parameters which agents possess and which evolves according to the following process

$$D_t = D_{t-1} + e_{2t} \quad \text{where} \quad e_{2t} \sim (0, Q) \tag{3}$$

1. A more general expectations term can be included which allows for expectations further into the future. In this paper we only deal with expectations one period ahead.

The change in the learning parameters is therefore determined by the value of the Q matrix, the hyperparameters of the state equation, where the coefficient on the lagged D term is always set to be equal to unity (or the identity matrix in a systems context). Having specified the mechanism which governs the evolution of these parameters through time it is possible to make the whole learning apparatus operational.

2.2 Method of updating

In adaptive learning schemes we assume that agents utilize a standard statistical or econometric procedure for estimating the expectations rule or the perceived law of motion of the system. The assumption is that some element of the rule is not known with certainty. This element of uncertainty is usually taken to be the parameters of the rule. The basic idea is that through time the economic agent will use the specified statistical method to increase his knowledge about the true value of these parameters.[2] The forecasts needed in decision-making are then computed from the estimated law of motion. Agents are therefore boundedly rational in that the economic agents use models that are misspecified while they are learning, i.e. outside the rational expectations equilibrium.

The statistical framework we adopt in this application for the updating of the learning parameters is the Kalman filter. Equation (2), the perceived law of motion, is the measurement equation and equation (3) is an AR(1) representation of the states of the system. The W and Q matrices are the hyperparameters of the system. Below, in equations (4) to (7), we define the recursive stochastic algorithm which determines the change in the learning parameters. The updating of the parameters is governed by the combination of the prediction and updating equations, which can be shown to be of the same form as those in Marcet and Sargent (1989a, 1989b). Therefore, their theorem regarding convergence can be applied.

The prediction equations are equal to[3]

$$\hat{D}_{t|t-1} = \hat{D}_{t-1} \tag{4}$$

$$P_{t|t-1} = P_{t-1} + Q \tag{5}$$

whereas the updating equations read[4]

---

2. The underlying parameters are assumed to be constant over time.
3. If the Q matrix is set to zero then the Kalman filter algorithm described in (4) to (7) becomes the familiar least-squares algorithm described in Harvey (1990, p. 53). In our case Q is an estimated matrix, where we restrict the off-diagonal elements to be zero but allow the elements on the diagonal to differ from one another. This amounts to weighted recursive least squares.
4. For simplicity we only present the formulas for the univariate case where D is $(n \times 1)$, P is $(n \times n)$, Z is $(n \times 1)$, Y is (1×1) and W is (1×1).

$$\hat{D}_t = \hat{D}_{t|t-1} + P_{t|t-1} Z_t (Y_t - Z_t' \hat{D}_{t|t-1}) / (Z_t' P_{t|t-1} Z_t + W) \tag{6}$$

$$P_t = P_{t|t-1} - P_{t|t-1} Z_t Z_t' P_{t|t-1} / (Z_t' P_{t|t-1} Z_t + W) \tag{7}$$

The solution sequence combines the learning algorithm described in (4) to (7) above with (1) to (3) in the following way. Assuming we know D_{t-1} (i.e. $\hat{D}_{t-1}$) we can solve (3) for the expected value of D_t (i.e. $\hat{D}_{t|t-1}$), which is simply given by the Kalman filter prediction equations for D, equation (4). Given the expected value of D_t we can solve (2) for the expected value of $Y^e_{t,t+1}$, and therefore we can solve (1) for Y_t. The matrix Q (the covariance matrix of the errors in the equations governing the evolution of the parameters, or in Kalman filter terms the state equation error terms) used in the prediction equation (5), is computed when estimating the expectations rule by time-varying parameter methods. The same estimation also provides us with the starting value for the matrix P_{t-1} (the uncertainty of the parameters or state variables). We can therefore use the Kalman filter prediction equation for P, in order to derive an estimate of $P_{t|t-1}$. Having solved the complete model equation (1) for Y_t, we can define $V_t = Z'_{t-1} D_{t-1} - Y_t = Y^e_{t-1|t} - Y_t$, i.e. the error which occurs between the expectation of the vector Y_t derived from the learning model and the model's final solution for Y_t. We then use the Kalman filter updating equations (6) and (7) in order to derive revised estimates of P_t and D_t. Hence the updating evolves according to the observed errors between the whole model's solution and the original expectations model forecast. The process can then be repeated for the next period, starting from the new updated estimates of D_t to predict D_{t+1}, and so on. In this way the learning model will adjust its own parameters to cope with any change in structure or regime of the whole model.[5]

The underlying assumptions of the learning process are really still quite strong and the spirit of the approach is not strongly divorced from that of the rational expectations approach. Agents are still assumed to process all available information in an optimal fashion and the degree of sophistication on the part of economic agents is still considerable. The only departure from the strong form of RE is that agents are not assumed to have full information. So they are likely to make mistakes in the short run. However, to converge on a rational expectations equilibrium agents are required not to make systematic errors over an extended period. The assumed informational demands are weaker and therefore more acceptable in the learning case than under the strong RE assumption.

5. Convergence is possible as we operate in a deterministic world, see Bullard (1992).

3 Some implementations of learning

The first application of learning in a large-scale macroeconomic model is in the work of Hall and Garratt (1992). This work used a learning model of the exchange rate sector in the London Business School (LBS) model of the UK economy, which is a large quarterly forecasting model. The incorporated expected exchange rate model had the following form

$$E^e_{t|t+1} = \gamma_{0t} + \gamma_{1t}E_{t-1} + \gamma_{2t}r^d_{t-1} + \gamma_{3t}INF^{uk}_{t-1} + \gamma_{4t}T^{uk}_{t-1} + \gamma_{5t}PO_{t-1} \tag{8}$$

where E is the log of the real Sterling-Deutsche Mark exchange rate, r^d is the real interest differential with Germany, INF is the annual rate of UK producer price inflation, T is the log of the ratio of UK exports to imports and PO is the log of the price of North-Sea oil.[6]

The specific experiment reported was a change of regime so as to peg the exchange rate against the Deutsche Mark in two different ways. First, by fixing the rate at the current level (2.91 DM/£) which entailed no obvious discrete change of policy and, second, by fixing the rate at a level (2.96 DM/£) higher than that prevailing, which implied an implicit announcement effect because of the immediate change. In both cases the learning parameters converged although, as expected, at rather different rates and the announcement effect led to faster convergence. The convergence of the constant and the parameter of the lagged exchange rate are illustrated in Figures 1 and 2. What actually occurred as a result of the UK entry into the ERM is that the risk premium on the Sterling remained large, narrowing only gradually as private agents learnt (perhaps erroneously, in fact) about the commitment to the ERM parity. Only over time the DM/£ interest differential did narrow. The learning approach is able to incorporate these effects through the updating of expectations as the actual model variables react to the new regime, which in turn effects the model's outcome in the next period. It is also able to assess the effect of the choice of the initial parity on subsequent learning and credibility issues. By contrast, the RE assumption cannot address these questions.

A further application of this form of learning is given in Barrel *et al.* (1994), where three learning rules are incorporated into the Global Econometric Model (GEM) – jointly maintained by the London Business School and the National Institute of Economic and Social Research – in the form of prices' expectations terms in the wage sectors of the UK, Italy and France. A range of experiments was carried out to illustrate the behavior of the learning mechanism: realignments were carried out for each of the countries' exchange rates and an oil price simulation was undertaken as a general world shock. This is possibly the first instance where a number of learning rules have been combined simultaneously in the same model, so that in

6. Note that information lagged one period, rather than current information was used in this instance.

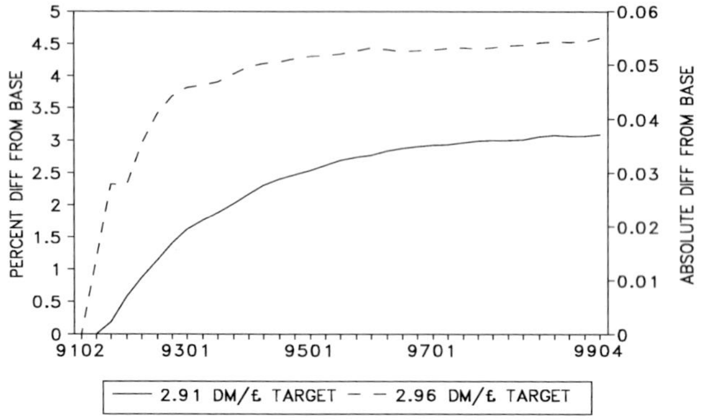

Figure 1: Effects of exchange rate regimes on the intercept of model (8)

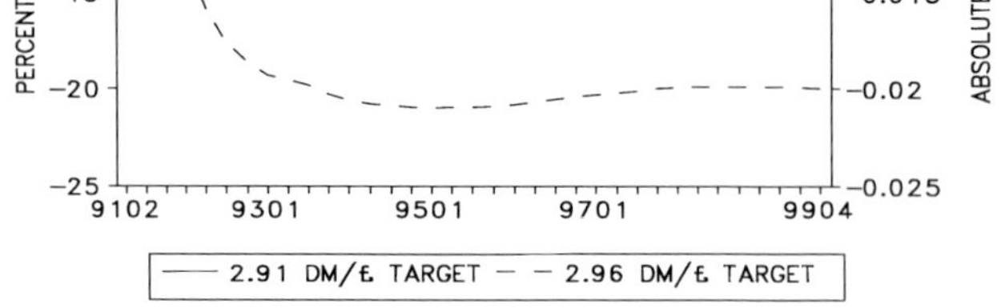

Figure 2: Effects of exchange rate regimes on the lagged exchange rate coefficient of model (8)

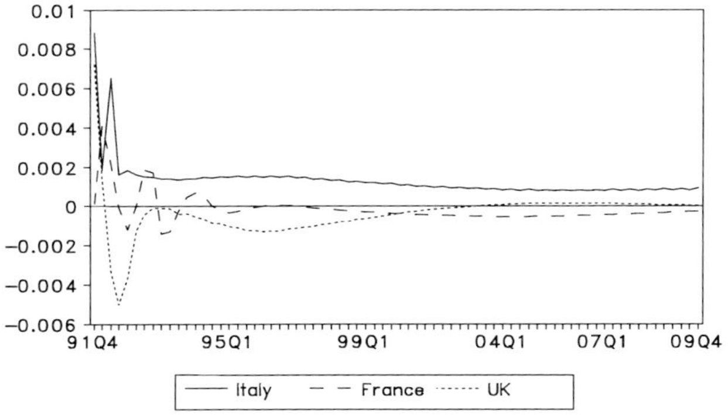

Figure 3: Expectations errors of prices. Realignments in Italy, France and the UK

effect the learning has not only to learn about the model but also about the other learning processes taking place. Despite this added dimension of complexity the model still seems to have achieved a RE solution. Figure 3 shows the behavior of the expectations errors made while forecasting prices in each of the own country realignments. In our view these represent a convergence towards zero and hence a RE solution. The parameters of the learning rules equally suggest convergence but for space reasons we will not report them here. Figure 4 reports the expectations errors made when forecasting prices in the face of an oil price shock where oil prices are raised for five years and then returned to their original value. The interesting feature here is that large errors occur both in case oil prices are raised and in case they are returned to their base values. In contrast with a model-consistent expectations solution the early part of the solution is not affected by the fact that eventually oil prices will return to their base values, as this is not part of the information set.

A third application of this approach to expectations formation may be found in Hall and Symansky (1993) where the RE terms in the IMF MULTIMOD model were replaced with learning rules. Here, once again convergence to an expectations equilibrium occurred fairly reliably and there was little change in the long-run properties of the model. The short-run adjustment path of the model was however significantly altered.

These three studies establish that learning in this way can work effectively with a number of obvious benefits over the standard model-consistent expectations assumption. However, they leave a number of questions unanswered. In particular: How can we test the appropriateness of the RE assumption? How can future

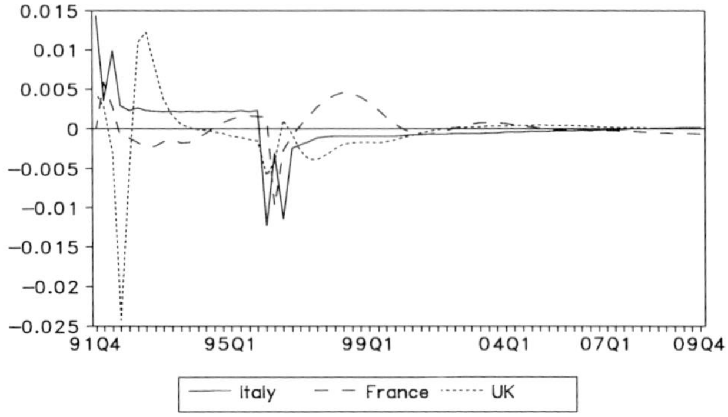

Figure 4: Expectations errors of prices. Oil price shock (of 100% for five years) in Italy, France and the UK

information be incorporated into the learning rule? And, how important is the specification of a particular learning rule to a model's properties? The next sections will address these questions.

4 Varying the learning rule

The applications of learning described above have been conducted conditional on particular expectations rules which have a given set of variables. These systems must always contain a degree of arbitrariness since there are many expectations rules we might have implemented. This raises questions of how this choice may affect the uniqueness of the equilibrium, and if it is attained, the likelihood of attaining the equilibrium and the uniqueness of the dynamic path to equilibrium. In this section we report on work carried out in Hall and Garratt (1993) to investigate the effects of varying the expectations rule on the results of a simple application to the London Business School model.

The starting point is the application of Hall and Garratt (1992) described in Section 3 and the expectations rule (8) for the exchange rate. This rule is incorporated, in conjunction with an uncovered interest parity condition for the determination of the exchange rate, into the LBS model. The experiment is then to subject the LBS model to a permanent increase in the price of oil of 100% for the period 1990Q1 to 2000Q4 (44 periods) under a number of alternative expectations rules.

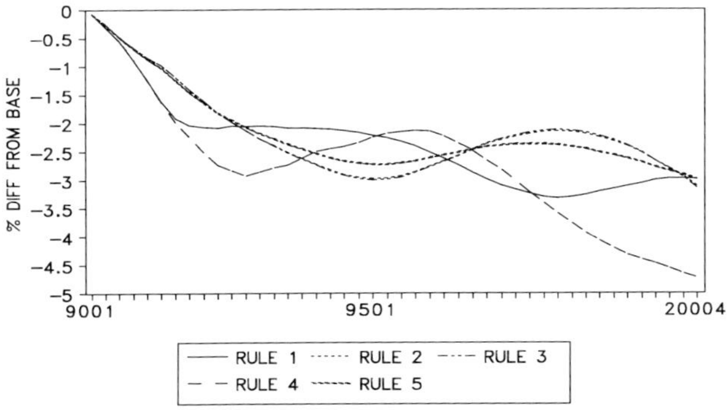

Figure 5: Comparison of learning rules. Change in % in GDP from 100% oil price shock

We proceed by examining a number of variants of the expectations rule. First, we investigate simplified versions of equation (8). Hence Rules 2-5 below are restricted versions of (8), where the variables not included are set to zero as opposed to remaining in the rule but with parameters which are constant over time. Second, we examined the effects of different hyperparameters and variance-covariance matrices used when updating the time-varying parameters. Third, we conducted a preliminary look at the effects of rules which are not nested by (8) but have endogenous parameters with varying degrees of theory-based relevance for expectations of the exchange rate.

The simple rules are of the following form:

(i) Rule 1 – equation (8), cf. Hall and Garratt (1992);
(ii) Rule 2 – time-varying intercept;
(iii) Rule 3 – time-varying intercept and lagged exchange rate only;
(iv) Rule 4 – time-varying intercept, lagged exchange rate and oil prices;
(v) Rule 5 – time-varying intercept, lagged exchange rate and inflation.

In Figure 5 we plot the response of output (as a percentage difference from base) to the oil price shock for the five variants of the rules. The most striking feature of Figure 5 is the tendency of the implied output fall (in four out of the five rules) to be of the same order of magnitude (in period 44), i.e. approximately 3% less than base. The exception to this result is Rule 4 where the effect on output is clearly not at the same value in the end period. In the case of Figure 5, the criteria for convergence (expectation errors tending to zero and constant movement of the time-varying parameters) are more clearly satisfied for the four rules that move

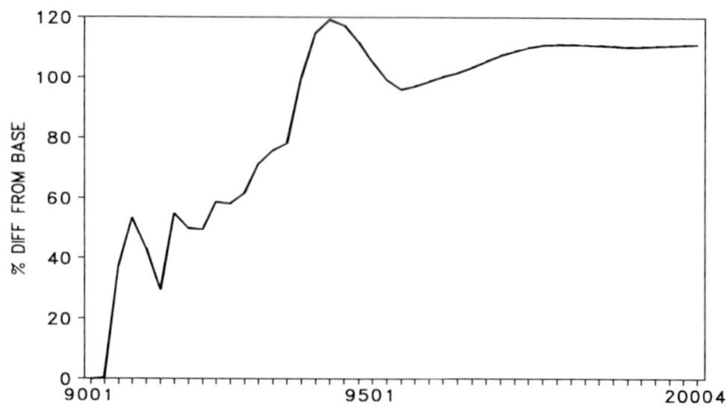

Figure 6: Oil learning coefficient – Rule 1 (oil price shock of 100%)

to the same output change than for Rule 4. Hence we might tentatively conclude that where convergence does occur the same equilibrium value for output results from a range of information sets used in forming expectations. Regarding Rule 4 it may well be the case in the very long run that all the different rules converge on the same value. Figure 6 plots what is a typical example of the movement of the learning parameters where convergence has been achieved. The period of learning is approximately five years with significant movements in the parameters ceasing after 1995 (a similar timing is apparent in the movement of output in Figure 4). A notable feature of the speed of adjustment to the long-run value is that there is little variation between the alternative rules. The paths during the movement to the long run do vary somewhat, with Rule 1, i.e. equation (8), being the least cyclical of the movements.

The results are very sensitive to the size of the hyperparameters and the related variance-covariance matrix. The combination of these two elements determines the extent of the change in the learning parameters conditional on a given error term. Hence if both the hyperparameter and the variance and related covariances of a particular variable are set to zero then the parameter ceases to vary over time. Figures 7 and 8 report the expectations error and movement in the time-varying parameter associated with the oil price variable for Rule 4 (for a 10% shock) where the modification is a small adjustment in the hyperparameters. The first six periods of the simulation solve but both the error and therefore the change in the learning coefficient become explosive in period 7 causing no solution to be found. Similar

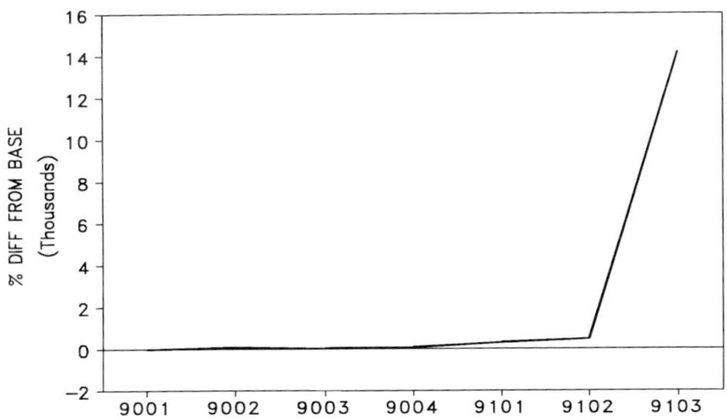

Figure 7: Expectations error – modified rule (oil price shock of 10%)

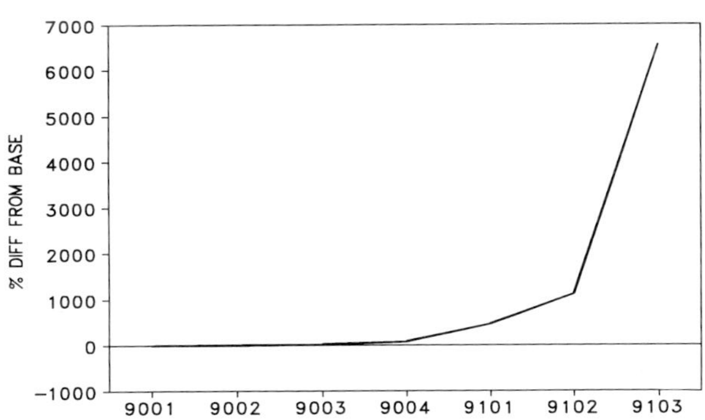

Figure 8: Oil learning coefficient – modified rule (oil price shock of 10%)

pictures can be shown for Rule 5 where relatively small changes in hyperparameters can cause no solution to be found. Generally it is the case that a range of hyperparameters exist such that for most rules a solution can be found. However, the results will vary significantly for the same rule but with different hyperparameters. As a further generalization we believe that sufficiently large hyperparameters (i.e. very fast learning) will always induce explosive behavior and non-convergence to an expectations equilibrium.

The values of the hyperparameters are therefore important and hence we require a method which gives the most efficient and neutral way of finding the range of values which give a solution. Statistical estimation is the most obvious way of doing this and it is interesting that the most robust rule is Rule 1 which was chosen on estimation criteria without any view to achieving a particular model solution. However, estimation alone does not always yield a stable rule. We have also found that it is important to find a rule which passes a broad range of diagnostics and which seems well specified (both Rule 4 and 5 did not solve using the estimated hyperparameters from what was evidently a poorly specified equation).

Finally, if we used in our investigations variables that were endogenous but not clearly related to the exchange rate the estimated values would not yield a solution, even for a 10% oil price shock, although again the relevant equations were clearly inadequate statistically.

5 Testing the strong form of RE

The standard approach of testing the RE assumption in many settings is to take some measure of the expectation of a series, such as the forward exchange rate as a measure of the expected future spot rate, and then to see if any information available in the information set is able to add explanatory power. Under the RE assumption all available information should be analyzed in the most efficient possible way, so nothing in the information set can add any extra explanatory power over the RE expectation itself, see e.g. Hodrick (1987). Hall and Symansky (1993) proposed a testing procedure which proceeds in exactly the same fashion but which allows a joint test of the RE assumption and the assumption that agents are using a particular model to form their expectations.

Under the strong RE assumption, i.e. (1) and $Y^e_{t,t+1} = Y_{t+1}$, we can restate the fully restricted solution to the model as

$$Y_{it} = h_i(X_1, \dots, X_T, Y_1, \dots, Y_{t-1}) \qquad i = 1, \dots, n; \;\; t = 1, \dots, T \tag{9}$$

Equation (9) represents the fully restricted reduced form forecast of the model based only on information available at time t (compared with equation (1) we exclude current values of Y). Hall and Symansky set up the null hypothesis that h is the true RE forecast of Y_t and therefore the expectations error should be a white noise innovation which is impossible to predict from the available information set. This may be tested simply by estimating a model of the following form

$$Y_t = B(L)X_t + \Gamma h(X_1, \ldots, X_T, D_t, Y_1, \ldots, Y_{t-1}) \tag{10}$$

where h is the fully restricted reduced form of the system and D_t defines the learning parameters. Under the null hypothesis, that we have the true model and agents know and use this model, we expect $B = 0$ and the coefficient on h to be unity (or the identity matrix in a systems context). If, however, we do not have the true model or if there is some real-world departure from rationality then this may be captured in the model by some of the parameters in the B-vector (or B-matrix in a systems context) being nonzero. This is an explicit test of the restrictions imposed in the h-formulation.

Hall and Symansky proposed to construct a time series of forecasts from a given model and to use these in a formal test such as (10). However, this test is a rather weak one as we are limiting the way the information set is being used rather severely. The alternative to the RE assumption is a simple fixed-parameter extrapolative rule and we know that if the data period has contained important regime changes this rule may not perform well. Therefore, they also proposed to set up a more general form of this test where the alternative is an explicit learning model. This would have the form of

$$Y_t = B_{t|t-1}(L)X_t + \Gamma h(X_1, \ldots, X_T, D_t, Y_1, \ldots, Y_{t-1}) \tag{11}$$

where the term $B_{t|t-1}$ is the time-varying parameter. If a test such as (11) rejects the RE assumption, how should we then proceed to deal with expectations in the model? Their suggestion is to work directly with the information set which has proved to be superior in the formal testing. I.e. if both parts of (11) hold some explanatory power then we should use both of them in the model to form expectations. In effect (11) will become the expectations generating equation in the model. This would nest the standard RE solution within it as a special case. It would modify the jump properties of the simple RE model however if the estimation found the non-RE parts of the model to be important. It would also retain the basic property of the RE model that a change in any future exogenous variable would potentially have a big impact on the present.

6 Combining learning with rational expectations

In this section we will consider how the modified expectations rule, which contains future information, can be incorporated into an econometric model. This can be done quite simply by using (11) directly as an equation which generates the expectations variables in the model. Equation (11) can be given a slightly different interpretation by reparameterizing it as follows as

$$Y_t = (1 - \Gamma)\zeta_{t|t-1}(L)X_t + \Gamma h(X_1, \ldots, X_T, D_t, Y_1, \ldots, Y_{t-1})$$
$$\text{where } (1 - \Gamma)\zeta_{t|t-1}(L) = B_{t|t-1}(L) \tag{12}$$

This then weights together two parts, the standard RE solution given by h and the learning expectation given by the time-varying parameter model. There is, however, a further complication which rests in the fact that h is the reduced form of model (1) and the expectations rule, taken to be $Y^e_{t,t+1} = Y_{t+1}$ under RE. There are three ways to proceed now. The first is to use the following algorithm to build up a solution for the periods $t, \ldots, T$. To begin with set $k = 0$. Next:

(a) Set $\Gamma = I$ and solve the model for periods $j = t + k, \ldots, T$. Define Y^{RE} as the solution and set it equal to h.

(b) Set $\Gamma = \Gamma^*$, the estimated value defined from equation (12). Then with $h(Y^{RE})$ fixed solve the model for periods $j = t + k, \ldots, T$.

(c) This gives the solution for period $t + k$. If $t + k = T$ stop, otherwise set $k = k + 1$ and go to (a).

A much easier alternative is simply to solve the model with the new expectations rule in it, although this will not be a true reflection of the dynamics of the rationality test because h will be modified by the new learning rule.

A final alternative is to recognize that the learning rule should be part of the model structure once we have rejected the simple RE assumption. The way to estimate this weighting pattern is to derive a time series of forward model solutions based on an arbitrary Γ, and next to estimate an equation which includes time-varying parameters along with endogenous and exogenous variables to derive a new value for Γ, and then to iterate over this procedure to convergence.

Our preferred procedure is to use expectations which arise from time-varying parameters combined with endogenous and exogenous variables to test the RE assumption and then to use the final one of the three options discussed above to estimate a parameter based on a combination of learning and model-consistent expectations. This reflects true rationality on the part of the rational agents.

7 Conclusion

Recent developments in the learning literature have emphasized the limitations of the rational expectations assumption. It is perhaps in the large empirical models where the weakness of the RE assumption has become most apparent. As a tool for analyzing long-run behavior in abstract, RE is both powerful and useful. But it is not a good representation of the short-run dynamic behavior of many markets and the large models have really emphasized this weakness. The natural progression of the treatment of expectations effects is to move from the strong RE assumption to a learning model which allows the possibility of making errors in the short run but rules out systematic errors over the long run. This gives rise to the introduction of learning models. These have remained to a large extent a side issue in the theoretical literature, but it is our view that these models will constitute an increasingly important feature of the empirical models. This represents a step back from the assumption of full rationality in expectations towards the ideas of bounded rationality which are more consistent with the psychological literature on learning processes. Current work suggests that where a learning rule is well specified, estimated and tested using reasonable statistical criteria it will converge to an expectations equilibrium. The equilibrium will probably be unique, assuming the model itself generates only a single equilibrium. However, the dynamic path to that equilibrium can vary significantly between different expectations rules and it seems certain that there are some values for the rate of learning which will preclude the possibility of an expectations equilibrium being reached.

References

Barrell, R., G.M. Caporale, A. Garratt, and S.G. Hall (1994), "Learning about monetary union: an analysis of boundedly rational learning in European labour markets", in S.G. Hall, editor, *Applied economic forecasting techniques*, Simon and Schuster, London.

Bray, M.M. (1983), "Convergence to rational expectations equilibrium", in R. Frydman and E.S. Phelps, editors, *Industrial forecasting and aggregate outcomes*, Cambridge University Press, Cambridge.

Bray, M.M. and D.M. Kreps (1984), "Rational learning and rational expectation", Mimeo, Cambridge University, Cambridge.

Bray, M.M. and N.E. Savin (1986), "Rational expectations equilibria, learning and model specification", *Econometrica*, **54**, 1129–1160.

Bullard, J. (1992), "Time-varying parameters and nonconvergence to rational expectations under least squares learning", *Economics Letters*, **40**, 159–166.

DeCanio, S.J. (1979), "Rational expectations and learning from experience", *Quarterly Journal of Economics*, **93**, 47–57.

Evans, G.W. (1983), "The stability of rational expectations in macroeconomic models", in R. Frydman and E.S. Phelps, editors, *Individual forecasting and aggregate outcomes*, Cambridge University Press, Cambridge.

Evans, G.W. (1986a), "Expectational stability and the multiple equilibria problem in linear rational expectations models", *Quarterly Journal of Economics*, **100**, 1217–1233.

Evans, G.W. (1986b), "Selection criteria for models with non-uniqueness", *Journal of Monetary Economics*, **12**, 147–157.

Evans, G.W. (1989), "The fragility of sunspots and bubbles", *Journal of Monetary Economics*, **23**, 297–317.

Evans, G.W. and S. Honkapohja (1990), "Learning, convergence and stability with multiple rational expectations equilibria", Discussion Paper TE/90/212, STICERD LSE, London.

Evans, G.W. and S. Honkapohja (1992a), "On the robustness of bubbles in linear RE models", *International Economic Review*, **33**, 1–14.

Evans, G.W. and S. Honkapohja (1992b), "Local convergence of recursive learning to steady states and cycles in stochastic nonlinear models", Discussion Paper TE/92/236, STICERD LSE, London.

Evans, G.W. and S. Honkapohja (1992c), "On the local stability of sunspot equilibria under adaptive learning rules", Discussion Paper TE/92/249, STICERD LSE, London, forthcoming in Journal of Economic Theory.

Evans, G.W. and S. Honkapohja (1994), "Adaptive learning and expectational stability: an introduction", in A. Kirman and M. Salman, editors, *Learning and rationality in economics*, Basil Blackwell, Oxford, forthcoming.

Friedman, B.M. (1975), "Rational expectations are really adaptive after all", Discussion Paper 430, Howard Institute of Economic Research.

Frydman, R. (1982), "Towards an understanding of market processes, individual expectations: learning and convergence to rational expectations equilibrium", *American Economic Review*, **72**, 652–668.

Hall, S.G. and A. Garrat (1992), "Model consistent learning: the Sterling Deutschmark rate in the London Business School model", Discussion Paper 92-02, LBS-CEF, London.

Hall, S.G. and A. Garrat (1993), "Convergence and stability of E-equilibria to varying learning rules", Mimeo, London Business School, London.

Hall, S.G. and S.A. Symansky (1993), "Modifying the rational expectations assumption in a large world forecasting model", Mimeo, International Monetary Fund, Washington DC.

Harvey, A. (1990), *The econometric analysis of time series*, second edition, Phillip Allan, Oxford.

Hodrick, R.J. (1987), *The empirical evidence on the efficiency of forward and futures exchange markets*, Harwood Academic Publishers, London.

Marcet, A. and T.J. Sargent (1988), "The fate of systems with adaptive expectations", *American Economic Review*, **80**, 168–171.

Marcet, A. and T.J. Sargent (1989a), "Convergence of least-squares learning in environment with hidden state variables and private information", *Journal of Political Economy*, **97**, 1306–1322.

Marcet, A. and T.J. Sargent (1989b), "Least squares learning and the dynamics of hyperinflation", in W.A. Barnett, J. Geweke, and K. Shell, editors, *Economic complexity, chaos, sunspots, bubbles and nonlinearity*, Cambridge University Press, Cambridge.

Radner, R. (1982), "Equilibrium under uncertainty", in K.J. Arrow and M.D. Intriligator, editors, *Handbook of mathematical economics, volume 2*, North-Holland, Amsterdam.

Townsend, R.M. (1978), "Market anticipation, rational expectation and Bayesian analysis", *International Economic Review*, **19**, 481–494.

Townsend, R.M. (1983), "Forecasting the forecast of others", *Journal of Political Economy*, **91**, 546–588.

Woodford, M. (1990), "Learning to believe in sunspots", *Econometrica*, **58**, 277–308.

Methods and Applications of Economic Dynamics
L. Schoonbeek, E. Sterken and S.K. Kuipers (editors)

Chapter 9

Policy simulations and long-run sustainability in forward-looking macroeconometric models [1]

Peter N. Smith and Kenneth F. Wallis

1 Introduction

The sustainability of fiscal policy is high on the agenda of policy makers and macroeconometric modelers. For policy makers in many OECD countries the size of the government budget deficit has become an important issue in recent years, while members of the European Community in particular are now required by the Maastricht Treaty to control both the size of the deficit and the volume of debt, as proportions of GDP. This policy concern has led to model-based assessments of the impact and feasibility of such criteria; for example Barrell *et al.* (1993), using the National Institute Global Econometric Model (NIGEM), estimate that the application of the Maastricht criteria will in general be contractionary. Such criteria can be thought of as providing a form of solvency requirement or financial closure rule, and the issues surrounding the use of such rules in large-scale macroeconometric models are the subject of this paper.

The government budget restraint, that total government expenditure must equal the total flow of financing from all sources, including printing money, was introduced into the standard IS/LM model in the classic article by Christ (1968). The government expenditure multiplier cannot then be defined without an assumption about how the expenditure is to be financed. Modelers have typically calculated such multipliers by means of simulation experiments conducted under one of two

1. The assistance of Peter Mitchell and the financial support of the Economic and Social Research Council are gratefully acknowledged.

polar assumptions, namely unchanged interest rates or unchanged monetary aggregates. The first implies that increases in money demand are fully accommodated and the rest of the deficit is financed by issuing bonds; the second implies purely bond finance. While these do not necessarily represent realistic monetary policy assumptions, they do provide standard settings within which simulation results can be readily interpreted and compared. Government bonds did not appear in Christ's original model; in a subsequent article (Christ, 1979), he extended the model to include them, and reviewed the growing body of results on the instability of bond finance. These concern the possibility that bond financing of the budget deficit may generate a cumulative downward spiral of income and tax revenue, leading to an ever widening budget deficit, requiring the issue of a yet larger volume of bonds, and so on; see, for example, Blinder and Solow (1973). Increased debt interest payments also cause a deterioration of the budget position, and some analyses, following Domar (1944), focus on the debt explosion that results from this source alone.

The requirement that such explosions do not occur, that is, that the government remains solvent, imposes an intertemporal budget constraint on the government. Discussion of the intertemporal budget constraint often takes taxation to be the "free" variable, and speaks of the constraint as a device for shifting the tax burden between generations, for example: low taxation at present leads to debt accumulation, which will require higher taxation in future to stabilize the debt and cover increased debt interest payments. Such discussion implicitly takes government expenditure and transfer payments as given, which is an additional behavioral assumption. The constraint itself is nothing more than an identity, however, and is silent on the question of which variable should be modified. The future adjustment could equally come from lower expenditure, and in the long run a change in the composition of government expenditure may be a more plausible means of adjustment than the tax rate. Nevertheless the closure rules that have been used to implement the constraint in macroeconometric models have typically adjusted tax rates, in response to deviations of the ratio of government debt to GDP from some "normal" or "target" level, for example.

Examples of closure rules are mostly found in multi-country macroeconometric models, in particular in several of the models that feature in the model comparison projects sponsored by the Brookings Institution, see Bryant *et al.* (1988, 1993). They are relatively rare in models of national economies, possibly for two reasons. First, in forecasting and policy analysis exercises these models usually focus on the short-to-medium term, during which potential debt explosions may not become apparent and hence, arguably, may not matter; indeed, it is relatively rare for the debt position to be monitored. Second, many mainstream forecasting models retain a backward-looking treatment of unobserved expectations variables, which contributes to the view that future potential disasters may have little impact on current behavior. On the other hand the incorporation of the rational expectations hypothesis or, to be more precise, the adoption of an explicit forward-looking treatment of unobserved future expectations, using model-consistent solution procedures, is a feature of several of the multi-country models mentioned above. This implies that the long-run effects of exogenous shocks may have a strong influence on short-run behavior, and so it is important to verify that the model has sensible long-run properties. For some kinds of shock a forward-looking model may not be able to reach a convergent solution without making some explicit assumption about how the government's intertemporal budget constraint is ultimately satisfied. Rational or model-consistent expectations were introduced into two mainstream models of the UK economy in the mid-1980s, see Wallis *et al.* (1986), but not fiscal closure rules, and one of these models is used in our simulation experiments below.

Augmenting the model with a financial closure rule or policy reaction function in order to stabilize a potentially unstable model is, at the simplest level, an example of the application of the control methods introduced into economics from engineering in the classic articles by Phillips (1954, 1957). But adoption of the rational expectations hypothesis breaks the analogy with engineering systems on which this early work rested. Economic systems are intelligent in ways that engineering systems are not. They can anticipate the likely actions of the controller, and react to those anticipations. Study of the dynamic implications of augmenting the model with a control rule that describes the setting of a policy instrument then requires a different set of techniques, in the linear case those developed by Blanchard and Kahn (1980) and used by Barrell *et al.* (1993, Appendix III) for example, and in the non-linear case the numerical model-consistent solution procedures referred to above.

Increased attention to the long-run properties of macroeconometric models has been stimulated not only by the increased use of model-consistent expectations but also by greater stress on a consistent and coherent underlying theoretical structure. This has been a reaction to criticism of the weak theoretical foundations of empirical models in general, and of their overemphasis on the demand side in particular. Since the supply side of a macroeconometric model determines its long-run properties, a shift of emphasis to the supply side has called for a sharper focus on the long-run or steady-state implications of the models. Formal macroeconomic theory then assumes a greater role, since this has most to say about the nature of the steady state, and somewhat less to say about the process of short-run adjustment. From a system perspective this has led to the development of techniques to analyze the model's steady-state properties directly, rather than through numerical solution over an extended forecast horizon; see, for example Malgrange (1989), Masson (1987), Murphy (1992), and Wallis and Whitley (1987). Procedures for reducing a large structural empirical model to a smaller structural model have also been devised (see, for example, Masson, 1988) with a similar objective, namely to make the theoretical structure more transparent and the core theoretical properties more tractable. Alternatively it might be insisted that key long-run properties should be built into the model structure from the beginning, as in the Australian models constructed at the Economic Planning Advisory Council, see Murphy *et al.* (1986), and subsequently by Murphy (1988, 1992) himself; the Murphy model also features in our experiments.

The remainder of this paper is organized as follows. In Section 2 we consider various issues of experimental design with forward-looking models, in particular reviewing the way in which closure rules have been implemented in multi-country models. In Section 3 we present the results of some simulation experiments, showing the impact of the introduction of closure rules in single-country models. Section 4 contains concluding comments.

This paper reports research that forms part of the general research programme of the ESRC Macroeconomic Modelling Bureau. This is a unique model-comparison project which, since 1983, has conducted its own independent comparative and methodological research, with full hands-on access to the different econometric models of a national economy, in this case the UK economy. Smith (1990) provides an independent appraisal of this activity; Wallis (1993) compares the more conventional style of model-comparison project. In addition to the Murphy model, the UK models of the National Institute of Economic and Social Research (NIESR) and the University of Strathclyde (STR) feature in the present exercise; further information on their general properties may be found in the Bureau's most recent comparative review, Church *et al.* (1993).

2 Experimental design

In this section we review existing approaches to several experimental design questions. The basic experiment we have in mind is a simulation of a permanent fiscal expansion. Dynamic multipliers are calculated by comparing the results of two solutions of a model, one a base run and the second a perturbed run in which the level of an exogenous component of government expenditure is held permanently above its base-run values. It is desired to prevent an explosive growth of government debt. The nature of the closure rule or policy reaction function, the timing of the reaction and the choice of terminal conditions are discussed in turn.

2.1 Closure rules

Four forward-looking models appear in the first Brookings multi-country model comparison, see Bryant *et al.* (1988), namely the MINIMOD, McKibbin Sachs Global (MSG), Liverpool and Taylor models, and other publications on the first two models give details of the fiscal closure rules that are employed.

In MINIMOD, see Haas and Masson (1986), the average aggregate tax rate T is changed according to the rule

$$T = T^* + 0.1(b - b^*)_{-1} \tag{1}$$

where b is the ratio of the government bond stock to nominal GNP and an asterisk denotes a "normal" (T^*) or "equilibrium" (b^*) value. Two "countries" are represented in the model, the United States and the rest of the world, and each has the same rule. For reasons discussed below, in the Brookings simulations these rules were only switched in after seven years. In a subsequent examination of the stability and steady-state properties of the model, Masson (1987) employs the rule

$$\Delta T = 0.015(b - b^*)_{-1} + 0.5\Delta b_{-1} \tag{2}$$

Dynamic analysis of a system augmented by such reaction functions implicitly assumes that they operate continuously.

In MULTIMOD, the successor to MINIMOD also developed at the International Monetary Fund, see Masson *et al.* (1988), rules of the same form appear, with coefficients 0.01 and 0.3, respectively. However, Masson *et al.* (1990) report that this rule "sometimes generated anomalous movements in tax rates owing to temporary divergences in nominal GNP from its equilibrium level, especially for countries with large baseline debt positions relative to GNP". A demand stimulus that increases output temporarily reduces the bond stock/GNP ratio, which can lead to a reduction in tax rates that reinforces the initial stimulus; this "occasionally caused problems with the dynamic stability of the model". Given that the objective is to ensure government solvency in the long run, such sensitivity to transitory changes is undesirable. The revised rule adopted by Masson *et al.* (1990) reduces their impact and is given as

$$\Delta T = 0.04\left(\frac{B - B^*}{Y}\right)_{-1} + 0.3\,\Delta\left(\frac{B - B^*}{Y}\right)_{-1} \tag{3}$$

where $b = B/Y$, in an obvious notation. Thus the target is expressed in terms of the debt stock, and B^* is adjusted where necessary "to reflect permanent changes in nominal GNP, such as those arising from money level or growth shocks". The quadrupling of the first coefficient ensures that debt returns to its base-run values over a typical simulation horizon.

In the MSG model, see McKibbin and Sachs (1991), taxes are adjusted to cover the interest burden of a changing debt stock, specifically by making interest payments an element of the lump-sum tax on households. In response to a permanent increase in government expenditure the overall fiscal deficit is permanently higher, but the primary deficit (spending net of interest payments less total tax receipts) eventually moves into surplus to prevent the explosive growth of government debt.

The NIGEM model referred to above, Barrell *et al.* (1993), uses a rule similar to that used in MULTIMOD, but expressed in terms of the deviation of the deficit, D, from its target value, namely

$$\Delta T = 0.01(D - D^*)_{-1} \tag{4}$$

where T is now the rate of personal income tax. This rule affects the path of the economy less rapidly than is the case with MULTIMOD, but Barrell *et al.* (1993) attribute this to the latter model's lower nominal inertia and the assumption of forward-looking consumers, rather than the change of rule. No direct analysis of the sensitivity of simulation results for a given model to different closure rules is presented by any of the authors cited in this section.

The closure rules discussed above have been calibrated by trial and error to achieve satisfactory dynamic properties overall, and this is the approach that we adopt below. It is in the spirit of Phillips' (1954, 1957) original approach to control theory, in which the objective – in his case, of correcting errors caused by unanticipated shocks as quickly and smoothly as possible – is formulated relatively informally. An alternative approach is that of formal optimization of an explicit objective function, specified as a scalar function, usually quadratic, of the deviations of actual values of endogenous variables and policy instruments from their desired values, possibly also including terms that penalize rapid changes in these quantities. In a non-linear model the optimal policy is then given as a sequence of instrument values rather than a feedback rule, unless the control problem is approached via a linear approximation to the non-linear model, whereupon a linear feedback rule can be obtained. A further possibility that is sometimes discussed in the literature is to estimate the parameters of the policy reaction function from time-series data. This requires a suitably long period of observation on the policy regime of interest, a condition that is unlikely to be met given the number of regime changes that have occurred over recent years. In any event its applicability is limited to actual policy regimes that have been observed, whereas many hypothetical "what-if" questions are of equal, if not greater, interest.

2.2 Jam today or jam tomorrow?

In the second Brookings exercise, Bryant *et al.* (1993), the guidelines on the simulation experiments asked model proprietors to keep fiscal policy unchanged from its base setting during the ten years of the simulation period. It was recognized that forward-looking models would require subsequent adjustments to ensure government solvency, but it was requested that these be delayed. This reflects a similar request to the four forward-looking models in the first exercise to confine such adjustments to the period after the simulation period of interest, in that case six years. No reason for these requests was given; presumably the organizers felt that this would achieve greater standardization of the policy environment and hence greater comparability of results, in particular between forward-looking and backward-looking models.

In the event, however, model proprietors "differed significantly in the ways that they did, or did not, implement these guidelines", see Bryant *et al.* (1993, p. 238). MULTIMOD and MSG, for example, "appear *not* to have suppressed their normal tax-rate reaction functions during the initial ten-year simulation period". While standardization of policy reaction functions is a prerequisite for diagnosis of "the many other causes of differences in results across models", these model proprietors are implicitly arguing that a delay in the introduction of the fiscal adjustment should not be a feature of the standard experimental design.

This position is supported by Sims (1993), in his invited comments and reflections on the exercise. Sims notes that when the fiscal policy reaction to the level of debt is postponed, the size of the adjustment that is eventually required increases exponentially with the delay. The larger the adjustment in taxation the more likely it is that this is non-neutral, and hence the more likely that the nature of the equilibrium is affected by the particular kind of fiscal policy that is specified. Moreover, a delay in adjustment raises credibility problems. "As recent U.S. political history makes clear, large, long-postponed fiscal adjustments are politically difficult and disruptive if they involve fiscal stringency. It therefore becomes hard to interpret the policy, because the fiscal adjustment is not inevitable. ... When the fiscal adjustment required is easing, it is even less realistic to imagine a long delay. That real governments will wait for ten years, allowing successor administrations to introduce large, long-delayed tax breaks or new spending, is unlikely" (Sims, 1993, p. 432).

Model-consistent expectations solutions assume full credibility of the policies being pursued, with the "full information" assumption covering policy reaction functions along with all other relations in the model. Departures from this can be modelled by specifying alternative expectations schemes, but these typically do not capture the uncertainty to which Sims draws attention. An appropriate response to his criticism is not to attempt to develop descriptions of economic agents' behavior during an interregnum in which they ponder the nature and timing of the eventual policy reaction but, at least in the first instance, to use policy reaction functions that operate continuously.

2.3 Terminal conditions

The numerical procedures used to solve a model with forward expectations variables in a consistent manner ensure that current expectations of future variables coincide with the future solution values over a finite sequence of periods. Terminal conditions that specify future expectations beyond this horizon are then required; in cases where there exists a multiplicity of consistent solution paths, these also ensure that the stable (saddlepoint) path is selected.

If the nature of the stable path is known *a priori*, from analysis of the steady-state properties of the model, for example, then the terminal conditions may explicitly incorporate this knowledge. This may require a relatively long solution period, however, to ensure that the model has reached an approximate equilibrium. In the absence of such information, or in a shorter solution period, terminal conditions should be specified that approximate the stable path after the end of the solution period, typically by requiring constant levels or constant growth rates of relevant variables. In order to ascertain whether the time period is sufficiently long or whether appropriate terminal conditions have been used, so that the solution over the period of interest is unaffected, numerical sensitivity analysis may be undertaken. The sensitivity of the solution to variations in the terminal date indicates how much of the solution can be regarded as a genuine product of the model rather than a product of the assumed terminal conditions. Changes in the type of terminal condition, together with evidence from the different solution periods, can also suggest whether or not a unique stable solution exists. For examples of such sensitivity analysis, see Wallis *et al.* (1986, Ch. 2.5).

The exchange rate is the most common forward-looking variable both in multi-country models and in single-country models of open economies. The most common specification adopts a modified uncovered interest parity (UIP) condition, relating future expected exchange-rate changes to the interest-rate differential between domestic and foreign assets and a risk premium term. In solving for future expectations variables in a model-consistent manner the exchange-rate equation then has a forward unit root if the interest rate is assumed fixed, and it is necessary that this be moderated by feedbacks in the remainder of the system so that a unique stable solution exists. Fisher *et al.* (1992) present applications of a model reduction procedure that explicitly focuses on this question. For the present purposes attention focuses on the choice of the risk premium term and the specification of an appropriate terminal condition, in the light of the requirement of long-run fiscal solvency.

In the NIESR and STR models the risk premium proxy variable is the ratio of net overseas assets to GDP, whereas Fisher *et al.* (1990) find that a specification in terms of the current balance to GDP ratio is preferred empirically. Barrell *et al.* (1993) argue that a flow variable is also preferable as the bearer of the terminal condition. In the perturbed solution the target values of relevant asset stock or flow variables are typically the base-run values. A flow variable will approach its base-run values in a shorter period than the stock variable to which it cumulates, hence a shorter solution period is required, and the imposition of an "equilibrium" terminal condition in these terms will require less of an extension beyond the period of interest.

3 Controlling government debt in single-country model simulations

In this section we report on experiments in which the level of government debt is controlled in two models of the UK economy, namely the NIESR and STR models, together with the Murphy model of the Australian economy. Of the current portfolio of models of the UK economy deposited at the Bureau these are the two models which employ forward-looking, model-consistent expectations, and hence in which the issues of the longer-run stability of government debt are of importance for the determination of short-run behavior. For related reasons, these are also the two models which are provided to the Bureau with long simulation databases. It can therefore be expected that any problems of the instability of government finances should appear within the simulation period. The Murphy model shares a number of features of the two UK models including forward-looking expectations in financial markets. While it differs in only being solved over a short, five-year, period, it has a well-defined long-run form which is used to provide terminal conditions. It is also a model which includes a government budget closure rule as part of its basic structure.

The policy simulation which we examine on the UK models is an unanticipated, permanent increase in government consumption expenditure of £360mn (1985 prices) per quarter, approximately £2bn per year in 1990 prices. Monetary policy is assumed to operate by keeping the short rate of interest unchanged from its base-run values. This is one of the standard set of policy simulations which forms the benchmark of comparison in the Bureau's recent systematic review of model properties, see Church *et al.* (1993), where more detail on the simulation results and the general properties of the two models can be found. The two models have been amended, however, to ensure that interest payments by the government to holders of debt more closely match those implied by the current distribution of government debt holdings; in the STR model an equation has been added to calculate the debt stock. A summary of the simulation results is given in Table 1; these very closely resemble the results in Church *et al.* (1993), the amendments having only minor effects in this simulation.

Broadly speaking, in the two models the fiscal expansion has substantial short-run expansionary effects on output, and these persist into the medium term, although it appears that the long-run effects are much smaller. The short-run impact in the STR model is amplified by the assumption that consumers have forward-looking expectations. The forward-looking nature of expectations in the foreign exchange market and sluggishness of goods prices leads to some initial depreciation of the nominal and real exchange rate, in turn bringing forward an expansion in net exports and therefore aggregate demand. The behavior of the government budget deficit and hence government debt relative to nominal GDP follows these responses; Figures 1 and 2 show the deviation from base of the debt/GDP ratio for each model

Table 1: Uncontrolled government expenditure simulation

	NIESR		STR	
GDP(a)				
Year 1	0.40		0.70	
3	0.70		0.57	
5	0.60		0.31	
Long run	0.20		−0.16	
Price Level(a)(b)				
Year 1	0.4	(0.4)	0.37	(0.37)
3	1.6	(0.5)	1.17	(0.36)
5	2.0	(0.1)	1.60	(0.18)
Long run	0.9	(0.1)	0.51	(−0.03)
Nominal Exchange Rate(a)(c)				
Year 1	−0.7	(−0.2)	−0.50	(−0.17)
3	−0.7	(1.1)	−0.50	(0.74)
5	−0.6	(1.5)	−0.49	(1.25)
Long run	−0.1	(0.8)	−0.12	(0.47)
PSBR/GDP(d)				
Year 1	0.31		1.13	
3	0.01		1.49	
5	0.07		2.10	
Long run	−0.26		9.12	
Real Current Account(e)				
Year 1	−1.40		−0.52	
3	−1.30		−0.74	
5	−1.20		−0.78	
Long run	−2.80		2.46	

Notes:

(a) Percentage difference from base

(b) Consumer prices; change in inflation in brackets

(c) Effective rate; real exchange rate, defined in terms of producer prices, in brackets

(d) Percentage point difference from base

(e) £billion 1990 prices: deflated by price index in (b)

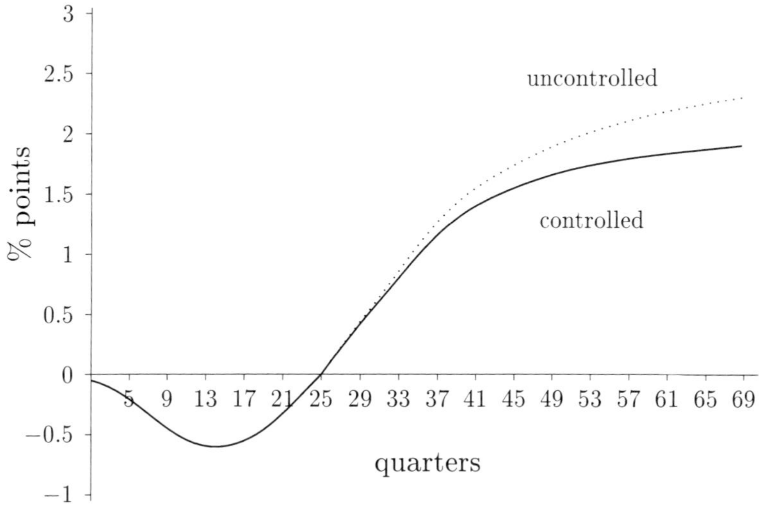

Figure 1: NIESR debt/GDP ratio (deviation from base)

in turn. The short-run behavior of the ratio reflects the size of the initial positive response of aggregate demand to the expansion in government spending. The ratio is lower than its base-run value for two years for STR and six years for NIESR, then in the following years both build up substantially. In both cases, the instability of the government debt/GDP ratio is clear after fifteen years. The fact that neither model has a mechanism which provides long-run closure of the government budget constraint is obvious. It also clear, however, that the instability does not cause problems in obtaining a solution in the time periods employed in standard simulation exercises. This is due to the fact that neither model uses the infinite-horizon or analytic long-run solution of the model to provide terminal conditions for forward-looking variables, but simply approximates the stable path.

We consider closure rules for the government budget deficit similar to those employed by the multi-country models discussed above. Control of government debt is achieved by requiring the income tax rate to rise in response to values of the ratio of the Public Sector Borrowing Requirement (PSBR) to GDP, d_t, above its base-run values. The rule we use is

$$\Delta T = \alpha \left[(d_{t-1} - d^*_{t-1}) + \cdots + (d_{t-4} - d^*_{t-4}) \right] / 4 \tag{5}$$

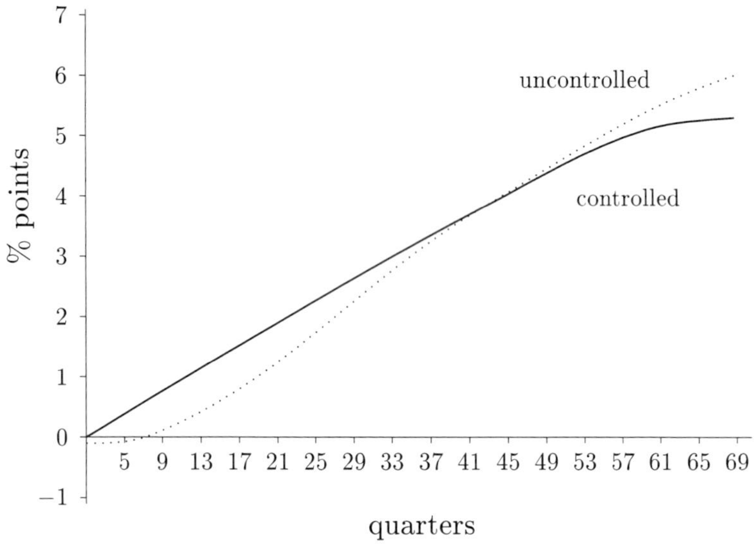

Figure 2: STR debt/GDP ratio (deviation from base)

where the income tax rate is changed in response to a four-quarter moving average of the deviation of the PSBR/GDP ratio from its target value. In the simulations the target value, d^*, is the base-run value. In each case the coefficient α has been chosen, after some experimentation, to ensure that the deviation from base of the debt/GDP ratio, b_t, has stopped rising by the end of the first fifteen years of the simulation period.

The impact of the use of the closure rule in the NIESR model, with $\alpha = 0.8$, can be judged from Figure 1 and from comparison of the first columns of Tables 1 and 2. The path of b_t following the government expenditure increase is damped in comparison with the uncontrolled simulation. The income tax rate rises very gradually, reaching a maximum increment of one half of one percentage point by the end of the simulation period. Thus it has little impact in the early years of the simulation but, as intended, substantially affects the growth of debt over the longer run, with the debt/GDP ratio following the uncontrolled path in the early years of the simulation and subsequently increasing at a declining rate. The multiplier effects of the expenditure increase are reduced in the medium and longer term. This is due in part to the impact of higher taxes on consumers' expenditure, but also on the smaller initial depreciation of the exchange rate. Control of public sector debt results in smaller current account deficits over time and lower overseas debt accumulation.

Comparison of Tables 1 and 2 shows that, for the STR model, the impact of the long-term control of public debt has more substantial effects in the short term. In common with the results for the NIESR model, the income tax rate rises little in the short run and by up to half a percentage point by the end of the simulation period. As shown in Figure 2, the debt/GDP ratio is higher in the initial period of the simulation under control than in the uncontrolled case, due to the reduced growth of GDP. The reason for this appears to be a combination of the impact of forward-looking consumption decisions and a forward-looking exchange rate. Just as the initial response of consumption to the increase in government expenditure was greatest for the STR model in the comparative exercise reported in Church *et al.* (1993), the negative effect of higher taxes over the period of this simulation has had an offsetting initial effect on consumption. There is also a substantially smaller initial depreciation in the exchange rate. In common with the results for the NIESR model, the lower current account deficits over the period of the simulation result in much smaller accumulation of overseas debt. A smaller initial depreciation in the exchange rate results from the interaction of the behavior of domestic government debt and overseas debt. This is translated into a smaller initial depreciation through the risk premium term in the exchange rate equation. Over the medium and longer term of this simulation, the effect of the control of government debt is very sensitive to the choice of the parameter α. These results are obtained with $\alpha = 0.1$; halving this stabilizes debt only after some fifty years.

Finally, we consider the implications of delay in the implementation of government budget closure rules within a model of the Australian economy which incorporates such a rule in its structure. This model is similar in underlying philosophy to the UK models discussed above, but is much more explicit about the form of long-run solution of the model. In particular, the model has an explicit long-run form which incorporates forms of equilibrium behavior by firms and households. This long-run solution is used to provide terminal conditions for the forward-looking variables in the model, namely the exchange rate and the long interest rate. The closure rule used in the model is

$$\Delta T_t = 0.028(b_t - b_t^*) + 0.48\, \Delta(b_t - b_t^*) \tag{6}$$

where the tax rate employed is the tax on labor income and b_t is the ratio of the outstanding stock of interest-bearing government debt to nominal GDP. The largest weight in this rule is placed on the change in the debt ratio, which is closely related to the level of the deficit. In addition, the level of b_t is targeted. The target path b_t^*, in common with the models discussed above, is the base path. The parameter values used in the rule were chosen, firstly, to ensure that the debt ratio ceases to rise after

Table 2: Controlled government expenditure simulation

	NIESR		STR	
GDP[(a)]				
Year 1	0.38		0.39	
3	0.61		0.29	
5	0.47		0.16	
Long run	−0.16		−0.35	
Price Level[(a)(b)]				
Year 1	0.41	(0.41)	0.15	(0.15)
3	1.56	(0.50)	0.52	(0.16)
5	1.92	(0.08)	0.69	(0.06)
Long run	0.60	(0.00)	−0.45	(−0.02)
Nominal Exchange Rate[(a)(c)]				
Year 1	−0.43	(−0.05)	−0.04	(−0.12)
3	−0.42	(1.31)	−0.04	(0.55)
5	−0.38	(1.65)	−0.04	(0.75)
Long run	−0.02	(0.53)	0.02	(−0.52)
PSBR/GDP[(d)]				
Year 1	0.30		1.59	
3	−0.01		1.76	
5	0.07		2.00	
Long run	0.11		−0.48	
Real Current Account[(e)]				
Year 1	−1.43		−0.36	
3	−1.73		−0.49	
5	−1.30		−0.49	
Long run	−1.54		0.18	

Notes:
(a) Percentage difference from base
(b) Consumer prices; change in inflation in brackets
(c) Effective rate; real exchange rate, defined in terms of producer prices, in brackets
(d) Percentage point difference from base
(e) £billion 1990 prices: deflated by price index in (b)

five years of a simulation of increased government consumption expenditure. The second criterion is that the ratio should achieve its target value by the end of five years in a simulation of a permanent change in the target. For further discussion of the model's properties see Murphy (1988, 1992).

The results of a simulation of a permanent, unanticipated, 1% of GDP increase in government consumption expenditure with the closure rule operating from the start of the simulation are given in the first column of Table 3. The standard monetary policy assumption in the Murphy model is that the nominal supply of narrow definition money is held at its base-run values. Consequently, the short interest rate can vary. Initially the interest rate rises and the exchange rate appreciates, followed by depreciation over the remainder of the simulation period. In the short run the increase in the PSBR is financed by issuing bonds. As the interest rate exceeds the growth rate of GDP the bond stock rises as a proportion of nominal GDP. However, this is ameliorated by the impact of increases in the tax rate which ensure that b_t reaches its largest value by the end of the five-year simulation period. In the long run the increase in government consumption crowds out private sector consumption. External debt increases and the exchange rate depreciates in order to satisfy the external constraint. In the long run b_t returns to the base solution, highlighting the fact that the increased government expenditure is financed in the long run by higher taxes.

The effects of delay in the implementation of the government budget closure rule are shown by comparison of columns 1 and 2 of Table 3. In the second simulation we hold the tax rate constant over the first three years of the simulation, and only allow the closure rule to operate thereafter. The result is that the tax rate is increased by nearly 2 percentage points in the fifth year of the simulation, and consequently has a severe expenditure-reducing effect at that time. GDP is somewhat higher than in the controlled case over the first three years of the simulation, although a higher interest rate and greater initial appreciation in the exchange rate also result. Following the argument of Sims (1993) discussed above, private agents may well not find credible such large corrective action by the government after three years of inaction. Clearly, were the corrective action delayed further, as in the Brookings exercises discussed above, the impact would be even more substantial.

4 Discussion

The results presented above show that augmenting a macroeconometric model with a policy reaction function intended to represent the imposition of the intertemporal budget constraint alters the inferences that are drawn about the short-run effects of a fiscal stimulus. The size of the alteration depends on the extent of forward-looking behavior in the model. The possibility that this may be small is not an argument

Table 3: Murphy model — government expenditure simulation

	With control	Control after 3 years
GDP[(a)]		
Year 1	0.56	0.51
3	0.25	0.46
5	0.05	−0.20
Long run	0.06	0.06
Consumer Prices[(a)]		
Year 1	−0.04	−0.12
3	0.13	0.19
5	0.50	1.11
Long run	0.33	0.33
Nominal Exchange Rate[(a)(b)]		
Year 1	3.37	3.86
3	1.55	1.82
5	0.37	−0.51
Long run	−0.45	−0.45
PSBR/GDP[(c)]		
Year 1	0.77	0.84
3	0.42	0.84
5	0.15	−0.05
Long run	0.0	0.00
Debt/GDP[(c)]		
Year 1	0.11	0.14
3	1.30	1.96
5	1.66	2.21
Long run	0.0	0.00
Tax Rate[(c)]		
Year 1	0.07	0.00
3	0.87	0.00
5	1.41	1.93
Long run	1.39	1.39

Notes:
(a) Percentage
(b) Effective, trade weighted
(c) Percentage points

for neglecting the intertemporal budget constraint, if it is desired to undertake comparative model analysis in a standardized, realistic policy environment.

Delaying the policy adjustment increases the size of the adjustment that is eventually required, raising credibility questions. Although such a delay was desired by the organizers of the Brookings comparative exercises, not all model proprietors concurred, and our experience with the Murphy model also suggests that the policy reaction functions should operate continuously. Since the policy reaction is an adjustment in taxation in all the cases considered, the issue is implicitly one of the balance between bond and tax finance of the deficit. The critical parameter which then requires further study in the context of the design of a standardized, realistic policy environment for comparative analysis of models is the speed with which such financial imbalances should be rectified.

References

Barrell, R., J. Sefton, and J.W. In't Veld (1993), "Interest rates, exchange rates and fiscal policy in Europe: the implications of Maastricht", Discussion Paper 44, NIESR, London.

Blanchard, O.J. and C.M. Kahn (1980), "The solution of linear difference models under rational expectations", *Econometrica*, **48**, 1305–1311.

Blinder, A.S. and R.M. Solow (1973), "Does fiscal policy matter?", *Journal of Public Economics*, **2**, 319–337.

Bryant, R.C., D.W. Henderson, G. Holtham, P. Hooper, and S.A. Symansky, editors (1988), *Empirical macroeconomics for interdependent economies*, Brookings Institution, Washington DC.

Bryant, R.C., P. Hooper, and C.L. Mann, editors (1993), *Evaluating policy regimes: new research in empirical macroeconomics*, Brookings Institution, Washington DC.

Christ, C.F. (1968), "A simple macroeconomic model with a government budget restraint", *Journal of Political Economy*, **76**, 53–67.

Christ, C.F. (1979), "On fiscal and monetary policies and the government budget restraint", *American Economic Review*, **69**, 526–538.

Church, K.B., P.R. Mitchell, P.N. Smith, and K.F. Wallis (1993), "Comparative properties of models of the UK economy", *National Institute Economic Review*, **145**, 87–107.

Domar, E.D. (1944), "The "burden of the debt" and the national income", *American Economic Review*, **34**, 798–827.

Fisher, P.G., S.K. Tanna, D.S. Turner, K.F. Wallis, and J.D. Whitley (1990), "Econometric evaluation of the exchange rate in models of the UK economy", *The Economic Journal*, **100**, 1230–1244.

Fisher, P.G., D.S. Turner, and K.F. Wallis (1992), "Forward unit root exchange-rate dynamics and the properties of large-scale macroeconometric models", in C.P. Hargreaves, editor, *Macroeconomic modelling of the long run*, Edward Elgar, Aldershot.

Haas, R.D. and P.R. Masson (1986), "MINIMOD: specification and simulation results", *IMF Staff Papers*, **33**, 722–767.

Malgrange, P. (1989), "The structure of dynamic macroeconomic models", in B. Cornet and H. Tulkens, editors, *Contributions to operations research and economics: the 20th anniversary of CORE*, MIT Press, Cambridge.

Masson, P.R. (1987), "The dynamics of a two-country minimodel under rational expectations", *Annales d'Economie et de Statistique*, **6/7**, 37–69.

Masson, P.R. (1988), "Deriving small models from large models.", in R.C. Bryant, D.W. Henderson, G. Holtham, P. Hooper, and S.A. Symansky, editors, *Empirical macroeconomics for interdependent economies*, Brookings Institution, Washington DC.

Masson, P.R., S.A. Symansky, R.D. Haas, and M.P. Dooley (1988), "MULTIMOD: a multi-region econometric model", in International Monetary Fund, editor, *Staff studies for the world economic outlook*, International Monetary Fund, Washington DC.

Masson, P.R., S.A. Symansky, and G. Meredith (1990), "MULTIMOD Mark II a revised and extended model", Occasional Paper 71, International Monetary Fund, Washington DC.

McKibbin, W.J. and J.D. Sachs (1991), *Global linkages: macroeconomic interdependence and cooperation in the world economy*, Brookings Institution, Washington DC.

Murphy, C.W. (1988), "An overview of the Murphy model", *Australian Economic Papers (Supplement)*, **27**, 175–199.

Murphy, C.W. (1992), "The steady-state properties of a macroeconometric model", in C.P. Hargreaves, editor, *Macroeconomic modelling of the long run*, Edward Elgar, Aldershot.

Murphy, C.W., I.A. Bright, R.J. Brooker, W.D. Geeves, and B.K. Taplin (1986), "A macroeconometric model of the Australian economy for medium-term policy analysis", Technical Paper 2, Economic Planning Advisory Council, Commonwealth of Australia.

Phillips, A.W. (1954), "Stabilisation policy in a closed economy", *The Economic Journal*, **64**, 290–323.

Phillips, A.W. (1957), "Stabilisation policy and the time-forms of lagged responses", *The Economic Journal*, **67**, 265–277.

Sims, C.A. (1993), "Comment", in R.C. Bryant, P. Hooper, and C.L. Mann, editors, *Evaluating policy regimes: new research in empirical macroeconomics*, Brookings Institution, Washington DC, 430–443.

Smith, R. (1990), "The Warwick ESRC Macroeconomic Modelling Bureau: an assessment", *International Journal of Forecasting*, **6**, 301–309.

Wallis, K.F. (1993), "Comparing macroeconometric models: a review article", *Economica*, **60**, 225–237.

Wallis, K.F., M.J. Andrews, P.G. Fisher, J.A. Longbottom, and J.D. Whitley (1986), *Models of the UK economy: a third review by the ESRC Macroeconomic Modelling Bureau*, Oxford University Press, Oxford.

Wallis, K.F. and J.D. Whitley (1987), "Long-run properties of large-scale macroeconometric models", *Annales d'Economie et de Statistique*, **6/7**, 207–224.

Methods and Applications of Economic Dynamics
L. Schoonbeek, E. Sterken and S.K. Kuipers (editors)

Chapter 10

The long run of macroeconometric models: the case of MULTIMOD[1]

Rahim Loufir and Pierre Malgrange

1 Introduction

Conventional dynamic macroeconometric models constitute a useful device, still widely used for shedding light on the preparation of quantitative economic policy. Their structure is generally based on the so-called "disequilibrium growth theory", an attempt to make a synthesis between short-run Keynesian theory and neoclassical growth theory. These models have been criticized on several grounds, the most dramatic one being the numerous defects in their theoretical foundations.

The basic idea of this paper is to exhibit the long-run structure of a model taking opportunity of the fact that, most of the time, the derivation of the typical behavioral relations starts from a long-run/equilibrium theory, on which dynamical mechanisms are plugged. We define the concept of the long run for macroeconometric models in the usual way as dynamic equilibrium of all adjustment mechanisms. Indeed, when the model is dynamically stable, this corresponds to its asymptotical behavior. Deriving long-run mechanisms associated with dynamical relationships is obviously not new. Most of the time, however, it has concerned single equation models and seldom an entire macroeconomic model, except a small number of studies, see e.g. Bergstrom and Wymer (1976), Gandolfo (1981), Currie (1982) and more recently Wallis and Whitley (1987), or Deleau *et al.* (1990). The search for long-run

1. We are grateful to Philippe Gudin de Vallerin and Steven Symansky for their very useful help. We benefited greatly from numerous remarks and suggestions from Jan Jacobs, Bert Schoonbeek and Elmer Sterken. Of course, the responsibility for any remaining errors is ours.

properties, if any, of a model has been reinforced recently by the introduction of rational expectations. Indeed, the logic of rational expectations imposes, through the necessity of setting terminal conditions, to have a clear perception of the long-run solution of a model.

This paper is divided into five sections. In Section 2, we present the methodology used for the derivation of the long run of a given macroeconometric model. Section 3 gives a brief description of the model analyzed, MULTIMOD, and describes how its long run is obtained. Section 4 shows the long-run properties of MULTIMOD. Section 5 concludes.

2 Methodology

In this section we recall briefly the methodology[2] we use for building the long-run version of a given macroeconometric model. A more detailed exposition can be found for instance in Deleau *et al.* (1990).

2.1 Formalization

Let us consider a dynamic macroeconometric model written as follows

$$y(t) = f(y(t),\ y(t-1),\ y(t+1),\ x(t); t) \tag{1}$$

with $y(t)$ the $(n \times 1)$ vector of endogenous variables, $y(t-1)$ and $y(t+1)$ lagged and forward looking endogenous variables, $x(t)$ the $(m \times 1)$ vector of exogenous variables, and t the index of discrete time.

The search for a Steady State Growth Path (SSGP) is equivalent to finding particular solutions of (1) of the type

$$\begin{aligned} x_i^*(t) &= x_i^*(0)a_i^t \qquad i = 1, \ldots, m \\ y_j^*(t) &= y_j^*(0)b_j^t \qquad j = 1, \ldots, n \end{aligned} \tag{2}$$

In other words, we look for a set of n initial conditions $y^*(0)$ and n growth rates $(b_1, \ldots, b_n)$ for the endogenous variables, the corresponding exogenous elements $x^*(0)$ and $(a_1, \ldots, a_m)$ being known, such that (2) satisfies the system (1) at each time period.

We immediately observe that a solution of (1) of the type (2) will exist only if each equation of this system fulfills certain homogeneity conditions. These conditions are imposed by an elementary mathematical property of exponentials: except for pathological cases, a sum of terms evolving through time at constant growth rates follows an exponential pattern only if all growth rates are identical.

2. Another way to obtain the long-run structure of macroeconometric models consists of running very long dynamic simulations. See e.g. Wallis and Whitly (1987).

2.2 Determination of growth rates

Almost all conventional macroeconometric models are based on the hypothesis that the long-term real growth of the economy results from the exogenously given growth rates of the population and technical progress. In the same way, long-term inflation of an open economy must be equal to foreign exogenous inflation, and in the case of a closed economy, follow from some – exogenous – money supply target growth. More generally, it is easy to see that all the growth rates a_i and b_j can be derived in a straightforward way from three independent basic exogenous growth rates which lie somewhere as parameters in the model:

ν : exogenous growth rate of population,
γ : exogenous growth rate of technical progress (necessarily Harrod neutral),
μ : exogenous growth rate of money supply,
or ρ : exogenous growth rate of foreign prices,
with the identity: $1 + \mu = (1 + \rho)(1 + \gamma)(1 + \nu)$.

For instance, the – common – rate of growth g of all quantities is given by the identity

$$1 + g = (1 + \nu)(1 + \gamma) \tag{3}$$

2.3 Determination of initial conditions

Once the growth rates, including those of the exogenous variables, are determined from the three basic growth rates (ν, γ, ρ), the principle of computation of the initial conditions $y(0)$, knowing $x(0)$, is straightforward. Rewriting the equations of model (1) at time $t = 0$, and substituting the lagged variables by their expression (2), yields

$$y^*(0) = f(y^*(0), (y_j^*(0)/b_j), (y_j^*(0)\, b_j),\ x^*(0); 0), \qquad j = 1, \ldots, n \tag{4}$$

or, omitting the time index

$$y^* = f(y^*, x^*, \nu, \gamma, \rho) \tag{5}$$

The system (5), which we call the "long-run system" associated with model (1), consists of a set of simultaneous equations, of which the solution y^*, given the exogenous vector x^*, defines a set of initial conditions for a SSGP.

One can notice that long-run (exogenous) growth rates intervene in this long-run system. The static multipliers associated with (5) correspond to the asymptotic effect of a sustained multiplicative shock on the exogenous variables, which could be obtained through long-run simulations of the initial model (1), provided it verifies the adapted stability conditions. Let us make a few preliminary remarks about this long-run system (5):

(i) An equation of model (1) written in terms of growth rates yields ultimately a long-run relationship between the three basic long-run growth rates only, without any implication for initial levels.

(ii) In an equation involving both rates and levels, only the last ones subsist in the long-run system. For instance an equation of the following type

$$\hat{y} = f(z), \quad z \in R, \quad \text{where } \hat{y} \text{ denotes the growth rate of } y, \tag{6}$$

implies an autonomous determination of z^*, i.e.

$$z^* = f^{-1}(\hat{y}^*) = g(\nu, \gamma, \rho) \tag{7}$$

A typical case is the Phillips curve. It links the growth of wages and prices to the level of the unemployment rate, and thus leads to a long-run determination of the unemployment rate independently from the rest of the system.

(iii) The relations involved in the system (5) may receive the interpretation of being a set of cointegrating relations that the original model (1) postulates to hold.

3 Implementation of the methodology to MULTIMOD

The version of the multi-national dynamic econometric annual model MULTIMOD (Masson *et al.* (1990), slightly revised in Masson *et al.* (1991)) we study describes the behavior of the whole world decomposed into eight industrial countries/zones (Canada, – denoted CA –, France – FR –, Germany – GR –, Italy – IT –, Japan – JA –, United Kingdom – UK –, United States – US –, and a zone, called "Small Industrial Countries" – SI –, collecting the rest of OECD), and the rest of the world comprising two developing zones: high-income oil exporters – HO – and other developing countries – DC. Three goods are distinguished: oil, primary commodities, and other goods called manufactures.

3.1 Methodological issues

It is important to note at this stage that MULTIMOD is not aimed at running baseline dynamic simulations, but has been designed mainly for evaluating effects of economic policy modulation or exogenous shocks, around a reference path given from outside. This reference path describes the transition of the world economy from the present state towards a SSGP in about ten years (the reference path presently available from the IMF is increasing at a constant rate from the year 2004 onwards). It is simulated with MULTIMOD by introducing systematic residuals in each behavioral equation. In other words, it is important to note that residuals are not given a reference value of zero but are computed such that the solution of the whole model coincides with the exogenously given baseline path.

The methodology described in the previous section has been applied to the model MULTIMOD by first simulating each country model in isolation, and next connecting all the blocks together (let us mention that this is the first time a model of this size – more than 450 equations – is processed with such a methodology). We must keep in mind that, contrary to the original dynamic model, where the weight of the lagged and the forward looking variables makes the system rather sluggish (system (1)), the interdependencies between variables in the long-run model are very strong because it is a purely simultaneous system (system (5)). Indeed it is our experience that this feature makes the solution much more sensitive to rather small errors than the solution of the corresponding original dynamic model. As a matter of fact, we found a few small inconsistencies between the reference path exogenously given and the version of MULTIMOD we used, which were easy to correct (namely through a slight modification of the normalization parameter in the production function of the industrial country models and the addition of supplementary residuals in the two investment equations of the model of the rest of the world).

The simulation of the whole long-run system has been able to reproduce the reference solution with an excellent numerical precision. Table 1 gives the errors between given and simulated data in per cent for the main variables. One can see that the errors are of a very small order of magnitude (about 10^{-5}), as compared to the convergence criterion of the resolution algorithm[3], and are not worsened in case we are considering the whole world model, relatively to the case of the country models in a non-linked mode.

As we have said above, contrary to usual macroeconometric models, MULTIMOD does possess one steady-state growth path solution by construction, through adequate values given to the residuals. However, in the present study, we are not looking for only one long-run path, but for a "long-run system" of the type (5), in order to be able to compute directly long-run effects of permanent shocks as well. In order to check the existence of such a system, we have to examine whether the equations verify the relevant homogeneity properties. In fact, it is easy to show here that the homogeneity conditions needed are less stringent than in the general case without built-in time-varying residuals, because equations are generally specified in log-linear terms.

To explain this, let us consider first the following *linear* equation linking a non-trended variable $R(t)$ to a trended one $X(t)$, i.e.

3. The software used for simulating MULTIMOD, TROLL, is based on Newton's algorithm. It considers that a simultaneous system has reached its equilibrium level at iteration n when the relative change of each variable with respect to iteration $n-1$ is less than 0.001. Tightening this criterion left the solution unaltered.

Table 1: Per cent errors between the given reference long-run path and the computed long-run solution

GNP_{CA}	0.0032	GNP_{FR}	0.0046
$PGNP_{CA}$	−0.0009	$PGNP_{FR}$	−0.0004
R_{CA}	−0.0019	R_{FR}	−0.0018
E_{CA}	0.0000	E_{FR}	0.0005
GNP_{GR}	0.0047	GNP_{IT}	0.0028
$PGNP_{GR}$	−0.0010	$PGNP_{IT}$	−0.0004
R_{GR}	−0.0018	R_{IT}	−0.0020
E_{GR}	0.0006	E_{IT}	0.0006
GNP_{JA}	0.0028	GNP_{SI}	0.0048
$PGNP_{JA}$	−0.0007	$PGNP_{SI}$	−0.0011
R_{JA}	−0.0018	R_{SI}	−0.0020
E_{JA}	0.0006	E_{SI}	0.0006
GNP_{UK}	0.0023	GNP_{US}	0.0053
$PGNP_{UK}$	0.0000	$PGNP_{US}$	−0.0004
R_{UK}	−0.0020	R_{US}	−0.0018
E_{UK}	0.0005	E_{US}	0.0000
GDP_{DC}	0.0004	$POIL$	−0.0002
$PGNP_{DC}$	0.0000	$PCOM$	0.0010
GDP_{HO}	0.0007	$WTRADE$	−0.0055

Notes: GNP = gross national product, $PGNP$ = GNP deflator, R = nominal interest rate, E = exchange rate, GDP = gross domestic product, $POIL$ = price of oil, $PCOM$ = commodity price index, $WTRADE$ = world trade discrepancy.

$$R(t) = a\,X(t) + b(t) + \varepsilon(t) \tag{8}$$

with the stationary reference solution (exogenously given) $R^*(t) = R^*$ and $X^*(t) = X^*(0)\,(1+g)^t$. The computation of the reference path for the residuals gives

$$\varepsilon^*(t) = R^* - a\,X^*(0)(1+g)^t - b(t) \tag{9}$$

Hence we can rewrite the equation as

$$R(t) = a\,(X(t) - X^*(0)(1+g)^t) + R^* \tag{10}$$

We observe that we cannot get a constant value for $R(t)$ even if $X(t)$ increases at the rate g, as soon as $X(0)$ differs from $X^*(0)$.

If we consider now the following equation, where the specification of the right-hand side is expressed in *log-linear* terms

$$R(t) = a\log(X(t)) + b(t) + \varepsilon(t) \tag{11}$$

with the same reference solution, the computation of the residuals $\varepsilon^*(t)$, consistent with the stationary path, leads to

$$R(t) = a\log(X(t)/(X^*(0)(1+g)^t)) + R^* \tag{12}$$

Now this specification obviously allows for a long-run structure of the type (5) even if $X(0) \neq X^*(0)$.

The homogeneity conditions that the model and the exogenous variables must fulfill do not need to be verified analytically but can be checked in a very straightforward way by simple simulation exercises. Indeed, this can be done by shocking some exogenous variables of the long-run system (5) (without changing the residuals), and simulating it over several periods, in order to see whether the shocked solution increases at a constant rate. This experiment has been carried out and led to the conclusion of the non-existence of any heterogeneous behavior.

At last, before getting into the presentation of the long-run structure, let us mention that the reference value for the long-run basic growth rates are (exogenously) given by the baseline path and amount to 3% for all the quantity variables and to 3.79% for all the price variables. The rate of growth of the labor force is not relevant in the model. In effect, demographic variables appear basically in the production function, through the labor force. Employment as well as wages are substituted for in the supply function. Hence only the growth rate of labor in efficient units (i.e. multiplied by productivity growth) matters. This rate is of course identically equal to the rate of growth of quantities: 3%.

3.2 Overview of the structure of MULTIMOD

The specification of the country models is the same across the eight industrial countries/zones, and includes about 50 equations. Their structure consists of an open economy Mundell-Fleming version of the standard IS/LM model. The short-run behavior of agents is almost systematically described through dynamic error-correction mechanisms toward their long-run, theory-based, equilibrium. The estimation has been carried out with pooled data for the main behavioral functions: consumption, capital, money demand, and price supply. The world trade equilibrium in volumes (respectively, values) is obtained, as is conventional when bilateral trade is not explicated, through a reallocation of discrepancies in export volumes (respectively, in import prices).

The aggregate supply side of the model is given by an inflation equation which is a reduced form summarizing supply and demand on the labor market, the augmented Phillips curve, and a mark-up pricing on unit labor costs varying with the degree of capacity utilization. Government intervention is represented by public expenditures, money supply, bonds supply, and taxes. However, due to the intertemporal government budget constraint, taxes are not exogenous and there is a dynamic reaction function of the tax rate to adjust progressively the government debt towards a nominal target value.

The rest of the world is aggregated into two regions, capital exporting countries comprising mainly high-income oil exporters, and other developing countries. The former region does not face any constraint on its balance of payments and its structure is modeled in a simple way because of the high proportion of its oil exports in gross national product. In contrast, the latter region, comprising dissimilar countries, is finance constrained and therefore its imports and its domestic investment depend on its ability to carry additional debt. In addition, the manufactured goods are split into tradable goods, and nontradable goods. The prices of these two goods are not perfectly flexible as opposed to oil and primary commodities which are considered as homogeneous goods with a single world price.

3.3 Equations of MULTIMOD for a typical country

Table 2 lists the main equations of the dynamic original model for a typical country and their transcription into the long-run static version. They are slightly stylized with respect to the full version of MULTIMOD in order to make them more readable: oil and primary commodities are omitted; we do not consider the time structure of interest rates which is irrelevant in the steady state. The interested reader will find a comprehensive presentation of MULTIMOD in Masson *et al.* (1990, 1991).

The first seven equations describe the IS-curve. Consumption C (eq. D1) is modeled through an adaptation of the Blanchard (1985) model, of finite but uncertain-horizon agents, to an open and growing economy. In addition to wealth W and the real interest rate RR, in the short run, disposable income influences consumption. The demand for capital K (eq. D2) is linked to the real value of capital WK in conformity with Tobin's q-theory. Foreign trade in manufactured goods is formalized with conventional export and import country functions (eqs. D4 and D5) with both demand and competitiveness effects. This ensures that the simulation of each country in isolation is economically meaningful. Equations D6 and D7 are accounting identities defining absorption A, and GDP, denoted as Q, respectively.

Equation D8 gives the definition of total real wealth W as the sum of human wealth WH, non-human wealth (itself composed of the real market value of domestic capital) WK, real value of money balances M, domestic government bonds B, and net foreign assets converted in domestic currency units NFA/E. The four following equations D9 to D12 describe the accumulation of these different stocks linked to

Table 2: Main dynamic and long-run equations of a typical country model of MULTIMOD

(D1) $\hat{C} = c_0 + c_1(\hat{Q} - \hat{T}) + c_2 RR + c_3 \log(W_{-1}/C_{-1}) + \varepsilon_C$

(D2) $\hat{K} = k_0 + k_1 \log(WK/K_{-1}) + k_2 \log(WK_{-1}/K_{-2}) + \varepsilon_K$

(D3) $I = K - (1-\delta)K_{-1} + \varepsilon_I$

(D4) $\hat{X} = x_0 + x_1(P/\widehat{PFM}) + x_2\widehat{FA} + x_3 \log(FA_{-1}/X_{-1}) + x_4 \log(P/PFM)_{-1} + \varepsilon_X$

(D5) $\widehat{IM} = i_0 + i_1(i'\hat{A} + (1-i')\hat{X}) + i_2(\widehat{PM}/P) + i_3 \log(A^{i'}X^{1-i'}/IM)_{-1} + i_4 \log(PM/P)_{-1} + \varepsilon_{IM}$

(D6) $A = C + I + G$

(D7) $Q = A + X - IM$

(D8) $W = WH + WK_{+}(M + B + NFA/E)/P$

(D9) $WH = WH_{+1}/(1 + rbar + 0.035) + (1-\beta)(Q - T) + rpr\ WK$

(D10) $WK = WK_{+1}/(1 + RR + g) + \beta(Q - T) - (rpr + \delta)WK$

(D11) $\Delta B + \Delta M = R.B_{-1} + P(G - T + \varepsilon_B)$

(D12) $\Delta NFA + E(P.X - PM.IM) + R_{US}NFA_{-1} + \varepsilon_{NFA}$

(D13) $\Delta R - r_3(R_{+1} - R_{-1}) = u.r_1 \log(MT/M) + (1-u)r_2(\log(E_{GR}/E))^3$

(D14) $\Delta TR = t_1(B - BT)/(P.Q) + t_2\Delta[(B - BT)/(P.Q)]$

(D15) $T = TR(Q - \delta K_{-1} + R.B_{-1}/P)$

(D16) $\log(M/P) = m_0 + m_1 \log A + m_2 R + m_3 \log(M_{-1}/P_{-1}) + \varepsilon_M$

(D17) $PM = (\Sigma\pi_i P_i E_i)/E$

(D18) $\log(PFM.E) = \Sigma\, \rho_i \log(P_i.E_i)$

(D19) $(1 + R_{US}) = (1 + R)(E_{+1}/E)$ or $E_{US} = 1$

(D20) $FA = \Sigma f_i A_i$

(D21) $CAP = (g_1 K^{-\sigma} + g_2((1+\gamma)^t L(1+\varepsilon_L))^{-\sigma})^{-1/\sigma}$

(D22) $\hat{P} - \hat{P}_{-1} = p_1(\hat{P}_{+1} - \hat{P}_{-1}) + p_2(Q/CAP)$

(D23) $\beta = g_1(CAP/K)^\sigma$

(D24) $(1 + R) = (1 + RR)P_{+1}/P$

(S1) $C = c(RR, g, \varepsilon_C)W$

(S2) $K = k(g, \varepsilon_K)\,WK$

(S3) $I = (g + \delta)K + \varepsilon_I$

(S4) $X = x(g, P/PFM, \varepsilon_X)FA$

(S5) $IM = i(g, PM/P, \varepsilon_{IM})A^{i'}X^{1-i'}$

(S6) $A = C + I + G$

(S7) $Q = A + X - IM$

(S8) $W = WH + WK + (M + B + NFA/E)/P$

(S9) $(rbar + 0.035 - g)\,WH = (1 - \beta)(Q - T) + rpr\,WK$

(S10) $(RR - g)\,WK = \beta(Q - T) - (rpr + \delta + g)\,WK$

(S11) $(R - gv)B = gvM - P(G - T + \varepsilon_B)$

(S12) $(R - gv)NFA = E(PM.IM - P.X) + \varepsilon_{NFA}$

(S13) $M = MT\,(u = 1)$ or $E = e\,E_{\mathrm{GR}}\,(u = 0)$

(S14) $B = BT$

(S15) $T = TR(Q - (\delta K - R.B/P)/(1 + g))$

(S16) $M/P = m(A, g, R, \varepsilon_M)$

(S17) $PM = (\Sigma \pi_i P_i E_i)/E$

(S18) $\log(PFM.E) = \Sigma \rho_i \log(P_i E_i)$

(S19) $R = R_{\mathrm{US}}$ or $E_{\mathrm{US}} = 1$

(S20) $FA = \Sigma f_i A_i$

(S21) $CAP = (g_1 K^{-\sigma} + g_2((1 + \gamma)^t L(1 + \varepsilon_L))^{-\sigma})^{-1/\sigma}$

(S22) $Q = CAP$

(S23) $\beta = g_1(CAP/K)^{\sigma}$

(S24) $(1 + R) = (1 + RR)(1 + \rho)$

Notation: $\hat{x}$ means log (x/x_{-1}), i.e. approximately the rate of growth of x; Δx means $x - x_{-1}$; ε_X denotes the residual associated with the equation defining X; g is the growth rate of quantities; gv is the growth of nominal values; γ is the growth rate of productivity. The summation indexed by i runs over all countries/zones except the home country.

Endogenous variables

A	Real domestic absorption
B	Government bonds
C	Real consumption expenditure
CAP	Capacity output
E	Exchange rate (US Dollars per local currency)
FA	Foreign real absorption
I	Real investment
IM	Real imports
K	Capital stock
M	Monetary base
NFA	Net foreign assets in US Dollars
P	Absorption deflator
PFM	Prices in foreign markets
PM	Import prices
Q	Real GDP
R	Nominal interest rate
RR	Real interest rate
T	Government real tax receipts
TR	Tax rate
W	Real total net wealth
WH	Human wealth
WK	Real value of capital stocks
X	Real exports
β	Optimal capital share in production

Exogenous variables

BT	Target level of government debt
G	Real government expenditures
L	Labor force
MT	Target level of the monetary base
rpr	Risk premium
σ	Exponent in the CES production function; $(1/(1+\sigma))$ = elasticity of substitution
δ	Depreciation rate for the capital stock

the agents' intertemporal budget constraints. One can note that the rate at which *WH* and *WK* are discounted are different, in conformity with the implications of the Blanchard (1985) theory of finite-horizon consumers, the main difference being the probability of death, which equals 0.035. The model also includes a risk premium at a rate *rpr* paid by firms to the consumers.

The two following equations D13 and D14 describe the government behavior. The money supply is written as a reaction function of the interest rate toward a nominal money target *MT* (case $u = 1$), except for the non-German members of the European Monetary System which adjust their money supply through a reaction function towards a given exchange rate *vis-a-vis* the Deutsche Mark ($u = 0$). The tax rate *TR* is endogenous and a function of the gap between the public debt *B* and an exogenously given nominal target level *BT*, which must be reached in the long run. Equation D15 is an accounting identity for taxes *T*.

The demand for real money balances *M* (eq. D16) is standard and is linked to absorption and the interest rate. Import prices are expressed as a weighted average of exports prices of other countries expressed in dollars, these last being in turn functions of *GDP* prices and import prices (eq. D17). Prices on foreign markets *PFM*, used as intermediate variables to define the competitiveness, are a double-weighted average of *GDP* and export prices of competitors (eq. D18). Equation D19 describes the open interest parity condition, in terms of an identity for the US, and, for other countries, in terms of an adjustment of their interest rate to the US interest rate. Foreign absorption *FA* (eq. D20) is defined as a weighted sum of the absorption of the other countries.

The supply side of the model is given by equation D21, a *CES* production function with labor-augmenting technical progress γ, and by an inflation equation which summarizes the working of the labor market. This price equation D22 ends up in the long run at an equilibrium between supply and demand in the goods market. The optimal capital share in production β is computed from the production technology (eq. D23). At last there is a straightforward relation between the nominal and real interest rate (eq. D24).

4 The long-run properties of MULTIMOD

It is worthwhile to present first the main multipliers associated with the country models taken into isolation, before analyzing the properties of the long-run version of the whole multi-national model MULTIMOD.

4.1 Main multipliers of the country models

The present subsection is devoted to the presentation of the multipliers obtained with some representative long-run country models, without taking into account the

Table 3: Permanent increase in government spending by 1% of GNP – per cent deviation

US model		German model		Small Industrial Countries model	
C_{US}	−1.67	C_{GR}	−1.65	C_{SI}	−1.72
I_{US}	−1.18	I_{GR}	−0.82	I_{SI}	−0.85
IM_{US}	0.03	IM_{GR}	0.07	IM_{SI}	0.04
X_{US}	−0.25	X_{GR}	−0.18	X_{SI}	−0.13
Q_{US}	−0.36	Q_{GR}	−0.24	Q_{SI}	−0.24
R_{US}	0.86	R_{GR}	0.00	R_{SI}	0.00
P_{US}	0.36	P_{GR}	0.17	P_{SI}	0.20
PM_{US}	0.03	PM_{GR}	−0.08	PM_{SI}	0.01
NFA_{US}	−22.94	NFA_{GR}	−22.93	NFA_{SI}	36.55
E_{US}	0.00	E_{GR}	0.09	E_{SI}	0.00

international feedbacks. These long-run multipliers may be interpreted as giving directly the asymptotic effects of sustained multiplicative shocks on the dynamic original MULTIMOD country models.

We have put forward in Subsection 3.3 that the foreign trade is specified in such a way that the simulation of each country in isolation is economically meaningful. However, there is one important exception concerning the US model. Indeed, all the exchange rates are defined in MULTIMOD as the price of the national currency expressed in US Dollars, and the US exchange rate is by definition equal to unity (see eq. S19). As a consequence, each simulation of the US model alone, without taking into account the reaction of the foreign exchange rates, must be interpreted as if the US were in a situation of fixed exchange rates.

Table 3 gives the results of a permanent increase by 1% of government spending in the US, Germany and the Small Industrial Countries respectively, calculated with the relevant country models. As money supply and public debt are fixed to their target values in the long run, this increase must be exactly balanced by a rise in real taxes.[4] This rise in taxes implies a drop in consumption. We observe that there is more than 100% crowding out, resulting in a decline in absorption. This is a result of the fact that the decrease in consumer's wealth goes beyond the increase in the present value of the additional taxes at the market interest rate. This mechanism, which is a typical consequence of the hypothesis of finite-horizon consumers, appears quantitatively fairly independent of the economy under

4. In the Small Industrial Countries there is no money target (see eq. S13), and the level of money supply results from the demand for money balances. The variation of this last variable is however rather small (0.05%) due to the opposite variation of quantities and prices.

Table 4: Permanent increase in money target by 1% – per cent deviation

US model		German model	
C_{US}	0.47	C_{GR}	0.00
I_{US}	0.75	I_{GR}	0.00
IM_{US}	1.09	IM_{GR}	0.00
X_{US}	−0.42	X_{GR}	0.00
Q_{US}	0.21	Q_{GR}	0.00
R_{US}	−1.45	R_{GR}	0.00
P_{US}	0.64	P_{GR}	1.00
NFA_{US}	47.54	NFA_{GR}	1.11
E_{US}	0.00	E_{GR}	−0.91

consideration: i.e. in the quasi-closed economy (US), and in the small open economy with a flexible exchange rate (Germany), or a fixed exchange rate (Small Industrial Countries). The price level increases, associated with LM-equilibration, but in the US case, the interest rate rises, which leads to an even higher price level.

The effects of a permanent augmentation of the money supply by 1% are given in Table 4. We first recall that in the Small Industrial Countries, as in other countries participating in the Exchange Rate Mechanism (ERM) of the European Monetary System, there is no concept of money target. If we consider the second column of Table 4 giving the effects of an increase of 1% of the money target in Germany, we observe that money is neutral: the shock induces a rise in prices of 1%, especially the DM price of the US Dollar, which is equal to $1/E$. The variation of nominal net foreign assets *NFA*, expressed in US Dollars, deserves specific comments because the behavior of this variable reveals an important feature of the model around the given long-run equilibrium. First, it must be observed that in equation S12, the relation between the stock of *NFA* and the flow of the trade balance degenerates if the nominal interest rate R is equal to the nominal growth rate gv as it is in the reference path: the variable *NFA* disappears from this equation.[5] The economic interpretation is that on a steady-state growth path the interest received at each period on *NFA* is exactly compensated by the yearly purchase of foreign assets. Then it is easy to see that, in that case, *NFA* does not belong any more to the simultaneous block of the model, but to the epilogue and is logically determined by the wealth equation S8. As a consequence, the variation of *NFA* can take any

5. This mathematical singularity of the reference path raised serious numerical problems during the simulations of the country models as well as of the whole model.

Table 5: Permanent increase in public debt target by 1% – per cent deviation

US model		German model		Small Industrial Countries model	
Q_{US}	0.00	Q_{GR}	0.00	Q_{SI}	0.00
R_{US}	0.00	R_{GR}	0.00	R_{SI}	0.00
P_{US}	0.00	P_{GR}	0.00	P_{SI}	0.00
NFA_{US}	0.21	NFA_{GR}	−0.12	NFA_{SI}	0.25
E_{US}	0.00	E_{GR}	0.00	E_{SI}	0.00

value contrary to other nominal variables of the simultaneous block which increase by 1%.

By contrast we see in the first column of Table 4 that money appears as being not neutral in the US long-run model. We recall that the way the exchange rates are defined in MULTIMOD implies that, when simulating the US economy in isolation, the system works as if exchange rates were fixed. Indeed US prices increase by less than 1% because of the stabilizing effect of import prices. Hence the interest rate must decrease because of the LM-mechanism, leading to an upward shift of the equilibrium level of capital and the output supply.

Table 5 gives the effects of a permanent increase in the public debt target BT of 1%. The special feature of the reference equilibrium path ($R = gv$), noted above, implies here that the variable B disappears from the government balance sheet identity, equation S11. Furthermore, in the wealth equation S8, the rise in B is exactly compensated by a symmetrical drop in NFA. Indeed, the change of this last variable produces no reaction on the simultaneous block of the system.

4.2 Multi-national interdependencies in the long-run multi-national model

We present in this subsection the multipliers obtained with the long-run version of the whole MULTIMOD.

Table 6 summarizes the incidence on the main variables of the model as a result of an increase in public spending by 1% of GDP in the US, Germany and Small Industrial Countries, respectively. We first observe that the own country effects are indeed rather close to those given in Table 3, which were obtained without taking into account international interdependencies. More precisely, the shocks depress slightly less their own economy. In the case of the US, the international transmission of the shock creates an upward shift in the US (hence world) interest rate, an appreciation of the US Dollar and a worldwide economic contraction. A public

Table 6: Permanent increase in government spending by 1% of GNP – per cent deviation

	G_{US}	G_{GR}	G_{SI}		G_{US}	G_{GR}	G_{SI}
C_{CA}	−0.25	0.04	0.01	C_{SI}	−0.02	−0.01	**−1.73**
IM_{CA}	−0.34	0.07	0.01	IM_{SI}	−0.05	−0.03	**0.03**
X_{CA}	0.03	0.02	−0.01	X_{SI}	−0.03	0.00	**−0.14**
Q_{CA}	−0.05	0.03	−0.01	Q_{SI}	−0.02	0.02	**−0.25**
R_{CA}	0.15	−0.21	0.02	R_{SI}	0.15	−0.21	**0.07**
P_{CA}	−0.01	−0.05	−0.01	P_{SI}	0.03	−0.10	**0.20**
E_{CA}	−0.25	0.02	0.02	E_{SI}	−0.05	0.02	**−0.02**
C_{FR}	−0.02	−0.01	−0.05	C_{UK}	−0.03	−0.06	−0.09
IM_{FR}	−0.04	−0.03	−0.09	IM_{UK}	−0.03	−0.08	−0.10
X_{FR}	−0.02	0.03	−0.01	X_{UK}	−0.07	0.19	0.04
Q_{FR}	−0.02	0.02	−0.02	Q_{UK}	−0.04	0.03	−0.04
R_{FR}	0.15	−0.21	0.07	R_{UK}	0.15	−0.21	0.07
P_{FR}	0.02	−0.12	−0.02	P_{UK}	0.09	−0.34	−0.07
E_{FR}	−0.05	0.02	−0.02	E_{UK}	−0.05	0.02	−0.02
C_{GR}	−0.01	**−1.66**	−0.05	C_{US}	**−1.63**	0.03	−0.01
IM_{GR}	−0.03	**0.07**	−0.10	IM_{US}	**−0.04**	0.06	−0.03
X_{GR}	−0.04	**−0.15**	−0.04	X_{US}	**−0.24**	0.02	−0.01
Q_{GR}	−0.02	**−0.21**	−0.02	Q_{US}	**−0.28**	0.03	−0.01
R_{GR}	0.15	**−0.21**	0.07	R_{US}	**0.15**	−0.21	0.07
P_{GR}	0.03	**0.12**	0.01	P_{US}	**0.18**	−0.05	0.02
E_{GR}	−0.05	**0.02**	−0.02	E_{US}	**0.00**	0.00	0.00
C_{IT}	−0.05	−0.01	−0.07	$CTOT_{DC}$	−0.08	0.00	−0.05
IM_{IT}	−0.07	−0.02	−0.08	IM_{DC}	−0.14	0.04	−0.04
X_{IT}	−0.01	0.06	0.01	X_{DC}	−0.10	0.02	−0.02
Q_{IT}	−0.03	0.03	−0.02	Q_{DC}	−0.05	0.00	−0.02
R_{IT}	0.15	−0.21	0.07	P_{DC}	−0.02	−0.06	0.02
P_{IT}	−0.01	−0.14	−0.04				
E_{IT}	−0.05	0.02	−0.02				
C_{JA}	−0.05	−0.01	0.00	X_{HO}	−0.22	0.04	−0.06
IM_{JA}	−0.12	−0.02	0.00	IM_{HO}	−0.13	0.01	−0.04
X_{JA}	−0.03	0.08	−0.03	Q_{HO}	−0.08	0.01	−0.02
Q_{JA}	−0.03	0.03	−0.01				
R_{JA}	0.15	−0.21	0.07				
P_{JA}	0.03	−0.06	0.02	$POIL$	0.03	−0.07	0.03
E_{JA}	−0.13	−0.07	0.02	$PCOM$	−0.12	−0.08	−0.05

Table 7: Permanent decrease of money supply target in the US by 1% – per cent deviation

	CA	FR	GR	IT	JA	SI	UK	US
IM	−0.23	−0.14	−0.11	−0.16	0.02	−0.17	−0.02	−0.23
X	−0.06	−0.11	−0.15	−0.12	−0.30	−0.11	−0.41	−0.09
Q	−0.10	−0.10	−0.10	−0.13	−0.10	−0.09	−0.17	−0.09
P	0.15	0.12	0.16	0.13	0.19	0.15	0.55	−0.83
R	0.71	0.71	0.71	0.71	0.71	0.71	0.71	0.71
E	−1.09	−0.92	−0.92	−0.92	−0.75	−0.92	−0.92	0.00

demand shock in the Small Industrial Countries induces contracting results qualitatively quite similar to those generated by the US. By contrast, results are reversed in the case of a shock in Germany which initiates a worldwide expansion through a drop in interest rates.

Concerning the role of public debt, we can deduce from the results obtained in the previous subsection, that a shock in the public debt Target BT will have here no more effect than in the country models in isolation.

The last and most puzzling experiment concerns the role of the money supply target. Indeed, as in the country models, there is no money supply target in the countries participating in the ERM. An increase in the money supply target in Germany has again no real effects, and produces a rise in the same proportion in prices and nominal variables in Germany, but implies now the same nominal evolutions in France, Italy, United Kingdom and the Small Industrial Countries whose exchange rates are supposed to be pegged to the German one. By contrast, it is impossible to find a solution of the system in the case of an increase of the money supply target in the US. However, a *decrease* of the same amount leads to the results displayed in Table 7. This result can be explained by the special feature of the long-run structure of MULTIMOD, which is not easy to exhibit: there is another equilibrium corresponding to the same exogenous data generating the baseline reference path given by the IMF, which is very close to the first. This equilibrium can be generated by making the US interest rate exogenous and by recomputing it through the US money demand equation (eq. S16). Figure 1 plots, for values of the nominal interest rate between 6.82% and 6.96%, the difference between the interest rate, computed from equation S16, and the exogenously "supplied" one. The bold line, which describes the baseline case, is almost tangential to the horizontal axis. Actually, it intersects this last one twice for the very close values of the interest rate 6.88% and 6.90%. The money shock curve of the figure corresponds

Figure 1: Long-run equilibria of MULTIMOD

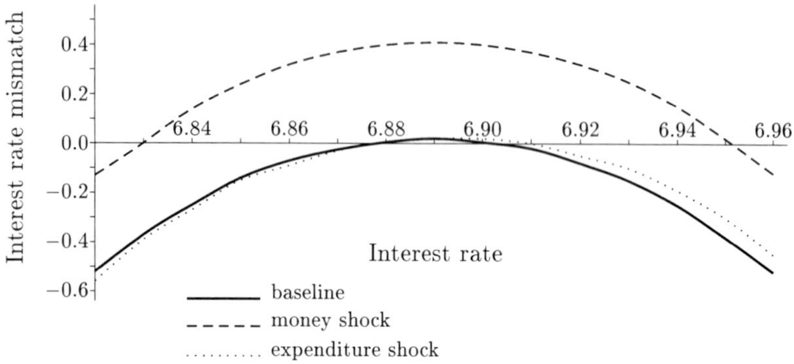

to a 1% permanent decrease of the US money target. The case of an increase is symmetrical and, indeed, does not allow for an equilibrium.

5 Conclusion

In the present paper we have shown that the determination of the long run of models is a workable framework for large-scale macroeconometric models. The problem is not the complexity of this task but the fact that most macroeconometric models do not have well-specified long-run properties, even models with rational expectations which should possess correctly defined terminal conditions. Our results confirm that MULTIMOD is one of the rare large-scale models to include a well-specified long-run. However, the complexity of its long run comes from two main peculiar features. First, the general interdependent nature of the (static) system gives no weight to the past and to the future as in the dynamic version. Second, the other source of complexity lies in stock-flow relations which lead to highly sensitive equations in the long run.

The most noticeable property of the steady-state structure of MULTIMOD is the existence of two close solutions. We do not understand well the reasons for this feature. They need careful investigations which are left for further research.

References

Bergstrom, A.R. and C.R. Wymer (1976), "A model of disequilibrium neoclassical growth and its application to the United Kingdom", in A.R. Bergstrom, editor, *Statistical inference in continuous time economic models*, North-Holland, Amsterdam.

Blanchard, O.J. (1985), "Debts, deficits and finite horizons", *Journal of Political Economy*, **93**, 223–247.

Currie, D.A. (1982), "The long-run properties of the Bank of England's small monetary model of the UK economy", *Applied Economics*, **14**, 63–72.

Deleau, M., C. Le Van, and P. Malgrange (1990), "The long run of macroeconometric models", in Champsaur, P. *et al.*, editors, *Essays in honor of Edmond Malinvaud, volume II, macroeconomics*, MIT Press, Cambridge.

Gandolfo, G. (1981), *Qualitative analysis and econometric estimation of continuous time dynamic models*, North-Holland, Amsterdam.

Masson, P.R., S.A. Symansky, and G. Meredith (1990), "MULTIMOD Mark II a revised and extended model", Occasional Paper 71, International Monetary Fund, Washington DC.

Masson, P.R., S.A. Symansky, and G. Meredith (1991), "Changes to MULTIMOD since the Occasional Paper no. 71. current model: MULTIAP", Internal Paper, International Monetary Fund, Washington DC.

Wallis, K.F. and J.D. Whitley (1987), "Long-run properties of large-scale macroeconometric models", *Annales d'Economie et de Statistique*, **6/7**, 207–224.

Methods and Applications of Economic Dynamics
L. Schoonbeek, E. Sterken and S.K. Kuipers (editors)

Chapter 11

Modeling the dynamics of net wages[1]

Lambert Schoonbeek and Elmer Sterken

1 Introduction

Macroeconometric models have been used for policy advice in the Netherlands for more than 55 years now. Since Tinbergen (1936) newer generations of models have become more sophisticated, see Barten (1991) and Fase *et al.* (1990) for an overview. A typical example of the Dutch variety is the CESAM model, the annual model of the CCSO-group, see Kuipers *et al.* (1988, 1990). Although most modern models claim to be eclectic, their properties are basically Keynesian. An exception is the MIMIC model, see Gelauff (1992), which can be labeled as an applied general equilibrium model. The Keynesian perception is sharply characterized by a Hicksian IS/LM-type expenditure modeling and the inclusion of a Phillips curve. The specification of the wage submodel is extremely important for the properties of the system, both in the short- and the long run. The majority of the models is used for short-term or medium-term analysis of the Dutch economy. Only a small number of long-term models has been developed. The Scientific Council for Government Policy has published the study Van Eijk and Veeneklaas (1987), and more recently the Central Planning Bureau (1992a) has published a long-term scenario-analysis. These studies are not based on standard macroeconometric models, however, and do not include econometric wage submodels.

An interesting line of research is the study of the long-run properties of existing macroeconometric models. A number of techniques for the analysis of long-run

1. We thank Johan Graafland for providing data and useful remarks and Jan Jacobs for helpful discussions.

properties has been developed, which we have reviewed in the introductory chapter. Let us shortly remind some of these techniques and "apply" them to CESAM.

First, one can carry out deterministic or stochastic simulation experiments with the model. Using (extended) smoothed numerical values for the exogenous variables, long-run deterministic simulated endogenous paths can give insight into the stability and oscillatory behavior of the model. It must be stressed, however, that numerical illustrations can hardly be seen as an explanation of the model's behavior. Applying this approach to the CESAM model, it comes to the fore that CESAM in its present form is not suited for long-term analysis, as the interaction between the supply-side submodel and expenditure submodel is troublesome in the long run. In particular, the interaction between wages, (un)employment, and capacity utilization deserves further attention.

Second, one can investigate the model with structural sensitivity analysis, see Kuh *et al.* (1985). The first step of this analysis consists of the linearization of the model around a reference solution. Next, the linearized model is analyzed with linear dynamic systems methods. In particular, the sensitivity of the eigensystem of the linearized model with respect to perturbations in the model parameters is investigated in detail. For a study of the eigensystem of CESAM, see Schoonbeek (1990).

A third line of research is more theoretical in nature. What are the theoretical essential characteristics of the model that drive the long-run solution? In new-classical models the long run of the model depends only on the specification of technology and preferences. New-Keynesian models, which assume imperfect competition, focus on wage and price formation on both the labor and the goods market, see Layard and Nickell (1986) and Layard *et al.* (1991). An example is the model wherein the wage level is determined by collective wage bargaining, whereas prices are set using mark-up factors over unit labor costs. A long-run equilibrium rate of unemployment (NAIRU) expressed in terms of exogenous variables – like tax rates of employers and employees, the real import price etc. – can then be computed. The convergence properties of the actual unemployment towards the NAIRU are essential for the model's characteristics, see Fisher and Henry (1992) and Turner (1991).

Since it turned out in simulations carried out by us (not reported here) that the long-run properties of the CESAM model heavily depend on the interaction of the wages and unemployment, we decide to proceed here with a detailed analysis of the dynamics of wage formation in the Netherlands. In Section 2, we therefore consider inspired by the NAIRU-literature the modeling of a wage level equation for the Netherlands using the cointegration approach. It comes out that Dutch data do not support the wage level approach after 1988. The sudden downturn in unemployment in the late eighties is shown to be responsible for this structural breakdown. In Section 3 we therefore consider the estimation of a Phillips-type wage growth equation. We sum up with conclusions in Section 4.

2 Modeling a wage level equation

In this section we model a wage level equation for the private sector of the Netherlands. We do not give a rigorous theoretical derivation of the wage level equation.[2] In Subsection 2.1 the empirical specification is discussed. Estimation of the equation is in Subsections 2.2 to 2.4, where we follow the cointegration approach. One of the attractive features of this approach is that a sharp distinction can be made between long-run and short-run dynamics. In particular, we apply the two-stage procedure developed by Engle and Granger (1987).[3] Related empirical studies on wage level equations for the Netherlands are those of Graafland and Huizinga (1988), Lever (1991), Graafland (1992) (the latter two studies are not based on cointegration theory, however), and Den Butter and Van de Wijngaert (1992). The recent model of the Dutch Central Bank, Fase *et al.* (1990), also contains a wage level equation; however, this equation is not derived with cointegration theory. Related studies for the United Kingdom are e.g. Hall (1986), Hall and Henry (1988, chapter 2) and Joyce (1990).

2.1 The specification of the wage equation

Starting point for the long-run part of our wage level equation is the model

$$WAGE/PCONS = f(UNEMPLOYMENT, TREND, WEDGE) \tag{1}$$

which can be considered as an exponent of the real wage resistance model as originally proposed by Sargan (1964). Without being very precise about their exact meaning, $WAGE$, $PCONS$, $UNEMPLOYMENT$, $TREND$ and $WEDGE$ denote some measure of respectively, the nominal wage, the consumption price, unemployment, a trend representing "desired" real wage, and the wedge. The model might be derived from a union bargaining framework, in which unions, representing the employees, bargain with the employers over the wages of their members. According to the model the level of the real wage is negatively dependent on the level of unemployment. This is a reflection of the weaker position of the unions during the wage negotiations in case unemployment is relatively high. The employees might fear a loss of their own jobs if the wage claims are too high. The real wage further depends on some "desired" or "target" trend level. Sargan (1964) simply used a time trend as the explanatory variable, but in more contemporaneous models some variable that measures productivity is commonly used. As argued by Hall (1986), from a theoretical point of view the latter choice is more appropriate. Finally, the real wage is influenced by the wedge term, which loosely speaking is the difference

2. See Layard *et al.* (1991).
3. For a description of various aspects of cointegration theory, we refer to Engle and Granger (1991) and Cuthbertson *et al.* (1992).

between the real wage costs of concern to the employers and the real take-home pay of the employees.

In order to apply model (1) in an empirical analysis, it is necessary to define the variables that are used more exactly. To illustrate the degrees of freedom in the definitions of the variables, consider e.g. the nominal wages. In practice, we can choose between the following three variables, W, WG and WN, which represent in nominal terms the wage sum, the gross wage rate, and the net wage rate per man-year of labor in the private sector, respectively. The variables are interrelated by means of the identities $WG \equiv W(1 - slwg)$ and $WN \equiv W(1 - slwn - slwg)$, in which $slwg$ denotes the social security contributions and pension premiums paid by the private sector employers as a fraction of W. Similarly, $slwn$ denotes, as a fraction of W, the social security premiums, pension premiums and taxes on wages and transfers paid by employees in the private sector. We simply refer to $slwg$ as the employment tax, and to $slwn$ as the direct tax. Associated with the three different nominal wage variables we can define the following wage variables in real terms, W_{real}, WG_{real} and WN_{real}, respectively. Here $W_{real} \equiv W/p_c$, where p_c is the price index-number of consumption of households. WG_{real} and WN_{real} are defined analogously. While specifying the wage level equation we must select one of these three real wage variables as the dependent variable. Obviously, given the values of $slwn$, $slwg$ and the chosen dependent variable, we can simply compute the values of the other two real wage variables. However, in practice, the estimation results will depend on the particular choice of the dependent variable.

Next, consider the explanatory variables of model (1). We consider as measures of unemployment the unemployment rate u, and the short-term (less than one year) unemployment rate us, both as a percentage of the labor supply excluding self-employed. The short-term unemployment rate can be used to investigate the relevance of so-called duration effects in the wage equation. Duration effects indicate an appreciable effect of the short-term unemployment rate only on the size of the real wage rate. In other words, we have duration effects in case the long-term unemployed have lost their influence on the determination of the wages. We also consider $\log u$ as an explanatory variable. The use of $\log u$ instead of u implies that at a higher rate of unemployment a larger absolute increase of unemployment is necessary to have the same moderating impact on the level of the real wage, see Joyce (1990). Therefore, the use of $\log u$ can point at duration effects. With respect to the trend variable that appears in model (1), we consider three indices measuring productivity. The ratio between gross value added and employment (excluding self-employed) in man-years in the private sector, denoted as $prod$, is mostly used. The other two productivity variables are simple smoothed versions of $prod$. They are defined as $prod1 \equiv (prod + prod_{-1})/2$ and $prod2 \equiv (prod + prod_{-1} + prod_{-2})/3$. The argument to include smoothed productivity measures is that smoothing rules out measurement errors. It should be noted that experimenting with various lag structures in the wage level is not essential, because theoretically it may not have an impact on the estimated cointegrating vector.

In order to discuss the concept of the wedge, we first remark that the dependent variable of the wage level equation is usually specified in logarithms. The log of the net wage rate WN is the important nominal wage variable for the employees. Ultimately, however, they will be concerned with the real purchasing power of their wage, i.e. they are concerned with the real net wage $\log(WN/p_c)$, which is also called the real consumption wage. The important nominal wage variable for the employers is the log of the wage sum W, as this represents their measure for total nominal labor costs. Assume for the moment that the employers deflate $\log W$ by using the same price index-number as the employees, p_c: $\log(W/p_c)$ is called the real product wage. The wedge is defined as the difference between the real product wage and the real consumption wage. Thus, it is given by $-\log(1 - slwn - slwg)$. The wedge must be included in the wage level equation if one expects that an increase in the wedge implies an increase in the wage sum W, because the employees will resist a fall in their real purchasing power as a result of higher taxes. To illustrate this, let us consider the following concrete example of a wage level equation, in which we take $\log WN_{real}$ as the dependent variable

$$\log WN_{real} = a_1 \log prod - a_2 u - a_3(-\log(1 - slwn - slwg)) + a_4 \qquad (2)$$

One expects with respect to the coefficients of this equation that $a_1 > 0, a_2 > 0$, and $0 < a_3 \leq 1$. The magnitude of a_3 reflects the extent to which the employees are able to resist a fall in their real purchasing power.

Three remarks are now in order. Firstly, the form in which the wedge enters into the wage equation depends on the particular choice of the dependent variable of this equation. To take a simple example, if the dependent variable in equation (2) would have been $\log W_{real}$, then the wedge term enters the equation as $-a'_3 \log(1 - slwn - slwg)$. Secondly, if the employers use a value-added price index-number in order to deflate the nominal wage sum, then the wedge also includes the difference between this price index-number and the consumption price index-number. In the literature one often rewrites this difference in terms of a real import price (possibly weighted with the ratio of imports to total value-added of the private sector) and the indirect tax rate. See e.g. Joyce (1990) and Layard *et al.* (1991). Thirdly, we remark that in practice one generally specifies the wedge while linearizing the terms that involve logarithms of the tax variables. To give an example here, instead of using the wedge as specified in equation (2), one simply specifies the wedge as $(slwn + slwg)$. In the context of this third remark, we also recall that the tax variables $slwn$ and $slwg$ are specified as a fraction of the wage sum W. However, alternative specifications of the tax variables are possible. Two straightforward examples are: (1) the pair of identities $WG(1 + slwg1) \equiv W$ and $WG(1 - slwn1) \equiv WN$ implicitly define an employment tax, $slwg1$, and a direct tax, $slwn1$, both as a fraction of the gross wage rate WG; and (2) the pair of identities $W(1 - slwg) \equiv WG$ and $WG(1 - slwn1) \equiv WN$, define the employment tax as a fraction of the wage sum W, and the direct tax as a fraction of the gross wage rate WG. We conclude that the wedge, and consequently the estimation results for the wage equation, might depend on the exact definition of the tax variables, in particular if we linearize the logarithms as described above.

2.2 Modeling the long run

We estimate the wage level equation with annual data for the Dutch economy covering the period 1953–1989. For details on the data used, we refer the reader to Jongbloed *et al.* (1991). The use of annual data clearly implies that the time series consists of only a limited number, namely 37, of observations. However, the following arguments in favor of using our annual data set can be given. First, the CESAM model used the same Jongbloed *et al.* data. Second, no official quarterly (macro) data are available for, amongst others, the Dutch wages over a reasonable period. Third, wage contracts in the Netherlands are primarily based on yearly periods. Finally, we remark that related studies of Graafland and Huizinga (1988), Lever (1991), Graafland (1992), and Den Butter and Van de Wijngaert (1992) are also based on annual data. The last year of the estimation period 1989 is chosen because in 1990 an important institutional change has been made in the tax-system in the Netherlands (the so-called "Plan Oort" has been introduced), which resulted in a structural break in the employment and direct taxes. After 1990 the National Accounts give rise to a structural break in the wage sum time series. A last remark should be made with respect to the unemployment series u. This series suffers from serious changes in definition. As we point out later on this can be a cause of problems in interpreting long-run parameters.

As a first step of the cointegration analysis, we have to establish the so-called order of integration of the variables involved.[4] Essentially, the order of integration of a variable equals d, if the variable must be differenced d times in order to produce a stationary time series. In that case we label the variable $I(d)$. Thus, in particular a stationary variable is $I(0)$. The order of integration of a variable can be determined by applying unit root tests. Following common practice, we use the well-known Dickey-Fuller (DF) and Augmented Dickey-Fuller (ADF) unit root tests. See Dickey and Fuller (1979, 1981). DF_c refers to the Dickey-Fuller test statistic including a constant, and DF_t to the Dickey-Fuller test statistic including a constant and a time trend. ADF_c and ADF_t are defined in an analogous way. Both ADF tests are specified with a one year lag. The null-hypothesis of all tests is the existence of a unit root. The null is rejected if the relevant test statistic is below its critical value.

4. For a formal discussion we refer to Engle and Granger (1987).

Critical values are derived from MacKinnon (1992).[5] Preceding the presentation of our results, we already remark here that it turns out that it is not possible to determine the order of integration of all variables unambiguously. Clearly, this is related to the fact that the length of our time series is rather limited. As a consequence, the discriminatory power of the unit root tests is low. Similar findings are reported by Graafland and Huizinga (1988) and Den Butter and Van de Wijngaert (1992).

In Table 1 we present the results of the unit root tests for the variables considered in this study. First we examine the logs of the three nominal wage variables W, WG and WN. Taking as an example $\log W$, we see that the second-order difference $\Delta\Delta \log W$ is stationary, i.e. it is an $I(0)$ variable. This implies that the first-order difference $\Delta \log W$ is $I(1)$, and that $\log W$ itself is $I(2)$. The same applies to $\log WG$ and $\log WN$. It further follows from Table 1 that the log of the consumption price, p_c, is $I(2)$. Turning to the real wage variables, we see that the order of integration of $\log W_{real}$ and $\log WG_{real}$ cannot be determined unambiguously. However, the order of integration of $\log WN_{real}$, the real net wage rate, apparently equals unity!

The ambiguity in the test statistics associated with the logs of the real wage sum and real gross wage rate can further be analyzed by considering the identities (i) $\log WN_{real} \equiv \log W_{real} + \log(1 - slwn - slwg)$ and (ii) $\log WG_{real} \equiv \log W_{real} + \log(1 - slwg)$. We observe from Table 1 that $\log(1 - slwn - slwg)$ is $I(1)$, whereas it is ambiguous whether $\log(1 - slwg)$ is $I(1)$ or $I(2)$. Now two remarks can be made. First, theoretically speaking it is likely to follow from (i) that $\log W_{real}$ should be $I(1)$ if $\log WN_{real}$ and $\log(1 - slwn - slwg)$ are both $I(1)$, except if the latter two form a cointegrating vector. The data do not support this very strongly, however. Second, from (ii) we see that the ambiguity found with respect to $\log W_{real}$ and $\log WG_{real}$ is particularly related to the unclear stationarity properties of the time series of $\log(1 - slwg)$.

Next, we examine in Table 1 the three productivity variables. It appears that $\log prod$ is $I(1)$, whereas $\log prod1$ and $\log prod2$ are $I(1)$ or $I(2)$. Turning to the unemployment measures, we see that the unemployment rate u is $I(1)$ or $I(2)$, whereas $\log u$ is $I(1)$. The short-term unemployment rate us as well as its log are obviously $I(1)$.

Next we consider the specification of the long-run equilibrium wage level equation. At first, it is convenient to delete the wedge term from our analysis. Later on the wedge is included again. See Joyce (1990) for a similar procedure. Given the results of Table 1, we first examine whether the variables $\log WN_{real}$, $\log prod$ and $\log u$ cointegrate, as these three variables are clearly $I(1)$. Therefore, we estimate with ordinary least squares the so-called cointegration regression with $\log WN_{real}$ as the dependent variable. In order to investigate the existence of cointegration

5. All calculations are carried out with MicroTSP, see Hall *et al.* (1990).

Table 1: DF and ADF statistics of model variables, 1953–1989

	DF_c	ADF_c	DF_t	ADF_t	order of integration
$\log W$	−2.87	−1.47	+1.89	−1.02	$I(2)$
$\Delta \log W$	−1.66	−1.51	−2.10	−1.95	
$\Delta\Delta \log W$	−6.21	−5.96	−6.14	−5.95	
$\log WG$	−2.20	−0.73	+0.50	−2.20	$I(2)$
$\Delta \log WG$	−2.23	−2.18	−2.13	−2.10	
$\Delta\Delta \log WG$	−4.96	−4.40	−4.85	−4.24	
$\log WN$	−2.39	−0.96	+0.64	−1.41	$I(2)$
$\Delta \log WN$	−2.50	−2.44	−2.57	−2.55	
$\Delta\Delta \log WN$	−5.99	−5.00	−5.91	−4.91	
$\log p_c$	−0.19	−0.60	−0.86	−2.21	$I(2)$
$\Delta \log p_c$	−2.27	−1.95	−2.23	−1.89	
$\Delta\Delta \log p_c$	−6.88	−5.11	−6.94	−5.24	
$\log W_{real}$	−4.98	−2.51	+0.85	−0.15	$I(1), I(2)$
$\Delta \log W_{real}$	−2.14	−2.28	−3.09	−3.61	
$\Delta\Delta \log W_{real}$	−5.60	−7.80	−5.50	−7.67	
$\log WG_{real}$	−5.23	−2.77	+0.08	−0.54	$I(1), I(2)$
$\Delta \log WG_{real}$	−2.67	−2.68	−3.59	−4.09	
$\Delta\Delta \log WG_{real}$	−6.02	−6.84	−5.95	−6.76	
$\log WN_{real}$	−3.87	−2.43	−1.27	−1.48	$I(1)$
$\Delta \log WN_{real}$	−3.51	−3.15	−3.87	−3.65	
$\Delta\Delta \log WN_{real}$	−7.00	−5.24	−7.00	−5.27	
$\log(1 - slwg)$	−1.16	−1.18	+0.04	−0.25	$I(1), I(2)$
$\Delta \log(1 - slwg)$	−4.38	−2.52	−4.58	−2.70	
$\Delta\Delta \log(1 - slwg)$	−9.90	−7.08	−9.93	−7.28	
$\log(1 - slwg - slwn)$	−1.32	−1.33	−0.17	−0.70	$I(1)$
$\Delta \log(1 - slwn - slwg)$	−4.20	−3.44	−4.39	−3.62	
$\log prod$	−2.13	−1.76	+0.29	−0.14	$I(1)$
$\Delta \log prod$	−4.21	−3.40	−4.60	−3.87	
$\log prod1$	−2.25	−1.34	+0.81	−0.81	$I(1), I(2)$
$\Delta \log prod1$	−2.64	−3.40	−2.92	−3.82	
$\Delta\Delta \log prod1$	−4.99	−8.10	−4.91	−8.07	
Critical values ($\alpha = 5\%$)	−2.94	−2.94	−3.53	−3.53	

Table 1: continued

	DF_c	ADF_c	DF_t	ADF_t	order of integration
$\log prod2$	−2.54	−1.43	+1.39	−0.94	$I(1), I(2)$
$\Delta \log prod2$	−1.66	−2.06	−2.07	−2.48	
$\Delta\Delta \log prod2$	−5.10	−5.15	−5.19	−5.39	
u	−0.79	−1.54	−1.63	−3.09	$I(1), I(2)$
Δu	−3.24	−2.77	−3.19	−2.72	
$\Delta\Delta u$	−6.90	−4.88	−6.74	−4.81	
$\log u$	−0.70	−1.25	−2.19	−3.09	$I(1)$
$\Delta \log u$	−4.14	−5.04	−4.06	−4.86	
us	−1.18	−1.69	−1.12	−2.46	$I(1)$
Δus	−3.83	−3.99	−3.85	−3.93	
$\log us$	−1.10	−1.51	−1.68	−2.80	$I(1)$
$\Delta \log us$	−4.46	−5.29	−4.48	−5.20	
$slwn$	−1.23	−1.21	−1.23	−1.49	$I(1)$
$\Delta slwn$	−5.58	−4.17	−5.81	−4.43	
$slwg$	−1.13	−1.11	−0.10	−0.40	$I(1), I(2)$
$\Delta slwg$	−4.58	−2.69	−4.68	−2.79	
$\Delta\Delta slwg$	−10.25	−7.46	−10.14	−7.42	
$(slwn + slwg)$	−1.72	−1.64	+0.14	−0.22	$I(1)$
$\Delta(slwn + slwg)$	−4.51	−3.34	−4.95	−3.77	
$slwn1$	−1.60	−1.56	−0.62	−0.92	$I(1)$
$\Delta slwn1$	−4.94	−3.78	−5.24	−4.09	
$slwg1$	−1.17	−1.18	+0.03	−0.25	$I(1), I(2)$
$\Delta slwg1$	−4.44	−2.56	−4.65	−2.74	
$\Delta\Delta slwg1$	−9.96	−7.22	−9.99	−7.41	
$\log p_{m,real}$	−1.82	−1.77	−1.74	−1.83	$I(1)$
$\Delta \log p_{m,real}$	−5.06	−4.68	−5.11	−4.83	
$(s \log p_{m,real})$	−1.29	−1.42	−2.12	−2.45	$I(1)$
$\Delta(s \log p_{m,real})$	−5.23	−4.85	−5.14	−4.76	
Critical values ($\alpha = 5\%$)	−2.94	−2.94	−3.53	−3.53	

Table 1: continued

	DF$_c$	ADF$_c$	DF$_t$	ADF$_t$	order of integration
$wedge$	−1.95	−2.12	−1.90	−2.07	$I(1)$
$\Delta wedge$	−5.09	−4.36	−5.03	−4.32	
$\log p_y$ [a]	−0.39	−0.49	−1.66	−2.13	$I(2)$
$\Delta \log p_y$	−2.65	−2.86	−2.52	−2.74	
$\Delta\Delta \log p_y$	−7.33	−6.00	−7.51	−6.11	
$\log(p_y/p_c)$	−0.23	−0.51	−2.84	−3.79	$I(0), I(1)$
$\Delta \log(p_y/p_c)$	−3.90	−4.25	−3.77	−4.10	
$\log rpl$ [b]	−1.74	−1.84	−0.40	−0.81	$I(1)$
$\Delta \log rpl$	−3.22	−2.82	−4.39	−4.34	
u_{cor}	−0.67	−1.90	−1.52	−3.09	$I(1), I(2)$
$\Delta \log u_{cor}$	−2.48	−3.60	−2.41	−3.48	
$\Delta\Delta \log u_{cor}$	−4.71	−4.75	−4.66	−4.74	
$\log u_{cor}$	−0.59	−1.21	−2.54	−3.37	$I(1)$
$\Delta \log u_{cor}$	−4.21	−5.43	−4.10	−5.26	
$1/u$	−1.00	−1.69	−3.16	−5.01	$I(0), I(1)$
$\Delta(1/u)$	−4.62	−7.61	−4.54	−7.42	
$slwn_{-1}(SL\mathring{W}N - \mathring{W}N)$	−5.40	−4.03	−5.81	−4.48	$I(0)$
$slwg_{-1}(SL\mathring{W}G - \mathring{W}N)$	−4.48	−2.81	−4.84	−3.16	$I(0), I(1)$
$\Delta(slwg_{-1}(SL\mathring{W}G - \mathring{W}N))$	−9.48	−7.66	−9.44	−7.71	
$\Delta slwn/(1 - slwn_{-1} - slwg_{-1})$	−4.95	−4.32	−4.98	−4.35	$I(0)$
$\Delta slwg/(1 - slwn_{-1} - slwg_{-1})$	−4.23	−2.38	−4.35	−2.49	$I(0), I(1)$
$\Delta(\Delta slwg/(1 - slwn_{-1} - slwg_{-1}))$	−9.89	−6.90	−9.96	−7.06	
$\{slwn_{-1}(SL\mathring{W}N - \mathring{W}N)+$ $slwg_{-1}(SL\mathring{W}G - \mathring{W}N)\}$	−4.83	−3.45	−5.31	−3.59	$I(0)$
$\Delta(slwn + slwg)/(1 - slwn_{-1} - slwg_{-1})$	−4.25	−3.48	−4.37	−3.59	$I(0)$
Critical values ($\alpha = 5\%$)	−2.94	−2.94	−3.53	−3.53	

[a] Series provided by Graafland

[b] Sample used: 1965–1989. The 5% critical values are −3.00, −3.00, −3.62 and −3.62, respectively

we have to test whether the residuals of the cointegration regression are stationary. This can be done by applying DF and ADF unit root tests with respect to the cointegration residuals. Cointegration is rejected if the residuals possess a unit root. The corresponding test statistics are denoted as EG (Engle-Granger) and AEG (Augmented Engle-Granger). The AEG test is specified with a one year lag. Critical values for these test statistics are somewhat larger in absolute value than the critical values of the DF and ADF tests used above in Table 1 while analyzing the stationarity properties of the time series of the model variables. See Engle and Granger (1987). In the present case, the 5% and 10% critical values of both tests amount to −3.52 and −3.17, respectively, if the number of variables involved equals two; if there are three variables, the corresponding critical values are equal to −4.00 and −3.64, respectively. As a unit root test of the cointegration residuals, one also often encounters in the literature the so-called Cointegrating Regression Durbin-Watson (CRDW), derived from Sargan and Bhargava (1983). Under the null-hypotheses of non-cointegration, the CRDW equals zero. The null is rejected if the CRDW is high enough. The 5% and 10% critical values of the CRDW used here equal 0.386 and 0.322, respectively, in the two variable case. The corresponding figures for the three variable case are 0.367 and 0.308, respectively. These numbers are only approximations and should be handled with great care. See Hall (1986). In our analysis below we also present the CRDW. We attach more weight on the outcomes of the EG and AEG tests, as these prove to be more selective.

In Table 2 we present the outcomes of a number of alternative cointegration regressions. In all cases we use $\log WN_{real}$ as the dependent variable. Consider first the equation presented in column (1) of the table. We see that the estimated coefficients of this equation satisfy *a priori* expectations. No economic interpretation should be attached to the constant term, as it depends on the choice of the basis year of the index-numbers (1980 =100 in our case). However, according to the associated EG and AEG statistics cointegration cannot be accepted. On the other hand, the CRDW is above its critical value. In column (2) we use $\log u_{-1}$ instead of $\log u$ as an explanatory variable. As compared with column (1) it turns out that the estimated coefficients do not change very much, while the values of the EG and AEG increase in absolute value. In particular, the AEG is now close to the 10% critical value (−3.64). In fact, it appears in general that the use of the log of the lagged instead of the current unemployment rate improves the values of the unit root test statistics. Therefore, from now on, we restrict our discussion primarily to cointegration equations specified with the variable $\log u_{-1}$. We remark that Graafland and Huizinga (1988), Graafland (1992) and Den Butter and Van de Wijngaert (1992) use a lagged unemployment variable as well (more specifically, they use u_{-1}). As argued by the latter authors, an economic justification for including lagged unemployment is that wages are usually negotiated at the beginning of the year, when

Table 2: Cointegration regressions using different productivity and unemployment variables, 1953–1989 (standard deviations between parentheses)

	Dependent variable $\log WN_{real}$						
	(1)	(2)	(3)	(4)	(5)	(6)	(7)
$\log prod$	1.04	1.03	.	.	1.00	1.00	1.00
	(0.05)	(0.03)	.	.	(-)	(-)	(-)
$\log prod1$	.	.	1.03	.	.	.	.
	.	.	(0.04)	.	.	.	.
$\log prod2$	.	.	.	1.05	.	.	.
	.	.	.	(0.05)	.	.	.
$\log u_{-1}$	.	−0.18	−0.19	−0.20	−0.17	.	.
	.	(0.01)	(0.01)	(0.02)	(0.01)	.	.
$\log u$	−0.18	.	.	.	.	−0.17	.
	(0.02)	.	.	.	.	(0.01)	.
us	.	.	.	.	.	.	−0.05
	.	.	.	.	.	.	(0.00)
constant	−5.84	−5.77	−5.76	−5.81	−5.68	−5.68	−5.73
	(0.18)	(0.13)	(0.14)	(0.18)	(0.01)	(0.01)	(0.02)
CRDW	0.81	0.98	1.00	0.91	1.04	0.69	0.46
EG	−2.46	−3.25	−2.88	−2.65	−2.99	−2.30	−1.07
AEG	−3.03	−3.50	−3.68	−3.44	−3.06	−2.61	−1.74
R^2	0.96	0.98	0.98	0.97	0.98	0.96	0.90

reliable data on current unemployment are not available and a forecast is made based on the lagged unemployment.

Next, examine the specification of the productivity variable. From columns (3) and (4) of Table 2, we conclude that the choice for a smoothed or an unsmoothed productivity variable is hard to make. We decide to adhere to the use of the unsmoothed $\log prod$. In column (2) of the table we further see that the coefficient associated with $\log prod$ does not differ significantly from unity. Therefore, we restricted the value of this coefficient to unity, and re-estimated the equation. This restriction is standard, and essential, in this model to derive the NAIRU property, see e.g. Fisher and Henry (1992), Joyce (1990) and Turner (1991). The result found is listed in column (5). The coefficient values in the columns (2) and (5) are clearly similar. According to the EG and AEG statistic of column (5) again there is no cointegration, although the AEG is close to the 10% critical value (−3.17). Comparing columns (5) and (6) we see that the use of $\log u$ instead of $\log u_{-1}$ again worsens the unit root test statistics. Finally, we remark that we have also estimated cointegration equations in which we use as a measure of unemployment the unemployment rate u, or the (log of the) short-term unemployment rate us, or one of these variables in lagged form. It appeared from our computations (not reported here) that in all cases the quality of the estimation results deteriorated. An illustrative example involving us is given in the last column of Table 2. Notice the large change in the values of the unit root statistics.

Concluding the analysis of Table 2, we decide to proceed our investigations while using the equation of column (5) as point of departure. We address next the inclusion of a wedge variable in this equation. For ease of presentation we first give the equation that, in the end, is preferred by us. This equation, with standard deviations between parentheses, reads as follows

$$\begin{array}{llll} \log WN_{real} = 1.00 \log prod & - \; 0.17 \log u_{-1} & - \; 0.20 \; wedge & - \; 5.59 \\ \qquad\qquad\qquad (-) & \qquad (0.01) & \qquad (0.07) & \quad (0.03) \end{array} \tag{3}$$

$$\mathrm{CRDW} = 1.08, \ \mathrm{EG} = -2.82, \ \mathrm{AEG} = -3.12, \ \mathrm{R}^2 = 0.98$$

where

$$wedge \equiv slwn + slwg + \log p_{m,real} \tag{4}$$

Here $\log p_{m,real}$ is the logged real import price derived as the log of the ratio of the (nominal) import price index-number and the producer price index-number.[6] The coefficients of the equation have *a priori* expected values. According to the EG and AEG statistics, the variables of the equation do not cointegrate. On the other hand, CRDW is above its critical value.

In Table 3 we present cointegration regressions with some alternative specifications of the wedge. Let us compare the results of that table with equation (3). In column (1) we see that if we skip the real import price from the wedge, then the coefficient associated with the wedge gets a wrong (but insignificant) sign. On the other hand, if we multiply the real import price in the wedge with the ratio s of imports to total value added of the private sector, then the values of the EG and AEG statistics decrease in absolute value, see column (2). In columns (3) and (4) we use the logarithm of the employment and direct tax. The result of column (3) is comparable with that of column (1); in particular, the parameter for the wedge term has a wrong (but insignificant) sign. The coefficients of the equation given in column (4) are similar to the coefficients of equation (3) above. In terms of the EG and AEG, equation (3) has to be preferred. Next, consider the last two columns of Table 3. Recall that the employment tax $slwg$ and direct tax $slwn$ are both

6. The log of the producer price, pp, satisfies $\log pp = \frac{1}{1+s} \log p + \frac{s}{1+s} \log p_m$, where p is the value added price index and s the ratio of imports to total value added, see Joyce (1990).

Table 3: Cointegration regressions including the wedge, 1953–1989 (standard deviations between parentheses)

Dependent variable $\log WN_{real}$

	(1)	(2)	(3)	(4)	(5)	(6)
$\log prod$	1.00	1.00	1.00	1.00	1.00	1.00
	(-)	(-)	(-)	(-)	(-)	(-)
$\log u_{-1}$	−0.18	−0.16	−0.18	−0.15	−0.16	−0.16
	(0.01)	(0.01)	(0.02)	(0.01)	(0.01)	(0.01)
$(slwn + slwg)$	0.08	.	.	.	.	.
	(0.10)	.	.	.	.	.
$(slwn + slwg + s\log p_{m,real})$	.	−0.16	.	.	.	.
	.	(0.14)	.	.	.	.
$-\log(1 - slwn - slwg)$	.	.	0.03	.	.	.
	.	.	(0.07)	.	.	.
$\{-\log(1 - slwn - slwg)$	.	.	.	−0.24	.	.
$+\log p_{m,real}\}$	.	.	.	(0.07)	.	.
$(slwn1 + slwg1 + \log p_{m,real})$	.	.	.	.	−0.22	.
	.	.	.	.	(0.07)	.
$(slwn1 + slwg + \log p_{m,real})$	.	.	.	.	.	−0.22
	.	.	.	.	.	(0.07)
constant	−5.70	−5.63	−5.69	−5.57	−5.58	−5.58
	(0.03)	(0.05)	(0.02)	(0.03)	(0.04)	(0.03)
CRDW	1.17	0.88	1.11	0.90	0.97	1.01
EG	−3.29	−2.49	−3.15	−2.17	−2.42	−2.57
AEG	−3.54	−2.41	−3.31	−2.15	−2.53	−2.75
R^2	0.98	0.98	0.98	0.99	0.98	0.98

defined as a ratio with the wage sum W in the denominator. Above we have also discussed two alternative methods to define the employment tax and direct tax. In the first method we used the variables $slwn1$ and $slwg1$, in the second method we used $slwn1$ and $slwg$. Here $slwg1$ and $slwn1$ are expressed as a ratio with the gross wage rate WG in the denominator. In the columns (5) and (6) of Table 3 we replace $slwn$ and $slwg$ of the wedge used in equation (3) by the tax variables corresponding to the two alternative methods. It turns out that the values of the coefficients do not change very much. The values of the EG and AEG statistics decrease in absolute value, however. Finally, we remark that we have also experimented with variants of a wage level equation in which (a) the real wage sum or real gross wage rate is used as the dependent variable, (b) the employment tax, direct tax and (weighted) real import price are included separately instead of put together in one single wedge term, (c) the difference of the log of the consumption price and the log of the value added price is included in the wedge (cf. Joyce (1990)), (d) the coefficient of $\log prod$ is estimated freely, or (e) the log of a producer price - consumer price ratio is included, see also Graafland (1992). In the latter experiments (e), use is made of the time series for the producer price, denoted p_y, provided by Graafland. Table 1 concludes that $\log p_y$ is $I(2)$, whereas it is ambiguous whether the ratio $\log(p_y/p_c)$ is $I(0)$ or $I(1)$. Although we used the same data for the producer price as Graafland (1992), we find unsatisfactory results with various specifications, similar to the ones presented in Table 3.[7] Moreover, the inclusion of the producer-consumer price ratio has a theoretical problem in determining the NAIRU, because the price level is not exogenous in the model. We do not report all the details of the variants listed above, but conclude here with the observation that we have not found an equation that is preferred to equation (3).

Finally, we have experimented with the inclusion of the replacement ratio rpl – i.e. the ratio of unemployment benefits and the wage rate – as a regressor, as Graafland (1992) has. In case the replacement ratio increases, the threat point for employees will increase, which will cause wage pressure. The time series for this variable runs only from 1965 onwards. We have tested $\log rpl$ for integration. It is concluded in Table 1 that $\log rpl$ is $I(1)$. For the 1966–1989 sample we have estimated

$$\begin{aligned}\log WN_{real} = \;& \underset{(-)}{1.00}\log prod \;-\; \underset{(0.01)}{0.20}\log u_{-1} \;-\; \underset{(0.07)}{0.09}\, wedge \\ & + \underset{(0.10)}{0.15}\log rpl_{-1} \;-\; \underset{(0.42)}{6.20}\end{aligned} \tag{5}$$

$$\text{CRDW} = 1.28,\ \text{EG} = -2.70,\ \text{AEG} = -3.01,\ \text{R}^2 = 0.87$$

The lag in the replacement ratio can be justified by the institutional fact that unemployment benefits are set in the autumn of the year, while wage bargaining is usually in the spring the year after. As the test statistics indicate non-cointegration cannot be rejected for this equation. The critical values at the 5% and 10% level are for EG and AEG −4.63 and −4.20, respectively, with this limited number of observations.

---

7. We included the sum of $slwn$, $slwg$ and the log of the producer-consumer price ratio as a wedge term, skipped the latter from the wedge, used logarithmic transformations like $-\log(1 - slwn - slwg)$, etc. All resulted in insignificant parameter estimates with the wrong sign for the producer-consumer price ratio if included separately.

2.3 Modeling short-run dynamics

As pointed out above, the EG and AEG associated with equation (3) indicate that the variables involved do not cointegrate (although the CRDW points to the opposite). Because we emphasize the use of the EG and AEG, we are inclined to adhere to the conclusion of non-cointegration. Strictly speaking, therefore, the second stage of the two-stage procedure of Engle and Granger need not be carried out; there is no corresponding error-correction representation. However, given the ambiguity in our findings and the low power of the cointegration tests given the limited size of our estimation period, we decide to proceed with the second stage. In doing so, we estimate an error-correction model in which $\Delta \log WN_{real}$ is the dependent variable and in which the computed residuals of equation (3), lagged one period res_{-1}, are included among the explanatory variables. Further explanatory variables are the dependent variable lagged one or two periods, and the differences of the right-hand side variables of equation (3) in current form and lagged one or two periods. A simple general-to-specific search procedure yields the following parsimonious error-correction model (with t-values between parentheses)

$$\begin{aligned} \Delta \log WN_{real} = \; & \underset{(2.27)}{0.26\, \Delta \log WN_{real_{-1}}} + \underset{(5.13)}{0.60\, \Delta \log prod} \\ & - \underset{(1.92)}{0.03\, \Delta \log u} - \underset{(3.17)}{0.06\, \Delta \log u_{-1}} \\ & - \underset{(2.72)}{0.21\, \Delta wedge} - \underset{(2.17)}{0.33\, res_{-1}} \end{aligned} \tag{6}$$

$$\mathrm{DW} = 2.03, \;\; \mathrm{DW/H} = -0.11, \;\; \mathrm{R}^2 = 0.68$$

Here, $wedge$ is again defined according to equation (4). Since the lagged dependent variable is included among the explanatory variables, we also present the Durbin h-statistic DW/H (or Durbin m-statistic DW/M), see Judge *et al.* (1980). The coefficients of equation (6) have plausible values and the statistical properties of the equation seem reasonably well. In particular, we observe that the negative coefficient associated with the lagged cointegration residuals is significant. This is a somewhat surprising result because above we have found evidence that there is no cointegration among the variables involved. This is supposed to imply that the coefficient of the lagged residuals will not differ significantly from zero. For a similar finding in a different context, see Jenkinson (1986). Proceeding, we have also estimated the error-correction model, while relaxing the restrictions with respect to the estimated coefficients implied by the cointegration regression equation (3). Instead of using res_{-1}, we include the explanatory variables $\log WN_{real-1} - \log prod_{-1}$, $\log u_{-2}$ and

$wedge_{-1}$ in an unrestricted way. The resulting equation reads (with t-values between parentheses)

$$
\begin{array}{rll}
\Delta \log WN_{real} = & -\ 0.09\ \Delta \log WN_{real_{-1}} & +\ 0.26\ \Delta \log prod \\
& \quad (0.52) & \quad (1.37) \\
& -\ 0.05\ \Delta \log u & -\ 0.07\ \Delta \log u_{-1} \\
& \quad (2.86) & \quad (4.06) \\
& -\ 0.23\ \Delta wedge & -\ 0.19\ \log WN_{real-1} \\
& \quad (2.95) & \quad (1.24) \\
& +\ 0.19\ \log prod_{-1} & -\ 0.05\ \log u_{-2} \\
& \quad (1.24) & \quad (1.93) \\
& -\ 0.07\ wedge_{-1} & -\ 1.02 \\
& \quad (1.26) & \quad (1.17)
\end{array} \tag{7}
$$

$$\mathrm{DW} = 1.76,\ \mathrm{DW/M} = 0.62,\ \mathrm{R}^2 = 0.75$$

while the long-run equilibrium relation implied by this equation is given by

$$\log WN_{real} = 1.00 \log prod - 0.25 \log u_{-1} - 0.34\ wedge - 5.32 \tag{8}$$

The interesting observation with regard to equation (7) is that all coefficients associated with the level terms of the long-run part are insignificant. Moreover, the joint restriction of the last five coefficients of equation (7) to zero is not rejected by the computed Wald χ^2 test statistic 12.60 (critical value 13.28 at 1%, four degrees of freedom). This finding again reinforces the conclusion of the EG and AEG tests that the variables of equation (3) are not cointegrated. On the whole, summarizing our investigations so far, we conclude that using the cointegration approach no appropriate wage level equation can be derived for the Netherlands covering the period 1953–1989.

2.4 Alternative estimation periods

Consider again the cointegration regression given by equation (3). Recall that the estimation period on which this equation is based equals 1953–1989. Now, let us re-estimate the same specification with some alternative estimation periods. In particular, we will examine the following five periods 1953–1988, 1953–1987, 1953–1986, 1953–1985 and 1953–1984. Thus, each time we delete the last year of the previously used estimation period. The estimation results are presented in Table 4. We see from this table that the coefficient associated with $\log u_{-1}$ and the constant term

Table 4: Cointegration regressions using different estimation periods (standard deviations between parentheses)

Dependent variable $\log WN_{real}$

	'53–'84	'53–'85	'53–'86	'53–'87	'53–'88	'53–'89
$\log prod$	1.00	1.00	1.00	1.00	1.00	1.00
	(-)	(-)	(-)	(-)	(-)	(-)
$\log u_{-1}$	−0.16	−0.16	−0.16	−0.16	−0.16	−0.17
	(0.01)	(0.01)	(0.01)	(0.00)	(0.00)	(0.01)
wedge	−0.26	−0.26	−0.26	−0.25	−0.23	−0.20
	(0.06)	(0.06)	(0.05)	(0.05)	(0.05)	(0.07)
constant	−5.57	−5.57	−5.57	−5.57	−5.58	−5.59
	(0.03)	(0.03)	(0.02)	(0.02)	(0.03)	(0.03)
CRDW	1.39	1.39	1.39	1.39	1.33	1.08
EG	−3.90	−4.05	−4.12	−4.13	−3.97	−2.82
AEG	−4.28	−4.38	−4.37	−4.36	−4.23	−3.12
R^2	0.99	0.99	0.99	0.99	0.99	0.98

hardly change. The coefficient of the *wedge* varies from −0.23 to −0.26. Most remarkable, however, is the large difference in the values of the cointegration test statistics associated with (i) on the one hand the periods 1953–1984 up to and including 1953–1988, and (ii) on the other hand the period 1953–1989. In particular, the computed EG and AEG statistics associated with all cases of (i) provide strong evidence that the variables $\log WN_{real}$, $\log prod$, $\log u_{-1}$ and *wedge* cointegrate during the chosen shorter estimation periods. Recall now our previous conclusion that the same variables do *not* cointegrate if we use the estimation period 1953–1989! We observe that the answer on the question whether these variables cointegrate crucially depends on the fact whether the year 1989 is included or is not included in the estimation period.

We have also re-estimated the short-run error-correction model (6) using the same alternative estimation periods. Doing this, we used each time the lagged residuals of the corresponding cointegration regression given in Table 4 as the error-correcting variable. The resulting error-correction models are summarized in Table 5. The statistical properties of the equations look reasonably well. Further, we observe that the magnitude of the negative coefficient of the lagged cointegration residuals increases in absolute value if we use shorter estimation periods. This indicates that the variables involved move faster towards their long-run equilibrium. Moreover, the t-value associated with the coefficient of the lagged residuals clearly increases if we delete the year 1989 from the estimation period.

Table 5: Error-correction models using different estimation periods (t-values between parentheses)

	Dependent variable $\Delta \log WN_{real}$					
	'53–'84	'53–'85	'53–'86	'53–'87	'53–'88	'53–'89
$\Delta \log WN_{real-1}$	0.24	0.23	0.23	0.19	0.20	0.26
	(2.00)	(1.98)	(1.99)	(1.65)	(1.66)	(2.27)
$\Delta \log prod$	0.67	0.67	0.67	0.70	0.67	0.60
	(5.53)	(5.70)	(5.81)	(6.00)	(5.50)	(5.13)
$\Delta \log u$	−0.05	−0.04	−0.04	−0.04	−0.03	−0.03
	(2.66)	(2.66)	(2.71)	(2.59)	(1.87)	(1.92)
$\Delta \log u_{-1}$	−0.08	−0.08	−0.08	−0.08	−0.08	−0.06
	(3.82)	(3.88)	(3.93)	(4.00)	(3.75)	(3.17)
$\Delta wedge$	−0.26	−0.25	−0.23	−0.23	−0.23	−0.21
	(2.97)	(2.97)	(3.18)	(3.15)	(2.99)	(2.72)
res_{-1}	−0.60	−0.57	−0.55	−0.54	−0.44	−0.33
	(3.14)	(3.31)	(3.35)	(3.23)	(2.67)	(2.17)
DW	2.07	2.12	2.15	2.03	1.91	2.03
DW/H	−0.26	−0.42	−0.55	−0.10	−0.34	−0.11
R^2	0.75	0.75	0.76	0.75	0.71	0.68

It is interesting to identify the reason why the inclusion of the year 1989 in the estimation period has such a large impact on the cointegration properties of the variables $\log WN_{real}$, $\log prod$, $\log u_{-1}$ and $wedge$. Therefore, we examine in some more detail the numerical values of these variables for 1989. Comparing with the numerical values in the preceding year, it turns out that the largest change occurs in the value of $\log u_{-1}$. For 1988 and 1989 we have $\log u_{-1} = 2.65$ and $\log u_{-1} = 2.24$, respectively. This corresponds to the change of the unemployment rate u of 14.20% in 1987 to 9.37% in 1988. The changes in the values of the other variables are much more moderate. In order to judge the separate effect of the change in the unemployment rate, we have carried out the following experiment. First, we have set the value of $\log u_{-1}$ in 1989 equal to the value of this variable in 1988 (i.e. 2.24). Leaving all other data unchanged, next we have re-estimated the cointegration regression (3) for the period 1953–1989. The corresponding EG and AEG statistics are computed as −3.96 and −4.23, respectively. Recalling that the EG and AEG of the (old) equation (3) are equal to −2.82 and −3.12, we see that the EG and AEG have changed considerably. We also notice the close correspondence between the EG and AEG computed in this experiment with the EG and AEG given in Table 4 pertaining to the estimation period 1953–1988. Doing analogous experiments with each of the other variables of equation (3), it appeared that the computed EG and AEG do not differ much from the EG and AEG of the (old) equation (3). Hence, we conclude that the relatively large fall in the unemployment rate in 1988 should be held responsible for our finding that the variables $\log WN_{real}$, $\log prod$, $\log u_{-1}$ and *wedge* do not cointegrate if we use the estimation period 1953–1989, whereas they do cointegrate if we use the alternative shorter estimation periods.

The large reduction in the unemployment rate u in 1988 requires further explanation. To a large extent this reduction is a result of a change, introduced in 1988, of the way in which the official number of registered unemployed is determined. Until 1988 this number was based on the number of people recorded at the employment bureaus in the Netherlands. However, according to the Central Bureau of Statistics the data of the employment bureaus were filthy, and therefore no longer adequate. It was estimated (roughly) that the employment bureaus overstated the "correct" number of registered unemployed with 40% in 1988, see Central Planning Bureau (1989, p. 46). Despite this data problem it is essential to notice that actual wage negotiations were based on data available at that moment of bargaining (and so on our original series). From 1988 onward the corrected number of registered unemployed is published officially, and used in our database.

Given the large impact of the reduction of u in 1988, we decide to construct a time series of the "correct" number of registered unemployed covering our estimation period 1953–1989. Obviously, it is very tedious to determine the percentage with which the employment bureaus overstated the correct number of registered unemployed in the years before 1988. The Central Planning Bureau *op cit.* gives an estimate of 15% for 1979; Kuipers (1991, p. 79) gives an estimate of 5% for 1971. Kuipers further supposes that the percentages for the years 1972–1978 and 1980–1987 can be found by interpolating between the percentages 5% and 15%, and 15% and 40%, respectively. Doing the same, and assuming furthermore that the percentage for each of the years 1953–1971 equals 5%, we can construct a time series of the corrected unemployment rate, denoted as u_{cor}, for the period 1953–1989. We remark that u_{cor} equals 10.76% in 1987 and 9.37% in 1988. Notice that the fall of u_{cor} in 1988 is much smaller than the corresponding fall of u. The stationarity properties of u_{cor} and $\log u_{cor}$ are analyzed in Table 1. They resemble the stationarity properties of u and $\log u$, respectively.

Using the corrected unemployment rate u_{cor} instead of the unemployment rate u, we have estimated a number of alternative cointegration regressions. In particular, we have estimated regressions analogously to equation (3) and the specifications that are analyzed in the Tables 2 and 3. It appears from our computations that the results obtained with the corrected unemployment rate are similar to the earlier results. To give an example, the analogue of equation (3) reads (standard deviations between parentheses)

Table 6: Cointegration regressions with the corrected unemployment rate, using different estimation periods (standard deviations between parentheses)

Dependent variable $\log WN_{real}$

	'53–'84	'53–'85	'53–'86	'53–'87	'53–'88	'53–'89
$\log prod$	1.00	1.00	1.00	1.00	1.00	1.00
	(-)	(-)	(-)	(-)	(-)	(-)
$\log u_{cor-1}$	−0.17	−0.17	−0.17	−0.17	−0.18	−0.18
	(0.01)	(0.01)	(0.01)	(0.01)	(0.01)	(0.01)
wedge	−0.28	−0.29	−0.28	−0.26	−0.24	−0.21
	(0.06)	(0.06)	(0.06)	(0.06)	(0.06)	(0.07)
constant	−5.56	−5.56	−5.56	−5.57	−5.58	−5.59
	(0.03)	(0.03)	(0.03)	(0.03)	(0.03)	(0.03)
CRDW	1.31	1.29	1.28	1.24	1.15	1.01
EG	−3.75	−3.87	−3.86	−3.75	−3.44	−2.99
AEG	−4.21	−4.28	−4.16	−4.03	−3.72	−3.28
R^2	0.96	0.97	0.97	0.97	0.97	0.97

$$\log WN_{real} = \underset{(-)}{1.00} \log prod - \underset{(0.01)}{0.18} \log u_{cor-1} - \underset{(0.07)}{0.21}\, wedge - \underset{(0.03)}{5.58} \tag{9}$$

$$\text{CRDW} = 1.08,\ \text{EG} = -2.99,\ \text{AEG} = -3.27,\ \text{R}^2 = 0.98$$

The EG and AEG statistics provide evidence that the variables $\log WN_{real}$, $\log prod$, $\log u_{cor-1}$, and *wedge* do *not* cointegrate over the period 1953–1989. Analogously to Table 4 we have also estimated the cointegration equation (9) using shorter estimation periods. The results are given in Table 6. For the period 1953–1988, the AEG statistic indicates that the variables involved do cointegrate at the 10% level of significance. For the periods 1953–1984 up to and including 1953–1987, the EG and AEG also indicate that the variables cointegrate (at the 5% level). We observe that, except for the period 1953–1989, all EG and AEG statistics of Table 6 are somewhat smaller in absolute value than the corresponding statistics of Table 4. In other words the tests of cointegration are passed in a somewhat less pronounced way in the case of Table 6. The main point, however, is that our conclusions as derived above on the basis of the unemployment rate u, do not change in an essential way if we use the corrected unemployment rate u_{cor}. In particular, the wage level equation approach breaks down as soon as we include the year 1989 in the estimation period.

3 Modeling a wage growth equation

The previous section has shown that a wage level specification breaks down in 1989. It appears that net wages, productivity, unemployment and the wedge do not form a long-term equilibrium relationship in levels. Therefore, we consider next a model explaining real net wages specified in first differences. This brings us back to modeling the Phillips curve, which is extensively discussed in the literature, see Graafland (1990).

Large-scale macroeconometric models of the Dutch economy, like CESAM and FKSEC, see Central Planning Bureau (1992b), include a wage growth equation, allowing for both the Phillips-curve effect (the level of the unemployment rate) and the Lipsey effect (the change in the unemployment rate). As we have shown in Table 1, we reject stationarity in the unemployment rate. So including the unemployment rate in levels in our dynamic equation is not allowed. This implies that we reject the Phillips-curve effect *a priori* on statistical grounds. Including the change in the unemployment rate in the specification is testing for hysteresis in unemployment. Hysteresis in unemployment implies that the current equilibrium level of the unemployment rate depends on lagged actual unemployment rates. See Graafland (1990) for a discussion of the literature on hysteresis.

As above we use a two-step procedure in identifying a proper equation. First, we explain real net wage growth using productivity and unemployment as explanatory variables. After that we add a specification of the wedge. The orders of integration of the variables used are examined in Table 1. Our strategy is to follow the CESAM-specification as good as possible. So our starting point is the wage growth equation of the most recent version of CESAM, see Jongbloed *et al.* (1990), i.e.

$$\begin{aligned} \mathring{W} = {} & \mathring{p}_c + 0.78\, \mathring{prod}_{-\frac{1}{2}} - 0.21\, u - 0.80\, \Delta u \\ & + 0.11\, \frac{\Delta slwg}{1 - slwn_{-1} - slwg_{-1}} + 0.36\, \frac{\Delta slwn}{1 - slwn_{-1} - slwg_{-1}} + 2.47 \end{aligned} \tag{10}$$

Note that the variables W, p_c and $prod_{-\frac{1}{2}}$ of the CESAM-specification are in relative first differenced form (denoted by a dot). It should be noted that the relative first difference of a variable can be approximated by the first difference (Δ) of the logarithm of the variable. There are differences in parameter estimates and unit root values if we use this approximation, but it appears that the magnitude of the differences is very small and that our conclusions to be derived below do not change. In this section we proceed with relative first differences. As shown in Table 1 we cannot accept stationarity of $\Delta \log W_{real}$. The same holds for the relative first difference of the real wages. Instead we will use the real net wages as dependent variable. Moreover, the inclusion of u as an explanatory variable and of an intercept

Table 7: Regressions using different unemployment variables, 1953–1989 (t-values between parentheses)

Dependent variable $\mathring{WN}_{real}$	(1)	(2)	(3)	(4)	(5)
$\mathring{WN}_{real_{-1}}$	.	0.28	.	.	.
	.	(2.22)	.	.	.
$\mathring{WN}_{real_{-2}}$	0.40	.	0.44	.	0.48
	(4.36)	.	(4.47)	.	(4.96)
$\mathring{prod}$	.	0.31	.	0.55	.
	.	(2.11)	.	(4.01)	.
$\mathring{prod}_{-1}$	0.60	0.41	0.56	0.45	0.52
	(-)	(-)	(-)	(-)	(-)
$\Delta \log u$	−0.08	.	.	.	.
	(4.81)	.	.	.	.
Δu_{-1}	.	−0.01	.	.	.
	.	(3.13)	.	.	.
$\Delta \log us$	.	.	−0.05	.	.
	.	.	(3.19)	.	.
$\Delta \log us_{-1}$	.	.	−0.03	.	.
	.	.	(2.17)	.	.
Δus_{-1}	.	.	.	−0.01	.
	.	.	.	(2.56)	.
Δus_{-2}	.	.	.	−0.02	.
	.	.	.	(3.98)	.
$\Delta(1/u)$	.	.	.	.	0.20
	.	.	.	.	(4.67)
DW	2.10	1.85	1.87	1.62	1.63
DW/H	−0.34	0.66	0.48	.	1.32
R^2	0.54	0.54	0.51	0.55	0.52

is not allowed. As shown above we cannot reject the hypothesis that the long-run elasticity of productivity equals unity.

In the first step of the estimation procedure we use various measures of unemployment: Δu, Δus, $\Delta \log u$, $\Delta \log us$, and the reciprocal $1/u$. Again a general-to-specific methodology is followed, including two lags for each variable. We assume long-run homogeneity in productivity. Table 7 presents the major results. Column (1) shows the best fit including $\Delta \log u$. Column (2) shows the alternative for Δu, etc. Table 7 shows that the inclusion of short-term unemployment is inferior to the inclusion of total unemployment (both in levels and in logs). The inclusion of $1/u$

does not improve the fit either. Therefore we decide to proceed with the log of the total unemployment rate.

The inclusion of a wedge variable is the next step in the estimation procedure. For the wedge term Brunia and Kuper (1990) have discussed a number of alternatives. In case we compute the difference between the wage sum and net wages, we obtain

$$\overset{\circ}{W} - \overset{\circ}{W}N = slwn_{-1}(SL\overset{\circ}{W}N - \overset{\circ}{W}N) + slwg_{-1}(SL\overset{\circ}{W}G - \overset{\circ}{W}N) \tag{11}$$

$$\equiv wedge_n + wedge_g$$

where $SLWN \equiv slwn.W$ and $SLWG \equiv slwg.W$. As proxies for $wedge_n$ and $wedge_g$, Brunia and Kuper derive two alternatives, i.e. (i) $\Delta slwn$ and $\Delta slwg$, and (ii) $\Delta slwn/(1 - slwn_{-1} - slwg_{-1})$ and $\Delta slwg/(1 - slwn_{-1} - slwg_{-1})$. We use these three different definitions (which correlate over 0.9), and also for each definition the summation of the direct tax and employment tax terms as a measure of total wedge pressure. Again we use a general-to-specific procedure, starting with two year lags at a maximum for all variables. This implies that we neglect the lag structure presented in column (1) of Table 7, because inclusion of the wedge term can evoke multicollinearity problems. The wedge terms have the same kind of interpretation as in the net wage level equation. So we expect the estimated coefficient to be in the $[-1,0)$-interval.

Table 8 shows estimated equations for various alternatives. A few comments are in line with this table. Firstly, we presume dynamic homogeneity in productivity. This is in accordance with our discussion above. Secondly, in case free estimation indicates the dynamic wedge parameters to be outside the $[-1, 0)$-interval, we have calibrated them on the edge value. In all cases dynamic wedge parameters tend to become larger than unity in absolute terms, so we have assumed minus unity. For instance, in column (1) we have $1 - 0.69 = 0.31 = -(-1.22 + 0.91) = -(-1.46 + 1.15)$. Thirdly, it appears that current productivity and the current unemployment rate are the most relevant overall variables, as is the one year lagged real net wage rate.

Columns (1) and (2) report the results for the inclusion of the proxies (i), i.e. $\Delta slwn$ and $\Delta slwg$. As shown, the one period lagged wedge term is relevant. This holds for the inclusion of the other wedge terms as well. The impact parameters of the wedge terms, i.e. the estimated coefficients of the current wedge variable, exceed unity in absolute terms, which is implausible. In column (2) we have assumed the same parameters for $slwg$ and $slwn$, which is equivalent to the inclusion of a total wedge variable. Again, the impact parameter exceeds unity in absolute value. So we reject the inclusion of $\Delta slwn$ and $\Delta slwg$ in the wage equation. Columns (3) and (4) show the results for the inclusion of the second proxies (as also used in CESAM).

Table 8: Regressions using different wedge variables, 1953–1989 (t-values between parentheses)

	Dependent variable $\mathring{W}N_{real}$					
	(1)	(2)	(3)	(4)	(5)	(6)
$\mathring{W}N_{real_{-1}}$	0.69	0.68	0.66	0.66	0.70	0.70
	(9.43)	(9.51)	(8.44)	(8.58)	(10.28)	(10.44)
$\mathring{prod}$	0.31	0.32	0.34	0.34	0.30	0.30
	(-)	(-)	(-)	(-)	(-)	(-)
$\Delta \log u$	−0.04	−0.04	−0.03	−0.03	−0.05	−0.05
	(3.85)	(3.89)	(2.76)	(2.80)	(3.85)	(3.91)
$\Delta slwn$	−1.22	−1.27	.	.	.	.
	(6.94)	(8.35)	.	.	.	.
$\Delta slwn_{-1}$	0.91	0.95	.	.	.	.
	(-)	(-)	.	.	.	.
$\Delta slwg$	−1.46	−1.27	.	.	.	.
	(4.19)	(8.35)	.	.	.	.
$\Delta slwg_{-1}$	1.15	0.95	.	.	.	.
	(-)	(-)	.	.	.	.
$\Delta slwn/(1 - slwn_{-1} - slwg_{-1})$	.	.	−0.79	−0.80	.	.
	.	.	(6.84)	(8.57)	.	.
$\Delta slwn_{-1}/(1 - slwn_{-2} - slwg_{-2})$	.	.	0.45	0.46	.	.
	.	.	(-)	(-)	.	.
$\Delta slwg/(1 - slwn_{-1} - slwg_{-1})$	.	.	−0.84	−0.80	.	.
	.	.	(4.01)	(8.75)	.	.
$\Delta slwg/(1 - slwn_{-2} - slwg_{-2})$	.	.	0.50	0.46	.	.
	.	.	(-)	(-)	.	.
$slwn_{-1}(SL\mathring{W}N - \mathring{W}N)$	.	.	.	.	−0.80	−0.77
	.	.	.	.	(5.14)	(8.27)
$slwn_{-2}(SL\mathring{W}N - \mathring{W}N)_{-1}$	.	.	.	.	0.50	0.47
	.	.	.	.	(-)	(-)
$slwg_{-1}(SL\mathring{W}N - \mathring{W}N)$	.	.	.	.	−0.72	−0.77
	.	.	.	.	(2.69)	(8.27)
$slwg_{-2}(SL\mathring{W}N - \mathring{W}N)_{-1}$	.	.	.	.	0.42	0.47
	.	.	.	.	(-)	(-)
DW	2.01	2.01	1.97	1.96	1.80	1.80
DW/H	−0.05	−0.05	0.11	0.13	0.65	0.64
R^2	0.80	0.80	0.79	0.79	0.77	0.77

Again column (4) includes the results for the inclusion of a total wedge term. It appears that all parameters have theoretically correct signs. The fit of equation (4) is somewhat better than that of equation (3). Equation (3) shows some more detail of the impact of the direct and employment taxes. In line with the previous section the inclusion of a total wedge term could be preferred. Columns (5) and (6) give results for the inclusion of the wedge terms $wedge_n$ and $wedge_g$. As before column (6) shows the results for the restricted case. Compared with columns (3) and (4) the fit is worse, the tendency towards autocorrelation larger. Concluding, columns (3) and (4) represent the preferred equations.

Summarizing, we conclude that a Phillips-type wage growth equation for the Netherlands can be derived that explains the growth rate of real net wages in terms of labor productivity growth, the change in the log of the unemployment rate (with a long-term elasticity of -0.1), and the direct tax and employment tax wedge terms. The impact parameters of the wedge terms show that an increase in both taxes leads to a reduction of the real net wage by about 80 per cent. In the long run the effect reaches 100 per cent. So employees have to carry the tax increases in their real take-home pay. This result is in contrast with previous studies for the Netherlands, see Fase *et al.* (1990, p. 125). The wage equation (10) of the CESAM model illustrates that employees carry 64 per cent of direct taxes and 89 per cent of employment taxes. An explanation of the differences in these results is the dynamic specification of the wage equation.

4 Conclusion

In this paper the dynamics of net wages in the Netherlands have been studied in detail. It is motivated that modeling the wage equation is essential in long-run analyses of Keynesian macroeconometric demand-oriented models. Modeling wages hits the core of the model specification. The econometric toolkit for studying dynamic equations has been improved in the last decade by the easy-to-handle cointegration approach. Following this approach we have shown that a long-run wage level equation for the Netherlands breaks down in 1989. There seems to be decisive evidence to reject the wage level equation, which can be based on union wage bargaining models. This implies that real net wages, productivity, unemployment and the wedge do not form an equilibrium process in levels. Data problems can cause this rejection of a long-run wage level equation. Unemployment figures are unreliable, the definition of the wedge changes dramatically in 1990, etc. Concluding we do not find evidence to support the wage level bargaining theory. This conclusion contrasts with Fase *et al.* (1990) and Graafland (1992).

The empirical rejection of the wage level equation hampers the quest for the Dutch NAIRU. Although our "proof" is not exact, we cannot trace an equilibrium level of unemployment driven by exogenous variables only. Apparently more need to be said about the institutional aspects of tripartite wage bargaining. And even in that case it is likely that unemployment, both the equilibrium and the cyclical component will be endogenous.

Modeling a wage growth equation shows that the growth of net wages can be explained out of productivity growth, the change in unemployment and a change in the wedge. In the short run employees carry 80 per cent of the tax increases; in the long run employees have to accept all tax increases as a reduction of their real net wages. The fact that the change in unemployment affects wage growth implies that we support the idea of hysteresis in unemployment. The traditional Phillips-curve effect is rejected *a priori*, as the time series of the unemployment rate demonstrates a unit root.

There can be several explanations of hysteresis in unemployment. Besides wage bargaining models, unemployment-vacancy models and age related wage structures can explain hysteresis. As we have shown Dutch aggregate data do not support a wage level approach. So research in wage structures, as is done in Gelauff (1992) is wanted to describe wage formation in the Netherlands.

References

Barten, A.P. (1991), "The history of Dutch macroeconometric modelling 1936-86", in R.G. Bodkin, L.R. Klein, and K. Marwah, editors, *A history of macroeconometric model-building*, Edward Elgar, Aldershot.

Brunia, N. and G.H. Kuper (1990), "De specificatie van de afwenteling van de collectieve lasten", *Maandschrift Economie*, **54**, 49–55.

Butter, F.A.G. den and R.F. van de Wijngaert (1992), "Wage inflation and labour conflicts in the Netherlands: an empirical investigation using the co-integration approach", *European Journal of Political Economy*, **8**, 527–541.

Central Planning Bureau (1989), "Een verkenning van de Nederlandse economie voor de periode 1991–1994", Working Paper 31, Central Planning Bureau, Den Haag.

Central Planning Bureau (1992a), *Scanning the future*, Staatsuitgeverij, Den Haag.

Central Planning Bureau (1992b), *FKSEC a macroeconometric model for the Netherlands*, Stenfert Kroese, Leiden.

Cuthbertson, K., S.G. Hall, and M.P. Taylor (1992), *Applied econometric techniques*, Phillip Allan, New York.

Dickey, D.A. and W.A. Fuller (1979), "Distribution of the estimators of autoregressive time series with a unit root", *Journal of the American Statistical Association*, **74**, 427–431.

Dickey, D.A. and W.A. Fuller (1981), "Likelihood ratio statistics for autoregressive time series with a unit root", *Econometrica*, **49**, 1057–1072.

Eijk, C.J. van and F.R. Veeneklaas (1987), "Optimization and the preparation of economic policy", in W. Driehuis, M.M.G. Fase, and H. Den Hartog, editors, *Challenges for macroeconomic modelling*, North-Holland, Amsterdam.

Engle, R.F. and C.W.J. Granger (1987), "Co-integration and error correction: representation, estimation, and testing", *Econometrica*, **55**, 251–276.

Engle, R.F. and C.W.J. Granger, editors (1991), *Long-run economic relationships: readings in cointegration*, Oxford University Press, Oxford.

Fase, M.M.G., P. Kramer, and W.C. Boeschoten (1990), *MORKMON II: het DNB kwartaalmodel voor Nederland*, Monetaire Monografieën nr. 11, De Nederlandsche Bank NV, Amsterdam.

Fisher, P.G. and S.G.B. Henry (1992), "Inflation and unemployment in the U.K.", Technical report, Bank of England, London [Paper presented at the congress of the European Economic Association, Dublin, August 1992].

Gelauff, G.M.M. (1992), *Taxation, social security and the labour market: an applied general equilibrium model for the Netherlands.*, PhD thesis, Tilburg University, Tilburg.

Graafland, J.J. (1990), *Persistent unemployment, wages and hysteresis*, PhD thesis, Erasmus University, Rotterdam.

Graafland, J.J. (1992), "From Phillips curve to wage curve", *De Economist*, **140**, 501–514.

Graafland, J.J. and F. Huizinga (1988), "Modelling a wage equation for the Netherlands: a cointegration approach", Research Memorandum 51, Central Planning Bureau, The Hague.

Hall, R.E., J. Johnston, and D.M. Lilien (1990), *MicroTSP user's manual*, Quantitative Micro Software, Irvine.

Hall, S.G. (1986), "An application of the Granger & Engle two-step estimation procedure to United Kingdom aggregate wage data", *Oxford Bulletin of Economics and Statistics*, **48**, 229–239.

Hall, S.G. and S.G.B. Henry (1988), *Macroeconomic modelling*, North-Holland, Amsterdam.

Jenkinson, T.J. (1986), "Testing neo-classical theories of labour demand: an application of cointegration techniques", *Oxford Bulletin of Economics and Statistics*, **48**, 241–251.

Jongbloed, B.W.A., D.J.P. Kerstens, G.H. Kuper, and E. Sterken (1991), "The CCSO database of annual data", CCSO Series 13, University of Groningen, Groningen.

Jongbloed, B.W.A., G.H. Kuper, and E. Sterken (1990), "De Nederlandse economie op de middellange termijn: voorspellingen met CESAM voor de periode 1990–1994", CCSO Series no. 9, University of Groningen, Groningen.

Joyce, M.A.S. (1990), "The determination of average earnings in Great Britain", Technical report, Bank of England, London.

Judge, G.G., W.E. Griffiths, R.C. Hill, and T.C. Lee (1980), *The theory and practice of econometrics*, John Wiley & Sons, New York.

Kuh, E., J.W. Neese, and P. Hollinger (1985), *Structural sensitivity in econometric models*, John Wiley and Sons, New York.

Kuipers, S.K. (1991), "Marktwerking en werkloosheid in Nederland in de jaren dertig en tachtig", *Mededelingen van de Koninklijke Nederlandse Akademie van Wetenschappen*, **54**, 69–103.

Kuipers, S.K., B.W.A. Jongbloed, G.H. Kuper, and E. Sterken (1988), *Het CCSO-jaarmodel van de Nederlandse economie*, Wolters-Noordhoff, Groningen.

Kuipers, S.K., B.W.A. Jongbloed, G.H. Kuper, and E. Sterken (1990), "CESAM: the CCSO annual model of the Dutch economy", *Economic Modelling*, **7**, 202–250.

Layard, R. and S. Nickell (1986), "Unemployment in Britain", *Economica*, **53**, S121–S169.

Layard, R., S. Nickell, and R. Jackman (1991), *Unemployment: macroeconomic performance and the labour market*, Oxford University Press, Oxford.

Lever, M. (1991), "Union wage setting and unemployment in the Netherlands (1965-1987)", *Applied Economics*, **23**, 1579–1585.

MacKinnon, J. (1992), "Critical values for cointegration tests", in R.F. Engle and Granger C.W.J., editors, *Long-run economic relationships: readings in cointegration*, Oxford University Press, Oxford.

Sargan, J.D. (1964), "Wages and prices in the United Kingdom: a study in econometric methodology", in P.E. Hart, G. Mills, and J.K. Whitaker, editors, *Econometric analysis for national economic planning*, Butterworth, London.

Sargan, J.D. and A. Bhargava (1983), "Testing residuals from least squares regression for being generated by the Gaussian random walk", *Econometrica*, **51**, 153–174.

Schoonbeek, L. (1990), "Eigenvalue analysis of the CESAM model", CCSO Series no. 10, University of Groningen, Groningen.

Tinbergen, J. (1936), "Kan hier te lande, al dan niet na overheidsingrijpen, een verbetering van de binnenlandse conjunctuur intreden, ook zonder verbetering van onze exportpositie?", in *Prae-adviezen van de Vereeniging Voor de Staathuishoudkunde en de Statistiek*, Martinus Nijhoff, 's Gravenhage.

Turner, D.S. (1991), "The determinants of the NAIRU response in simulations on the Treasury Model", *Oxford Bulletin of Economics and Statistics*, **53**, 225–242.

Methods and Applications of Economic Dynamics
L. Schoonbeek, E. Sterken and S.K. Kuipers (editors)

Chapter 12

The dynamics of investment: an application to Dutch manufacturing industries

Gerard H. Kuper

1 Introduction

There is little agreement on modeling aggregate investment: Blanchard and Fischer (1989, p. 301) observe that the empirical characteristics of investment are still not well understood. This paper tries to model investment behavior by deriving factor demand equations from an intertemporal optimization problem. We formulate the theoretical model, analyze its dynamics, and estimate the model for five manufacturing industries for the Netherlands.

The dynamic analysis allows us to study the behavior of entrepreneurs as time passes. We restrict ourselves to analyzing investment behavior, which plays a prominent role both in theoretical classical and Keynesian models, and in empirical macroeconometric models (since the pioneering work of Tinbergen in the thirties). Volatility of investment is the prime contributor to aggregate demand fluctuations in the short and medium run. Furthermore, net investment affects the stock of capital, and hence the productive capacity of the economy in the long run. In general, an investment equation can describe the discrepancies between a firms' actual and desired stock of capital at any moment. We develop a model in which the dynamics are explicit elements in the optimization problem. Recently, Chirinko (1993) refers to this kind of models as *explicit models*, as opposed to *implicit models* in which the dynamics in the specification do not follow from the optimization problem.

Before turning to the characteristics of our model, we first assess the role of dynamics in mainstream investment theories. For a more detailed discussion on investment theory we refer to Kuper and Visser (1993). We start with discussing the simplest model of all, namely the accelerator model developed by Clark and others.

The accelerator model links net investment I_t to the change in demand for goods $\Delta Y_t = Y_t - Y_{t-1}$, i.e.

$$I_t = \Delta K_t = \alpha \Delta Y_t$$

This formulation implies that investment adjusts immediately to changes in demand, and that the production technique is fixed. In various papers, Clark admits that reality is much less mechanical and much more complicated than the simple dynamics implied by the acceleration principle, see Clark (1917, 1936, 1944). From his work it becomes clear that notions like time-to-build, sluggish adjustment and idle capacity are not unfamiliar. Koyck (1954) generalizes the accelerator model by allowing for sluggish adjustment of the stock of capital. In his view, instantaneous adjustment of the stock of capital is limited due to imperfect information, institutional rigidities and technological factors like production time. The accelerator theories – whether fixed or flexible – clearly lack theoretical foundation: if we allow for substitution possibilities between inputs and if relative prices are not fixed, then it will be unlikely that an entrepreneur invests according to the acceleration principle, see Tsiang (1951) and Knox (1952).

Jorgenson (1967), amongst others, challenges the accelerator theories of investment. He stresses the role of relative prices by deriving an investment demand function from optimal capital accumulation. He assumes a neoclassical setting with perfect competition taking prices as given. His approach is criticized by for instance Griliches. Griliches (1967) attacks the dynamics of Jorgenson's model. Only by assuming that prices change continuously Jorgenson can derive an investment demand equation. Discontinuous jumps to new accumulation paths are not possible. Another line of criticism is the static nature of the investment decision implied by Jorgenson's theoretical model: every quantity can be bought or sold instantaneously and without costs. In his empirical work, however, Jorgenson adds some *ad hoc* delivery lags by specifying a partial adjustment process. His reasoning is that although firms try to adjust instantaneously, they are hindered to do so because of unforeseen delivery delays. Demand for capital which follows from profit maximization is interpreted as the long-run desired capital stock K^d. In discrete time Jorgenson estimates

$$I_t = \sum_{i=0}^{\infty} \lambda_i \Delta K^d_{t-i} + \delta K_{t-1}$$

In Jorgenson (1972) convex costs of adjustment are added, introduced by Eisner and Strotz (1963), to arrive at a theoretically more satisfactory model.

Abel (1979) has shown that the neoclassical model with convex costs of adjustment is equivalent to another postwar theory of investment, namely Tobin's q-theory. Tobin (1969) – following Keynes and Wicksell – assumes that the ratio (called q) between the value of existing capital goods and their current reproduction costs can diverge significantly from unity for extended periods of time. Values of q above unity stimulate investment. Dynamics are introduced since q can exceed unity for a long period of time. Although theoretically attractive, the empirical performance of q-models is weak, see Abel and Blanchard (1986), because on the one hand the value of the firm and the replacement value of a firm is hard to quantify, and on the other hand it is even more difficult to measure *marginal* q.

Another line of research to introduce dynamics in an investment model assumes that investment decisions are irreversible, see Pindyck (1991). The implication is that investment becomes sensitive to uncertainty over future prices. Not only uncertainty about future prices affect the firms' optimization problem, uncertainty about future demand also changes the firm's attitude towards the future.

In this paper we discuss another type of model. In our model the production technique is irreversible rather than investment. The model is conceptually simple. In our approach a distinction is made between the *ex ante* and *ex post* technology available to a firm. The basic assumption is that capital is no longer homogeneous as in standard neoclassical models, but consists of vintages of capital goods, see Johansen (1959). Within one vintage homogeneity is assumed. Every year new equipment is installed and old equipment is scrapped if it has become obsolete, although physically it may not have been used up. The introduction of economic obsolescence is one of the advantages of the vintage model. Another advantage is that the vintage approach allows for embodiment of technical progress. This means that newer vintages will always be more efficient than older vintages.

The putty-clay type of vintage model, developed by Bliss (1968) and others, is an intermediate case between the pure neoclassical model with smooth substitution possibilities (which might be true in the long run) and the accelerator model in which relative prices do not play an explicit role. *Ex ante* the firm is free to choose a production technique (putty). *Ex post* factor inputs are complementary: the decision made *ex ante* determines the factor proportion over the remainder of the economic lifetime of the machine (clay). The putty-clay hypothesis implies that investment reacts to both output and relative prices. However, the capital stock responds more quickly to an increase in output than to a decrease in relative prices, because changes in relative prices only affect new vintages. As far as empirical evidence for the putty-clay hypothesis is concerned, we refer to Bischoff (1969, 1971a) who produces empirical support for the putty-clay hypothesis and Hausman (1973) who concludes that the putty-clay model is superior to both the (accelerator) clay-clay and the (Jorgenson) putty-putty models, in terms of goodness of fit and predictive power. The theoretical advantages of vintage models and the realism of the concept together with the empirical evidence clearly favor the putty-clay approach as a theory of production.

The remainder of this paper is organized as follows. The next section discusses vintage modeling. In Section 3 we present some stylized facts for sectors of the economy of the Netherlands. Section 4 presents the model. It describes the production structure and derives expressions for the net present value and the factor demand equations implied by the model. Section 5 presents some estimation results. Finally, Section 6 concludes the paper.

2 Vintage modeling

As far as empirical modeling is concerned there are essentially two ways to take account of the characteristics of a putty-clay vintage structure: a reduced-form approach and a structural approach. The reduced-form approach models putty-clay by incorporating output and a lagged function of relative prices directly into an investment equation. An example is the Bischoff (1971b) approach in which the lagged function of relative prices captures the notion that relative prices only affect new vintages. Bischoff's model is based on Jorgenson's neoclassical investment model. However, there are differences. First, Bischoff adopts a putty-clay production structure. Second, *ex ante* he uses a CES production function, rather than a Cobb-Douglas production function on the aggregate level. Third, expectations are modeled by means of a distributed lag function. In Jorgenson's model expectations are static. Finally, technical progress is modeled as a time trend and (expected) profitable lifetime of equipment is assumed to be constant. The models by Artus *et al.* (1981) as well as the ones by Ando *et al.* (1974), De Ménil and Yohn (1977), Schiantarelli (1983), and Helliwell *et al.* (1986) use the Bischoff approach. Another way is to explicitly model vintage bookkeeping in order to keep track of individual vintages during their lifetime. We call this approach the structural approach. We prefer the latter approach because it is the only way to really model the vintage approach while retaining all of its characteristics. Brute-force vintage modeling also has some disadvantages. The most important being the fact that it is more cumbersome.

Table 1 gives an overview of empirical putty-clay vintage models for (sectors of) the Netherlands' economy showing large differences in estimated parameters. See Den Hartog (1984) for a survey of empirical vintage models in the Netherlands. Although, basically the models are similar, they differ with respect to some adjustments made to make the model fit the data and to the underlying production structure. Gelauff *et al.* (1985) endogenize technical progress by relating technical progress to growth rates of exports and output. Muysken and Van Zon (1987) split the sample period in two subperiods using dummy variables in order to improve the empirical performance of the model. Meijers (1992) introduces sluggish adoption of

Table 1: Empirical putty-clay vintage models for the Netherlands*

		Elasticity of substitution			Technical progress (%) embodied			disembodied			
		I/N	J/I	$(I,J)/N$	I	N	J	I	N	J	P
Exogenous investment											
Sandee (1976)											
macro	'50–'74	0.90			0.5	0.5					1
Kuipers and Van Zon (1982)											
macro	'50–'77	0.32				4.75		−1.75	−1.75		13
Gelauff et al. (1985)											
macro	'60–'82		0.23	0.44		2–3			2–3	2.4	15
Kuipers et al. (1985)											
manufact.	'50–'80	0.74			7.6	5.5					14
food	'50–'80	0.19			1.5	5.9					8
textiles	'50–'80	0.36			5.3	5.6					6
chemical	'50–'80	0.16			2.4	8.2					12
metal	'50–'80	0.12			2.3	4.8					5
Muysken and Van Zon (1987)											
macro	'60–'82	0.38			1.13	4.77		1.25	0.4		25–8
Meijers (1992)											
macro	'60–'88	0.55			1.04	3.38		0.01	0.04		15–8
Endogenous investment											
Broer (1985)											
manufact.	'56–'76	0.44				5.24					±18
macro	'56–'76	0.40				4.83					±16
Kuper and Kroonenberg (1993)											
macro	'53–'89		0.79	0.74	1.8	0.3	0.7	0.1	0.1	0.1	±16

* I is investment, J is energy, N is labor, and (I,J) is the investment-energy bundle. P is the expected planning period in years.

new technologies in the production process. Muysken and Van Zon and Meijers observe a reduction in the length of the expected planning period from 25 and 15 years, respectively, to 8 years at the end of the estimation period. Broer (1985) and Kuper and Kroonenberg (1993) conclude that the expected planning period is fairly constant, on average. As far as the production structure is concerned, most models have only two inputs, labor and capital, combined in a CES production function to produce a single output. Gelauff *et al.* include energy as a third input in a two-level CES production function, assuming that capital and energy are separable from labor.

The earlier putty-clay vintage models have in common that investment is exogenous. Broer (1985) and Kuper and Kroonenberg (1993) on the other hand, assume convex costs of adjustment to introduce sluggish investment behavior. Introducing sluggishness in this way has the advantage that decisions with respect to various inputs in the production process – like investment and employment – on the one hand, and output on the other hand are integrated. In other words investment, employment, and demand for other inputs are endogenous.

Kuper and Kroonenberg (1993) present estimation results based on the putty-clay vintage model for the economy of the Netherlands as a whole. This paper uses the same model to describe investment behavior for industrial sectors. Before we present the model, we start off by discussing the stylized facts.

3 Stylized facts

The model presented in the next section will be estimated for various manufacturing industries for the period 1953–1987. Kuper (1991, 1994) discusses the data we use in this paper. Before we discuss the stylized facts, we will pay some attention to the sectoral classification.

The sectoral classification we employ depends on theoretical desirability, and on empirical feasibility. Or, in other words, on the questions we want to answer using a model, and on the availability of data. From a theoretical point of view data on a low level of aggregation are desirable because of differences in growth patterns and differences in production structure between sectors. Unfortunately, data on a low level of aggregation are neither available nor very reliable. This implies that we have to base our sectoral classification on the data available.

Concerning the availability of data we rely on I/O-tables published by the Central Bureau of Statistics (CBS) in the National Accounts and The Production Structure of the Netherlands' Economy. The CBS presents I/O-tables from 1969 on, based on the 58-sectoral Standard Industrial Classification (SBI) breakdown at current prices. For the years 1948 up to 1969 I/O data based on the International Standard Industrial Classification (ISIC) are available for 34 industrial sectors. Linking ISIC data and SBI data provides some difficulties. For instance, crude petroleum and natural gas production is part of the chemical industry in the ISIC classification, whereas in SBI it is a separate sector. Another example is rubber industry which according to ISIC is included in leather industry. Another source of data is the Central Economic Plan and the Economic Prospects published by the Central Planning Bureau (CPB) on a yearly basis. The CPB provides additional data based on a 25-sectoral breakdown. So, there are two sources of data. Clearly, we want to use both.

As far as modeling investment concerns we restrict our attention to manufacturing industries, excluding the petroleum industry, that is we explain investment behavior for the following five sectors: food *FB*, textiles *TE*, wood *OI*, chemical *CR* and metal *ME*. For each of the sectors we present some stylized facts with respect to the input-output structure and employment. The choice for these sectors is motivated by one of the assumptions underlying our model, i.e. we assume firms to be price-takers in all markets. This assumption applies to manufacturing industries, which are relatively exposed to foreign competition, and perhaps to some, but certainly not all, services industries.

"Food" (FB)

In 1985, more than half of total output of the food sector is produced by diary and meat manufacturing and grain-processing industry, although the latter produces mainly for intermediate consumption by other industries. Not surprisingly, the food sector produces mainly for exports and consumption, either intermediate or final. Diary and meat manufacturing accounts for more than fifty per cent of total exports and final consumption by the total food sector. When looking at the input structure of the food sector about one third is imported, this implies that two thirds is produced at home. In 1985, less than four per cent of the total number of employed (in man-years) was employed in the food sector.

"Textiles" (TE)

The input structure of the textiles sector differs from the input structure of food: in 1985, two thirds is imported and only one third is produced domestically. As far as output is concerned, more than 70% of total output is exported, only 13% is final consumption. Manufacturing of carpets, rugs, floor covering and other textiles, including clothing is by far the largest subsector, accounting for more than 65% of total output of the textiles sector. About one per cent of total employment in the Netherlands is related to the textiles sectors.

"Wood" (OI)

The input structure of the wood sector is similar to that of the food sector: in 1985, one third of inputs is imported. About one quarter of output is exported, about three quarters is consumed. Most consumption is intermediate consumption. Printing and publishing industries is the largest subsector. The wood sector accounts for about four per cent of total employment.

"Chemical" (CR)

Chemical industries import about half of their inputs, and produce mainly for exports (in 1985 about 70%). 80% of domestic output is used by other industries. By far the largest chemical industry is producing basic chemical products. Final chemical products, about 18% of total output of the chemical industry, are mainly exported. Employment in the chemical industry is only 2.4 per cent of total employment.

"Metal" (ME)

In 1985, the input structure for the metal sector is the same as the input structure of the chemical sector: about 50% of inputs is imported. About 60% of total output is exported, and about 30% of total output are final capital goods used as input by other industries. Manufacturing of electrotechnical products and machinery is the most important subsector as far as output is concerned. Employment in the metal sector is about 8.5% of total employment.

To put these sectors in perspective, note that in 1985 only 19% per cent of the total number employed was employed in manufacturing industries (excluding the petroleum industry) producing 19% of total gross value added (at factor costs). About 50% was employed in services industries, and 16% was employed in the government sector. Services industries and government produced 51%, respectively 13%, of total value added.

4 The model

The model is described in full detail in Kuper and Kroonenberg (1993). Here we present the main assumptions and derive the major equations. Throughout this paper we depart from:

Assumption 1. A putty-clay technology with a production function *ex ante* which exhibits constant returns to scale. *Ex post* the technology is characterized by fixed capital/labor, capital/output and capital/energy ratios; fixed coefficients in short.

Assumption 2. Firms are price-takers in all markets.

Assumption 3. There are convex adjustment costs associated with the sale and purchase of investment goods, and with the installation and maintenance of capital.

Assumption 4. Demand constraints, financing constraints and capacity constraints are not taken into account.

Each year, entrepreneurs make investment decisions with which they attempt to maximize income given the production function. They can choose both a level of investment and a production technique, i.e. ratios between capital, labor, energy and production. The dependence of investment costs on the capital stock introduces an intertemporal element, and the entrepreneur attempts to maximize expected discounted aggregated net yield minus investment costs over all future vintages.

The production structure *ex ante* is described by a twice-differentiable production function

$$X_\tau = F(\tau, N_\tau, I_\tau, J_\tau)$$

where X_τ is capacity output, N_τ is capacity demand for labor, I_τ is gross investment, J_τ is energy input, and τ indicates the year of installation of capital goods. *Ex post* $(t > \tau)$ input coefficients (ratios) are fixed, except possibly for disembodied technical progress. Capital goods deteriorate physically: after $t - \tau$ years only a fraction $D(t-\tau)$ of vintage τ remains. So

$$K_t = \sum_{\tau=S(t)}^{t} D(t-\tau) I_\tau$$

where K_t is the total stock of capital goods at time t, $D(t-\tau)$ is the survival rate of capital goods, with $D(0) = 1$ and $dD(t-\tau)/dt \leq 0$, and $S(t)$ is the oldest vintage in use at time t determined by relative prices and marginal productivities. For productive capacity and capacity demand for labor and energy we have the following equations

$$Q_t = h_t^\epsilon \sum_{\tau=S(t)}^{t} B(t-\tau) D(t-\tau) X_\tau$$

$$L_t = \sum_{\tau=S(t)}^{t} D(t-\tau) N_\tau$$

$$E_t = h_t^\epsilon \sum_{\tau=S(t)}^{t} D(t-\tau) J_\tau$$

where Q_t is productive capacity at time t, aggregated over all vintages still in use, L_t is capacity demand for labor, E_t is capacity demand for energy, function $B(t-\tau)$ indicates disembodied technical progress, h_t is the index of working hours, and ϵ is the elasticity of capacity output with respect to working hours. The index of working hours is included by simply multiplying aggregated productive capacity and capacity demand for energy by the working hour index. More intuitively this means that for a given amount of labor and capital, less energy is needed and less output is produced due to a reduction in the number of hours worked.

4.1 Net yield

Entrepreneurs maximize at time t the total expected discounted net present value of investment, i.e. net yield V_τ minus investment costs U_τ

$$\sum_{\tau=t}^{\infty} R(\tau-t)[V_\tau - U_\tau]$$

where $R(\tau-t)$ is the discount rate. At time t we only consider new vintages $\tau \geq t$, old vintages are already installed, and are not part of the optimization process. The expected total (summed over its lifetime) discounted net yield of vintage τ is

$$V_\tau = (1-\omega_\tau)\sum_{s=\tau}^{P(\tau)} R(s-\tau)D(s-\tau)[p_{X,s}B(s-\tau)h_s^\epsilon X_\tau - p_{N,s}N_\tau - p_{J,s}h_s^\epsilon J_\tau]$$

where ω_τ is the corporate tax rate, $p_{i,s}$ are prices of output and inputs ($i = X, N, J$), and $P(\tau)$ is the expected last productive date of vintage τ. The equation above needs some explanation. Net yield for vintage τ at time $s \geq \tau$, discounted from time τ, is

$$(1-\omega_s)R(s-\tau)D(s-\tau)\left[p_{X,s}B(s-\tau)h_s^\epsilon X_\tau - p_{N,s}N_\tau - p_{J,s}h_s^\epsilon J_\tau\right]$$

Summing this over its lifetime, and assuming that the tax rate is expected to be constant from time τ on, we can remove $1-\omega_s = 1-\omega_\tau$ from the summation.

We define the "values"

$$\begin{aligned}
\tilde{p}_{X,\tau} &= \sum_{s=\tau}^{P(\tau)} R(s-\tau)D(s-\tau)B(s-\tau)h_s^\epsilon p_{X,s} \\
\tilde{p}_{J,\tau} &= \sum_{s=\tau}^{P(\tau)} R(s-\tau)D(s-\tau)h_s^\epsilon p_{J,s} \\
\tilde{p}_{N,\tau} &= \sum_{s=\tau}^{P(\tau)} R(s-\tau)D(s-\tau)p_{N,s}
\end{aligned}$$

and write expected aggregated discounted net yield as

$$V_\tau = (1-\omega_\tau)\left[\tilde{p}_{X,\tau}F(\tau, I_\tau, J_\tau, N_\tau) - \tilde{p}_{N,\tau}N_\tau - \tilde{p}_{J,\tau}J_\tau\right] \tag{1}$$

A number of additional assumptions must be made, with $s > \tau$:

- The discount rate is constant

$$R(s-\tau)=e^{-\theta(s-\tau)};\ \theta>0$$

We mean by constant that the entrepreneur assumes that the parameter will remain constant: at time t he assumes that $\theta_s=\theta_t$ for $s>t$; at time τ he assumes that $\theta_s=\theta_\tau$ for $s>\tau$.

- Prices are expected to grow at a constant rate π_i

$$p_{i,s}=p_{i,\tau}e^{\pi_i(s-\tau)};\ i=X,I,J,N$$

- Expectations as to the index h of working hours are exponential

$$h_s=h_\tau e^{\zeta(s-\tau)}$$

- The rate of disembodied technical progress is constant

$$B(s-\tau)=e^{\beta(s-\tau)}$$

- Decay follows a cumulative gamma distribution with positive δ and positive integer α

$$D(s-\tau)=1-\Gamma(s-\tau;\alpha,\delta)=e^{-\delta(s-\tau)}\sum_{j=0}^{\alpha-1}(\delta(s-\tau))^j/j!$$

The cumulative gamma distribution is both realistic and mathematically tractable. For $\alpha=1$, it reduces to the exponential distribution; for larger α the curve is S-shaped, which means that decay is initially slow but accelerates later, until there is almost nothing left. Recent estimates of the Central Bureau of Statistics, see CBS (1987), indicate that the gamma decay provides a good approximation of the actual decay of capital goods.

4.2 Investment costs

Total investment costs for a vintage $\tau\geq t$ consist of the investment expenditures themselves, $p_{I,\tau}I_\tau$, and adjustment costs $p_{I,\tau}C_\tau$. *Adjustment costs* C_τ are convex with respect to investments: $\partial C_\tau/\partial I_\tau\geq 0$ and $\partial^2 C_\tau/\partial I_\tau^2\geq 0$. If the adjustment costs are related not only to newly installed capital (installation costs) but also to the existing capital (the relative size of expansion), then the problem faced by the entrepreneur is really intertemporal. For examples, see Lucas (1967), Gould (1968), Treadway (1969), Uzawa (1969), Hayashi (1982) and Broer (1985).

From the total investment costs we should subtract investment credits and discounted tax deductions. *Investment credits* are a tax deduction of a fraction

$0 \le \nu \le 1$ of investment in the year of the purchase. This amounts to a tax reduction of $\nu_\tau p_{I,\tau} I_\tau$. As for *tax deductions* it is assumed that investment expenditures are deducted linearly in S_ω years. As usual, tax deductions are discounted.

Thus, we can summarize investment expenses for vintage $\tau \ge t$ as

$$U_\tau = p_{I,\tau}[M_\tau I_\tau + C_\tau(I_\tau, K_{\tau-1})] \tag{2}$$

with

$$M_\tau = 1 - \nu_\tau - \omega_\tau \sum_{s=\tau}^{\tau+S_\omega-1} R(s-\tau)/S_\omega$$

Now, we have assembled all the pieces for computing the net present value NPV of any vintage $\tau \ge t$. Combining equations (1) and (2), the net present value equals

$$\begin{aligned} NPV_\tau &= V_\tau - U_\tau \\ &= (1-\omega_\tau)\big[\tilde{p}_{X,\tau} F(\tau, I_\tau, J_\tau, N_\tau) - \tilde{p}_{J,\tau} J_\tau - \tilde{p}_{N,\tau} N_\tau\big] \\ &\quad - p_{I,\tau}[M_\tau I_\tau + C_\tau(I_\tau, K_{\tau-1})] \end{aligned}$$

4.3 Production function and first-order conditions

We use a twice-differentiable two-level CES production function which satisfies a number of assumptions that will simplify the analysis. These assumptions are:

- Constant returns to scale and concavity in its inputs.
- Separability between labor N and the capital-energy bundle $Z = (I, J)$. Artus and Peyroux (1990) indicate that this separability is one of the most naturally plausible: machines representing a mix of capital and energy combined with labor. Formal testing of this assumption is not possible because data on energy use and labor demand of the newest vintages are not available.
- Embodied technical progress at a constant rate: $A_{i,t} = a_i e^{\alpha_i t}$, $\alpha_i > 0$, $i = I, J, N$, where a_i are scaling parameters.

The nested production function reads

$$F(\tau, I_\tau, J_\tau, N_\tau) = \Big[[Z(\tau, I_\tau, J_\tau)]^{-\rho} + [A_{N,\tau} N_\tau]^{-\rho}\Big]^{-1/\rho}; \ \rho \ge -1$$

with

$$Z(\tau, I_\tau, J_\tau) = \Big[[A_{I,\tau} I_\tau]^{-\rho_1} + [A_{J,\tau} J_\tau]^{-\rho_1}\Big]^{-1/\rho_1}; \ \rho_1 \ge -1$$

Both the inner production function Z and the outer production function F exhibit constant returns to scale. The parameters ρ and ρ_1 are the substitution parameters. The elasticity of substitution between the capital-energy bundle Z and labor N

equals $\sigma = 1/(1+\rho)$. The elasticity of substitution between capital and energy is $\sigma_1 = 1/(1+\rho_1)$.

We have to maximize

$$\begin{aligned}
&\sum_{\tau=t}^{\infty} R(\tau - t)[V_\tau - U_\tau] \\
&= \sum_{\tau=t}^{\infty} R(\tau - t)\Big[(1-\omega_\tau)[\tilde{p}_{X,\tau}F(\tau, I_\tau, J_\tau, N_\tau) - \tilde{p}_{N,\tau}N_\tau - \tilde{p}_{J,\tau}J_\tau] \\
&\quad -p_{I,\tau}[M_\tau I_\tau + C_\tau(I_\tau, K_{\tau-1})]\Big]
\end{aligned}$$

subject to a constraint consisting of a capital accumulation equation. Kuper and Kroonenberg (1993) show that for gamma decay the following recursive relations can be derived

$$\begin{aligned}
K_\tau &= \sum_{j=0}^{\alpha-1} K_{j,\tau} \\
K_{0,\tau} &= \kappa_{0,0} K_{0,\tau-1} + I_\tau \\
K_{j,\tau} &= \sum_{k=0}^{j} \kappa_{j,k} K_{k,\tau-1} \text{ with } 0 < j < \alpha
\end{aligned}$$

where $\kappa_{0,0}$ and $\kappa_{j,k}$ are positive constants. The capital accumulation equation can now be written in vector notation as

$$\vec{K}_\tau = \begin{bmatrix} K_{0,\tau} \\ \vdots \\ K_{\alpha-1,\tau} \end{bmatrix} = \vec{g}\,(\vec{K}_{\tau-1}, I_\tau)$$

given initial values $\vec{K}_0$.

Before deriving the first-order conditions, we specify the following cost function

$$C_\tau = C_\tau(I_\tau, \vec{K}_{\tau-1}) = \frac{1}{2}\varphi \frac{I_\tau^2}{\sum_{j=0}^{\alpha-1} K_{j,\tau-1}} = \frac{1}{2}\varphi I_\tau^2 / K_{\tau-1}$$

where φ is a positive constant.

Solving the model gives the following system of first-order conditions

$$\begin{aligned}
0 &= -p_{I,\tau}[M_\tau + \varphi I_\tau / K_{\tau-1}] \\
&\quad + \tilde{p}_{X,\tau}\,(1-\omega_\tau)\, A_{I,\tau}^{-\rho_1} (X_\tau/Z_\tau)^{1+\rho} (Z_\tau/I_\tau)^{1+\rho_1} + \lambda_{0,\tau} && (3) \\
0 &= \tilde{p}_{X,\tau}\, A_{J,\tau}^{-\rho_1} (X_\tau/Z_\tau)^{1+\rho} (Z_\tau/J_\tau)^{1+\rho_1} - \tilde{p}_{J,\tau} && (4) \\
0 &= \tilde{p}_{X,\tau}\, A_{N,\tau}^{-\rho} (X_\tau/N_\tau)^{1+\rho} - \tilde{p}_{N,\tau} && (5) \\
0 &= \Theta\, p_{I,\tau} \frac{1}{2} \varphi I_\tau^2 / K_{\tau-1}^2 - \lambda_{k,\tau-1} + \Theta \sum_{j=k}^{\alpha-1} \lambda_{j,\tau} \kappa_{j,k}
\end{aligned}$$

$$\text{with } 0 \leq k < \alpha \tag{6}$$

$$\vec{0} = \vec{K}_\tau - \vec{g}(\vec{K}_{\tau-1}, I_\tau) \tag{7}$$

$$X_\tau = \left[Z_\tau^{-\rho} + [A_{N,\tau}N_\tau]^{-\rho}\right]^{-1/\rho} \tag{8}$$

$$Z_\tau = \left[[A_{I,\tau}I_\tau]^{-\rho_1} + [A_{J,\tau}J_\tau]^{-\rho_1}\right]^{-1/\rho_1} \tag{9}$$

where $\Theta = e^{-\theta}$, and $R(\tau - t) = \Theta^{\tau-t}$.

Equation (3) of this system means that marginal yield from investment equals marginal cost, i.e.

$$\partial F/\partial I_\tau = \frac{p_{I,\tau}[M_\tau + \partial C_\tau/\partial I_\tau] - \lambda_{0,\tau}}{\tilde{p}_{X,\tau}(1 - \omega_\tau)} \tag{10}$$

where the marginal productivity of newest vintage capital is calculated as

$$\partial F/\partial I_\tau = A_{I,\tau}^{-\rho_1}(X_\tau/Z_\tau)^{1+\rho}(Z_\tau/I_\tau)^{1+\rho_1} \tag{11}$$

Observe that $\lambda_{0,\tau}$ represents the reduction of adjustment costs from investing an additional unit of capital. Equations (4) and (5) are the marginal productivity relations with respect to energy and labor, i.e.

$$\begin{aligned} \partial F/\partial J_\tau &= \tilde{p}_{J,\tau}/\tilde{p}_{X,\tau} \\ \partial F/\partial N_\tau &= \tilde{p}_{N,\tau}/\tilde{p}_{X,\tau} \end{aligned}$$

where the marginal productivities related to the newest vintage are calculated as

$$\begin{aligned} \partial F/\partial J_\tau &= A_{J,\tau}^{-\rho_1}(X_\tau/Z_\tau)^{1+\rho}(Z_\tau/J_\tau)^{1+\rho_1} \\ \partial F/\partial N_\tau &= A_{N,\tau}^{-\rho}(X_\tau/N_\tau)^{1+\rho} \end{aligned}$$

Equations (6) are the partial derivatives with respect to the components $K_{j,\tau}$ of the stock of capital. These equations produce a set of recursive equations for $\lambda_{k,\tau}$

$$\begin{aligned} \lambda_{k,\tau} &= \Theta \sum_{j=k}^{\alpha-1} \lambda_{j,\tau+1}\kappa_{j,k} + \Theta\, p_{I,\tau+1}\frac{1}{2}\varphi I_{\tau+1}^2/K_\tau^2 \\ &= \Theta\left[\sum_{j=k}^{\alpha-1} \lambda_{j,\tau+1}\kappa_{j,k} + p_{I,\tau+1}\frac{1}{2}\varphi I_{\tau+1}^2/K_\tau^2\right] \\ &\quad \text{with } 0 \leq k < \alpha \end{aligned} \tag{12}$$

Equation (3) can be rewritten to produce an equation for the level of investment

$$I_\tau = \frac{K_{\tau-1}}{\varphi}[q_\tau - M_\tau] \tag{13}$$

where q_τ can be interpreted as Tobin's marginal q and is defined as

$$q_\tau = \frac{\tilde{p}_{X,\tau}(1-\omega_\tau)(\partial F/\partial I_\tau) + \lambda_{0,\tau}}{p_{I,\tau}}$$

The λ-term introduces dynamic effects in the investment equation, it relates actual investment to lagged investment. The marginal productivity of investment $\partial F/\partial I_\tau$ can be calculated by eliminating Z_τ from equation (11)

$$\partial F/\partial I_\tau = A_{I,\tau}^{-\rho}(X_\tau/I_\tau)^{1+\rho}\left[1+\left(\frac{A_{J,\tau}J_\tau}{A_{I,\tau}I_\tau}\right)^{-\rho_1}\right]^{-(\rho_1-\rho)/\rho_1}$$

According to equation (13) investment depends on q_τ and on the fiscal regime M_τ. In turn, q_τ is related – through the marginal productivity of investment – to the output/capital ratio X_τ/I_τ and the energy/capital ratio J_τ/I_τ. It depends on the elasticities of substitution, ρ and ρ_1, whether the marginal productivity of investment, and hence investment, is more sensitive to X_τ/I_τ than to J_τ/I_τ. It can be shown that if

$$\left|\frac{1+\rho}{\rho_1-\rho}\right| > 1 \tag{14}$$

investment is more sensitive to the output/capital ratio X_τ/I_τ. Condition (14) is equivalent to $-1 < \rho_1 < 1+2\rho$ or $\sigma < 2\sigma_1$, where $\sigma = 1/(1+\rho)$ and $\sigma_1 = 1/(1+\rho_1)$.

Changes in current relative prices not only affect new vintages purchased now – through the marginal productivities – but new vintages to be bought in the future as well, because expected prices change and because changes in the stock of capital K_τ influence investment costs, and hence future investment. Besides expectations concerning future prices and the capacity effect there are two more channels through which future decisions are affected by current price shocks. These have to do with expected and actual economic decay. First, changes in relative prices alter the entrepreneurs' expectations with respect to the lifetime of equipment $P(\tau)$. Second, actual scrap of old vintages depends on current prices and on the existing stock of capital.

4.4 The dynamic working of the model

Table 2 shows what happens if, for instance energy J_τ, becomes relatively more expensive. It is assumed that all other prices remain unaffected. First, recall that the level of investment depends on $\partial F/\partial I_\tau$. Second, $\partial F/\partial I_\tau$ is related to the output/capital ratio X_τ/I_τ and to the capital/energy ratio I_τ/J_τ. Which of the ratios dominates depends on the elasticities of substitution. There are two possibilities.

Table 2: Working in case energy J becomes relatively expensive

	I/J	N/J	X/N	I/N		X/I		$\partial F/\partial I$
$0 \leq \sigma \leq \sigma_1 \leq 1$	+				$\Longrightarrow$			+
	+	+	$\Longrightarrow$	+				
			0	+	$\Longrightarrow$	−	$\Longrightarrow$	−
							I :	−
$0 \leq \sigma_1 < \sigma \leq 1$	+				$\Longrightarrow$			−
	+	+	$\Longrightarrow$	−				
			0	−	$\Longrightarrow$	+	$\Longrightarrow$	+
$\sigma_1 < \sigma < 2\sigma_1$							I :	+
$\sigma \geq 2\sigma_1$							I :	?

Case i: $0 \leq \sigma \leq \sigma_1 \leq 1$. Energy J_τ is substituted for both capital I_τ and labor N_τ. So, I_τ/J_τ and N_τ/J_τ increase. Since it is easier to substitute energy for capital, I_τ/N_τ increases and hence X_τ/I_τ decreases (note that X_τ/N_τ remains unchanged since only the price of energy changes). There are contradicting effects on the marginal productivity of capital $\partial F/\partial I_\tau$. The negative effect dominates since $\sigma \leq \sigma_1 < 2\sigma_1$, and investment decreases. What happens to other inputs and output is listed in Table 3.

Case ii: $0 \leq \sigma_1 < \sigma \leq 1$. Now, it is easier to substitute labor for capital. So, I_τ/N_τ decreases. In this case we only arrive at unambiguous results if $\sigma_1 < \sigma < 2\sigma_1$, i.e. investment increases as illustrated in Table 3.

What happens with aggregate inputs and output is already discussed above. Furthermore, it depends on the nature of the shock; is the shock temporary or permanent.

4.5 Long-run properties

While studying long-run dynamics it is convenient to define first the long run and discuss the different concepts of equilibrium. In accordance with Deleau *et al.* (1990) the short run is defined as a situation in which prices and the stock of capital are fixed. In the medium run prices adjust while keeping the stock of capital fixed. In the long run both prices and the stock of capital adjust. The definition of short and long

Table 3: Results in case energy J becomes relatively expensive*

		I	J	N	X
$0 \leq \sigma \leq \sigma_1 \leq 1$		$-$	$---$	$--$	$--$
$0 \leq \sigma_1 < \sigma \leq 1$	$\sigma_1 < \sigma < 2\sigma_1$	$+$	$0/-$	$++$	$++$
	$\sigma \geq 2\sigma_1$	$0/-$	$-$	$0/+$	$0/+$

Note that $++$ exceeds $+$, and $-$ exceeds $--$, etc.
$0/-$ means zero or a decrease, and $0/+$ means zero or an increase.

run coincides with Kuipers (1991, p. 76), except that Kuipers does not explicitly define a medium-run situation. The steady state is defined as the long-run situation in which all variables are growing at the same constant rate or are not growing at all. The situation in which all variables are not growing at all implies constant values and is called stationary by Wan (1971). A more general concept, again according to Wan (1971, p. 3), is a dynamic equilibrium, that is: "... a dynamic path in which no variable ... is arbitrarily held constant, yet certain economic variables ... and the ratios or limiting ratio between other economic variables ... take self-perpetuating values ...".

In this study we do not prove the existence or uniqueness of a steady state. For examples of that we rather refer to Broer (1985) and Van Hilten (1991). However, it should be noted that both Broer and Van Hilten only allow for labor-augmenting embodied technical progress in a one-level, two-inputs *ex ante* production structure. Technical progress plays a pivotal role in the characterization of long-run equilibrium. We do not restrict ourselves *a priori* to situations in which technical progress is only labor-augmenting. In other words we allow for a more general long-run concept. i.e. a dynamic equilibrium. To keep the analysis simple we first analyze a situation in which the elasticities of substitution between the various inputs are assumed to be the same, i.e. $\sigma = \sigma_1$ or $\rho = \rho_1$. We show under which conditions a dynamic equilibrium can be derived. Finally, if elasticities of substitution are not the same, we argue that similar conclusions apply.

If $\rho = \rho_1$, the *ex ante* production function collapses into a one-level production function

$$X_\tau^{-\rho} = A_{I,\tau}^{-\rho} I_\tau^{-\rho} + A_{J,\tau}^{-\rho} J_\tau^{-\rho} + A_{N,\tau}^{-\rho} N_\tau^{-\rho}$$

Multiplication by X_τ^ρ gives

$$1 = (A_{I,\tau} I_\tau / X_\tau)^{-\rho} + (A_{J,\tau} J_\tau / X_\tau)^{-\rho} + (A_{N,\tau} N_\tau / X_\tau)^{-\rho} \tag{15}$$

The first-order conditions (4) and (5), with $\rho = \rho_1$, are

$$\begin{aligned} \partial F / \partial J_\tau &= A_{J,\tau}^{-\rho} (X_\tau / J_\tau)^{1+\rho} = \tilde{p}_{J,\tau} / \tilde{p}_{X,\tau} \\ \partial F / \partial N_\tau &= A_{N,\tau}^{-\rho} (X_\tau / N_\tau)^{1+\rho} = \tilde{p}_{N,\tau} / \tilde{p}_{X,\tau} \end{aligned}$$

Now, we assume that

$$\begin{aligned} (A_{J,\tau} J_\tau / X_\tau)^{-\rho} &= (\tilde{p}_{J,\tau} J_\tau) / (\tilde{p}_{X,\tau} X_\tau) = c_J \\ (A_{N,\tau} N_\tau / X_\tau)^{-\rho} &= (\tilde{p}_{N,\tau} N_\tau) / (\tilde{p}_{X,\tau} X_\tau) = c_N \end{aligned}$$

where c_J and c_N are constants. If we define μ_i as the constant rate of growth of variable $i = X, I, J, N$, the latter assumptions imply that $\pi_J - \pi_X = \mu_X - \mu_J = \alpha_J$ and $\pi_N - \pi_X = \mu_X - \mu_N = \alpha_N$. From equation (15) it then follows that

$$c_I = (A_{I,\tau} I_\tau / X_\tau)^{-\rho} = 1 - c_J - c_N$$

or $\mu_X - \mu_I = \alpha_I$. Using

$$\partial F / \partial I_\tau = A_{I,\tau}^{-\rho} (X_\tau / I_\tau)^{1+\rho} = c_I (X_\tau / I_\tau)$$

the first-order condition (10) can be written as

$$c_I (X_\tau / I_\tau) = \frac{p_{I,\tau} [M_\tau + \partial C_\tau / \partial I_\tau - \lambda_{0,\tau} / p_{I,\tau}]}{\tilde{p}_{X,\tau} (1 - \omega_\tau)}$$

Assuming that, analogously to the rates of growth for other prices, $\pi_I - \pi_X = \alpha_I$, the term between square brackets in the last equation has to be constant. M_τ is constant if investment credits ν_τ are a constant fraction of investment and if the corporate tax rate ω_τ is constant. The λ-term is a bit more complicated. If we write equation (12) as

$$\frac{\lambda_{k,\tau}}{p_{I,\tau}} = \Theta e^{\pi_I} \left[\sum_{j=k}^{\alpha-1} \frac{\lambda_{j,\tau+1}}{p_{I,\tau+1}} \kappa_{j,k} - \partial C_{\tau+1} / \partial K_\tau \right]$$

with $0 \leq k < \alpha$, then $\lambda_{0,\tau} / p_{I,\tau}$ is constant if $\partial C_{\tau+1} / \partial K_\tau$ is constant, and vice versa. In that case $\partial C_\tau / \partial I_\tau$ is constant as well. In other words $\mu_I = \mu_K$.

Summarizing, we now have a long-run situation – which we call a dynamic equilibrium – were prices are assumed to grow according to

$$\begin{aligned} \pi_J &= \pi_X + \alpha_J \\ \pi_N &= \pi_X + \alpha_N \\ \pi_I &= \pi_X + \alpha_I \end{aligned}$$

and inputs and output grow according to

$$\begin{aligned} \mu_J &= \mu_X - \alpha_J \\ \mu_N &= \mu_X - \alpha_N \\ \mu_I &= \mu_X - \alpha_I = \mu_K \end{aligned}$$

This outcome needs not be surprising since it is assumed that prices and quantities move in such a way that the income distribution remains constant, in other words

$$\pi_J + \mu_J = \pi_I + \mu_I = \pi_N + \mu_N = \pi_X + \mu_X$$

Without technical progress it is easy to see that we arrive in a steady state. Furthermore, if price levels are constant, the long-run situation can be depicted as a stationary state.

If we no longer assume that the elasticities of substitution between the various inputs are the same, we arrive at similar conclusions. Assume that energy and capital are separable from labor. In this case the production function is again the nested one. Redefine c_J, c_N and c_I as follows

$$\begin{aligned} c_J &= (A_{J,\tau} J_\tau / X_\tau)^{-\rho_1} \\ c_N &= (A_{N,\tau} N_\tau / X_\tau)^{-\rho} \\ c_I &= (A_{I,\tau} I_\tau / X_\tau)^{-\rho_1} = (1 - c_N)^{\rho_1/\rho} - c_J \end{aligned}$$

The marginal productivity of capital can be rewritten as

$$\partial F / \partial I_\tau = c_I^{\rho/\rho_1} \left(1 + \frac{c_J}{c_I}\right)^{-(\rho_1 - \rho)/\rho_1} (X_\tau / I_\tau)$$

and the same conclusions apply.

5 Estimation results

The model is estimated by optimizing a quadratic maximum likelihood function which measures the fit of the following quantities:

- Investment I_t,
- Capacity output $Q_t = h_t^\epsilon \sum_{\tau=S(t)}^{t} B(t-\tau) D(t-\tau) X_\tau$,
- Capacity demand for labor $L_t = \sum_{\tau=S(t)}^{t} D(t-\tau) N_\tau$,
- Capacity demand for energy $E_t = h_t^\epsilon \sum_{\tau=S(t)}^{t} D(t-\tau) J_\tau$.

Note that I_t is the only observed, non-aggregate, quantity. X_τ, N_τ and J_τ are non-observed variables related to vintage τ. The aggregates of Q_t, L_t and E_t are not observed either, but are related through the utilization rates to observed gross output, labor demand and energy use. The rate of capacity utilization is – in accordance to CPB estimates – assumed to be 85% on average.

There are seventeen parameters in the model, some of which are set in advance rather than being estimated. The parameters relate to:

- the embodied technical progress: α_I, α_N, α_J,
- the rate of neutral disembodied progress: β,
- the substitution elasticities: $\sigma = 1/(1+\rho)$ and $\sigma_1 = 1/(1+\rho_1)$,
- the gamma decay function: δ and α,
- the cost function: φ,
- a relaxation factor in the investment relation: γ (see below),
- scaling: a_I, a_N, a_J; and initial stocks: K_0, L_0,
- elasticity of productive capacity with respect to hours worked: ϵ,
- tax deduction period: S_ω.

Three parameters are fixed in all experiments, these are ϵ, S_ω and α. The value for ϵ is based on estimates by Den Hartog and Tjan (1976). A value of 10 for S_ω is probably most usual. As far as α is concerned, CBS (1987) shows that 3 is a reasonable value. The estimated values of the other parameters are assumed to be restricted to a feasible region.

The second parameter in the decay function δ is estimated and determines the shape of the decay function. In order to facilitate convergence we have introduced a parameter γ. The higher γ, the more investment is determined by the model outcomes. Parameter γ has a lower bound. It is assumed, rather arbitrarily, that $0.5 \leq \gamma \leq 1$.

The model is estimated by optimizing the likelihood function using a quasi-Newton method. The estimation results for the period 1953-1987 are given in Table 4.

Some remarks with respect to the estimation results are in order. First, α en δ are parameters in the gamma decay function, they indicate the rate of technical decay: the estimated value of these parameters reflect an expected average technical lifetime of about $\alpha/\delta = 15$ years.

Second, the actual lifetime $t - S(t)$ is not constant but varies with profitability of vintages. The expected lifetime of equipment $P(\tau)$ is assumed to be constant since preliminary calculations indicated that this is a plausible assumption.

Third, the parameters α_i $(i = I, J, N)$ represent embodied technical progress. Technical progress is mainly labor-augmenting. The rate of capital-augmenting technical progress is much lower, less then 1%. Energy-augmenting technical progress is high in the chemical sector. Disembodied technical progress β is assumed to be neutral and is negligible, except for the chemical industry.

Fourth, the elasticity of substitution between capital and energy σ_1 averages about 0.85. The elasticity of substitution between capital/energy and labor σ is

Table 4: Estimation results

Fixed parameters					
α	3				
ϵ	0.75				
S_ω	10				
Estimated parameters					
	FB	*TE*	*OI*	*CR*	*ME*
a_I	1.17	4.27	1.67	0.95	0.59
a_J	13.29	26.11	39.58	7.38	7.90
a_N	10.21	8.82	20.76	7.27	1.95
α_I	-[a]	0.007	0.006	-	-
α_J	-	0.011	-	0.104	0.021
α_N	0.070	0.029	0.087	0.005	0.051
β	0.001	-	-	0.072	-
σ	0.83	0.88	0.88	0.54	0.11
σ_1	0.79	0.87	0.94	0.89	0.71
φ	73.67	81.98	115.14	71.79	69.65
γ	0.50	0.50	0.50	0.50	0.50
δ	0.21	0.19	0.22	0.22	0.21
K_0	1157	611	770	1284	223
L_0	138	56	181	61	139
Quality of fit					
	FB	*TE*	*OI*	*CR*	*ME*
Likelihood	1188	1038	1215	1321	1266
$U(I)$	0.62	0.66	0.77	0.67	0.60
$U(L)$	0.63	0.43	0.78	0.39	0.57
$U(E)$	0.64	0.58	0.57	0.75	0.67
$U(Q)$	0.42	0.56	0.50	0.64	0.52

[a] value set equal to 0 (the lower bound)

Table 5: Technical progress

	Food	Textiles	Wood	Chemical	Metal
capital-augm.	-	low	low	-	-
energy-augm.	-	medium	-	high	medium
labor-augm.	high	medium	high	low	medium
disembodied	low	-	-	high	-

somewhat lower, especially for chemical industries and metal manufacturing industries. These values are considerably higher than the elasticities of substitution found in other studies, see Table 1.

Fifth, the other parameters are scale parameters (a_i, $i = I, J, N$), initial stocks (K_0, L_0), a technical parameter in the cost function (φ), and a relaxation factor in the estimated investment function (γ). The values for most of the parameters do not seem unrealistic, except for φ. Estimated values for φ imply unrealistically high adjustment costs associated with investment.

The quality of fit is measured by a differenced Theil inequality coefficient

$$U(x) = \frac{\sqrt{\sum_{t=2}^{n}(\Delta x_t^a - \Delta x_t)^2}}{\sqrt{\sum_{t=2}^{n}(\Delta x_t^a)^2} + \sqrt{\sum_{t=2}^{n}(\Delta x_t)^2}} \tag{16}$$

where x_t^a is an observed variable and x_t is the computed series. Δ is the difference operator. $U(\cdot)$ ranges from 0 (perfect) to 1 (bad). Table 4 lists values for U for each variable in the likelihood function. It should be emphasized that the likelihood function is optimized in the estimation procedure and not the Theil inequality coefficients.

Finally, we interpret some of the conclusions. The most interesting parameters are the technical progress parameters and the elasticities of substitution. The results will be summarized here. If we label technical progress at a rate exceeding 7% as *high*, and *low* if technical progress proceeds at a rate lower than 1%, we can summarize technical progress as in Table 5.

As far as the estimation results with respect to the elasticities of substitution are concerned, these are visualized in Figure 1. Along the axes are the elasticities of substitution. It is shown that the elasticities of substitution σ and σ_1 in the nested production function determine what happens in case relative prices change.

Suppose that, initially, we are in point A in Figure 2. If, for instance, energy becomes relatively expensive, the expansion path in Figure 2 becomes steeper. Price

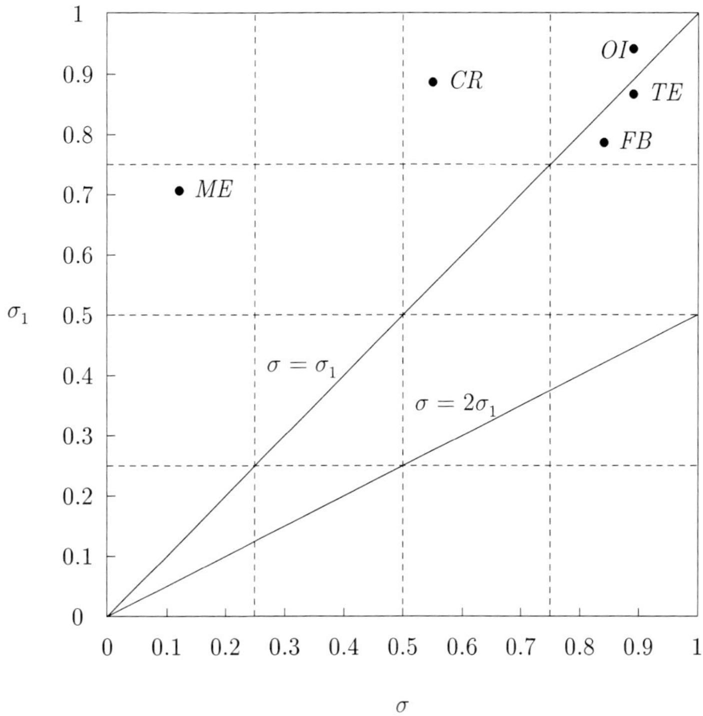

FB	Food, beverages and tobacco
TE	Textiles, clothing, shoe and leather industry
OI	Other industry: wood, furniture and publishing
CR	Chemical industry and rubber industry
ME	Metal industry

Figure 1: Elasticities of substitution

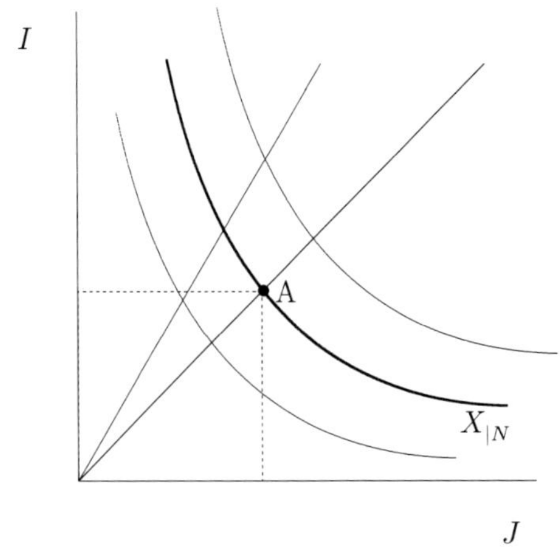

Figure 2: Optimal production technique

changes induce substitution processes, so levels of inputs adjust to the new relative prices, and so does output. If, as a result, the isoquant – drawn for a given level of labor input N – moves inward, then input J is reduced. However, it is ambiguous what happens to investment I. On the other hand, if the isoquant moves outward, investment increases, and it is not clear what happens to energy use. Our analysis of Section 4.4 leads to the conclusion that if $\sigma \leq \sigma_1$ investment decreases, and that if $\sigma_1 < \sigma < 2\sigma_1$ investment increases. If $\sigma \geq 2\sigma_1$ then the results are ambiguous.

If we look at the estimation results, we conclude that $\sigma < 2\sigma_1$ in all sectors. Diagrammatically, all sectors are in the area above the $\sigma = 2\sigma_1$-line in Figure 1. Two sectors fall within the area enclosed by the $\sigma = \sigma_1$-line and the $\sigma = 2\sigma_1$-line. These sectors are the food sector and textiles manufacturing. In these sectors investment increases in case energy becomes relatively expensive. However, while interpreting these results, one should bear in mind that the analysis is partial in nature, since the demand side is not modeled and output prices are assumed to be unaffected by changes in the price of energy.

What will happen after the price shock depends on whether the shock is temporary or not. Even if the shock is temporary there are some forces that prevent the model from returning immediately to its pre-shock values. One force has to do with expectations formation and scrap, another because the stock of capital adjusts, and this in turn affects future investment due to the fact that adjustment costs are assumed to be dependent on the capital stock.

6 Conclusion

The main purpose of this paper is defined as gaining insight into the dynamics of investment behavior on a sectoral level. We do not compare various investment models empirically but rather consider the vintage model as theoretically superior to alternative models. This presumption is supported by a large literature.

In the present study we stay close to economic theory and rigorously derive input demand equations from present value optimization. Unlike in most standard neoclassical models we do not assume homogeneous capital, but we assume that the stock of capital consists of capital of different vintages. The production structure is based on a putty-clay vintage framework with a two-level, three inputs *ex ante* production function. Besides capital and labor we add energy as a factor of production. In simple vintage models only the optimal production technique – the ratio between inputs – is determined. In our model adjustment costs are introduced in order to derive levels of inputs and output simultaneously and consistent with the optimal production technique. Technical lifetime of equipment is modeled by a flexible S-shaped gamma decay function. Actual economic lifetime of equipment is endogenous, and aggregation over profitable vintages yields total capacity demands for inputs and output. Furthermore, vintage modeling allows for a more elaborate modeling of technical progress.

Finally, we make some critical remarks. Obviously, the value of the model depends on the relevance of the assumptions underlying the model. The assumptions are partly motivated by our goal to describe analytically the dynamic investment behavior of firms, and partly by conclusions reached in the literature. Our attempt to keep the analysis manageable perhaps goes to a certain extent at the expense of empirical relevance. Introducing market imperfections undoubtedly broadens the applicability of our model, but analyzing investment behavior along the lines of this paper surely becomes untractable. The usefulness of our approach might be increased further by comparing the results of our analysis with those of competing investment models. For this purpose a benchmark model should be developed in which the dynamics are also modeled explicitly.

References

Abel, A.B. (1979), *Investment and the value of capital*, Garland, New York.

Abel, A.B. and O.J. Blanchard (1986), "The present value of profits and cyclical movements in investment", *Econometrica*, **54**, 249–273.

Ando, A., F. Modigliani, R. Rasche, and S.J. Turnovsky (1974), "On the role of expectations of price and technological change in an investment function", *International Economic Review*, **15**(2), 384–414.

Artus, P. and P-A. Muet, editors (1990), *Investment and factor demand*, North-Holland, Amsterdam.

Artus, P., P-A. Muet, P. Palinkas, and P. Pauly (1981), "Economic policy and private investment since the oil crises: a comparative study of France and Germany", *European Economic Review*, **16**, 7–51.

Artus, P. and C. Peyroux (1990), "Production functions with the energy factor: estimations for the major OECD countries", in P. Artus and P-A. Muet, editors, *Investment and factor demand*, North-Holland, Amsterdam.

Bischoff, C.W. (1969), "Hypothesis testing and the demand for capital", *Review of Economics and Statistics*, **51**, 354–368.

Bischoff, C.W. (1971a), "Business investment in the 1970s: a comparison of models", *Brookings Papers on Economic Activity*, **1**, 13–58.

Bischoff, C.W. (1971b), "The effects of alternative lag distributions", in G. Fromm, editor, *Tax incentives and capital spending*, North-Holland, Amsterdam.

Blanchard, O.J. and S. Fischer (1989), *Lectures on macroeconomics*, MIT Press, Cambridge.

Bliss, C. (1968), "On putty-clay", *Review of Economic Studies*, **35**, 105–132.

Broer, D.P. (1985), *Neoclassical theory and empirical models of aggregate firm behaviour*, PhD thesis, Erasmus University, Rotterdam.

Central Bureau of Statistics, *National Accounts* (in dutch: Nationale Rekeningen), Staatsuitgeverij, 's-Gravenhage [various issues].

Central Bureau of Statistics, *The production structure of the Netherlands' economy* (in dutch: De produktie-structuur van de Nederlandse volkshuishouding), Staatsuitgeverij, 's-Gravenhage [various issues].

Central Bureau of Statistics (1987), *Bijdragen tot de statistieken betreffende de kapitaalgoederenvoorraad 1986*, Staatsuitgeverij, 's-Gravenhage, 65–72.

Central Planning Bureau, *Central Economic Plan* (in dutch: Centraal Economisch Plan), Staatsuitgeverij, 's-Gravenhage [various issues].

Central Planning Bureau, *Economic Prospects* (in dutch: Economisch Beeld), Staatsuitgeverij, 's-Gravenhage [various issues].

Champsaur, P. *et al.*, editors (1990), *Essays in honor of Edmond Malinvaud, volume II, macroeconomics*, MIT Press, Cambridge.

Chirinko, R.S. (1993), "Business fixed investment spending: modeling strategies, empirical results, and policy implications", *Journal of Economic Literature*, **31**, 1875–1911.

Clark, J.M. (1917), "Business acceleration and the law of demand: a technical factor in economic cycles", *Journal of Political Economy*, **25**, 217–235 [Reprinted in Haberler, G. (1944)].

Clark, J.M. (1936), "Additional note on "business acceleration and the law of demand"", in J.M. Clark, editor, *A preface to social economics*, Farrar and Reinhart, New York [Reprinted in Haberler, G. (1944)].

Clark, J.M. (1944), "Business acceleration and the law of demand: a technical factor in economic cycles", in G. Haberler, editor, *Readings in business cycle theory*, Blakiston, Philadelphia.

Commission on Money and Credit (1963), *Impacts of monetary policy*, Prentice-Hall, Englewood Cliffs, New Jersey.

Deleau, M., C. Le Van, and P. Malgrange (1990), "The long run of macroeconometric models", in Champsaur, P. *et al.*, editor, *Essays in honor of Edmond Malinvaud, volume II, macroeconomics*, MIT Press, Cambridge.

Eisner, R. and R.H. Strotz (1963), "The determinants of business investment", in Commission on Money and Credit, editors, *Impacts of monetary policy*, Englewood Cliffs, New Jersey, Prentice-Hall, 59–236.

Ferber, R., editor (1967), *Determinants of investment behavior, a conference of the Universities-National Bureau Committee for Economic Research*, New York, NBER.

Fromm, G., editor (1971), *Tax incentives and capital spending*, North-Holland, Amsterdam.

Gelauff, G.M.M., A.R.M. Wennekers, and A.H.M. de Jong (1985), "A putty-clay model with three factors of production and partly endogenous technical progress", *De Economist*, **133**, 327–351.

Gould, J.P. (1968), "Adjustment costs in the theory of investment of the firm", *Review of Economic Studies*, **35**, 47–56.

Griliches, Z. (1967), "Comment on Jorgenson", in R. Ferber, editor, *Determinants of investment behavior, a conference of the Universities-National Bureau Committee for Economic Research*, New York, NBER.

Haberler, G., editor (1944), *Readings in business cycle theory*, Blakiston, Philadelphia.

Hartog, H. den (1984), "Empirical vintage models for the Netherlands in the postwar period: a review in outline", *De Economist*, **132**, 326–349.

Hartog, H. den and H.S. Tjan (1976), "Investment, wages, prices and demand for labour (a clay-clay vintage model for the Netherlands)", *De Economist*, **124**, 32–55.

Hausman, J.A. (1973), *Theoretical and empirical aspects of vintage capital models*, PhD thesis, Oxford University, Oxford.

Hayashi, F. (1982), "Tobin's marginal q and average q: a neoclassical interpretation", *Econometrica*, **50**, 213–224.

Helliwell, J.F., P. Sturm, P. Jarrett, and G. Salou (1986), "The supply side in the OECD's macroeconomic model", OECD Economic Studies no. 6, OECD, Paris.

Hilten, O. van (1991), *Optimal firm behaviour in the context of technical progress and a business cycle*, volume 352 of *Lecture Notes in Economics and Mathematical Systems*, Springer-Verlag, Berlin.

Johansen, L. (1959), "Substitution versus fixed production coefficients in the theory of economic growth: a synthesis", *Econometrica*, **27**, 157–176.

Jorgenson, D.W. (1967), "The theory of investment behavior", in R. Ferber, editor, *Determinants of investment behavior, a conference of the Universities-National Bureau Committee for Economic Research*, New York, NBER, 129–175.

Jorgenson, D.W. (1972), "Investment behaviour and the production function", *Bell Journal of Economics and Management Science*, **3**, 220–251.

Knox, A.D. (1952), "The acceleration principle and the theory of investment: a survey", *Economica*, **19**, 269–297.

Koyck, L.M. (1954), *Distributed lags and investment analysis*, North-Holland, Amsterdam.

Kuipers, S.K. (1991), "Marktwerking en werkloosheid in Nederland in de jaren dertig en tachtig", *Mededelingen van de Koninklijke Nederlandse Akademie van Wetenschappen*, **54**, 69–103.

Kuipers, S.K., C.M. Andriesen, J.P.A.M. Jacobs, and G.H. Kuper (1985), "A putty-clay vintage model for sectors of industry in the Netherlands", *De Economist*, **133**, 151–175.

Kuipers, S.K. and A.H. van Zon (1982), "Output and employment growth in the Netherlands in the postwar period: a putty-clay approach", *De Economist*, **130**, 38–70.

Kuper, G.H. (1991), "Data structure of a multisectoral model of the Dutch economy: description and listing of input-output data (version '91)", CCSO Series no. 14, University of Groningen, Groningen.

Kuper, G.H. (1994, forthcoming), *Investment behaviour and vintage modelling*, PhD thesis, Groningen University, Groningen.

Kuper, G.H. and N.S. Kroonenberg (1993), "The dynamics of investment: a putty-clay approach", CCSO Series no. 18, University of Groningen, Groningen.

Kuper, G.H. and B. Visser (1993), "Investment theory: a survey", Research Memorandum no. 526, Institute of Economic Research, University of Groningen, Groningen.

Lucas, R.E. (1967), "Adjustment costs and the theory of supply", *Journal of Political Economy*, **75**, 321–334.

Meijers, H.H.M. (1992), "On the slowdown of productivity growth in the Netherlands 1960–1988: a macroeconomic vintage diffusion approach", Research Memorandum no. 3, MERIT, Maastricht.

Ménil, G. de and F. Yohn (1977), "La formation de capital fixe par les enterprises", *Annales de l'INSEE*, **26-27**, 115–161.

Muysken, J. and A.H. van Zon (1987), "Employment and unemployment in the Netherlands", *Recherches Economiques de Louvain*, **53**, 101–133.

Pindyck, R.S. (1991), "Irreversibility, uncertainty, and investment", *Journal of Economic Literature*, **29**, 1110–1148.

Sandee, J. (1976), "A putty-clay model for the Netherlands", unpublished manuscript [Conference Paper: European Meeting of the Econometric Society].

Schiantarelli, F. (1983), "Investment models and expectations: some estimates for the Italian industrial sector", *International Economic Review*, **24**(2), 291–312.

Tobin, J. (1969), "A general equilibrium approach to monetary theory", *Journal of Money, Credit and Banking*, **1**, 15–29.

Treadway, A.B. (1969), "On rational entrepreneurial behaviour and the demand for investment", *Review of Economic Studies*, **36**, 227–239.

Tsiang, S.C. (1951), "Accelerator, theory of the firm and the business cycle", *Quarterly Journal of Economics*, **65**, 325–341.

Uzawa, H. (1969), "Time preference and the Penrose effect in a two-class model of economic growth", *Journal of Political Economy*, **77**, 628–652.

Wan, H.Y. Jr. (1971), *Economic growth*, Harcourt Brace Jovanovich, New York.

Methods and Applications of Economic Dynamics
L. Schoonbeek, E. Sterken and S.K. Kuipers (editors)

Chapter 13

On the empirics of endogenous economic growth[1]

Anton van Schaik

1 Introduction

In industrial countries real GDP per capita grows by about 2% a year on average. As documented by Maddison (1991), this historically unprecedented increase in the wealth of the nations dates back to the start of the second industrial revolution (1870). In addition, by testing endogenous growth theory on Maddison's data, Van de Klundert and Van Schaik (1993), further referred to as K&S, found the process of economic growth to be steady over eight countries and eight distinct subperiods since 1870. The steady growth is interrupted only by some events like the second world war (WW II) and the impact of convergence towards the United States in productivity during the fifties and the sixties. After 1973 the impact of convergence of technological knowledge has disappeared, which explains the growth slowdown in the European countries and Japan. This idea of "back to normal" does not fit with the results of many other empirical growth studies, which indicate a process of ungoing convergence over the whole post WW II period. Standard growth studies focus on the role of an attractor, like the steady state in the neoclassical model, which leaves little room for testing a break around 1973. On the other hand, following Scott (1989, 1993), K&S consider growth to be endogenous in the sense that the investment ratio and the rate of growth of labor explain differences in growth of output across countries and across time periods. They also found that the constant

1. I like to thank Theo van de Klundert, the editors of this book and the participants of the Groningen workshop for useful comments.

term of Scott's fundamental growth equation does not differ significantly from zero, so that technological progress is indeed endogenous.

A natural way to investigate the robustness of the K&S findings that after 1973 there is no longer a role for an attractor and that technological change is endogenous, is to extend the Maddison sample or to fit the equation to a different data set. K&S have already put a step on this road by extending the "Maddison" countries (1870–1989) with post WW II observations of eight other countries. In this paper we choose the other road and apply Scott's growth equation on a sample derived from the Summers and Heston data base (1991), which contains much more countries than the Maddison data, but is restricted to post WW II observations only. In order to understand the estimation results properly, we give in Section 2 an illustrative overview of relevant empirical evidence. The K&S equation is introduced in Section 3. In Section 4 we put the K&S results in a worldwide perspective by estimating the fundamental growth equation on a sample of 107 countries and 3 distinct subperiods over the period 1950–1986, derived from the Summers and Heston set. In this broader context we discuss "lost opportunities for growth", the "switch" in the relation between growth and cycles at the beginning of the seventies and exceptions to the normal pattern of economic growth as described by our growth equation. The main conclusion is that the constant term of the linear growth equation does not differ significantly from zero, so that endogenous growth theory stands up to the facts.

2 Growth by convergence

With hindsight a common starting point of the literature on empirical growth equations is the test of the convergence prediction, i.e. the tendency for poor countries to grow faster than rich countries, which is implied by the following log-linearized approximation to the neoclassical growth model with a Cobb-Douglas technology (cf. Barro and Sala-I-Martin, 1992, and Barro *et al.*, 1992)

$$\frac{\ln y - \ln y_0}{T} = \frac{1 - e^{-\beta T}}{T} (\ln y^* - \ln y_0) \tag{1}$$

Here T denotes the length of the observation period, β the convergence rate, y_0 the initial level of labor productivity, y the present level of labor productivity and y^* the level of labor productivity to which the economy is assumed to be attracted. The growth rate of output per capita is a negative function of initial output per capita, y_0, after controlling for the attractor y^*. The speed of adjustment, β, depends on the parameters of the model, which predicts y^*.

It should be noted that in the older work on economic growth by convergence, cf. Baumol (1986), the attractor is implicit in the constant term of the regression equation, so that convergence is supposed to be unconditional in that the poor economies grow faster than the rich ones. In recent empirical work, cf. Mankiw *et al.* (1992), the attractor is specified by the steady-state solution of the neoclassical model. This theory, see e.g. Solow (1956) and Swan (1956), assumes that technological progress is exogenous and that there are diminishing returns with respect to reproducible factors. It is assumed that the knowledge incorporated in the production function at every point in time is freely available to everyone. Countries may nevertheless grow at a different rate, not only because there is a mismatch between the initial output per capita and its long-run equilibrium value, but also because savings rates or rates of change of labor input are different. The Solow-Swan model predicts that during the transition to the steady state economic growth is governed by the difference between investment (= savings) at time t and investment needed to maintain output per capita at that very moment in time. During the transition growth is endogenous, cf. Brander (1992), but in the steady state growth is fully determined by the exogenous natural rate of growth.

The core of the neoclassical theory of economic growth is a production function with constant returns to scale. Assuming a Cobb-Douglas specification the function can be written in terms of rates of change as

$$g = \alpha g_k + (1-\alpha)g_\ell + \epsilon \tag{2}$$

where g denotes the growth rate of output, g_ℓ the growth rate of labor input, g_k the growth rate of capital input and the parameter α stands for the production elasticity of capital. Technological change is constant and is denoted by the parameter ϵ. If estimates for the capital stock are lacking, equation (2) can be estimated after replacing g_k by the Harrod-Domar identity $g_k = \sigma/\kappa$, with the share of investment in output denoted by σ and the capital-output coefficient denoted by κ (e.g. Dowrick and Nguyen, 1989)

$$g = \frac{\alpha}{\kappa}\sigma + (1-\alpha)g_\ell + \epsilon \tag{3}$$

In this equation there is no role for an attractor so that the convergence hypothesis cannot be tested. In contrast, the convergence prediction is tested by Mankiw *et al.* (1992), who model the attractor by a Cobb-Douglas production function and country-specific steady-state investment ratios, σ^*, and growth rates of labor, g_ℓ^*, which leads to

$$\frac{\ln y - \ln y_0}{T} = \frac{1-e^{-\beta T}}{T}\left[\frac{\alpha}{1-\alpha}\left(\ln\sigma^* - \ln(g_\ell^* + \rho + \delta)\right) - \ln y_0\right] \tag{4}$$

Estimation of equation (4) requires *a priori* knowledge about the uniform rate of Harrod-neutral labor-augmenting technological change $\rho = \epsilon/(1-\alpha)$ and the depreciation rate of capital δ. In this case convergence is conditional on the parameters

Table 1: Summary of a cross-section sample of 95 countries, 1960–1988*

Group		Rank	g	g_ℓ	σ	sec_{1960}	$(y_0/y_{us})_{1960}$	$(y_0/y_{us})_{1988}$
I		1–19	3.9	1.3	26.2	56.1	56.9	71.6
	var		0.35	0.68	0.17	0.28	0.34	0.16
II		20–38	4.5	2.2	20.5	21.9	30.2	36.3
	var		0.39	0.49	0.26	0.43	0.36	0.28
III		39–57	5.1	2.5	16.5	14.8	15.2	18.8
	var		0.35	0.15	0.34	0.70	0.44	0.31
IV		58–76	3.3	2.4	12.6	3.5	9.5	8.0
	var		0.43	0.27	0.63	0.81	0.28	0.28
V		77–95	2.9	2.1	10.7	3.3	4.9	3.6
	var		0.52	0.24	0.41	1.42	0.54	0.26
		1–95	3.9	2.1	17.3	19.9	23.4	27.7
	var		0.44	0.40	0.46	1.09	0.92	0.93

* The columns show the average values of the growth rate of output (g), the growth rate of labor input (g_ℓ), the investment ratio (σ), the secondary enrollment rate in 1960 (sec_{1960}), the initial level of labor productivity relative to US labor productivity and the ultimate level of labor productivity in each group of countries relative to US labor productivity. For each figure the coefficient of variation (*var*) is given.

of the model, which predicts the attractor, i.e. the set of country-specific steady states.

We now give an illustrative overview of the standard growth equations, by regressing them, as usual, on a cross-section sample of post WW II data (1960–1988). The sample, summarized in Table 1, is an update of the sample (1960–1985) in Mankiw *et al.* (1992), and is taken from Van Schaik (1992). The data come from Summers and Heston (1991) and Barro (1991). Summers and Heston have compiled observations for 138 countries over the period 1950–1988, but for a number of countries the series start in 1960. To test convergence the observation period must be of equal length for every country, so that only the series from 1960 onwards can be used. The number of countries is reduced from 138 to 95 for the reasons, discussed in Mankiw *et al.* (1992) and the availability of data in the Barro set.[2]

Table 1 distinguishes 5 groups of 19 countries which are ranked according to productivity levels in 1985. Productivity is defined as real GDP *per worker*. The bottom line reports the figures for all 95 countries together. The classification implies that group I comprises the *ex post* richest and group V the *ex post* poorest

2. The main oil-producing countries are left aside, because GPD per capita cannot be traced back to production circumstances prevailing in the other countries. Further, countries with populations smaller than 1 million are excluded.

countries. The columns show the average values of the growth rate of output, g, the growth rate of labor input, g_ℓ, the investment ratio, σ, the initial secondary enrollment rate, sec_{1960}, the initial level of labor productivity relative to US labor productivity, $(y_0/y_{us})_{1960}$, and the ultimate level of labor productivity in each group of countries relative to US labor productivity, $(y_0/y_{us})_{1988}$. The averages are unweighted. For each figure the coefficient of variation, *var*, is mentioned. The table expresses the well-known fact that investment ratios and enrollment rates are lower as countries are poorer. The two rightmost columns show that from an *ex post* point of view the first three groups have catched up with the US. However, the relative position of group III *vis a vis* group II has hardly changed, whereas the position of II *vis a vis* I has worsened somehow. In other words, among the five groups distinguished here we do not observe β-convergence, i.e. there is no tendency for poor countries to grow faster than rich countries, although the wealth of nations measured in absolute productivity levels has clearly increased; measured in 1985 international prices, mean labor productivity increased from 14032 dollars to 26943 in group I, from 7455 to 13641 in group II, from 3743 to 7071 in group III, from 2343 to 2997 in group IV and from 1217 to 1369 in group V.[3] On the other hand β-convergence is observable within each group as appears from the declining values of the coefficients of variation between 1960 and 1988. This does not change the fact that relative to the US the poor countries are put back during the considered period.

Table 2 provides a survey of the test of the Baumol-type equation on the data of Table 1, which leaves the attractor implicit in the constant term. The dependent variable is percentage labor productivity growth, $g - g_\ell$, which approximately equals the LHS of equation (1). Basically, Baumol (1986) estimated an equation like 2A, focusing on the *ex post* richest countries only. The explained variance of this equation is high. Baumol found it striking that only *one* variable, i.e. a country's initial GDP per capita, mattered so much for explaining growth, implying that other variables could have only a peripheral influence. His interpretation was that spillovers from leader economies to followers are large, at least among the group of industrial nations, thus pointing at the influence of some kind of attractor.

As argued by de Long (1988), Baumol's finding of convergence is subject to the *ex post* selection bias criticism. This critique is recapulated here by the equations 2B–2E. After subsequently extending the sample with the less richer countries, convergence becomes weaker and weaker and after all even completely disappears. This is in accordance with the observation that global β-convergence is absent. The presence of local β-convergence is confirmed by regressions on each group of 19 countries separately (not reported here): the coefficient of determination is high,

3. The tendency for poor countries to grow faster than rich countries, termed β-convergence, need not imply a reduction in the dispersion of income levels, termed σ-convergence, if each country's level of income is continually subject to random disturbances, cf. Barro and Sala-I-Martin (1992).

Table 2: Unconditional convergence and the *ex post* selection bias, 1960–1988*

OLS estimation of productivity growth $g - g_\ell$ on	(2A)	(2B)	(2C)	(2D)	(2E)	(2F)
Constant	29.85	15.84	11.45	3.31	0.49	6.24
	(10.82)	(4.72)	(5.20)	(1.65)	(0.35)	(3.91)
	[9.61]	[5.80]	[4.90]	[1.51]	[0.42]	[4.00]
Convergence ($\ln y_{1960}$)	−2.88	−1.46	−1.02	−0.14	0.16	−0.85
	(9.90)	(4.00)	(4.08)	(0.61)	(0.95)	(3.66)
	[8.63]	[5.03]	[3.95]	[0.58]	[1.19]	[3.87]
Human capital ($prim_{1960}$)						0.04
						(5.67)
						[6.42]
Numb. of obs. (N)	19	38	57	76	95	95
Countries (see Table 1)	1–19 richest	1–38 +subrich	1–57 +middle	1–76 +subpoor	1–95 +poorest	1–95
$\bar{R}^2$	0.84	0.29	0.22	0.00	0.00	0.25

* Absolute t-statistics are shown in parentheses ( ), whereas brackets [ ] give White's heteroscedasticity-consistent t-statistics.

viz. 84% (I), 59% (II), 67% (III), 42% (IV) and 70% (V). The differences between these figures are in line with the magnitude of the decrease of the coefficients of variation between the last columns in Table 1.

Equation 2F is an example of the Barro-type equation. Barro (1991) starts from an estimation equation like 2E, showing that the hypothesis of global β-convergence is inconsistent with cross-country evidence. Then he adds school-enrollment rates as proxies for human capital to the equation. As equation 2F shows it suffices to add the initial primary enrollment rate, $prim_{1960}$, to "save" the convergence hypothesis: the coefficient of initial labor productivity has the right sign and is significant. The coefficient of determination as compared with equation 2A is low, but can be increased by adding other "Barro-variables", such as the initial adult-literacy rate and the initial student-teacher ratio in primary schools. The extended "Barro-equation" is, however, subject to the critique of Levine and Renelt (1992), who found that a large assortment of economic and political indicators, other than the initial enrollment rate, are not robustly correlated with growth.

One of the few encouraging conclusions of Levine and Renelt (1992) is a positive and robust correlation between average growth rates and the share of investment in GDP. This is recapulated here in Table 3. Applying equation (3), which is equation

(2) after substituting the Harrod-Domar identity in it, leads to equation 3A. The coefficient of the investment ratio is highly significant. It should be noted, however, that this equation is inconsistent from a theoretical perspective, because one has to assume that the capital-output coefficient is constant, which during the transition to the steady state is not predicted by the model. Equation (4), which stresses the attraction by country-specific steady states, does more justice to neoclassical transitional dynamics. Equation 3B is the MRW-type equation, cf. Mankiw *et al.* (1992). We did not restrict the parameters of σ and g_ℓ to be equal, because the parameter of the labor-input variable does not differ significantly from zero.[4] This reveals one problem with respect to the estimation of equation (4). Another problem is the low value of the speed of adjustment. Barro *et al.* (1992) propose to open the neoclassical growth model for the closed economy to allow for full capital mobility, which raises the speed of adjustment. The last problem we mention here has to do with the assumption that countries converge to positions with different marginal products of capital. So the question is: why is the marginal product of capital not high in countries where it is scarce? The answer Lucas (1988) proposes is that other inputs are also scarce in such countries, in particular, capital inputs complementary to physical capital.

The last equation of Table 3 extends equation 3A by introducing a logarithmic catch-up variable ($\ln cu$) in the form of the ratio of the initial level of labor productivity in each country, y_0, and the initial level of labor productivity in the US: $cu_{1960} \equiv (y_0/y_{us})_{1960}$. This does not alter the coefficients of the investment ratio (σ) and the growth rate of labor input (g_ℓ), but the interpretation is quite different. In equation 3C the dimensional homogeneity of the estimation equation is not destroyed, so that the constant term can be interpreted as a pure measure for exogenous technological change.

3 Endogenous technological change

It should be observed that Mankiw *et al.* (1992) introduce human capital along with unskilled labor to improve the empirical results, but technological change remains exogenous in this approach. Human capital accumulation also plays an important role in the so-called new growth theories. Some models, e.g. Rebelo (1991), introduce human capital and schooling along with the accumulation of physical capital. Endogenous growth in the long run prevails if there is a "core" of capital goods that is produced without the direct or indirect contribution of nonreproducible factors.

4. Country-specific natural growth rates are approximated here by the growth rates of employment, averaged over 1960–1988. Apart from the effect of changing participation rates, cf. Dowrick (1992), other proxies such as the growth rates of total population come down to the same results, cf. Levine and Renelt (1992).

Table 3: Conditional convergence, 1960–1988*

OLS estimation of productivity growth $g - g_\ell$ on	(3A)	(3B)	(3C)
Constant	0.17	3.32	0.94
	(0.29)	(2.20)	(1.40)
	[0.28]	[2.54]	[1.61]
Investment ratio (σ)	0.09	0.12	0.12
	(4.67)	(5.22)	(5.22)
	[4.36]	[4.00]	[4.00]
Growth rate of labor input (g_ℓ)	0.04	−0.01	−0.01
	(0.23)	(0.06)	(0.06)
	[0.25]	[0.06]	[0.06]
Convergence ($\ln y_{1960}$)		−0.43	
		(2.26)	
		[2.26]	
Catch-up ($\ln cu_{1960}$)			−0.43
			(2.26)
			[2.26]
Number of observations (N)	95	95	95
$\bar{R}^2$	0.18	0.22	0.22

* Absolute t-statistics are shown in parentheses ( ), whereas brackets [ ] give White's heteroscedasticity-consistent t-statistics.

Other new growth models, e.g. Grossman and Helpman (1991), allocate inputs for research and development activities, which can be directed at process or at product innovations. In learning models the principal cause of growth is embodied in firms who learn by doing things. Accumulated knowledge by learning from what has been done in the past can be related to the stock of capital, e.g. Romer (1986). In a world with perfect competition and a constant returns to scale production function at the firm level learning has to take the form of an externality. Knowledge of firms increases by watching other producers. The production function at the firm level could then be augmented by a multiplicative term in the aggregate capital stock with exponent γ. Aggregating over firms and logarithmic differentiation with respect to time results then in the equation

$$g = (\alpha + \gamma)g_k + (1 - \alpha)g_\ell \tag{5}$$

There is no constant term as knowledge is endogenized completely. As appears from equation (5) this new growth model predicts that the estimated coefficient on g_k

must exceed the production elasticity of capital. However, there are problems with respect to the long-run implications of equation (5). For $\alpha + \gamma < 1$ there exists a steady-state solution

$$g = \frac{1 - \alpha}{1 - (\alpha + \gamma)} g_\ell \tag{6}$$

In this case the growth rate of output is fully determined by the growth rate of labor. In the opposite case with $\alpha + \gamma \geq 1$ (associated with Romer, 1986) growth accelerates over time as can be shown easily. Assume $\alpha + \gamma = 1$ for expositional purposes. Taking account of the definition $g_k \equiv \sigma/\kappa$, equation (5) can then be reformulated as (cf. Van de Klundert and Meijdam, 1993)

$$g = \frac{\sigma}{\kappa} + (1 - \alpha)g_\ell. \tag{7}$$

For a constant investment ratio and a fixed growth rate of labor, equation (7) implies an accelerating growth of output. An increase in labor can be absorbed by adopting a relatively more labor-intensive production technique. As a result output increases and the capital-output coefficient declines. A given level of savings then translates into a higher growth rate of capital. This is an unappealing result, which is reinforced in case of increasing returns to capital, $\alpha + \gamma > 1$. It should be noted that in this model there are no transitional dynamics. The capital stock does not have to adjust to some long-run equilibrium level and the instantaneous rate of growth is derived from equation (7).

The theory of endogenous growth of Scott (1989) likewise puts a strong emphasis on learning. However, in this theory there is no need for a concept as the stock of capital traditionally defined. If one wants to link Scott's theory with the learning model discussed above, it could be postulated that the capital-output ratio in equation (7) does not fall because with $g_\ell > 0$ adjustment costs have to be incurred, which counterbalance a decline in κ resulting from changing to less capital intensive techniques of production. In this way a linear relation is obtained, explaining the rate of growth in terms of the gross investment ratio and the growth rate of labor input with no need for a residual factor. Economic growth and investment always involve some form of qualitative change. This is not to say that firms have no choices to make. What must be decided upon is the level of investment in relation to the ongoing production process and the bias towards more or less labor saving these investment projects will have. Scott's fundamental growth equation or investments possibility curves, as he calls it, shows within which constraints these choices have to be made. Forward-looking firms maximize the present value of the cash flow for given time paths of wages, prices and interest rates. Depending on these time paths economic growth will be predominantly expansionary, requiring additional labor to realize plans, or more defensive, rationalizing on variable labor input. The options for firms can thus be summarized by the *fundamental growth equation* (cf. Van de Klundert and Meijdam, 1993)

$$g = f(\sigma, g_\ell), \qquad f_1, f_2 > 0,\ f_{11}, f_{22} < 0 \tag{8}$$

where f_i and f_{ii} $(i = 1, 2)$ represent the first and second order partial derivatives of the non-linear function f with respect to its i-th argument, and the other symbols have the same meaning as before. Notice that this growth equation is concave in σ and g_ℓ, but when the curves are relatively flat a linear approximation may be acceptable in empirical work. The equation to be estimated can therefore be written as

$$g = a_0 + a_1\sigma + a_2 g_\ell + \mu \tag{9}$$

where μ is a random error term and the constant a_0 is predicted to be zero, because technological change is fully endogenous in the model. Equation (9) is reminiscent of equation (3), i.e. equation (2) after that the Harrod-Domar identity is substituted in the latter. Now there is, however, no need to assume that the capital-output ratio is constant, because the neoclassical production function is abandoned entirely. According to Scott (1989) the best one can do is to use changes in capital, i.e. gross investment to explain changes in output. Equation (9) refers to a "normal" pattern of economic growth. The equation may temporarily shift under the impact of the international transfer of labor, cf. Inkster (1990). Technology transfer may give rise to catch up if a country is *socially capable* of it, cf. Abramovitz (1989). This is identified here by adding a logarithmic catch-up variable $(-a_3 \ln cu)$ to the estimation equation. Equation (9) applies for each subperiod within the entire period of observation, because there are no transitional dynamics apart from catching up. This makes it possible to test stability over time of all parameters, including the coefficient of the catch-up variable.

Van de Klundert and Van Schaik (1993) have estimated equation (9) for eight countries (Germany, Japan, France, the Netherlands, Australia, the United Kingdom, Canada and the United States). The data come from Maddison (1991, 1992). The business cycle has been eliminated by calculating exponential growth rates of output and labor input from peak to peak level (1870, 1890, 1913, 1929, 1938, 1950, 1960, 1973 and 1989). This made it possible to split the observation period (1870–1989) into eight subperiods. The series for Australia, the United Kingdom, Canada and the United States cover the whole period from 1870 onwards. Data are missing for Germany, Japan, France and the Netherlands for the "war period" 1938–1950, whereas the Japanese series starts in 1890 and the Dutch series starts in 1913. This reduces the sample to 57 observations. Estimation proceeded as follows. First, K&S tested the significance of country-specific factors and stability over time of the coefficients. The test reveals that country-specific influences can only be assigned to Australia and that the coefficient of the investment ratio is stable over time, with exception of the "war period" 1938–1950. Further it appears that the catch-up variable is insignificant in the periods before 1950 and after 1973. The resulting equations are reproduced here in Table 4. The post-1973 catch-up variable is shown to emphasize the conclusion that catching up after 1973 is not significant for the countries under consideration.

In Table 4 the growth rate of labor input is captured by two different measures: persons (4A) and man-hours (4B). This distinction has to do with the fact that annual hours worked per person have been approximately halved since 1870. When hours of work are long, a reduction can generally be expected to result in some offsetting increase in output per man-hour. Scott (1989) mentions several studies showing that such an offset exists. Authors disagree, however, as to how much should be allowed for increased productivity as hours fall. That is the reason K&S present two equations. Equation 4A implicitly assumes a complete compensation for change in hours, whereas equation 4B implies that the offset is absent. It is to be expected that the truth lies somewhere in between these extremes. The main conclusion is that the constant term does not differ significantly from zero, so that the hypothesis of endogenous technological change cannot be rejected. In the following section we put the K&S results in a broader perspective by estimating the fundamental growth equation on a sample derived from the dataset of Summers and Heston (1991).

4 The normal pattern of growth in worldwide perspective

The observations cover the period 1950–1986. The number of countries is 107. Most economies show cyclical peaks around 1960 and 1973, so that the total period is split into 3 subperiods, 1950–1960, 1961–1973 and 1974–1986. An additional argument to separate the fifties and the sixties is that the subperiods must be of equal length for all countries and that for many countries data are lacking for the fifties. In total we come to 275 observations, which are reproduced in the Appendix.

Following Dowrick and Nguyen (1989), trend growth rates of output, g, and labor input, g_ℓ, have been estimated by regressing the logarithm of output and employment respectively on a time trend 1950–1986, spliced at 1960 and 1973. The figures for the investment ratio, σ, are the subperiod averages. The catch-up variable, cu, is the ratio of a country's level of labor productivity and the US productivity level in 1950, 1961 and 1974, respectively. The Appendix also shows the ratios R_{1985} and R_{1974}. For countries with *three* entries in the sample these ratios are defined as

$$R_{1985} = \frac{cu_{1985}}{cu_{1950}}, \quad R_{1974} = \frac{cu_{1974}}{cu_{1950}} \tag{10}$$

Table 4: Pooled time-series and cross-section regression, 1870–1989*

OLS estimation of output growth g on	(4A)	(4B)
Constant	−0.07	0.34
	(0.15)	(0.73)
	[0.20]	[0.98]
Investment ratio (σ)	0.11	0.14
	(2.68)	(3.46)
	[2.97]	[3.97]
Growth rate of labor input in persons (g_ℓ)	1.07	
	(8.36)	
	[7.40]	
Growth rate of labor input in man-hours (g_ℓ)		0.83
		(9.04)
		[12.51]
Catch-up 1950–1960 ($\ln cu_{1950}$)	−2.77	−2.19
	(6.95)	(6.37)
	[6.26]	[4.10]
Catch-up 1960–1973 ($\ln cu_{1960}$)	−3.72	−3.13
	(5.60)	(5.76)
	[6.62]	[6.96]
Catch-up 1973–1989 ($\ln cu_{1973}$)	−0.30	0.19
	(0.28)	(0.22)
	[0.35]	[0.28]
$\sigma Dummy_{1938-1950}$	0.14	0.21
	(3.15)	(5.13)
	[2.22]	[3.83]
$\sigma Dummy_{Australia}$	−0.07	−0.06
	(3.39)	(3.09)
	[4.28]	[4.42]
Number of observations (N)	57	57
$\bar{R}^2$	0.86	0.87

* Absolute t-statistics are shown in parentheses ( ), whereas brackets [ ] give White's heteroscedasticity-consistent t-statistics.

For countries with *two* entries these ratios are

$$R_{1985} = \frac{cu_{1985}}{cu_{1961}}, \quad R_{1974} = \frac{cu_{1974}}{cu_{1961}} \tag{11}$$

The data give rise to a number of interesting observations. In the Appendix countries are ranked according to productivity levels in 1985. Thus it appears that some OECD-countries (Ireland, Greece, Portugal and Turkey) do not belong to the top-24. Non-OECD-countries in the top-24 are Israel, Singapore, Trinidad & Tobago and Hong Kong. The subtop is a mixture of strongly growing economies such as Taiwan and stagnating economies such as Uruguay. The data confirm what we have already seen before: many countries have increased their productivity level relative to the US ($R_{1985} > 1$). What is shown now in more detail is that the exceptions are among the poorest countries and among countries in South America. There are major winners which more than doubled productivity levels relative to the US ($R_{1985} > 2$) as well as losers which lagged behind US productivity growth ($R_{1985} < 1$). Great winners were Taiwan, Gabon and Botswana. In contrast, countries like Uruguay, Argentina and Chile strongly felt back.

The division of the post WW II data into 3 subperiods leads to the important observation that the acceleration of output growth in the sixties and the slowdown afterwards is quite general. In many countries, even among the richest of the top-24, the slowdown in output growth has been more dramatic than in the US. This observation is somewhat underexposed in the literature on the American slowdown in growth, cf. Williamson (1991). In contrast, the number of countries where post-1973 output-growth accelerated is restricted to 10: Egypt, Paraguay, Sri Lanka, Cameroon, Indonesia, Lesotho, Benin, Somalia, Nepal and Burkina Faso. These countries also show a substantial rise of the investment ratio after 1973, so that there is no *a priori* reason to attach country-specific elements to these exceptions. A country has catched up with the US after 1973, if $R_{1985} > R_{1974}$. This is the case for approximately half of the number of countries (53 out of 107). It should be noted that after 1973 catch up of rich countries like Canada, Switzerland, the Netherlands, Australia, France, Belgium, Germany and the UK has become very weak or has even come to a halt. This corresponds with the K&S results for the "Maddison" countries that after 1973 the impact of convergence of technological knowledge has disappeared. The data also reveal a wide spectrum of output growth rates. There are 35 observations with $g > 7\%$ and 21 observations with $g < 1\%$. Most of these exceptional growth rates are found in the last subperiod, 1974–1986. It should be noted that for a sample of 102 countries Parente and Prescott (1993) observe that the distance between the richest and poorest countries remained essentially the same throughout the 1960–85 period and that the wealth distribution (wealth measured by GDP per capita) has shifted up: the richer got richer, but the poor did too. However, analysis of our data for subperiods recommend caution with this.

Table 5: Pooled regression, data Summers and Heston, 1950–1986*

OLS estimation of output growth g on	(5A)	(5B)	(5C)	(5D)
Constant	−0.09	0.13	0.24	0.24
	(0.15)	(0.21)	(0.40)	(0.40)
	[0.15]	[0.21]	[0.38]	[0.38]
Investment ratio (σ)	0.12	0.09	0.09	0.09
	(6.25)	(5.02)	(5.17)	(5.20)
	[5.98]	[4.92]	[4.64]	[4.62]
Growth rate of labor input (g_ℓ)	0.68	0.70	0.78	0.78
	(4.91)	(5.15)	(5.79)	(5.81)
	[4.99]	[5.18]	[6.12]	[6.14]
Catch-up 1950–1960 ($\ln cu_{1950}$)	−0.81	−1.40	−1.45	−1.42
	(3.54)	(4.87)	(4.32)	(4.96)
	[3.74]	[4.92]	[5.01]	[5.12]
Catch-up 1961–1973 ($\ln cu_{1961}$)	−0.91	−1.50	−1.03	−1.03
	(5.20)	(6.30)	(4.04)	(4.13)
	[5.00]	[5.59]	[3.82]	[3.93]
Catch-up 1974–1986 ($\ln cu_{1974}$)	0.04	−0.37	−0.83	−0.84
	(0.20)	(1.76)	(3.74)	(3.81)
	[0.20]	[1.64]	[3.51]	[3.58]
Primary enrollment ($\ln prim$)		1.27	1.16	1.15
		(3.14)	(2.95)	(2.96)
		[3.17]	[2.95]	[2.97]
Secondary enrollment ($\ln sec$)		0.34	0.49	0.50
		(1.36)	(1.95)	(2.04)
		[1.11]	[1.58]	[1.66]
Cycle 1950–1960 ($cind_{1950-1960}$)			−1.85	
			(0.17)	
			[0.20]	
Cycle 1961–1973 ($cind_{1961-1973}$)			18.94	19.07
			(3.04)	(3.09)
			[3.08]	[3.13]
Cycle 1974–1986 ($cind_{1974-1986}$)			−17.12	−17.02
			(3.68)	(3.69)
			[2.91]	[2.92]
Number of observations (N)	275	275	275	275
$\bar{R}^2$	0.24	0.29	0.35	0.35

* Absolute t-statistics are shown in parentheses ( ), whereas brackets [ ] give White's heteroscedasticity-consistent t-statistics.

Table 5 gives the estimation results. Equation 5A is directly comparable with equation 4A in Table 4, because in both equations labor input is measured in persons. It appears that the main K&S results stand upright: there is no indication of a significant constant term, so that technological change is endogenous and there is no catch up after 1973. The latter does however not fit very well with the observation that about half of the countries has been catching up with the US after 1973. Presumably, this may be due to international differences in social capability for catching up. However, it is not clear how we should measure the social and economic environment of countries in a robust way. The extended "Barro-equation" is subject to the critique of Levine and Renelt (1992), who found that a large assortment of economic and political indicators, other than the initial enrollment rate, are not robustly correlated with growth. Therefore social capability is here only approximated by the logarithmic enrollment rates, which is reminiscent of investment in human capital. There is no effect on growth if $prim = 1$ and $sec = 1$, but enrollment rates smaller than unity depress growth. Countries with low initial productivity levels have big opportunities for growth, but in general exhibit low enrollment rates. In this way, $\ln prim$ and $\ln sec$ express "lost opportunities for growth". In India for instance, where $cu_{1961} \approx 0.05$, the potential for output growth by catching up is 3%.[5] This is offset however by the inability of this country to create a social and economic environment similar to that of leading countries. As appears from equation 5B this effect is picked up by the enrollment rates quite well: the fit of the equation is increased by about 25%.[6] This result is of course not unexpected as the *positive* relation between growth and enrollment rates has widely been documented. Adding the enrollment rates improves the performance of the process of catching up as can be seen from the higher t-values. The catch-up variable now better reflects the potential for growth by technological convergence, even for the period 1974–1986, although after 1973 the effect is considerably smaller than in the fifties and the sixties. The constant term of equation 5B does not differ significantly from zero, so that the finding of K&S that technological change is endogenous is still standing.

Intuitively, one would expect the absolute extent of catching up to be stronger in the earlier years, so that the coefficient of $\ln cu$ is greater for the fifties than for the sixties. The equations 5A and 5B do not confirm this presumption: the absolute value of the coefficient of the catch-up variable is largest for the sixties. One may wonder whether this is due to the working of period-specific factors. For most countries the sixties are characterized by historically large trend-growth rates and a considerable slowdown in growth afterwards. An explanation is given by Scott (1989), who attributes a part of the slowdown in growth after 1973 to lower rates

5. According to equation 5A the elasticity of the catch-up variable is about -1.
6. The data on enrollment rates are borrowed from Barro (1991).

of capacity utilization and higher rates of scrapping, which mitigate the effects of the investment ratio on growth. In contrast economic growth in the sixties may be favored by high rates of capacity utilization. To test this hypothesis we need additional information on capacity utilization rates. However, this information is not readily available for the large number of countries we are dealing with here. Therefore, as a first step on this route, we approximate the cyclical indicator by the standard deviations of the residuals of the trend regressions on the time series of output.

The effects of the addition of the cyclical indicator, *cind*, are found in equation 5C: compared with equation 5B the coefficient of determination has increased from 29% to 35%. Catch up is now stronger in earlier years: the absolute value of the coefficient of the catch-up variable declines from 1.45 in the fifties over 1.03 in the sixties to 0.83 in the seventies and eighties. In equation 5C all coefficients are significant with exception of the constant term and the coefficient of $cind_{1950-1960}$. In equation 5D the latter variable has been omitted, which slightly improves the regression results. It appears that the cyclical indicator emphasizes the differences between the "golden" sixties and the stagnation of the world economy afterwards: the relation between growth rates and the variability of growth rates is positive in the sixties and negative afterwards. A positive relation is also found by Kormendi and Meguire (1985), who consider the variability of growth rates as a measure of risk. In terms of equation (8) firms have to choose from a set of investment projects which are not equally risky. From the projects with given growth and employment characteristics the least risky ones are chosen first. Hence expected growth can be increased at a given rate of investment and employment change only at the cost of a higher risk. It should be observed that Kormendi and Meguire only consider the 1950–1977 period, so that the post-1973 observations are given insufficient weight in the sample. Grier and Tullock (1989) also find a positive relation in a pooled regression on five-year averaged data for 89 countries over 1961–1980. In addition they distinguish several subsamples, which shows that the relation is strongly negative for Asian countries and weakly positive for OECD. In contrast with these studies, our results point at a "switch" in the relation between growth and cycles at the beginning of the seventies, which asks for a more encompassing theory to explain this relation.

We now come to a discussion of the implications of our estimation results. The coefficient of determination of equation 5D is 35%, while the coefficients on the investment ratio (0.09) and the growth rate of labor input (0.78) are highly significant and robust with respect to the addition of variables as compared with equation 5B. Inspection of the residuals shows that there are about 60 residuals in the neighborhood of zero (between −0.5 and +0.5), which are not clustered for groups of countries or for subperiods. To see how equation 5D works out, Table 6 describes

Table 6: The proximate causes of growth in 4 selected countries

Obser-vation	Period	Actual g	Explained by (according to eq. 5D) σ	g_ℓ	cu	soc	$cycle$	Residual equation (5A)	(5B)	(5D)
	USA									
1	50–60	3.09	1.51	0.84		0.11		0.57	0.53	0.39
2	61–73	3.71	1.55	1.52		0.10	0.46	0.54	0.55	−0.16
3	74–86	2.33	1.65	1.52		0.01	−0.52	−0.96	−0.83	−0.55
	Singapore									
61	61–73	9.18	2.18	2.72	1.20	−0.33	1.62	3.11	2.87	1.55
62	74–86	7.58	3.49	2.85	0.61	−0.01	−0.50	0.85	1.05	0.90
	Hong Kong									
66	61–73	8.37	1.96	2.90	1.42	−0.27	0.70	2.23	1.71	1.42
67	74–86	8.15	1.98	2.88	0.79	−0.13	−0.86	3.29	3.16	3.25
	Ethiopia									
273	50–60	3.35	0.27	1.52	5.51	−5.75		−1.36	1.54	1.57
274	61–73	4.23	0.48	1.72	3.98	−3.65	0.23	−1.29	−0.34	1.23
275	74–86	2.79	0.40	1.47	3.24	−2.24	−0.44	1.24	1.56	0.12

the proximate causes of growth in 4 selected countries. (In the table *soc* is the contribution of both enrollment rates together.) We have chosen the US, because this is the leading country. The last country in the sample is Ethiopia, which is taken as illustrative for the explanation of growth in the poorest countries. Singapore and Hong Kong are chosen, because recently they have got much interest in empirical growth studies, cf. Young (1992). The last column of Table 6 shows that the residuals of equation 5D are relatively small for the US, Singapore, Hong Kong in the sixties and Ethiopia in the seventies. This means that in the mentioned subperiods these economies have grown according to the "normal" pattern of growth, as implied by the fundamental growth equation. In the US – and this holds for the other rich countries as well – the investment ratio contributes a large part to output growth. In Ethiopia – as in many other poor countries – the investment ratio plays a more modest role. In the fifties, Ethiopia's potential for growth as measured by the catch-up variable has fully been lost, but in the periods afterwards the differences between the effects of *cu* and *soc* are positive.

The Appendix shows that there are 35 observations with $g > 7\%$ and 21 observations with $g < 1\%$. Let us call these "winners" and "losers", respectively. In addition we consider residuals larger than 2.5 and smaller than -2.5 as outliers. According to equation 5D there are 14 positive and 14 negative outliers. All positive outliers are among the winners and all negative outliers among the losers. This means that 21 out of the 35 winners are explained rather well. The positive outliers are (numbers in parentheses refer to the numbers of the observations in the Appendix): Japan (59), Trinidad & Tobago (63), Hong Kong (67), Algeria (86), Taiwan (98), South Korea (131), Botswana (150, 151), Egypt (154), Paraguay (157), Cameroon (189), Indonesia (191), Cape Verdian Islands (195) and Lesotho (213). The negative outliers are Nicaragua (165), Jamaica (172), Bolivia (173), Papua New Guinea (200), Guyana (205), Liberia (217), Zambia (223), Ghana (227), Angola (232), Madagascar (241), Mozambique (243), Chad (248), Guinea (261) and Zaire (269). The effect of these outliers on the coefficient of determination of equation 5D is high: adding two dummies, one for the positive outliers and the other for the negative outliers, doubles the coefficient of determination. All t-values are higher, but the constant term remains small and insignificant. It is more appropriate however to attach country-specific circumstances such as wars to the outliers and remove the observations from the sample. This is put on our agenda for further research, but at first glance our rough estimate is that only a restricted number of winners, such as Hong Kong (67), will be left.

5 Concluding remarks

We investigated the robustness of our earlier findings for the "Maddison" countries, see Van de Klundert and Van Schaik (1993), that after 1973 the process of catching up with the US has come to an end and that technological change is endogenous by estimating the fundamental growth equation of Scott (1989) on a sample of 107 countries and 3 distinct subperiods over the period 1950–1986. The main conclusion still is that the constant term of the growth equation does not differ significantly from zero, so that the hypothesis of endogenous technological change cannot be rejected. This favors Scott's equation above its neoclassical counterpart. These equations have the same independent variables in common, but do not share the prediction that the constant term should be zero.

The other conclusion must now be put in the right perspective however. In many countries the productivity level relative to US productivity has increased after 1973. The exceptions to this rule are among the richest and the poorest countries and the middle-income countries in South America. We found that the fundamental growth equation can handle this. The stylized fact is that technological catch up seems to be important for some time in some countries, but does not characterize the world as a whole. After 1973 the process of catching up appears to be very weak in the richest countries and is counterbalanced by inadequate preconditions for catching up in the poorest countries. Given the apparent importance of technology transfer, it seems that the most promising message of new growth theories concerns the implications of international economic linkages and communication in the process of economic growth.

Since the beginning of the second industrial revolution European countries have catched up with the technological leader *only* during the fifties and the sixties of the twentieth century. After 1973 this process has come to an end, which can be seen as an important cause of the slowdown of economic growth in these countries. In traditional macroeconometric models the slowdown of economic growth is usually captured by lowering the exogenous rate of technical progress. This is an unsatisfactory way of dealing with economic growth, especially in the light of the recent attention for the long-run characteristics of macroeconometric models. New growth theories try to explain the proximate sources of growth, in particular technological progress, as the outcome of more ultimate individual and market level economic processes and incentives. This may have consequences for macroeconometric modelbuilding. The long-run properties of traditional macroeconometric models usually come down to a neoclassical steady state with exogenous technological change. A natural way to extend such models is to endogenize the rate of labor-saving technical progress. Technical change may depend among other things on the degree of capacity utilization and the development of real wages, cf. Van de Klundert and Van Schaik (1978). In these models the factors driving the demand for goods also influence the rate of growth in a steadily growing economy. Trying to explain technological progress by both demand and supply factors may contribute to a better understanding of the historically unprecedented variation in economic growth across time periods and across countries that has occurred over the past forty years.

References

Abramovitz, M. (1989), "The catch-up factor in postwar economic growth", *Economic Inquiry*, **27**, 1–18.

Barro, R.J. (1991), "Economic growth in a cross section of countries", *Quarterly Journal of Economics*, **106**, 407–443.

Barro, R.J., N.G. Mankiw, and X. Sala-I-Martin (1992), "Capital mobility in neoclassical models of growth", Working Paper Series 4206, NBER.

Barro, R.J. and X. Sala-I-Martin (1992), "Convergence", *Journal of Political Economy*, **100**, 223–251.

Baumol, W. (1986), "Productivity growth, convergence, and welfare: what the long-run data show", *American Economic Review*, **76**, 1072–1085.

Brander, J.A. (1992), "Comparative economic growth: evidence and interpretation", *Canadian Journal of Economics*, **25**, 792–818.

Dowrick, S. (1992), "Technological catch-up and diverging incomes: patterns of economic growth 1960-88", *The Economic Journal*, **102**, 600–610.

Dowrick, S. and D.T. Nguyen (1989), "OECD comparative economic growth 1950-85: catch-up and convergence", *American Economic Review*, **79**, 1010–1030.

Grier, K.B. and G. Tullock (1989), "An empirical analysis of cross-national economic growth, 1951-80", *Journal of Monetary Economics*, **24**, 259–276.

Grossman, G.M. and E. Helpman (1991), *Innovation and growth in the global economy*, MIT Press, Cambridge.

Inkster, I. (1990), "Mental capital: transfer of knowledge and technique in eighteenth century Europe", *Journal of European Economic History*, **19**, 403–441.

Klundert, Th. van de and L. Meijdam (1993), "Endogenous growth and income distribution", *Journal of Economics*, **58**, 53–75.

Klundert, Th. van de and A. van Schaik (1978), "Demand and supply as factors determining economic growth", *De Economist*, **126**, 370–389.

Klundert, Th. van de and A. van Schaik (1993), "On the historical continuity of the process of economic growth", Discussion Paper 850, CEPR.

Kormendi, R.C. and P.G. Mequire (1985), "Macroeconomic determinants of growth: cross-country evidence", *Journal of Monetary Economics*, **16**, 141–163.

Levine, R. and D. Renelt (1992), "A sensitivity analysis of cross-country growth regressions", *American Economic Review*, **82**, 942–963.

Long, B.J. de (1988), "Productivity growth, convergence, and welfare: comment", *American Economic Review*, **78**, 1138–1154.

Lucas, R.E. (1988), "On the mechanics of economic development", *Journal of Monetary Economics*, **12**, 3–42.

Maddison, A. (1991), *Dynamic forces in capitalist development*, Oxford University Press, Oxford.

Maddison, A. (1992), "A long-run perspective on saving", *Scandinavian Journal of Economics*, **94**, 181–196.

Mankiw, N.G., D. Romer, and D.N. Weil (1992), "A contribution to the empirics of economic growth", *Quarterly Journal of Economics*, **107**, 407–437.

Parente, S.L and E.C. Prescott (1993), "Changes in the wealth of nations", *Quarterly Review Federal Reserve Bank of Minneapolis*, **17**, 3–16.

Rebelo, S. (1991), "Long-run policy analysis and long-run growth", *Journal of Political Economy*, **99**, 500–526.

Romer, P.M. (1986), "Increasing returns and long-run growth", *Journal of Political Economy*, **94**, 1002–1037.

Schaik, A. van (1992), "Productivity and labor force participation in a cross section of 95 countries (in dutch)", *Maandschrift Economie*, **56**, 475–492.

Scott, M.F. (1989), *A new view of economic growth*, Oxford University Press, Oxford.

Scott, M.F. (1993), "Explaining economic growth", *American Economic Review, Papers and Proceedings*, **83**, 412–425.

Solow, R.M. (1956), "A contribution to the theory of economic growth", *Quarterly Journal of Economics*, **70**, 65–94.

Summers, R. and A. Heston (1991), "The Penn World Table (Mark 5): an expanded set of international comparisons, 1950-1988", *Quarterly Journal of Economics*, **106**, 327–368.

Swan, T.W. (1956), "Economic growth and capital accumulation", *Economic Record*, **32**, 343–361.

Williamson, J.G. (1991), "Productivity and american leadership: a review article", *Journal of Economic Literature*, **29**, 51–68.

Young, A. (1992), "A tale of two cities: factor accumulation and technical change in Hong Kong and Singapore", in NBER, editor, *NBER macroeconomics annual 1992*, MIT Press, Cambridge.

Appendix: pooled time-series cross-section sample, 1950–1986

The data are derived from that given in Summers and Heston (1991). Real GDP per worker is taken from RGDPW (1985 international prices); the investment share is taken from I (investment share of GDP, 1985 international prices). Output and labor input (workers) are obtained by using the series for real GDP per capita in constant dollars (RGDPCH) and population (POP). The main oil-producing countries are left aside. The remaining 107 (out of 134) countries are listed below. The countries are ranked according to productivity levels in 1985 (Rank). Integers immediately before the country names are the indexes in the Summers-Heston data base. The underlined indexes identify the countries in the sample of Table 1. The total period (1950–1986) is split into 3 subperiods, 1950–1960, 1961–1973 and 1974–1986. For a number of countries data are lacking for the fifties so that in total we come to 275 observations.

The trend-growth rates of output, g, and labor input, g_ℓ, are estimated by piecewise linear trend regression. The figures for the investment ratio, σ, are the subperiod averages. The catch-up variable, cu, is the ratio of a country's level of labor productivity and the US productivity level in 1950, 1961 and 1974, respectively. The other columns show the ratios R_{1985} and R_{1974}. For countries with three entries in the sample these ratios are defined as

$$R_{1985} = \frac{cu_{1985}}{cu_{1950}}, \quad R_{1974} = \frac{cu_{1974}}{cu_{1950}}$$

For countries with two entries these ratios are

$$R_{1985} = \frac{cu_{1985}}{cu_{1961}}, \quad R_{1974} = \frac{cu_{1974}}{cu_{1961}}$$

It can be observed that a country has catched up with the US after 1973, if $R_{1985} > R_{1974}$. US GDP per worker, measured in 1985 international prices, has developed as follows: 20244 (1950), 24753 (1961), 31155 (1974), 34374 (1985), 37608 (1988).

Table A: Pooled time-series cross-section sample, 1950–1986

Rank	Country		g	g_ℓ	σ	cu	R_{1985}		R_{1974}
1–1	66	USA	3.09	1.07	16.12	100.00	1.00		1.00
2			3.71	1.94	16.59	100.00			
3			2.33	1.94	17.58	100.00			
4–2	50	CANADA	3.81	1.96	22.54	86.26	1.01	>	0.97
5			4.71	2.87	21.34	83.28			
6			3.27	2.50	23.89	83.31			
7–3	119	LUXEMB.	2.26	−0.53	33.45	68.32	1.25		1.31
8			3.73	0.33	29.00	70.32			
9			2.26	1.24	23.85	89.56			
10–4	127	SWITZERL.	4.98	1.73	24.35	72.41	1.18		1.32
11			4.07	1.42	31.59	85.83			
12			0.62	0.27	28.11	95.36			
13–5	122	NORWAY	3.47	−0.02	32.72	49.24	1.63	>	1.36
14			4.40	1.56	33.20	58.06			
15			4.03	1.61	32.93	66.75			
16–6	121	NETHERL.	4.61	0.15	23.35	49.82	1.58		1.69
17			5.46	1.47	27.97	65.03			
18			1.87	1.44	20.49	84.27			
19–7	131	AUSTRALIA	4.38	1.99	28.54	70.45	1.11		1.13
20			5.16	2.50	29.76	69.07			
21			2.58	2.08	26.74	79.77			
22–8	118	ITALY	6.20	0.12	27.13	28.83	2.68	>	2.31
23			5.05	0.15	30.72	46.55			
24			3.16	0.58	25.31	66.74			
25–9	112	FRANCE	4.64	0.25	19.92	39.54	1.88		1.88
26			5.69	0.88	26.83	52.22			
27			1.94	0.87	25.34	74.23			
28–10	108	BELGIUM	2.73	−0.03	20.07	50.56	1.45		1.55
29			4.79	0.41	24.08	57.29			
30			1.61	0.88	22.23	78.30			
31–11	89	ISRAEL	9.89	4.39	32.02	32.19	2.21		2.27
32			8.43	3.53	30.14	48.16			
33			3.36	2.46	23.30	72.94			
34–12	126	SWEDEN	3.80	0.61	21.00	55.98	1.27	>	1.22
35			3.81	1.31	24.65	62.39			
36			1.71	0.79	20.68	68.31			
37–13	113	GERMANY	7.42	1.15	27.95	33.16	2.12	>	2.07
38			4.15	0.31	29.76	54.08			
39			1.80	0.60	24.15	68.60			
40–14	133	NEW ZEAL.	5.08	1.96	20.00	72.63	0.90		1.13
41			4.09	2.11	21.03	77.31			
42			1.03	1.85	22.70	82.08			
43–15	116	ICELAND	4.82	0.83	24.72	48.97	1.31	>	1.22
44			4.76	2.61	27.67	54.21			
45			4.63	2.44	24.50	59.73			

Table A: continued

Rank	Country		g	g_ℓ	σ	cu	R_{1985}		R_{1974}
46–16	107	AUSTRIA	5.82	−0.37	20.54	25.02	2.58	>	2.47
47			5.00	−0.50	26.76	40.04			
48			2.43	0.97	28.04	61.73			
49–17	111	FINLAND	4.57	0.08	33.05	31.07	2.07	>	1.84
50			4.61	0.81	36.26	44.74			
51			3.20	0.81	32.46	57.09			
52–18	129	UNI. KINGDOM	2.82	0.38	13.50	53.12	1.21	>	1.15
53			2.91	0.47	18.43	56.96			
54			1.68	0.47	17.71	61.01			
55–19	110	DENMARK	4.15	0.04	23.10	45.83	1.40	>	1.31
56			4.32	1.33	31.88	54.76			
57			1.83	1.01	24.63	59.97			
58–20	90	JAPAN	8.48	2.08	18.08	14.36	4.40	>	3.50
59			9.37	1.52	31.57	25.83			
60			3.41	0.66	30.96	50.24			
61–21	100	SINGAPORE	9.18	3.48	23.34	31.19	2.12	>	1.54
62			7.58	3.65	37.30	48.14			
63–22	65	TRIN. & TOBA.	9.28	1.88	22.31	32.72	1.75		1.98
64			5.88	1.40	16.72	58.77			
65			3.24	2.46	21.49	64.94			
66–23	84	HONG KONG	8.37	3.71	20.93	25.24	2.33	>	1.54
67			8.15	3.69	21.17	38.97			
68–24	125	SPAIN	5.14	0.77	20.83	23.48	2.23		2.52
69			6.83	0.38	28.91	32.86			
70			1.11	0.98	24.11	59.18			
71–25	78	VENEZUELA	6.08	3.09	22.21	42.89	1.13		1.74
72			7.17	3.30	14.55	50.57			
73			3.69	4.47	18.64	74.45			
74–26	60	MEXICO	5.36	2.10	16.35	34.57	1.35		1.50
75			7.07	3.10	19.01	40.61			
76			4.26	4.03	21.01	51.70			
77–27	117	IRELAND	1.20	−1.46	18.41	29.68	1.52		1.60
78			5.02	0.23	25.85	34.48			
79			2.19	1.44	28.49	47.57			
80–28	114	GREECE	5.45	0.85	15.67	14.81	2.95	>	2.50
81			7.29	0.22	28.02	21.05			
82			2.69	0.74	24.40	37.02			
83–29	109	CYPRUS	4.77	0.94	36.87	17.73	2.42	>	1.62
84			4.76	0.97	35.71	22.29			
85			4.60	1.31	28.53	28.75			
86–30	1	ALGERIA	8.14	1.01	18.24	22.36	1.63	>	1.58
87			6.66	3.59	33.65	35.24			
88–31	120	MALTA	6.91	1.56	30.09	20.99	2.20	>	1.28
89			6.67	1.69	24.77	26.81			

Table A: continued

Rank	Country		g	g_ℓ	σ	cu	R_{1985}		R_{1974}
90–32	38	SOUTH AFR.	3.89	1.46	22.24	31.83	1.18		1.33
91			5.54	2.31	25.67	33.91			
92			2.17	1.67	26.47	42.38			
93–33	49	BARBADOS	5.84	0.74	17.33	35.00	1.01		1.25
94			1.05	2.50	18.88	43.87			
95–34	94	MALAYSIA	6.58	2.98	23.66	21.74	1.91	>	1.34
96			7.27	3.47	33.93	29.06			
97–35	103	TAIWAN	6.94	1.78	11.11	7.77	4.24	>	3.06
98			9.98	2.77	19.49	12.15			
99			7.57	3.39	26.71	23.78			
100–36	77	URUGUAY	1.31	1.07	17.75	44.09	0.75		0.84
101			1.50	0.62	12.93	43.82			
102			1.14	0.32	18.63	37.16			
103–37	67	ARGENTINA	2.97	1.36	9.75	36.55	0.88		1.10
104			4.09	1.32	12.35	37.13			
105			0.65	0.99	11.69	40.22			
106–38	69	BRAZIL	7.95	2.60	26.39	14.66	2.16		2.35
107			9.03	3.17	19.76	25.08			
108			4.24	3.02	19.81	34.47			
109–39	132	FIJI	6.25	3.38	23.39	35.40	0.90		1.07
110			3.04	2.62	21.82	37.91			
111–40	70	CHILE	4.05	1.43	14.19	37.08	0.84		1.06
112			3.80	1.79	14.74	40.41			
113			1.03	2.53	11.72	39.14			
114–41	62	PANAMA	5.65	2.02	17.68	16.92	1.80	>	1.67
115			7.66	2.84	26.20	20.14			
116			4.07	2.55	23.93	28.23			
117–42	71	COLOMBIA	3.89	1.87	21.57	23.87	1.24		1.28
118			5.78	2.61	18.62	25.95			
119			4.02	2.58	15.90	30.60			
120–43	43	TUNISIA	5.83	1.85	17.13	21.04	1.46	>	1.25
121			5.78	3.65	14.04	26.32			
122–44	124	PORTUGAL	4.16	−0.43	17.57	12.60	2.33		2.48
123			6.70	0.59	24.19	18.40			
124			3.15	2.19	23.15	31.20			
125–45	51	COSTA RICA	6.24	2.48	11.56	23.68	1.22		1.45
126			6.92	3.53	12.98	28.93			
127			2.96	3.55	14.98	34.25			
128–46	28	MAURITIUS	1.38	2.39	9.56	39.67	0.72		0.72
129			3.56	2.63	10.48	30.04			
130			4.97	2.72	12.89	28.51			

Table A: continued

Rank	Country		g	g_ℓ	σ	cu	R_{1985}		R_{1974}
131–47	92	SOUTH KOREA	10.11	2.96	20.54	11.29	2.74	>	1.83
132			6.57	2.53	29.53	20.63			
133–48	72	ECUADOR	4.09	2.29	23.21	16.90	1.58	>	1.49
134			6.72	2.58	24.10	18.70			
135			5.51	2.77	26.21	25.20			
136–49	75	PERU	4.63	1.94	18.25	25.78	0.96		1.37
137			5.84	2.25	15.07	28.49			
138			1.61	3.27	16.62	35.36			
139–50	15	GABON	10.83	0.60	28.46	6.64	4.07	>	2.91
140			6.04	0.78	46.63	19.31			
141–51	56	GUATEMALA	3.71	2.26	8.20	22.17	1.01		1.12
142			5.65	2.33	8.16	21.42			
143			3.23	2.35	8.87	24.84			
144–52	128	TURKEY	5.68	1.55	13.77	9.43	2.32	>	2.18
145			6.18	1.44	18.55	13.61			
146			3.96	1.97	23.60	20.58			
147–53	53	DOM. REP.	4.42	1.64	11.07	15.02	1.41		1.75
148			6.65	2.31	11.13	16.97			
149			3.74	3.28	17.62	26.26			
150–54	4	BOTSWANA	11.11	1.62	21.51	4.61	4.75	>	2.61
151			10.10	3.32	27.53	12.03			
152–55	13	EGYPT	3.53	1.71	5.25	7.93	2.63	>	1.68
153			7.10	1.98	5.24	7.78			
154			8.13	2.26	7.33	13.29			
155–56	74	PARAGUAY	2.39	1.71	5.30	18.03	1.14	>	0.89
156			4.66	2.62	8.13	15.56			
157			7.24	3.42	14.59	16.03			
158–57	12	CONGO	6.45	1.93	13.95	9.77	2.13	>	1.30
159			6.35	2.01	14.20	12.68			
160–58	29	MOROCCO	4.37	2.13	9.06	14.38	1.35	>	1.22
161			6.27	2.23	6.60	15.10			
162			4.51	3.48	10.72	17.54			
163–59	61	NICARAGUA	5.54	2.45	14.66	20.79	0.87		1.61
164			6.03	2.74	18.22	25.15			
165			−1.09	3.19	19.57	33.51			
166–60	101	SRI LANKA	3.79	1.78	14.49	15.28	1.00	>	0.86
167			2.23	2.12	16.85	14.69			
168			3.96	2.05	25.88	13.21			
169–61	40	SWAZILAND	6.74	1.83	20.15	10.83	1.80	>	1.35
170			2.99	2.14	26.60	14.64			
171–62	59	JAMAICA	6.67	1.22	27.59	18.18	1.21		1.40
172			−1.49	3.07	15.53	25.53			
173–63	68	BOLIVIA	−0.24	1.56	14.69	17.80	0.82		0.98
174			6.50	1.77	19.19	13.46			
175			1.40	2.32	15.55	17.43			

Table A: continued

Rank	Country		g	g_ℓ	σ	cu	R_{1985}		R_{1974}
176–64	98	PHILIP.	6.08	1.83	15.67	9.65	1.47		1.58
177			5.62	2.52	18.22	12.87			
178			3.97	2.45	20.91	15.25			
179–65	104	THAILAND	4.04	2.11	7.90	8.52	1.67	>	1.21
180			7.40	2.85	14.79	7.99			
181			5.92	2.64	15.45	10.29			
182–66	97	PAKISTAN	4.36	0.73	12.24	9.39	1.45	>	1.14
183			4.61	2.14	20.53	10.10			
184			4.36	2.96	11.14	10.72			
185–67	54	EL SALV.	4.58	2.10	6.13	15.46	0.86		1.14
186			6.05	3.31	7.47	15.81			
187			0.84	2.87	8.04	17.57			
188–68	7	CAMEROON	5.14	1.67	8.75	6.29	2.20	>	1.27
189			7.64	1.63	12.30	8.00			
190–69	86	INDONESIA	5.30	1.97	11.91	7.33	1.77	>	1.12
191			8.22	2.21	26.23	8.22			
192–70	58	HONDURAS	3.27	2.77	12.33	13.00	0.93		0.95
193			5.40	2.54	13.16	11.42			
194			4.23	3.44	13.74	12.29			
195–71	20	CAPE V. IS.	8.14	2.79	9.29	7.92	1.39		1.44
196			3.49	2.55	11.02	11.37			
197–72	47	ZIMBABWE	6.53	3.30	19.99	8.81	1.18	>	1.08
198			4.84	2.72	15.27	9.53			
199–73	134	PAPUA N. G.	6.52	1.80	25.00	9.07	1.19		1.36
200			0.27	2.00	23.80	12.38			
201–74	39	SUDAN	2.03	1.96	1.65	11.66	0.83	>	0.72
202			3.12	2.77	2.00	8.35			
203–75	73	GUYANA	2.65	1.37	32.10	21.43	0.40		0.88
204			5.21	2.48	37.03	22.26			
205			−2.38	3.61	25.82	18.84			
206–76	32	NIGERIA	6.41	4.66	9.42	12.21	0.81		1.14
207			1.06	1.90	15.40	13.88			
208–77	27	MAURIT.	5.20	1.73	6.64	10.44	0.79		1.08
209			0.25	2.10	20.18	11.27			
210–78	36	SIERRA L.	4.49	0.81	2.55	7.95	1.05		1.29
211			−0.58	1.02	2.01	10.26			
212–79	22	LESOTHO	7.41	1.54	7.71	2.56	2.92	>	1.93
213			8.28	2.01	14.98	4.93			
214–80	34	SENEGAL	1.77	2.91	7.03	11.22	0.69		0.71
215			2.71	2.77	7.34	7.99			
216–81	23	LIBERIA	3.88	2.50	36.88	11.13	0.79		0.88
217			0.85	2.45	19.63	9.80			

Table A: continued

Rank	Country		g	g_ℓ	σ	cu	R_{1985}		R_{1974}
218–82	81	BANGLAD.	1.22	1.53	6.61	7.62	1.00	>	0.82
219			4.53	2.32	5.16	6.25			
220–83	3	BENIN	2.03	1.58	3.77	7.22	1.00	>	0.91
221			2.86	2.07	7.56	6.57			
222–84	46	ZAMBIA	5.00	2.51	39.15	12.90	0.48		0.99
223			−2.16	2.88	19.05	12.72			
224–85	37	SOMALIA	1.99	2.39	5.78	9.21	0.76	>	0.64
225			4.53	3.20	13.42	5.85			
226–86	17	GHANA	2.72	1.68	9.11	10.12	0.66		0.92
227			0.41	2.54	5.92	9.31			
228–87	21	KENYA	1.41	2.89	24.89	6.51	0.92		1.10
229			7.28	3.30	14.62	5.04			
230			3.63	3.54	13.80	7.18			
231–88	2	ANGOLA	2.16	1.62	12.01	11.18	0.52		0.98
232			−3.41	2.56	11.73	11.00			
233–89	85	INDIA	3.51	1.51	11.56	5.43	0.98	>	0.90
234			2.70	1.52	15.69	5.34			
235			2.75	1.82	17.51	4.89			
236–90	95	NEPAL	2.28	1.22	6.51	4.89	1.08	>	0.93
237			4.24	2.00	13.93	4.56			
238–91	42	TOGO	7.50	2.41	14.12	3.63	1.31		1.45
239			2.15	2.08	20.19	5.27			
240–92	24	MADAGAS.	2.41	1.99	9.21	7.97	0.56		0.78
241			−0.39	2.08	8.06	6.18			
242–93	30	MOZAMB.	4.30	2.46	14.37	10.51	0.41		0.94
243			−3.03	3.29	10.86	9.84			
244–94	82	BURMA	5.49	1.33	12.91	2.62	1.62	>	1.24
245			4.25	2.01	10.84	3.00			
246			4.78	2.14	12.32	3.24			
247–95	10	CHAD	1.05	1.45	16.01	8.24	0.52		0.71
248			−2.08	1.76	13.94	5.88			
249–96	33	RWANDA	5.92	2.64	3.28	3.68	1.08	>	0.96
250			5.39	2.98	5.60	3.55			
251–97	9	C. AFRICA	2.11	0.97	10.44	5.59	0.76		0.82
252			0.81	1.30	6.56	4.60			
253–98	25	MALAWI	5.90	2.08	14.01	3.78	1.29	>	1.10
254			2.58	2.37	10.76	4.14			
255–99	26	MALI	1.33	1.56	6.48	5.34	0.71	>	0.70
256			3.96	2.02	6.60	3.72			
257–100	31	NIGER	3.81	2.05	8.69	4.19	0.88		1.01
258			1.16	1.99	9.32	4.23			
259–101	5	BURK. FASO	2.83	1.50	14.15	2.53	1.24	>	1.05
260			4.15	1.83	18.61	2.66			

Table A: continued

Rank	Country		g	g_ℓ	σ	cu	R_{1985}		R_{1974}
261–102	18	GUINEA	0.43	1.59	14.64	3.82	0.84	>	0.76
262			3.71	1.76	13.78	2.92			
263–103	6	BURUNDI	2.70	1.20	4.33	3.05	0.91	>	0.77
264			5.01	1.58	10.53	2.34			
265–104	41	TANZANIA	6.60	2.67	19.89	1.91	1.40	>	1.29
266			4.69	2.81	18.72	2.47			
267–105	45	ZAIRE	4.36	2.06	8.25	2.82	0.96		1.41
268			4.16	1.41	5.85	3.03			
269			−0.53	2.05	13.33	3.97			
270–106	44	UGANDA	3.32	2.99	4.17	3.53	0.74		0.75
271			3.85	3.55	5.12	2.88			
272			0.84	2.49	2.75	2.63			
273–107	14	ETHIOPIA	3.35	1.95	2.84	2.04	1.05	>	1.03
274			4.23	2.20	5.15	2.11			
275			2.79	1.88	4.28	2.11			

Author index

Subject index